The Future of Finance

Henri Arslanian • Fabrice Fischer

The Future of Finance

The Impact of FinTech, AI, and Crypto on Financial Services

Henri Arslanian
University of Hong Kong
Hong Kong, Hong Kong

Fabrice Fischer
Blu ltd
Hong Kong, Hong Kong

ISBN 978-3-030-14532-3   ISBN 978-3-030-14533-0   (eBook)
https://doi.org/10.1007/978-3-030-14533-0

This Palgrave Macmillan imprint is published by the registered company Springer Nature Switzerland AG
The registered company address is: Gewerbestrasse 11, 6330 Cham, Switzerland

Preface

We are going through perhaps the most exciting period in the modern history of financial services. The rapid acceleration of technology is enabling a fundamental reinvention of the structure of the financial institution, while at the same time inviting the entrance of new competitors with the potential to upend the traditional order of the industry. As with any revolution, there will be winners and there will be losers; some will be able to adapt and thrive in the face of these changes, while others will struggle to reinvent themselves in the ways necessary to remain relevant. It is impossible for us to know for certain who will emerge victorious from this period of tumultuous change, but we can examine the forces that have shaped the transformation so far, and consider what the future might hold. This book is written for those who want to understand the transformation that technology is driving in financial services and to consider the impact these forces might have on the future of the industry and on themselves.

We believe that three key areas of innovation are poised to have an outsized impact on the shape of the financial services ecosystem. These are the fintech revolution, the advent of crypto-assets, and the rise of artificial intelligence (AI). In the chapters that follow, we will explore each of these subjects independently, helping the reader to understand the context, background, and fundamentals of these trends. Grasping these basic concepts in detail is critical as it provides the foundational knowledge to explore further.

Armed with these basic concepts, we will consider the trends shaping the future of these areas of innovation. What might the future of fintech look like? What could be the implications of AI playing a larger role in financial decision-making? Will crypto-assets make their way into daily use by individuals around the world? We hope that the examination of these and many more questions will provide useful insights to a wide range of readers, from the bank CEO debating the strategic direction of her organization to a student considering where to focus studies or start her career.

Finally, while we believe that fintech, crypto-assets, and artificial intelligence could each have a significant and long-lasting impact on the structure of the financial system, it is the combined interaction of these three that stands to have the most transformative impact. While the confluence of these three areas of innovation may still be over the horizon, we devote our final chapter to the examination of several plausible scenarios for how they could intersect, in the hope of illustrating their potential combined power.

We hope you are as excited as we are to embark on this journey on the future of finance!

Hong Kong   Henri Arslanian
Hong Kong   Fabrice Fischer

Acknowledgments

Writing a book is an intense journey. It devours all of your "spare" time, energy, and focus. We knew this going in, but we still underestimated it (as every author does!). However, we did it with great passion and pleasure knowing that many may benefit, and that is very rewarding. We hope that you will enjoy reading this book as much as we enjoyed writing it.

Thanking everyone who inspired us to write this book would be impossible, but we would like to take the time to thank some individuals who really made a difference and helped us bring this book to fruition.

A big thank-you to Jesse McWaters for his valuable support throughout the book. Without his priceless insights and feedback, this book would have never been the same. To Alessandro Di Lullo, who helped us enormously in writing the fintech section. His passion and dedication to making this book happen was exemplary. To Antony Lewis, for his priceless help in reviewing the crypto and blockchain sections. To Kevin Pereira, for his review and comments on the artificial intelligence chapters. And to Nikita Mathur and Nayantara Bhat, for their amazing support when it came to aspects of research and editing.

To the entire team at our publisher Palgrave Macmillan, including Tula Weis and Jacqueline Young, for their incredible support during this journey—this book would have never been possible without their continuous support and backing.

To Michael Wykoff, for his patience and meticulous proofreading and editing work. To Belinda Esterhammer and her team, for the awesome work on the graphics. And to Lisa Rivero, for the help on the indexing.

And the most important thank-you to you, dear reader, for your passion and interest in the fields of fintech, crypto, and artificial intelligence. Welcome to the future of finance!

Personal Acknowledgment from Henri Arslanian

This book would have never seen the light of day without the support of my amazing family. To my dad, from whom I learned the values of hard work and integrity. To my mom, who taught me the importance of intellectual curiosity and giving back. To my parents-in-law, for their incredible understanding and support.

But most important, to my wife Lara Setrakian (and my baby daughter Vera-Maria Arslanian!), for their patience and understanding for the entire weekends and holidays during which I was physically with them, but mentally and practically in front of the computer working on this book.

Personal Acknowledgment from Fabrice Fischer

Writing this book has been both a joy and a massive endeavor. It could not have happened without the support of my family, the support of and enlightening discussions with my colleague and friend Kevin Pereira, who is as passionate as I am about artificial intelligence, and the kind attention of Guillaume Huet. My warmest thanks to them and to the many others who contributed to the success of this book.

Your authors
Henri and Fabrice

Contents

List of Figures

List of Tables

List of Boxes

Part I

The Fundamentals of Fintech, Crypto, and AI

Financial services and the technological context in which it operates are changing rapidly, so rapidly that it can be difficult to track the emergence of new business models, the entry of new competitors, and applications of new technologies to the business of financial services. In this section, we will seek to provide a foundational understanding of the most important forces currently transforming the operational structure, competitive dynamics, and regulatory treatment of the financial system.

The content that follows is divided into four subsections. First, we provide a high-level survey of the changing technological landscape, considering the impact of exponential improvements in computing power, storage, and connectivity on the dynamics of the business sector. From there, we will explore the fundamentals of fintech, considering the landscape of new fintech competitors, the response of incumbent financial institutions, and the potential for entry by large technology companies into the financial ecosystem. In our third subsection, we will dive into the world of crypto-assets, exploring the workings, history, and proliferation of these new instruments and establishing a taxonomy for organizing their many variants. Finally, in our fourth subsection, we will explore the emerging technology of artificial intelligence, first providing a high-level overview of its definition and workings, before exploring the ways this technology is being applied to within the financial ecosystem.

The Fundamentals of a Rapidly Changing Technological Landscape

To understand how new technologies and their applications are changing the future of financial services, it is imperative that we understand the foundations of how technology itself is evolving. In the following two chapters, we will first explore the relationship between the exponential increase of computational power, new networks of connectivity, and the rise of the data economy before considering the advent of new human-to-machine interfaces and their implications for our interactions with digital technologies. This background will help set the scene for this book and help us better understand the changes that will affect the financial services industry in the future.

1

The Digital Triumvirate of Computation, Data, and Connectivity

The past 50 years have seen rapid technological change that has fundamentally shifted the boundaries of human possibility, enabling radical improvements in productivity, new scientific advances, and the advent of both new communities and new divisions within society. These changes have forced a rapid transformation of both the operational structure and the core tenets of competitiveness for every industry, creating a host of new challenges and opportunities for businesses, their customers, and the policymakers responsible for governing them.

The following chapter will consider the rapid increase in the capacity and accessibility of computational power, data, and networks of digital connectivity, as well as the implications of the confluence of these three forces.

1.1 Increasing Computational Power

In 1965, Intel co-founder Gordon E. Moore made a radical prediction. He argued that the number of transistors in an integrated circuit would double every two years. These circuits are crucial to any electronic device; made of a network of transistors and other components, they perform the complex calculations that keep a device running and completing tasks. As the number of transistors on every integrated circuit goes up, computing power increases in step.

Moore's prediction proved correct and forms the basis for what is now called Moore's law in his honor. This increase in computational power has been the primary driver of the rapid advancement in technology that we have seen over the past 50 years. At the same time, the cost of computational power

© The Author(s) 2019
H. Arslanian, F. Fischer, *The Future of Finance*,
https://doi.org/10.1007/978-3-030-14533-0_1

has fallen spectacularly: between 1980 and 2010, the number of transactions per second purchasable for a single US dollar has increased 10 millionfold.[1]

The result is a world in which the average person has in their pocket a device whose computational power is millions of times more powerful than the combined computing power used by NASA to complete the Apollo 11 mission to the Moon.[2] In fact, it is the reason that almost every device used in your life today, from your toaster to your electric toothbrush, likely contains several microchips.

But Moore's law cannot persist forever. There are fundamental physical limits to how small a transistor can be and we are already pushing those boundaries. For example, Intel's advanced 'Skylake' transistor is only 100 atoms across. Pushing up against these boundaries increases both the cost and the complexity of the development of new chips, suggesting that sooner or later new approaches will need to be found if computational power is to continue increasing exponentially.[3]

One frontier of exploration that has captured the attention and imagination of many is an entirely different approach to computing called quantum computing that relies on insights from a complex branch of physics called quantum mechanics. A quantum computer would radically shift the boundaries of what a machine can do, potentially allowing us to encrypt data with near-perfect security as well as predict changes to complex systems such as the climate.[4]

Box 1.1   What Is Quantum Computing?

Experimentation in the field of quantum computing seeks to deliver new computational capabilities by harnessing the complex, and often counterintuitive world of properties of subatomic particles, through a branch of physics called 'quantum mechanics'. These subatomic particles don't behave in the same way as physical objects in our daily activities, which have well-defined positions and characteristics. Instead, subatomic particles exhibit a property called 'superposition' where they can effectively exist in multiple places at the same time.

This property turns out to be important for computing. Traditional computers, from the most basic calculator to the most powerful supercomputer, all perform calculations using something called 'binary code' where all data is encoded as a series of ones or zeros called bits. A quantum computer also uses ones and zeros,

(continued)

---

[1] "One Dollar's Worth of Computer Power, 1980–2010," accessed January 5, 2019, http://www.hamiltonproject.org/charts/one_dollars_worth_of_computer_power_1980_2010.

[2] Tibi Puiu, "Your Smartphone Is Millions of Times More Powerful than All of NASA's Combined Computing in 1969," *ZME Science*, September 10, 2017, https://www.zmescience.com/research/technology/smartphone-power-compared-to-apollo-432/.

[3] "After Moore's Law | Technology Quarterly," *The Economist*, February 25, 2016, https://www.economist.com/technology-quarterly/2016-03-12/after-moores-law.

[4] Larry Greenemeier, "How Close Are We–Really–to Building a Quantum Computer?," *Scientific American*, May 30, 2018, https://www.scientificamerican.com/article/how-close-are-we-really-to-building-a-quantum-computer/.

Box 1.1   (continued)

but through 'super-position', a quantum bit, or qubit, can in some sense be one and zero at the same time.[5]

If that doesn't make any sense, don't worry. Physicist Richard Feynman, who won a Nobel prize for his contributions to the field, once quipped that 'nobody understands quantum mechanics'.[6] What matters is that a quantum computer would enable us to quickly solve problems that are extremely difficult for conventional computing systems.

For example, take the classic challenge of the 'traveling salesperson problem' where a sales agent who needs to visit a dozen cities on a trip wishes to chart the most efficient route. Because of the enormous number of permutations of possible trips, this turns out to be an extremely difficult problem to solve for conventional computers and proves impossible to fully optimize at the level of a shipping company like FedEx. However, using a quantum computing system, such calculations could be completed much more quickly.[7]

A range of potential applications for quantum computing exists in financial services, most notably the optimizing of large investment portfolios and the identification of arbitrage opportunities. They may also be able to accelerate the process of deep learning in financial services and more broadly.[8]

However, these new computational capabilities could also pose challenges. Today's data encryption techniques (discussed more in Chap. 8) mostly rely on a branch of mathematics called 'one-way functions', which are easy to compute if you already have the answer (also known as the private key), but where reverse engineering that key through guess work might take millions of years for a conventional computer. However, a powerful quantum computer could theoretically break through the encryption that secures our most valuable data (and, as we will see in Chaps. 9 and 11, the majority of crypto-assets) in seconds.[9]

But don't go out and try to buy a quantum computer just yet. While an array of technology firms, including big names like IBM, Google, and Microsoft, are making sizable investments in the technology, today's prototype systems lack the power to deliver on any of the applications discussed above.[10] Estimates of how long it will take to build a fully-fledged quantum computer are uncertain, but some experts imagine that it may take until 2030 or 2040 at the earliest.[11] Even then, the highly specialized applications of these devices, combined with the complex mechanisms required to harness subatomic particles for computation, mean you are unlikely to have a quantum computer in your pocket any time soon.

---

[5] Tom Simonite, "What Is Quantum Computing? The Complete WIRED Guide," *WIRED* (WIRED, August 24, 2018), https://www.wired.com/story/wired-guide-to-quantum-computing/.

[6] Ibid.

[7] Dominic J. Moylett, Noah Linden, Ashley Montanaro., "Quantum Speedup of the Traveling-Salesman Problem for Bounded-Degree Graphs," *Physical Review*, 2017, https://people.maths.bris.ac.uk/~csxam/papers/tsp.pdf.

[8] Roman Orus, Samuel Mugel, and Enrique Lizaso. "Quantum computing for finance: overview and prospects." *arXiv preprint arXiv:1807.03890* (2018).

[9] "Quantum Computers Will Break the Encryption That Protects the Internet," *The Economist* (The Economist, 2018), https://www.economist.com/science-and-technology/2018/10/20/quantum-computers-will-break-the-encryption-that-protects-the-internet.

[10] Note 6.

[11] Note 9.

Extensive research is currently underway to develop a quantum computer by large firms such as Google, IBM, and Microsoft as well as small specialists such as Rigetti, IonQ, and Dwave.[12] Unfortunately, the technical challenges to building a reliable quantum computer with sufficient processing power to be useful are significant.[13]

1.2   Increasing Data Collection and Availability

Not so long ago the storage of digital data faced two significant barriers: price and size. In 1956, the IBM 305 RAMC, which represented the cutting edge of data storage technology, needed the space of two refrigerators to store five megabytes (at a cost of US$10,000 per megabyte). Today a 500-gigabyte hard drive with 100,000 times that capacity can fit in the palm of your hand and costs less than a hundred dollars (a cost of less than two cents per megabyte[14]).

The extremely low cost of data storage has encouraged both individuals and businesses to accumulate data almost without limit. Where once storage was a resource to be judiciously rationed, today it is not unusual for users to refrain from deleting anything at all. Consider, for example, how many poorly lit or blurry photos you might have on your phone and the last time you deleted them.

The availability of data storage, combined with the ubiquity of microchips, has driven an enormous proliferation of sensors. Almost every device today has built-in sensors that analyze everything from sound to light to acceleration. These sensors create an endless flow of data that enable the aggregation of a nexus of data points around the simplest actions to create a universe of insights.

The confluence of these trends means that data is being accumulated at a truly unprecedented rate. According to former Google CEO Eric Schmidt, every two days we now create as much new data as we did from the beginning of recorded history up to 2003.[15] This radical increase in the quantity and availability of data is transforming the priorities of companies across almost

---

[12] "The Race to Build a Quantum Computer | NIST," NIST, accessed January 30, 2019, https://www.nist.gov/topics/physics/introduction-new-quantum-revolution/race-build-quantum-computer.

[13] Peter Gwynne, "Practical Quantum Computers Remain at Least a Decade Away," *Physics World*, December 12, 2018, https://physicsworld.com/a/practical-quantum-computers-remain-at-least-a-decade-away/.

[14] Jennifer Dutcher, "Data Size Matters [Infographic]," *What Is Data Science?*, November 6, 2013, https://datascience.berkeley.edu/big-data-infographic/.

[15] M. G. Siegler, "Eric Schmidt: Every 2 Days We Create as Much Information as We Did Up to 2003," *TechCrunch*, August 4, 2010, https://techcrunch.com/2010/08/04/schmidt-data/.

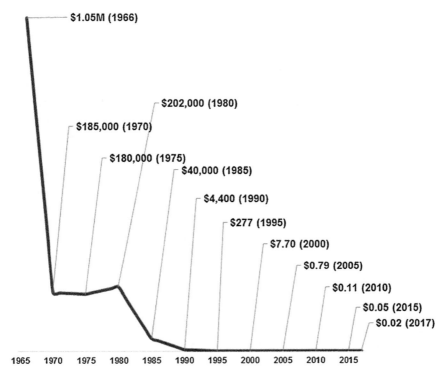

$1.05M (1966)

$202,000 (1980)

$185,000 (1970)

$180,000 (1975)
$40,000 (1985)

$4,400 (1990)

$277 (1995)

$7.70 (2000)

$0.79 (2005)

$0.11 (2010)

$0.05 (2015)
$0.02 (2017)

1965   1970   1975   1980   1985   1990   1995   2000   2005   2010   2015

Fig. 1.1 Cost per gigabyte of storage over time; Once extraordinarily expensive, the cost of storing large quantities of data has dropped to fractions of a cent. Source(s): Lucas Mearian, "CW@50: Data Storage Goes from $1M to 2 Cents per Gigabyte (+video)," Computerworld, March 23, 2017, https://www.computerworld.com/article/3182207/data-storage/cw50-data-storage-goes-from-1m-to-2-cents-per-gigabyte.html

every industry as well as placing extreme strain on the governance and regulatory regimes intended to protect this often-sensitive data.

Data is becoming central to the business models of firms around the world. Obvious examples include data services firms like Dow Jones, Factiva, and Bloomberg, as well as large technology companies like Google and Facebook whose ability to generate valuable consumer data drives their core business of advertising. However, the growing importance of data is also deeply impacting the priorities of more traditional manufacturing or services firms.

Take, for example, the automotive industry. In the past, automotive manufacturers would focus on the final assembly of a component like a dashboard and the production of the plastic molding, while using a subcontractor to handle the production of the wiring assemblies to go inside. Today, automotive manufacturers view the streams of data coming from the numerous

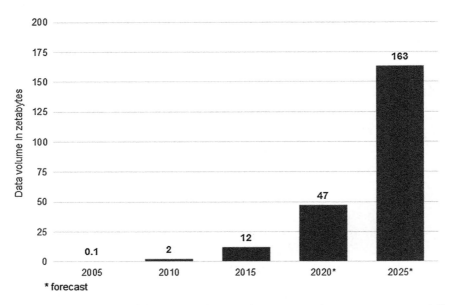

Fig. 1.2 Global volume of data created in zettabytes; Data is increasing exponentially, with more new data now created each year than from the beginning of recorded history to 2003. Source(s): "Data Created Worldwide 2005–2025 | Statistic," Statista, accessed January 30, 2019, https://www.statista.com/statistics/871513/worldwide-data-created/

sensors located in the car as a cornerstone of their competitive positioning. As a result, the supply chain has inverted with the dashboard plastic often being handled by a subcontractor while the automaker focuses on design and installation of the sensors to go inside.

The data produced by the automotive manufacturer can also be quite useful in at least one corner of financial services. The car's sensors capture detailed information on the behavior of the driver, painting a picture of all of the driver's choices from whether she is prone to speeding to whether she drives mostly during the day or at night. With access to this data, car insurers have the opportunity to calibrate the driver's premiums in a much more personalized way than offered by traditional actuarial tables that simply account for the type of individuals (e.g. sex, age, history).

The competitive importance of data produced by sensors such as these, combined with its often-sensitive and personal nature, makes the governance and protection of this data a fraught but important issue. Clearly the insurer will want access to the car's data, but who should have a say in whether or not they do? The automotive manufacturer may feel they should have a say, given that they built the sensors and may demand some kind of fee to access the data.

At the same time, the driver might not like the idea of her every turn or poor parallel parking attempt being monitored and might also argue she should have the final say on whether or not the data is used.

Protection, governance, and ownership of the terabytes of data being generated every day are of growing concern to policymakers around the world. The General Data Protection Regulation (GDPR) recently enacted by the European Union is a particularly notable example of a sweeping set of regulations that establish strict guidelines on the use and storage of data with significant fines of up to 4% of global revenues for firms who fail to comply.[16]

Ultimately these regulations need to strike a delicate balance between competing goals such as privacy and public security. Moreover, they must both encourage innovation in the development of new 'data economy' business models and meet goals for customer enfranchisement and competition. Getting the rules right will be far from simple, but is necessary to ensure that the current explosion of data is a force for public good.

1.3   Increasing Digital Connectivity

In the early days of computing, all of an organization's data would likely be stored on a single computer, which could only be accessed by one person at any time. But as the number of computers being used by an organization grew, so did the need to share data between people and offices. A digital network was needed to facilitate the exchange of data between points of computational power, both in a particular location via a local area network (LAN) and between locations around the world on a wide area network (WAN).

The sharing of data between devices may seem like a trivial problem, but it is in fact quite an elaborate process. Data first needs to be read by the sending device before being transported. It also then needs to be received and written on the new device, before being read again in order to compute it. This means that hundreds of calculations are run at every step, and that the larger the quantity of data being transferred, the more computationally intensive the process, making the creation of data networks particularly challenging for early computers.

As a result, the first packet of data sent over a digital network back in 1969 turned out to be very small indeed, just the two letters 'lo'. These were the first two letters of the word 'login', a word which a graduate student at UCLA was

---

[16] "Compliance Fines and Penalties," *GDPR EU.ORG*, accessed January 5, 2019, https://www.gdpreu.org/compliance/fines-and-penalties/.

trying to transmit to a computer at Stanford.[17] Before he could send the entire word, his system crashed. This inauspicious start is the foundation of what we now call the Internet.

Today over a million miles of fiber-optic cables crisscross the globe,[18] providing the backbone for the data connectivity network that transfers 640 terabytes of data per minute[19] and connects almost half of the world's population.[20] Ultimately this network has allowed data to become decentralized—shifting from an architecture of data being stored in an organization's server for a unique use to it being shared, exchanged, and combined with other data from other sources around the world.

The past 50 years have seen radical accelerations in the speed of data transfer across digital networks as well as the emergence of new mediums of transferring data from copper wire, to fiber optics, to the wireless networks that connect our mobile phones and other mobile devices. The cutting edge of these developments today is the development of the 5G, or fifth generation, wireless network. The vision for this new network seeks to enable the transfer of data at previously unimaginable speeds, allowing an individual to, for example, download an entire ultra-high definition film in just a few seconds on their mobile phone.

Such a network will do more than simply provide consumers with faster download speeds; they are set to enable a new level of connectivity between devices. Already the laptops, cars, fridges, and children's toys that populate our lives are not individual islands of computational power: they are part of an emergent network often called the internet of things (IoT). The advent of 5G wireless networks will allow much larger quantities of data to be transferred near instantaneously between devices and will be a critical enabler of a range of technologies currently being developed such as autonomous vehicles.[21]

---

[17] Mike McDowall, "How a Simple 'hello' Became the First Message Sent via the Internet," *PBS*, February 9, 2015, https://www.pbs.org/newshour/science/internet-got-started-simple-hello.

[18] Nick Routley, "MAPPED: The World's Network of Undersea Cables," *Business Insider*, August 26, 2017, https://www.businessinsider.com/map-the-worlds-network-of-undersea-cables-2017-8.

[19] Rick Burgess, "One Minute on the Internet: 640TB Data Transferred, 100k Tweets, 204 Million E-Mails Sent," *Techspot*, March 20, 2013, https://www.techspot.com/news/52011-one-minute-on-the-internet-640tb-data-transferred-100k-tweets-204-million-e-mails-sent.html.

[20] Adam Taylor, "47 Percent of the World's Population Now Use the Internet, Study Says," *Washington Post* (The Washington Post, November 22, 2016), https://www.washingtonpost.com/news/worldviews/wp/2016/11/22/47-percent-of-the-worlds-population-now-use-the-internet-users-study-says/.

[21] Amy Nordrum, Kristen Clark and IEEE Spectrum Staff, "Everything You Need to Know About 5G," *IEEE Spectrum*, January 27, 2017, https://spectrum.ieee.org/video/telecom/wireless/everything-you-need-to-know-about-5g.

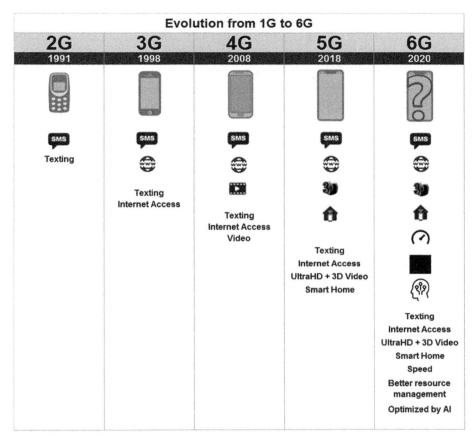

Fig. 1.3 Evolution from 1G to 6G mobile networks; Rapid improvements in mobile connectivity are enabling the formation of new data-rich networks

Of course, increased connectivity creates its own share of challenges. As high bandwidth, low latency connectivity becomes more and more central to our daily lives, our vulnerability to the failure of the infrastructure that enables this connectivity increases as well. For example, in 2010, the accidental severing of the African Coast to Europe (ACE) submarine cable, likely by a fishing trawler, left the entire country of Mauritania offline for 48 hours and disrupted connectivity of nine other West African nations.[22]

---

[22] Chris Baynes, "Entire Country Taken Offline for Two Days after Undersea Internet Cable Cut," *The Independent*, April 10, 2018, https://www.independent.co.uk/news/world/africa/mauritiana-internet-cut-underwater-cable-offline-days-west-africa-a8298551.html.

At the same time, the frequent movement of data across national and sub-national boundaries adds an additional layer of complexity to the challenges of data privacy discussed earlier in this chapter. The landscape of data regulation is a patchwork of varying, and sometime conflicting, requirements. How should data be treated as it moves between jurisdictions? How should data about a user in one jurisdiction be treated when moved to another jurisdiction? These questions have prompted close examination by regulators, and in some cases, have triggered strict data-residency requirements that limit the ability of data to move across borders. Given the limitations these residency requirements place on the many emerging business models predicated on the free flow of global data, they are likely to remain key regulatory flashpoints in the years to come.

1.4   Bringing Computation, Connectivity, and Data Together in the Cloud

Exponential increases in computational power, dramatic decreases in the size and cost of storage, and a dizzying acceleration in data transfer speeds: any one of these alone is revolutionary, but together they can be truly disruptive. These capabilities can be combined in many ways, but there is perhaps no better distillation of their combined power than the rise of cloud computing.

You might think of the cloud in terms of consumer services like Dropbox or iCloud that allow you to remotely store data such as photos, making them accessible from multiple devices at a moment's notice. You might also think of it in terms of collaboration tools like Google Docs that allow teams of people in multiple locations around the world to edit a document in real time. However, while cloud services certainly facilitate collaboration and access to remote storage, its full impact runs much deeper.

Cloud computing enables organizations to dynamically scale their data storage, computational power, and bandwidth. Put simply, it does this by chopping a given computational task into many smaller processes and using a vast shared pool of servers in a data center operated by the cloud provider to complete the task. The computing resources of these cloud computing providers can be massive. Amazon Web Services, one of the largest providers of cloud computing in the world, has as many as 80,000 servers in a single data center with 28 data centers around the world.[23]

---

[23] Jack Clark, "5 Numbers That Illustrate the Mind-Bending Size of Amazon's Cloud," *Bloomberg*, November 14, 2014, https://www.bloomberg.com/news/2014-11-14/5-numbers-that-illustrate-the-mind-bending-size-of-amazon-s-cloud.html.

While many companies were initially hesitant about the idea of entrusting their data and IT operations to third-party infrastructure, preferring 'on-premises' solutions, the value proposition of cloud computing has proven highly compelling.

One reason for this is that the computational and storage demands of an organization are not static. They fluctuate over time depending on a wide range of factors. For example, an online retailer may experience much higher traffic around key holiday gift buying seasons than any other time of the year. If information technology infrastructure is kept on premises, the firm would need to purchase a sufficient number of servers to meet their maximum demand leaving most of these machines inactive except during peak seasons. If instead the firm 'rents' computing cycles from a cloud data center, they can scale their usage up and down dynamically, paying only for what they need and potentially achieving significant cost advantages.

In fact, this very narrative is how Amazon found itself in the business of cloud computing. Having built out massive data centers to address times of peak demand, they realized that an opportunity existed to monetize their idle computing cycles (as well as the competencies they had developed in running data centers) by providing IT infrastructure 'as a service'. In 2006, the company launched Amazon Elastic Compute Cloud, now a sub-offering of Amazon Web Services (AWS), making them first to market with a modern cloud infrastructure service. The service posted remarkable year-over-year growth at an average of 57%[24] and now accounts for a significant portion of Amazon's total profitability with operating income of over US$5 billion in the first three quarters of 2018.[25] Its clients past and present include Netflix, Airbnb,[26] and even the CIA.[27]

The flexibility offered by cloud computing is particularly important for high-growth digitally focused startups. Prior to the existence of cloud services, a new company would need to make significant capital outlays in the purchase of servers and the hiring of staff to maintain those servers. Moreover, if growth exceeded expectations, they might struggle to bring new servers online quickly

[24] Ron Miller, "How AWS Came to Be," *TechCrunch*, July 2, 2016, https://techcrunch.com/2016/07/02/andy-jassys-brief-history-of-the-genesis-of-aws/.

[25] Amazon.com, Inc., "Amazon.com Announces Third Quarter Sales up 29% to $56.6 Billion," October 25, 2018, https://ir.aboutamazon.com/news-releases/news-release-details/amazoncom-announces-third-quarter-sales-29-566-billion.

[26] Amazon, "All Customer Success Stories," *Amazon Web Services (AWS)*, accessed January 5, 2019, https://aws.amazon.com/solutions/case-studies/all/.

[27] Amazon, "Public Sector Customer Success Stories," *Amazon Web Services (AWS)*, accessed January 5, 2019, https://aws.amazon.com/solutions/case-studies/government-education/.

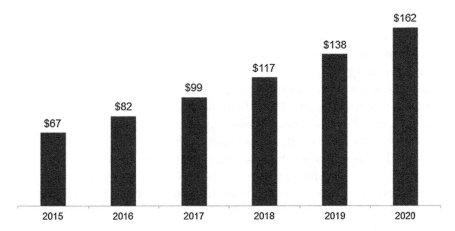

Fig. 1.4 Forecasted global spending on cloud computing, 2015–2020 (US$B); Public cloud computing resources provide access to scalable computing and data storage resources. Source(s): "Data Created Worldwide 2005–2025 | Statistic," Statista, accessed January 30, 2019, https://www.statista.com/statistics/871513/worldwide-data-created/

enough, leading to operational failures and dissatisfied new or potential customers. By using cloud computing, a single individual can easily design and deploy a new application or service and scale their computational usage dynamically according to demand. This has dramatically reduced the investment required to start new digital services businesses and has arguably encouraged significantly greater innovation in this sector over the past decade.

Capital efficiency and scalability are not the only advantages of cloud computing. Cloud-based IT arguably offers higher levels of security than on-premises infrastructure, which may be more vulnerable to cyberattacks or disgruntled employees. It also offers an environment that enables the increased reuse of code and makes data integration across an organization's lines of business and with other firms much easier. Most importantly, the cloud provides a more suitable environment for the analysis of large datasets and the deployment of sophisticated algorithms such as machine learning models.

Take for example the deployment of evolutionary algorithms. These models are designed to work like natural selection—eliminating inefficient methods to arrive at an optimized solution. They are increasingly used in the trading of securities to predict the movements of stocks based on a range of variables. This technique requires massive amounts of data and processing power best delivered in a cloud environment to continuously track variables and identify patterns.

It should be noted that cloud computing is not ideal for all tasks, as it may sometimes make more sense to conduct computations where data is being created rather than transporting it to another location with more powerful and efficient computational resources. In cases where new data must be analyzed as quickly as possible—for example, autonomous vehicles where fast response times could be the difference between life and death—data may be analyzed in place rather than in the cloud.

2

New Interfaces for the Digital World

The previous chapter detailed the rapid acceleration of computational power, data creation, and connectivity, as well as the impact of these three trends. However, the new capabilities of these technologies are only useful if humans can easily and effectively interact with them. Interfaces are critical to the success of any technology product. They collect data, facilitate user requests, and deliver the processed information back to the user. Moreover, creating interfaces that gather new and richer sets of data on their users is increasingly central to the business models of many firms.

In this chapter, we will explore the history of human-machine interfaces and how emerging interface technologies are making engagement with technology both easier and richer.

2.1 The Evolution of Visual Displays

The medium of the computer display has evolved significantly over the past 100 years. It might be hard to imagine a computer without a visual display, and while the technology of the cathode ray tube (CRT) monitor has existed since 1897,[1] the first use of this technology for a computer display was actually in the 1950s for a system called SAGE (Semi-Automatic Ground Environment), developed by the US military to detect Soviet bombers and

---

[1] Stephanie Walden, "Tech Time Machine: Screens and Display," *Mashable*, accessed January 5, 2019, https://mashable.com/2015/01/06/screen-display-tech-ces/#e.WJ5m0AguqQ.

© The Author(s) 2019
H. Arslanian, F. Fischer, *The Future of Finance*,
https://doi.org/10.1007/978-3-030-14533-0_2

guide American intercept missiles.[2] Prior to this, computing systems such as the Zuse 23 Terminal developed in 1941[3] or the UNIVAC 1 Console developed in 1951,[4] used punch cards, teletape, or an automatic typewriter to physically print all computational outputs.

The invention of the light-emitting diode in 1961 followed closely by the development of the first working liquid crystal display (LCD) and plasma display in 1964 enabled the development of much flatter and thinner displays[5] than the bulky CRT. While these technologies, like early cathode ray tubes, were initially monochrome, color-compatible versions were developed over time. Indeed, these are the foundation of many of today's interfaces, including the displays of most TVs, laptops, and smartphones.

The development of these displays has been critical to the democratization and proliferation of computing technology. The integration of the CRT monitor with the invention of the computer mouse enabled the development of the graphical user interface (GUI), first commercially launched by Apple in 1983.[6] The advent of GUIs made computing experiences more visually appealing to consumers, and significantly reduced the complexity of interacting with these systems by removing the need to engage with a less intuitive command line interface.

The evolution of display technology has also been critical to the miniaturization of our devices. The ability to pack the massive computational power and connectivity of a smartphone into a device little larger than a pack of cards is not particularly useful if you also need to carry around a CRT monitor and a physical keyboard in order to interact with it.

The development of touchscreens, first invented in 1965,[7] has been particularly impactful in enabling our interaction with small devices and the subsequent smartphone revolution. The commercial launch of the Apple iPhone in 2007,[8] followed by the development of similar devices by Samsung and

---

[2] "SAGE: Semi-Automatic Ground Environment Air Defense System | MIT Lincoln Laboratory," MIT Lincoln Laboratory (Massachusetts Institute of Technology), accessed January 30, 2019, https://www.ll.mit.edu/about/history/sage-semi-automatic-ground-environment-air-defense-system.

[3] "Computer History Museum—Zuse Computer Z23," Computerhistory.org, accessed January 30, 2019, https://www.computerhistory.org/projects/zuse_z23/.

[4] Michael R. Swaine and Paul A. Freiberger, "UNIVAC | Computer | Britannica.Com," Britannica, October 7, 2008, https://www.britannica.com/technology/UNIVAC.

[5] Walden, "Tech Time Machine: Screens and Display."

[6] Andrew Pollack, "APPLE'S LISA MAKES A DEBUT," *The New York Times*, January 19, 1983, https://www.nytimes.com/1983/01/19/business/apple-s-lisa-makes-a-debut.html.

[7] Note 5.

[8] Apple Inc., "Apple Reinvents the Phone with iPhone," January 9, 2007, https://www.apple.com/newsroom/2007/01/09Apple-Reinvents-the-Phone-with-iPhone/.

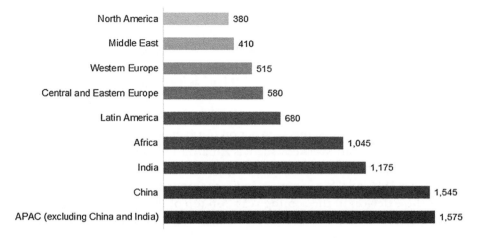

Fig. 2.1 Total mobile subscriptions as of Q3 2018; Global mobile subscriptions now exceed 7.9 billion, with 5.7 billion of those providing broadband connectivity. Source(s): "Mobile Subscriptions Worldwide Q3 2018—Ericsson Mobility Report November 2018," Ericsson.com, November 20, 2018, https://www.ericsson.com/en/mobility-report/reports/november-2018/mobile-subscriptions-worldwide-q3-2018

others, has triggered a technological and behavioral revolution. Ninety-eight million new mobile subscriptions were added worldwide in the first quarter of 2018 alone,[9] and the nature of these devices and their displays changes, among other things, users' purchasing behavior, enabling anywhere/anytime browsing and shopping (Fig. 2.1).[10]

Moving forward, the development and refinement of new display technologies such as flexible displays and organic LEDs can be expected to continue to change the way in which we interact with our devices.

2.2   Voice as a User Interface

Our hands, whether typing, clicking, or tapping, are the most frequent means by which we interact with our digital devices and communicate electronically today. However, our in-person interactions continue to use another interface that has been honed over countless millennia—our voice.

---

[9] "Ericsson Mobility Report" (Ericsson, June 2018), https://www.ericsson.com/assets/local/mobility-report/documents/2018/ericsson-mobility-report-june-2018.pdf.

[10] Theo Anderson, "How We Shop Differently on Our Phones," *KelloggInsight* (Kellogg School of Management, Northwestern University), accessed January 5, 2019, https://insight.kellogg.northwestern.edu/article/how-we-shop-differently-on-our-phones.

Voice is a natural and intuitive way for us to express ourselves, so it unsurprising that we have a desire to communicate with our digital devices through this same medium. A computer's ability to understand spoken human language has increased significantly in recent years, and English voice-to-text now boasts an accuracy rate of over 94%, as good as professional human transcribers.[11]

The implications of this technology are profound, enabling us to interact verbally with virtual assistants who act on our behalf in the digital realm. The proliferation of 'smart speakers' such as Amazon Echo or Google Home provides a strong indication of consumers' demand for these types of interactions, with 19% of US consumers indicating that they planned to purchase one of these devices in the coming year[12] on top of the 24% who already own such a device.[13]

Of course, aspects of this new interface medium present challenges. While a smart speaker may seem to understand what a user is saying, today's natural language processing systems use a process of picking out keywords and using them to construct a response. This can be challenging in instances where words have multiple meanings depending on context and tone.

Persistent difficulties also exist around efforts to use the voice as an authentication medium. In a notable news case, a BBC reporter asked his twin brother to attempt to breach a voice authentication system used by HSBC. His brother managed to trick the system and get access to the account.[14]

Designing voice authentication is challenging, because it is difficult to determine how stringent the system should be given that the 'voice print' of a customer might change after, say, a couple of pints of beer or a night out at a rock concert. Too stringent, and the system will cause issues for legitimate customers, but too lenient and it risks authenticating someone who isn't you.

---

[11] Devin Coldewey, "Microsoft Hits a Speech Recognition Milestone with a System Just as Good as Human Ears," *TechCrunch* (TechCrunch, October 18, 2016), http://social.techcrunch.com/2016/10/18/microsoft-hits-a-speech-recognition-milestone-with-a-system-just-as-good-as-human-ears/.

[12] Brian Heater, "Smart Speaker Sales on Pace to Increase 50 Percent by 2019," *TechCrunch* (TechCrunch, August 14, 2018), http://social.techcrunch.com/2018/08/14/smart-speaker-sales-on-pace-to-increase-50-percent-by-2019/.

[13] Micah Singleton, "Nearly a Quarter of US Households Own a Smart Speaker, according to Nielsen," *The Verge* (The Verge, September 30, 2018), https://www.theverge.com/circuitbreaker/2018/9/30/17914022/smart-speaker-40-percent-us-households-nielsen-amazon-echo-google-home-apple-homepod.

[14] Patrick Collinson, "HSBC Voice Recognition System Breached by Customer's Twin," *The Guardian*, May 19, 2017, https://www.theguardian.com/business/2017/may/19/hsbc-voice-recognition-system-breached-by-customers-twin.

2.3   Wearables and the Body as an Interface

The idea of wearable digital devices has been around for several decades. For example, the 1977 International Watch and Jewellery Trade Fair in London saw the launch of the world's first calculator watch.[15] While technically impressive, these devices have only recently begun to see large-scale usage as their sophistication has increased. Smart watches such as the Apple Watch and fitness tracking bands such as the Fitbit or the Xiaomi Mi Band have seen significant growth in recent years with some forecasts predicting the global market to grow from 84 million units in 2015 to 245 million units in 2019.[16]

These devices boast the ability to perform a range of functions from displaying emails to tracking your heart rate. As the sophistication of these devices grows, and as networks of sensors become integrated into other wearable objects such as clothing, it is likely that these devices will have the ability to keep our bodies under constant measurement, tracking vital statistics like blood pressure and respiratory rate. Together with other physical augmentation devices currently being explored, such as smart prosthetics and advanced hearing aids, wearable technologies can be expected to have significant implications for the health ecosystem.

As the sophistication of these sensors improves, they will increasingly be able to capture a range of visual, audio, olfactory, and biochemical inputs from our body, perhaps even including the ability to monitor and derive useful signals from our brainwaves themselves. While traditional display interfaces continue to evolve, and voice interfaces become more and more ubiquitous, it may be the direct interface with our bodies that could perhaps present the most impactful shift in our relationship with digital devices in the years to come.

---

[15] Erica Schwiegershausen, "A Brief History of Wearable Tech," *The Cut*, April 24, 2015, https://www.thecut.com/2015/04/brief-history-of-wearable-tech.html.

[16] Marina Koytcheva, "Wearables Market to Be Worth $25 Billion by 2019," accessed January 5, 2019, https://www.ccsinsight.com/press/company-news/2332-wearables-market-to-be-worth-25-billion-by-2019-reveals-ccs-insight.

Part II

The Fundamentals of Fintech

In the previous two chapters, we considered how the rapid pace of technological advancement is transforming the way in which businesses interact with their customers, social groups interact with each other, and how we interact with our own bodies. In the following chapters, we will turn our attention to the core focus of this text: the implications these technologies are having on the operational structure, competitive dynamics, and governance requirements of the financial services industry.

Before diving into a focused exploration of two particularly transformative technologies—crypto-assets and artificial intelligence—let's take a moment to consider the broader impacts of technological advancement on financial services, and in particular, the way in which these advancements enable new forms of competition. In Chap. 3, we will explore the rise of fintechs, agile startups seeking to disrupt incumbent financial institutions, and in Chap. 4, we will explore the response of the incumbents as they seek to preserve their position. In Chap. 5, we will consider the position of large technology firms entering the realm of financial services, paying particular attention to the instructive lessons of developments in China. In Chap. 6, we will consider how the combination of these three categories of competitors is evolving. Finally, in Chap. 7, we will consider how the increased use of technology in financial services is supporting the goal of a more inclusive global financial system.

3

The Rise of Fintech

The decade since the financial crisis has seen an explosion of new entrants into financial services. Agile, technology-focused 'fintech' firms have sought to upend the established order of financial services, changing the dominant operating models and competitive dynamics of an industry that, in the 50 years prior, had seen remarkably little change in market structure.

The speed of fintech's growth has been remarkable. The first half of 2018 saw global investments in fintech companies totaling US$57.9 billion across 875 separate deals,[1] and as of 2018, 28 separate venture capital–backed companies have private market valuations in excess of US$1 billion,[2] giving them the coveted title of 'unicorns'.

Many argue that these firms are the beginning of a revolution that will reshape the financial ecosystem, creating new winners and losers in the process. While fintech is often portrayed by the media as a battle between incumbent institutions and new entrants, the reality is far more complex. The ecosystem extends far beyond the most boisterous fintechs directly challenging incumbent firms for customer ownership to include a range of players transforming the back office, middle office, and regulatory workings of the financial system.

---

[1] Anton Ruddenklau Ian Pollari, "The Pulse of Fintech—2018" (KPMG, July 31, 2018), https://home.kpmg.com/xx/en/home/insights/2018/07/pulse-of-fintech-h1-2018.html.
[2] "Global Fintech Report Q2 2018," *CB Insights*, July 2018, https://www.cbinsights.com/research/report/fintech-trends-q2-2018/.

© The Author(s) 2019
H. Arslanian, F. Fischer, *The Future of Finance*,
https://doi.org/10.1007/978-3-030-14533-0_3

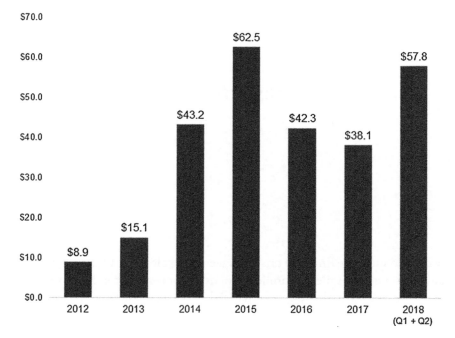

Fig. 3.1 Global investment activity in Fintech (venture capital, private equity, and M&A); From 2012 to the middle of 2018, over US$260 billion in venture capital, private equity, and M&A investments have been made into fintech companies. Source(s): "The Pulse of Fintech 2018" (KPMG, July 31, 2018), https://assets.kpmg/content/dam/kpmg/xx/pdf/2018/07/h1-2018-pulse-of-fintech.pdf

3.1   Drivers of the Fintech Revolution

But why is the fintech revolution happening now? In our view, the current environment of rapid change has three catalysts: a changing macroeconomic and regulatory environment, the rapid evolution of technology, and shifting customer expectations.

3.1.1   A Changing Economic/Regulatory Landscape

In the wake of the global financial crisis in 2008, a number of economic and regulatory factors converged to facilitate the growth of fintech. As regulators sought to improve the safety and soundness of the financial system, they drastically increased the regulatory burden on financial institutions, forcing them to divert the majority of their internal focus and resources to 'must-have' risk management and compliance initiatives that caused product and process innovation to take a back seat.

Name	Valuation (US$ billion)	Country
Lu.com	18.5	
Stripe	9.2	
Paytm - One97	7.0	
Robinhood	5.3	
SoFi	4.5	
Credit Karma	4.0	
Oscar	3.2	
Circle	3.0	
Klarna	2.5	
Zenefits	2.0 (as of Q2'15)	
Avant	1.9	
Affirm	1.8	
Revolut	1.7	
TransferWise	1.6	
Coinbase	1.6	
Nubank	1.0 - 2.0	
Tuandaiwang	1.5	
Dataminr	1.2 - 1.6	
AvidXchange	1.2	
Clover	1.2	
UiPath	1.1	
51 Credit	1.0	
Funding Circle	1.0	
Gusto	1.0	
Kabbage	1.0	
PolicyBazaar	1.0	
Symphony	1.0	
Tongdun Technology	1.0	
Tradeshift	1.0	

Fig. 3.2 Global VC-backed Fintech Companies with a private market valuation of $1B+; Recent years have seen an explosion of Fintech 'unicorns'. Source(s): "The Fintech 250: The Top Fintech Startups Of 2018," CB Insights Research, October 22, 2018, https://www.cbinsights.com/research/fintech-250-startups-most-promising/

Simultaneously, a number of regulators sought to encourage the emergence of nontraditional competition, such as the newly formed Financial Conduct Authority in the United Kingdom, that included the promotion of competition as one of its three core operational objectives alongside protecting customers and enhancing market integrity. Finally, the extremely low interest rates in the years following the financial crisis created a low-yield environment that significantly increased the flow of funds into alternative asset classes like venture capital. These flows helped increase the availability of funding for a wide range of new innovators including fintech entrepreneurs.

3.1.2   A Rapidly Evolving Technology Environment

At the same time, rapid technological advancements were enabling new approaches to a range of financial activities, from onboarding bank customers to deploying ultra-high-speed trading strategies. While financial institutions were among some of the earliest private sector entities to make significant investments in information technology, and while that technology remains at the core of their business, most large institutions have acquired significant legacy technical debt. This means these institutions are deeply invested in inflexible systems that are often 40 or more years old. Migration away from these systems would be extremely challenging and costly for these institutions, and following the financial crisis, investments of this sort bordered on impossible.

These legacy systems made it difficult for financial institutions to keep pace with some of the exciting new opportunities presented by the rapid evolution of technology. While some financial institutions recognized the potential of engaging with customers via new platforms like smartphones, leveraging cloud computing, or even exploring new trading strategies enabled by artificial intelligence (AI), actual implementation was extremely difficult within an operating model constrained by 40-year-old mainframe systems.

3.1.3   Shifting Customer Expectations

While banks struggled to prioritize resources for innovation and wrangle their legacy systems, nonfinancial digital offerings were changing rapidly. Digital natives like Uber, Airbnb, WhatsApp, Facebook, and WeChat were revolutionizing not only their respective industries, but customers' expectations for digital experiences across the board. These technology companies conditioned consumers to expect digital services to be timely, personalized, and on-demand. When compared to these offerings, a growing number of consumers began to see financial services as outdated and resistant to change.

Younger customers have proven to be particularly frustrated with the banking experiences offered by incumbents. In fact, the millennial disruption index found that 71% of millennials would rather go to the dentist than listen to their bank.[3] This environment, particularly when compounded with the frustration felt toward banks by many in the years following the global financial crisis, has likely expanded the pool of individuals willing to 'take the leap' to trying new fintech offerings.

The confluence of these three catalysts has forced banks, insurers, asset managers, and a host of other incumbent financial institutions to re-evaluate the competitive threats they face. It has also forced them to begin reimagining the ways in which technology could aid them in delivering value to their customers.

This shift has caused many to reflect on a quote from technology visionary Bill Gates, the founder of Microsoft, who suggested in 1994 that 'banking is necessary, banks are not'. A second quote from almost a decade later echoes this sentiment. In 2013, Jack Ma, the founder of Alibaba, argued, "There are two big opportunities in the future of the financial industry. One is online banking, all the financial institutions go online; the other one is internet finance, which is purely led by outsiders."

We believe that it is a certainty that the future of financial services will be characterized by rapid change with technology as the central driver of new customer offerings and competitive strategies. What is much less clear is who stands to 'win' in the remaking of the financial ecosystem that is to come. Incumbent financial institutions can no longer claim it to be theirs by right, but as discussed in the following chapter, their hold on the industry is far from lost.

3.2   Types of Fintechs

Financial services make up a massive chunk of the global economy. In the United States alone, financial services comprise 7% of the country's US$19 trillion GDP.[4] That's a lot for any fintech startup to take on in one bite. Instead, successful fintechs have taken a focused approach, developing products and services that take aim at the areas of the current system where they believe they can offer significantly better value propositions than incumbent financial institutions. Most of the time this means targeting areas where customers feel they are paying a lot for unsatisfactory experiences and then using technology to deliver a significantly improved experience at lower cost.

---

[3] "The Millennial Disruption Index," *Viacom Media Networks*, 2013, https://www.bbva.com/wp-content/uploads/2015/08/millenials.pdf.

[4] "Value Added by Private Industries: Finance, Insurance, Real Estate, Rental, and Leasing: Finance and Insurance as a Percentage of GDP (VAPGDPFI)," *Federal Reserve Bank of St Louis*, accessed January 5, 2019, https://fred.stlouisfed.org/series/VAPGDPFI.

In the pages that follow, we will explore the strategies that leading fintechs are using in their efforts to reshape some of the most important subsectors of financial services: payments, lending, wealth management, insurance, and banking itself. We will also explore how a different breed of fintech focused on managing regulatory compliance across all of these subsectors is having a profound impact on both startups and incumbents.

3.2.1   Fintech and Payments

The impact of technology on the way we pay is readily apparent. We have come a long way from the days of so-called knuckle busters designed to make imprints of physical credit cards and facilitate the paper-based processing of credit card slips. New payment form factors including QR codes, contactless credit cards, and mobile wallets are increasingly integrated into our daily lives.

The growing ubiquity of these digital payment methods are making the use of cash less and less frequent in both developed and emerging economies. Global noncash transaction volumes grew by 40.1% from 2011 to 2015 and reached a total of $433.1 billion. In advanced economies, this is the continuation of a long-standing trend of digitization where accepting digital payments has become both easier and less expensive for merchants—increasing the variety of sellers who accept noncash payments and decreasing the minimum ticket size they require for customers to use these payment methods.[5]

Indeed, in some European countries, digital payments have become so ubiquitous that cash is becoming a rare commodity. In just over ten years, the amount of cash in circulation in Sweden has halved from 112 billion Swedish kronor to 50 billion (US$6.14 billion).[6] Indeed, academics at the Copenhagen School of Economics have gone so far as to suggest that by 2023, cash will no longer be used or accepted by Swedish retailers, potentially making Sweden the world's first cash-free country.[7]

But the biggest changes in the use of cash can be found in the developing world, where the proliferation of mobile phones has driven a digital payment revolution, enabling the rapid rollout of SMS and QR code-based payments

---

[5] Rachel Green, "Global Merchant Card Acceptance Grew 13% in 2017," *Business Insider*, December 2018, https://www.businessinsider.com/global-merchant-card-acceptance-growing-2018-12.

[6] Reuters Editorial, "Cash Still King: Swedish Central Bank Urges Lawmakers to Protect Cash Payments," *U.S.*, February 26, 2018, https://www.reuters.com/article/sweden-cenbank-cash-idUSL8N1QG79Y.

[7] "Will Sweden Become the First Nation to Go Cash-Free?," *NBC News*, accessed January 5, 2019, https://www.nbcnews.com/mach/science/will-sweden-become-first-country-go-cash-free-ncna809811.

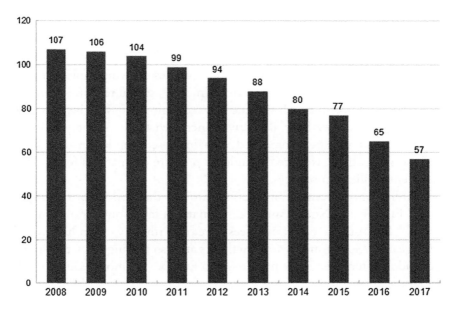

Fig. 3.3   Average value of banknotes and coins in circulation (SEK billion); In Sweden, digital payments have become so ubiquitous that cash is becoming a rare commodity. Source(s): "Statistics," *Sveriges Riksbank*, January 2, 2018, https://www.riksbank.se/en-gb/notes-and-coins/statistics/

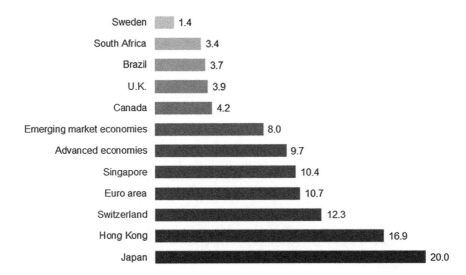

Fig. 3.4   Value of cash as a percentage of GDP (2016); Sweden has the world's lowest share of cash in circulation as a percentage of GDP. Source(s): Morten Bech and Umar Faruqui, "Payments are a-changin' but cash still rules" *Bis Quarterly Review*, March 11, 2018, https://www.bis.org/publ/qtrpdf/r_qt1803g.pdf

infrastructure. Central Europe, the Middle East, and Africa saw a 77% spike in noncash transactions from 2011 to 2015, while growth over the same period in emerging Asia was a remarkable 182%.[8]

With digital payments acceptance and volumes growing rapidly, it is no surprise that payments are a big business. In 2017, global revenues from payments were US$1.9 trillion.[9] But while new technologies have driven increased payment volumes, they have also driven increased levels of competition for payment revenues. When combined with increased regulation of payment transaction fees, this has placed significant pressure on margins for providers of payment facilitation services.

This trend can be seen in jurisdictions around the world. For example, in Western Europe and North America, fee margins fell about 20% from 2007 to 2013.[10] In Australia, credit card fees have been roughly cut in half over the last ten years.[11] Governments and regulators are also playing a key role in driving the adoption of electronic payments. In Europe, the most recent round of payments regulation, the second Payment Services Directive (PSD2), introduced a cap on interchange fees at 0.2% and 0.3% for debit and credit card transactions, respectively.[12]

But payments aren't only important to incumbent financial institutions because of the fees that they generate. Payments are the starting point of a typical client's banking journey and an individual's most frequent and visceral connection with their financial institutions. Consequently, they are viewed as the cornerstone of a 'sticky' relationship between banks and their customers.

The centrality of technology to the payments business, combined with the large revenues associated with this space, made many early fintech commentators suspect that payments would be a first port of call for disruptors and a beachhead for future incursions into the core business of banks.

---

[8] "World Payments Report 2018," *World Payments Report* (blog), October 4, 2018, https://worldpaymentsreport.com/resources/world-payments-report-2018/.

[9] "Global Payments: Expansive Growth, Targeted Opportunities," accessed January 5, 2019, https://www.mckinsey.com/industries/financial-services/our-insights/global-payments-expansive-growth-targeted-opportunities.

[10] Marc Niederkorn, Phil Bruno, Grace Hou, Florent Istace, Sukriti Bansal, "Global Payments 2015: A Healthy Industry Confronts Disruption" (McKinsey & Company, October 2015), https://www.mckinsey.com/~/media/mckinsey/industries/financial%20services/our%20insights/how%20the%20payments%20industry%20is%20being%20disrupted/global_payments_2015_a_healthy_industry_confronts_disruption.ashx.

[11] Rob Galaski R. Jesse McWaters, "Beyond Fintech: A Pragmatic Assessment of Disruptive Potential in Financial Services" (World Economic Forum, August 2017), http://www3.weforum.org/docs/Beyond_Fintech_-_A_Pragmatic_Assessment_of_Disruptive_Potential_in_Financial_Services.pdf.

[12] European Commission, "Payment Services Directive and Interchange Fees Regulation: Frequently Asked Questions," July 24, 2013, http://europa.eu/rapid/press-release_MEMO-13-719_it.htm.

But disrupting payments is no easy task. The business is characterized by network effects—meaning that the value of using the service increases as the number of users increases. A phone isn't a useful innovation until someone you want to call also has a phone, and in the same way, a payment network isn't useful until someone you want to pay also uses that network. Merchants in developed economies have made significant investments in the payment terminals of incumbent payment networks and have established agreements with a variety of service providers such as merchant acquirers that facilitate their integration into existing card networks.

At the same time, in regions where payments systems are relatively mature, customers have been less eager to adopt new technologies than their emerging market counterparts. According to surveys of US consumers conducted at the end of 2017, only 12.8% of adult smartphone users had ever used Apple Pay and only 3% of smartphone users visiting a store that accepts Apple Pay had chosen to use it.[13]

When asked why they had not tried Apple Pay, 37% of those who had not used the service said they were happy with their existing payment methods and of those who had used Apple Pay, more than half of users rated its ease of use as equivalent as, or less easy than, swiping a card.[14] When contrasted with the rapid shift of Chinese consumers from cash to mobile payments (discussed further in part 5.2), this highlights how difficult it can be for even one of the world's most successful technology firms to shift consumers' payment behavior when existing services are viewed by consumers as 'good enough'.

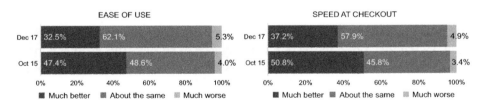

Fig. 3.5 How would you rate the convenience of Apple Pay versus swiping a card?; Apple Pay has struggled to convince US consumers to shift away from payment by card. Source(s): "2018 Apple Pay Adoption Stats," PYMNTS.com, accessed January 5, 2019, https://www.pymnts.com/apple-pay-adoption/

---

[13] "2018 Apple Pay Adoption Stats," *PYMNTS.com*, accessed January 5, 2019, https://www.pymnts.com/apple-pay-adoption/.
[14] Ibid.

This makes attempting to go toe-to-toe with the core business of incumbent payment networks a big challenge for even the largest of corporations, let alone a scrappy bunch of fintech startups. There is however one area of payments where incumbent service offerings in many jurisdictions have continued to be weak or nonexistent. In spite of the numerous advances in payments technology, peer-to-peer transactions between consumers through incumbent payment networks have been characterized by high levels of friction and expense, particularly when funds must cross international borders. This has created a perfect entry point for fintechs to disrupt both domestic and international peer-to-peer payments.

On the domestic side, payment systems like Venmo in the United States (now a subsidiary of PayPal) and PayMe in Hong Kong make it easy for users to solve 'the brunch problem'—that is, the challenge of splitting the bill for brunch, or indeed any expense, with friends. These systems provide seamless onboarding for new users and make it easy to find friends on the network via integration with social networks like Facebook and WhatsApp. Moreover, these services typically do not charge customers a fee for transactions paid from the app's wallet, or funded directly from a bank account, charging them only if they top up the account using a credit card.

Venmo has grown rapidly in popularity, particularly among the millennial age group. According to a 2018 survey, 44% of millennials had used the app,[15] and in 2017, the service processed US$35 billion worth of transactions, an increase of 97% from the preceding year.[16]

One interesting driver of Venmo's success has been their savvy integration of lessons learned from leading social media platforms like Facebook and Instagram into their product design. Unlike traditional financial offerings which are private by default, Venmo lets you see what you friends are doing (and paying for), often in the popular language of emojis. This enables a marrying of the social and financial elements of life that have traditionally been separate in the Western world and creates a less awkward way for users to remind a friend that she owes you money for last night's pizza, beer, or this month's rent (the first, second, and fourth most popular emojis[17]). It also creates a venue for the sharing of cryptic (and sometimes lewd) inside jokes.

---

[15] Mike Brown, "Best Mobile Payment Apps—Survey & Report," *LendEDU*, April 21, 2017, https://lendedu.com/blog/best-mobile-payment-app.

[16] "PayPal Reports Fourth Quarter and Full Year 2017 Results," Press Release (BusinessWire, January 31, 2018), https://www.businesswire.com/news/home/20180131006195/en/PayPal-Reports-Fourth-Quarter-Full-Year-2017.

[17] "LendEDU's Venmo Transaction Study: Pizza, Drinks, Fantasy Football … and Sometimes Strippers," *LendEDU*, 2016, https://lendedu.com/blog/venmo.

While these services have made domestic peer-to-peer transfers easier, they are typically restricted to payments between two individuals in the same country. International transfers of funds remain remarkably frustrating and expensive for users. The legacy system for the cross-border transfer of funds is complex and inefficient, with money often being routed through multiple intermediary banks before arriving at the recipient's bank account.[18]

United Kingdom–based fintech startup TransferWise is one of the most successful examples of a new entrant seeking to rectify these inefficiencies and build a successful business in the process. TransferWise bills itself as a peer-to-peer solution for international funds transfer that can deliver money quickly and with a flat transparent fee structure that can be as low as 0.35%.

The system is simple. Imagine you live in the United Kingdom and want to send money to a friend who lives in France. Using the TransferWise mobile app or website, you initiate a free domestic transfer of funds from your UK account to the UK account of TransferWise. Once the money is received, TransferWise initiates a domestic transfer of funds from their French bank account to your friend's bank account (note that this system does not require your friend to have an account with TransferWise, making life even easier for both sender and receiver).[19] TransferWise charges a transparent flat fee for the service and uses the mid-market exchange rate to calculate the number of euros that will be delivered to your friends account—all before the transfer is initiated.

In practice, this means that your money never actually crosses the border and TransferWise only needs to initiate international transfers via the legacy banking systems on an occasional basis to rebalance accounts (e.g. if the volume of transactions from the United Kingdom to France exceeds those from France to the United Kingdom for an extended period, necessitating a 'top up' of TransferWise's UK account). While this approach to cross-border transfers is not unique, TransferWise has combined a low-friction mobile app experience with edgy guerrilla advertising to capture the attention of a growing, and predominantly millennial, user base that now collectively transfer over two billion British pounds every month between 69 countries in 47 currencies.[20]

---

[18] Ibid.; "Fintech and Cross-Border Payments," *IMF*, November 1, 2017, https://www.imf.org/en/News/Articles/2017/11/01/sp103017-fintech-and-cross-border-payments.

[19] TransferWise Content Team, "How TransferWise Works: Your Step-by-Step Guide," *TransferWise*, March 14, 2018, https://transferwise.com/gb/blog/how-does-transferwise-work.

[20] "TransferWise Mission Report Q1 2018," *TransferWise*, April 24, 2018, https://transferwise.com/gb/blog/transferwise-mission-report-q1-2018.

3.2.2   Fintech and Lending

In the environment of increased restrictions on traditional lending that followed the financial crisis of 2008, many individuals and small businesses found themselves excluded from traditional sources of capital, creating an opportunity for the entry of new lenders. Perhaps the most intriguing of these were fintech innovators promoting the idea of peer-to-peer lending.

The idea of peer-to-peer lending capitalized on the momentum building in the early 2010s around the potential of a range of sharing economy business models. At its core, the model proposed removing banks as an intermediary between those with excess capital and those in need of capital. The resulting marketplace would, at least in theory, offer the borrower a lower interest rate than they would receive from a traditional financial institution, while at the same time delivering to the lender a higher rate than they could expect to receive from traditional investments of comparable risk. Some platforms such as Lending Club offer users the ability to pick and choose which individuals and businesses to extend loans to, while others allow investors to hedge their risks by investing in a diverse portfolio of debt held by many individuals.

While the community-based narrative of peer-to-peer lending may be compelling, it ultimately proved challenging as a business model and few, if any, true peer-to-peer lenders remain in operation today. The reasons for this are manifold. While peer-to-peer networks enjoyed several cost advantages over traditional banks, most notably the absence of fixed costs associated with a branch network, these costs were ultimately more than offset by the higher funding costs of loans.[21] Simply put, while banks were able to lend customers' deposits, on which they paid very low interest rates, peer-to-peer lenders needed to pay premium rates to attract capital from potential investors.

These new platforms also frequently faced higher customer acquisition costs than incumbents, and challenges in effectively balancing the demand for loans and availability of capital on their platforms. As a result, many lending platforms, particularly those in the United States, shifted rapidly away from individuals as a source of financing for their loans and instead relied on capital from institutional sources such as hedge funds, as well as the sale of securitized loans to institutional investors.[22]

---

[21] Kadhim Shubber, "Peer-to-Peer May Have Changed Banking, but Banking Still Won," *Financial Times*, November 17, 2016, https://ftalphaville.ft.com/2016/11/16/2179884/peer-to-peer-may-have-changed-banking-but-banking-still-won/.

[22] Boris Vallee and Yao Zeng, "Marketplace Lending: A New Banking Paradigm?," Working Paper (Harvard Business School, January 2018), https://www.hbs.edu/faculty/Publication%20Files/18-067_1d1e7469-3a75-46a0-9520-bddbfda0b2b9.pdf.

However, this is not to say that new fintech entrants into the domain of lending have not had a significant impact on the operating models and competitive dynamics of this space. In addition to exploring new mechanisms of financing loans, fintech lenders have explored new mechanisms of originating and underwriting loans, allowing them to offer borrowers access to a faster and more streamlined digital loan application experience. Many online lenders now offer end-to-end online loan application processes and have reduced the time from application to fulfillment of loans significantly, in some cases from weeks to minutes.

These fintechs have also explored novel credit evaluation mechanisms that may be less likely to exclude certain good credit risks than the traditional credit bureau data used by incumbent financial institutions. This often includes social, mobile, and bill payment data. Fintechs argue that these models allow for better underwriting of established borrowers, and in particular extend their ability to confidently lend to 'thin-file' borrowers with limited credit bureau history, such as new immigrants who may have the appropriate risk profile despite a lack of historical data with their new home's credit bureau. For small businesses, who lack reliable credit bureau data in many jurisdictions, detailed inputs from their accounting and invoice management systems have provided an opportunity to automate underwriting processes, significantly reducing the cost of writing these loans.

3.2.3   Fintech and Wealth Management

If you were to ask a random person on the street to describe their financial goals, she might talk to you about when she hoped to retire and the type of lifestyle she hoped to enjoy in retirement. A younger person with retirement too far away to imagine might be more focused on saving to buy her first home, and a young parent might be focused on saving funds for her child's education.

Our long-term goals form the center of our financial aspirations; however, navigating the path to achieving those goals is no easy feat. Despite being one of the wealthiest countries in the world, over 40% of Americans don't have enough money on hand to cover a $400-dollar emergency expense, and less than two-fifths of non-retired adults feel that their retirement savings are on track to meet their goals.[23]

---

[23] "The Fed-Report on the Economic Well-Being of U.S. Households in 2017–May 2018," *Board of Governors of the Federal Reserve System*, accessed January 5, 2019, https://www.federalreserve.gov/publications/2018-economic-well-being-of-us-households-in-2017-preface.htm.

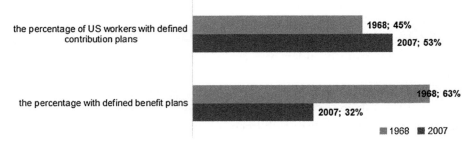

Fig. 3.6 Share of US workers with defined benefit versus defined contribution retirement plans; The shift toward defined contribution retirement plans has increased savers' responsibilities around the management of their investments. Source(s): "The Shift from Defined Benefit to Defined Contribution Plans," Greenbush Financial Planning (blog), July 17, 2015, https://www.greenbushfinancial.com/the-shift-in-retirement-and-importance-of-education/

To make matters worse, a significant knowledge gap exists around individual wealth management. In past decades, many workers could rely on so-called defined benefit pensions which promised to pay a certain percentage of income upon retirement for the remainder of an individual's life. However, over the past 50 years, economies around the world have seen a shift away from these plans toward 'defined contribution' schemes where employers and employees both make contributions to a pot of money saved for retirement and hope that the amount saved at the time of retirement will be sufficient. Schemes like the 401(k) plans in the United States and Individual Savings Accounts (ISA) in Great Britain are both examples of defined contribution plans. From 1968 to 2007, the percentage of US workers with defined contribution plans increased from 45% to 53%, while the percentage with defined benefit plans declined from 63% to only 32%.[24]

The shift to defined contribution plans puts more responsibility on average savers to choose their investments and to ensure that they have put aside enough for retirement, even though they cannot be sure how long they will live. Unfortunately, the complex array of financial products available to investors, combined with the limited transparency of those products, makes meeting this responsibility extremely difficult.

To illustrate this challenge, let's imagine a typical visit to the grocery store. With a varied selection of cereals in front of you to choose from, it is easy to review the different brands and their nutritional information. If you want to

---

[24] "The Shift from Defined Benefit to Defined Contribution Plans," Greenbush Financial Group, LLC, accessed January 30, 2019, https://www.greenbushfinancial.com/the-shift-in-retirement-and-importance-of-education/.

buy fruits or vegetables, it is easy to tell where they originate from and you could probably find some information about their cultivation methods, such as whether they are certified organic. Most importantly, when you head to the cash register, you know exactly what you are paying for, how much it will cost, and (hopefully) have a plan in mind for how you will put these ingredients together when you get home.

Unfortunately, the same is rarely true for investments. The financial literacy of the average consumer is weak; on average, Americans answered fewer than three out of five basic financial literacy questions correctly.[25] Moreover, it is difficult for even an expert to effectively compare available financial products and plans. While the nutritional information of two cans of soup is easily comparable, it can be much more complicated to assess the impact of the litany of fees (transaction fees, bookkeeping fees, legal fees, custody fees, subscription and redemption fees, and many more often hidden expenses) that make up the traditional wealth management experience.

Often, investors are not aware of the spectrum of fees or do not know and/ or understand the reasoning behind these added fees. These costs may initially appear to be affordable as they are just a small percentage of the expenses involved, but over time they can significantly erode returns. Take two investors for example: one paying a total of 1% in fees, and another paying 2%. Over a typical lifetime of savings, the person paying 2% in fees will run out of retirement savings a decade earlier than the one paying 1% in fees.[26]

Clearly, people need help navigating the complex landscape of wealth management products to achieve their long-term financial goals. The trouble is that doing so can often be expensive. The fees associated with obtaining even a basic financial plan from a certified professional typically range between US$1000 and US$3000 in the United States.[27] This is a significant expenditure, especially when we recall that 40% of the country's population may actually struggle to come up with even $400 for an emergency.

Of course, some planners will offer to prepare a financial plan for free, but as with many things in life, free can be expensive in the long run. These planners are typically paid through commissions on the sale of financial securities, and many jurisdictions may not have fiduciary duty requirements—meaning

---

[25] Note 23.

[26] Lorie Konish, "Fees Could Sink Your Retirement Savings. Here's What to Do about It," *CNBC* (CNBC, February 20, 2018), https://www.cnbc.com/2018/02/20/fees-could-sink-your-retirement-savings-hereswhat-to-do-about-it.html.

[27] Andrea Coombes Arielle O'shea, "How Much Does a Financial Advisor Cost?," *Nerd Wallet*, December 7, 2018, https://www.nerdwallet.com/blog/investing/how-much-does-a-financial-advisor-cost/.

that they are not required to recommend what is in the best interest of their clients. As a result, such planners may have a strong incentive to steer clients toward higher fee products that may ultimately erode customers' lifetime savings significantly.[28]

Fintech innovators are trying to answer questions of how to deliver high-quality advice at low cost through the development of the 'robo-advisor'. In their basic form, robo-advisors are essentially a set of tools to help individuals manage their accumulation and investment of wealth, by automating many of the basic activities traditionally performed by a human advisor. They help users understand their financial needs and risk preferences, and then identify financial products that are suitable to those needs, often low-fee products such as exchange traded funds. They then automate the ongoing rebalancing of that user's portfolio as her age, risk tolerance, and financial goals change over time. Many robo-advisors also automate tax reporting and the execution of tax optimization strategies, such as tax loss harvesting.

The majority of these tools are not new innovations. They have, in fact, been used by financial advisors for decades to help drive efficiency in their business. The goal of robo-advisors has been to democratize access to these tools, creating easily navigable and low-cost self-service tools for financial planning.

Based on these compelling value propositions, customer awareness of robo-advisor offerings has grown rapidly. In the United States, early movers like Betterment and Wealthfront managed $14.14 billion and $11.17 billion, respectively, as of Q3 2018.[29] That's only a small fraction of the over $37 trillion in total US assets under management,[30] but certainly sufficient to join the ranks of mid-sized asset managers, and with a clear appetite for further growth.

In some cases, robo-advisors have also sought to democratize access to products. In February 2018, Wealthfront announced plans for a new investment product available on their platform that replicated a popular fund created by Bridgewater Associates, one of the world's largest hedge funds. Given that most Wealthfront clients presumably did not have the US$100 million

---

[28] Szifra Birke, "Is Your Financial Advisor Working in Your Best Interest?," *Birke Consulting*, January 30, 2017, https://birkeconsulting.com/is-your-financial-advisor-working-in-your-best-interest/.

[29] Brittney Grimes, "10 Largest Robo-Advisers by AUM," accessed January 5, 2019, https://www.investmentnews.com/gallery/20181107/FREE/110709999/PH/10-largest-robo-advisers-by-aum&Params=Itemnr=11).

[30] "Global Asset Management 2018: The Digital Metamorphosis," Https://www.bcg.com, accessed January 5, 2019, https://www.bcg.com/en-ch/publications/2018/global-asset-management-2018-digital-metamorphosis.aspx.

account minimum required by Bridgewater clients to invest, this approach represented a unique opportunity for them to pursue an exciting and potentially profitable strategy.[31]

Of course, none of this means that robo-advisors will fully displace human advisors in the near future. It is clear that some customers with complex financial needs, such as high-net-worth individuals, still require the customization and knowledge that, at least for now, are only available from an experienced human advisor. Others may simply prefer the human touch and be willing to pay a premium for it.

3.2.4 Fintech and Insurance

For an industry with a long-standing reputation for being risk averse and slow to change, it is perhaps surprising that some of the most exciting and innovative fintech applications are emerging in the realm of insurance. While other areas of financial services have sought to reinvent the delivery, pricing, and behind-the-scenes operations of their businesses for greater efficiency, fintech being deployed in the insurance space—often referred to as 'insurtech'—is going even further by introducing fundamentally new products.

Traditional consumer insurance offerings have been built on the notion of pooling risks across a large number of people, typically providing 'one-size-fits-all' policies that protect against a wide variety of undesirable events. These policies are typically offered for a fixed term, and do not change as new information about the risk landscape emerges. Finally, traditional insurance products are reactive, rather than proactive, meaning that they are almost universally focused on providing compensation when unfortunate events occur, and not on preventing those events in the first place.

Insurtech startups seek to upend many of these assumptions. For example, offerings like Trōv and Metromile are exploring ways to make insurance policies more flexible to users' needs. Trōv allows users to quickly insure an individual possession, such as a camera or a bicycle, for a specific duration of time. Using the mobile app, users can toggle the insurance for a product on and off, enabling them to pay for insurance only when they feel the product is at risk—for example, when a bike is being ridden, or a camera is being used, but not when stored at home (and perhaps covered by the owner's blanket home or renters' insurance).

---

[31] The Wealthfront Team / 02.22.18, "Investing Just Got Better with Wealthfront," Wealthfront Blog, February 22, 2018, https://blog.wealthfront.com/risk-parity/.

Metromile offers users a similar kind of flexibility, by giving drivers access to 'pay-as-you-go' automobile insurance. Traditional insurers generally ask applicants about the length of their daily commute, as there is a strong causal relationship between the number of miles driven and the likelihood that the driver, no matter how responsible or skilled, will experience some sort of accident. Metromile takes a different approach, pricing insurance by the mile, and using sensors within the car to keep track of the policyholder's bill.

Other insurtech startups are seeking opportunities to be more proactive, offering insurance products that continuously track policyholders' risky behaviors and attempt to play an active role in reducing those risks. An early example of this is the use of 'telematics' in automotive insurance, an idea initially developed by the incumbent US auto insurer Progressive in the early 2000s. Under this system, the driving behavior of policyholders is constantly monitored, allowing cautious drivers to enjoy lower premiums while penalizing higher-risk behavior.

As sensors like these become more common in our homes, offices, and on our person, a growing number of insurance products are considering how the IoT can be used to more proactively respond to risks, influencing risk-related behaviors and intervening to limit damage. For example, Nest, a subsidiary of Alphabet that produces a range of 'smart devices', including smart smoke alarms, offers the option to communicate directly with insurers to confirm that the alarm's battery is charged, and the sensors are functional.[32]

In the realm of individual health, the South African company Vitality offers insurers a suite of technologies that let policyholders opt-in to an incentives program that rewards healthy lifestyle choices. The incentives come in the form of premium savings, retail discounts, and rewards, and limit users' interference by tracking their physical activity via wearable technologies such as a Fitbit or Apple Watch.[33]

Of course, the development of new products is not the only sort of innovation taking place in the realm of insurance. As with other areas of financial services, active efforts are underway to onboard new customers rapidly and seamlessly. This is of particular importance given that insurance is a product few people—especially younger people—are excited to purchase.[34] Insurtech companies are also working hard to make filing for claims faster and easier.

---

[32] "Homepage," *Nest*, accessed January 5, 2019, https://nest.com/insurance-partners/.

[33] "How Vitality Works," *Vitality Group*, accessed January 5, 2019, https://www.vitalitygroup.com/how-vitality-works/.

[34] Dan Kadlec, "Why Millennials Resist Any Kind of Insurance," *Money* (Time Inc, August 27, 2014), http://time.com/money/3178364/millennials-insurance-why-resist-coverage/.

San Francisco–based insurtech firm Lemonade, which specializes in home-owner and renters' insurance, endeavors to make everything instant with clients taking as little as 90 seconds to get insured. Claims are also built for speed with users able to submit claims via the Lemonade app by providing a text or video description of damages which is then analyzed by an automated system. In December 2017, Lemonade announced to great fanfare that their AI-enabled claims agent had set a new 'world record' by processing an insurance claim in only seven seconds.[35]

Lemonade also provides an interesting example of insurtech innovation in nontraditional pricing. Lemonade's business model is deceptively simple. The company takes a transparent fixed fee out of clients' monthly payments to cover reinsurance and expenses, and then uses the rest to pay out claims.[36] Any funds left at the end of the year are donated to nonprofit organizations selected by policyholders. Lemonade argues that this approach ensures they are never in conflict with customers filing insurance claims,[37] since they only take a flat fee, while also discouraging policyholders from claims fraud since they know any excess funds will be donated to a cause that matters to them.

3.2.5   Fintech and Digital Banking

Each of the fintech innovations discussed so far in this chapter seeks to revolutionize some slice of financial services. But in our day-to-day lives, most of us obtain our payments services, lending products, wealth products, and sometimes even our insurance products from a single provider—our bank—with our checking account (in some jurisdictions called a 'current account') living at the center of all these products. It is therefore natural that the fintech revolution should endeavor to disrupt the heart of banking itself.

The names of these innovators differ from region to region, called virtual banks, digital banks, challenger banks, or neo-banks to distinguish them from their incumbent competitors. Examples of such challenger banks include Revolut, Starling Bank, WeBank, MyBank, Monzo, N26, Atom, Fidor Bank, Holvi, Compte Nickel, Loot, and Nubank. Each of these examples is pursuing

---

[35] Daniel Schreiber, "Lemonade Sets a New World Record," *Lemonade Inc*, January 1, 2017, https://www.lemonade.com/blog/lemonade-sets-new-world-record/.

[36] "FAQ," *Lemonade Inc*, accessed January 5, 2019, https://www.lemonade.com/faq#service.

[37] Jordan Crook, "Lemonade Wants to Rewrite the Insurance Policy Itself," *TechCrunch*, May 2018, https://techcrunch.com/2018/05/16/lemonade-wants-to-rewrite-the-insurance-policy-itself/.

a unique strategy, but at their core they share a desire to reinvent the banking experience, making it digitally native, data-driven, and customer-centric.[38]

Some are even going so far as to explore innovative new business models that rethink the business of banking by providing customers with a digital platform to access the best products for them, rather than trying to build and sell every product from scratch. For example, the German neo-bank N26 has directly integrated their bank accounts with the fintech startup TransferWise, discussed earlier in this chapter, to facilitate easier and cheaper cross-border payments.[39] They have also partnered with large incumbent insurer Allianz to provide travel insurance for customers of select credit card products.[40]

Many of these digital banks have rapidly grown their user numbers. Revolut, founded in the United Kingdom in 2013, is a digital banking alternative that gives its users prepaid debit cards, currency exchange facilities, a cryptocurrency exchange, and peer-to-peer payments.[41] Revolut's multicurrency accounts, which offer free international money transfers and fee-free global spending at the interbank exchange rate, have been of particular interest to consumers.[42] Combined with an attractive and easy to use mobile app, Revolut has been able to acquire more than two million European customers[43] in less than five years. They have also processed more than 100 million transactions with monthly volumes of approximately US$2 billion.[44] Seeking to capitalize on this momentum, Revolut is, at the time of writing, in the process of expanding to the United States.[45]

While these numbers tell an exciting story, it is important that we consider them in the proper context. While adoption rates for digital banking products have been impressive, this does not mean that customers are abandoning incumbent banks in droves. The majority of users who have signed up for these services use them, at least for now, as a secondary account, the most notable indicator of this being the fact that users have largely shied away from

---

[38] "Who Are You Calling a 'challenger Bank'?," *PWC*, accessed January 5, 2019, https://www.pwc.co.uk/industries/banking-capital-markets/insights/challenger-banks.html.

[39] "Seamless International Money Transfers with TransferWise," *N26*, accessed January 5, 2019, https://n26.com/en-eu/transferwise.

[40] "N26 Black," *N26*, accessed January 5, 2019, https://n26.com/en-de/black.

[41] https://en.wikipedia.org/wiki/Revolut

[42] "About Revolut," *Revolut*, accessed January 5, 2019, https://www.revolut.com/it/about.

[43] Ryan Browne, "Fintech Start-up Revolut Grabs 2 Million Users and Plans to Launch Commission-Free Trading Service," *CNBC* (CNBC Europe, April 25, 2018), https://www.cnbc.com/2018/06/07/revolut-has-2-million-users-to-launch-commission-free-trading-service.html.

[44] James Cook, "UK Fintech Start-up Revolut Reaches 2 Million Users Save," *The Telegraph*, June 7, 2018, https://www.telegraph.co.uk/technology/2018/06/07/uk-fintech-start-up-revolut-reaches-2-million-users/.

[45] Ibid.

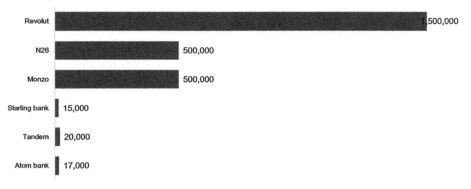

Note: Based on latest publically reported numbers from each challenger bank

Fig. 3.7 Challenger bank customers acquired since launch (2018); Challenger bank Revolut has seen strong customer acquisition growth since its launch in 2015. Source(s): "The Challenger Bank Playbook: How Six Challenger Bank Startups Are Taking On Retail Banking," CB Insights Research, March 8, 2018, https://www.cbinsights.com/research/challenger-bank-strategy/

having their salaries deposited into their neo-bank accounts. For example, UK-based neo-bank Monzo had an impressive 870,000 current account holders as of August 2018, and while more than 45% of these users were driving deposit base growth of more than £500 per month, only 20% used it as a destination for their payroll deposits,[46] suggesting that the remainder used Monzo only as a secondary service.

In spite of these impediments, it is clear that the potential of these digital banks continues to intrigue consumers. With new users signing up daily and new features continuing to be added, incumbent banks are watching these fintech innovators closely. At the time of writing, regulators in Hong Kong were looking at approving new virtual banking licenses for some of the incumbent banks and technology firms. That will be a very interesting development to follow in the coming years and a good example of the potential of digital banks.

3.2.6   Regtech: A Different Sort of Fintech Innovation

In the wake of the 2008 global financial crisis, governments around the world sought to restructure their existing regulatory frameworks and introduce new regulations with the aim of both curtailing the excesses that lead up to the crisis and preventing future crises.

---

[46] Martin Arnold, "Monzo Poised to Join Ranks of Europe's Fintech 'unicorns,'" *Financial Times*, August 17, 2018, https://www.ft.com/content/ef54082c-a16a-11e8-85da-eeb7a9ce36e4.

The result has been an absolutely massive rollout of new and onerous regulations; for example, the US Dodd-Frank Act alone is over 2300 pages, and includes thousands of other pages filled with detailed rules.[47] Postcrisis regulatory measures in the United States include: new procedures for the Federal Reserve to inject liquidity into the system, the ability for the government to infuse capital into troubled companies,[48] rescue plans to manage state-backed mortgage conglomerates Fannie Mae and Freddie Mac, initiation of tougher bank stress-tests, and new management methods for the resolution of distressed financial institutions.

To deal with these new requirements, banks in turn had to resort to hiring armies of consultants or adding headcount to their compliance and legal teams. In the years following the crisis, Citi had about 30,000 employees working in their compliance division,[49] while JPMorgan announced 13,000 new hires in compliance and control.[50]

While these are extremely high costs for any financial institution, there is reason to believe that the costs are disproportionately borne by smaller institutions, especially small regional banks or credit unions that play an outsized role within their communities. According to recent research, compliance costs amount to 8.7% of noninterest expenses at banks with less than US$100 million in assets, whereas banks with assets between US$1 and 10 billion only face costs of 2.9%.[51]

An excellent illustration of how resource-intensive it can be to meet regulatory obligations is the labyrinth of complex anti-money laundering (AML) processes at financial institutions, where up to 80% of costs are headcount-related.[52] Today, these processes can be highly manual and inaccurate. In some

---

[47] Frank Holmes, "These Are the 5 Costliest Financial Regulations of the Past 20 Years," *Business Insider*, May 2017, https://www.businessinsider.com/these-are-the-5-costliest-financial-regulations-of-the-past-20-years-2017-5?IR=T#march-2010-foreign-account-tax-compliance-act-fatca-3.

[48] Sean Ross, "What Major Laws Regulating Financial Institutions Were Created in Response to the 2008 Financial Crisis?," *Investopedia*, October 25, 2017, https://www.investopedia.com/ask/answers/063015/what-are-major-laws-acts-regulating-financial-institutions-were-created-response-2008-financial.asp.

[49] Sital S. Patel, "Citi Will Have Almost 30,000 Employees in Compliance by Year-End," *MarketWatch*, July 14, 2014, http://blogs.marketwatch.com/thetell/2014/07/14/citi-will-have-almost-30000-employees-in-compliance-by-year-end/.

[50] David Henry, "JPMorgan's Dimon Calls Settling Legal Issues 'Nerve-Wracking,'" *Reuters*, April 9, 2014, https://www.reuters.com/article/us-jpmorganchase-dimon-idUSBREA3822W20140409.

[51] Jackson Mueller Dan Murphy, "RegTech: Opportunities for More Efficient and Effective Regulatory Supervision and Compliance" (Milken Institute, July 11, 2018), https://www.milkeninstitute.org/publications/view/919.

[52] "Uncover the True Cost of Anti-Money Laundering & KYC Compliance" (LexisNexis Risk Solutions, June 9, 2016), https://www.lexisnexis.com/risk/intl/en/resources/research/true-cost-of-aml-compliance-apac-survey-report.pdf.

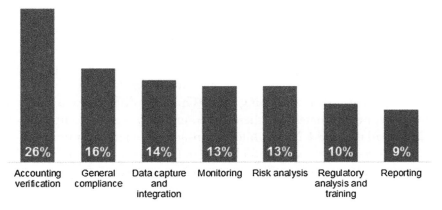

Fig. 3.8 Regtech firms by area of focus; Emerging regtech firms seek to address a range of pain points for financial institutions. Source(s): "World of Regtech" (Raconteur, 2018), https://www.raconteur.net/infographics/world-of-regtech

circumstances, the false positive rate for transactions—where the system incorrectly flags a legitimate transaction as suspicious—can exceed 90%.[53]

The resulting effect is the creation of a system that is both extremely expensive and not particularly effective. In the United States alone, banks collectively spend more than US$50 billion each year on AML compliance. However, in spite of this expenditure, global money laundering transactions are estimated to total US$1–2 trillion dollars a year, with less than 1% seized by authorities.[54] This suggests that in spite of all of the time and expense dedicated to compliance with these regulations, current efforts to limit money laundering are failing.

These challenges are not restricted to AML-related regulations. In spite of the enormous efforts and funds directed toward adapting to new regulations, financial institutions continue to run afoul of regulators and end up incurring even more costs in the form of fines. In 2016 alone, the U.S. Securities and Exchange Commission (SEC) issued 868 enforcements in disgorgement and penalties that exceeded US$4 billion.[55]

---

[53] Bain Insights, "Cutting Through Complexity in Financial Crimes Compliance," *Forbes* (Forbes, February 14, 2018), https://www.forbes.com/sites/baininsights/2018/02/14/cutting-through-complexity-in-financial-crimes-compliance/.

[54] Preeta Bannerjee, "UNODC Estimates That Criminals May Have Laundered US$ 1.6 Trillion in 2009," October 25, 2011, https://www.unodc.org/unodc/en/press/releases/2011/October/unodc-estimates-that-criminals-may-have-laundered-usdollar-1.6-trillion-in-2009.html.

[55] U.S. Securities and Exchange Commission, "SEC Announces Enforcement Results for FY 2016," October 11, 2016, https://www.sec.gov/news/pressrelease/2016-212.html.

In response to all of these issues, financial institutions began looking for more innovative ways to face the challenges imposed by their evolving and ever-increasing compliance needs. Many believe they found the answer in regulatory technology (regtech), which refers to the use of new technology to solve compliance burdens more effectively and efficiently.[56]

Regtech has been a fast-growing area. While it is difficult to exact precise figures, Deloitte estimates that there are around 240 regtech companies currently around the world. Meanwhile, CB Insights estimates that from 2012 to 2017, the regtech sector saw US\$5 billion in funding across 500 deals.[57]

These regtech providers offer solutions across many different use cases, including know your customer (KYC), onboarding, AML, transaction monitoring, regulatory reporting, compliance training, and analytics. A recent example of regtech in AML is the machine learning solution developed by Singapore-based United Overseas Bank and regtech startup Tookitaki that will help the bank to better detect and prevent money laundering activities in the bank's systems. Once the solution is fed with suspicious activity data, it will be able to identify similar patterns for future alerts.[58]

Box 3.1   How Is Regtech Different from Fintech?

Apart from the obvious distinctions that regtech is focused on the regulatory world, and fintech on the financial sector, certain characteristics set them apart.

- **Business-to-business (B2B) sales model**: Unlike fintech, which has both Business-to-customer (B2C) and B2B offerings, regtech solutions are almost exclusively sold to incumbent financial institutions. Since regtech innovation is seen as an ally to financial incumbents rather than a threat, the industry may at times be quicker to embrace these technologies.
- **No licensing required**: Many fintech verticals require regulatory licenses (e.g. P2P lending, digital banking). Regulatory licenses are generally not required in the regtech space. Most solutions are technology offerings that are designed to benefit clients.

(continued)

---

[56] "Regtech," *The Institute of International Finance*, accessed January 5, 2019, https://www.iif.com/topics/regtech.

[57] "The State of Regtech" (CB Insights, September 20, 2017), https://www.cbinsights.com/research/briefing/state-of-regulatory-technology-regtech/.

[58] "UOB Unveils Machine Learning Solution to Combat Financial Crime," *Singapore Business Review*, August 24, 2018, https://sbr.com.sg/financial-services/news/uob-unveils-machine-learning-solution-combat-financial-crime.

Box 3.1   (continued)

- **Cooperation between financial institutions**: When not seen as a competitive threat, fintech is often pursued to gain an edge over other competing financial institutions. However, compliance is seen as a collective burden, increasing costs for every industry player. There have been many instances of institutions wanting to work together with the idea of collectively reducing costs. The various initiatives around KYC utilities are an example of this.
- **Lengthier sales cycles**: Selling fintech solutions to banks takes a long time, but selling regtech solutions takes even more time. Not only are many of the regulatory teams at banks still unfamiliar with new technologies, but in many cases they are more conservative and unwilling to take risks. This is in part due to dire consequences of a mistake or compliance misstep, which can cause issues with regulators. Additionally, plugging the latest regtech solutions into labyrinthine systems of a bank is no easy task. This is why some of the best beneficiaries of regtech solutions have been new digital banks or crypto firms that are free of the legacy problems faced by the incumbents.
- **Regulators' support**: Aware of the high stakes of any changes in regulatory functions, regulators have been at the forefront of endorsing regtech development. They are aware that tools that allow financial institutions to better perform their compliance and monitoring obligations will benefit the entire ecosystem, including regulators.
- **Funding**: While raising capital is difficult for any startup, regtech startups face a specific challenge. Investors know that 'hockey stick' growth is almost impossible with regtech due to very long sales cycles and the natural reluctance from financial institutions to work with startups.
- **Fragmented regulatory environment**: Fragmentation in regulatory regimes is a key pain point for regtech startups. Minute variations in regulation from one country to the next pose a huge challenge; some of the most basic regulations between the United States and the United Kingdom, for example, are different. Such cases are even worse in regions like Asia-Pacific, where the average regional bank is active in a dozen different jurisdictions and needs a slightly different solution for each one.
- **Lack of standardized data**: As we will see later in this book when discussing artificial intelligence, the principle of 'garbage in, garbage out' applies to regtech as well. If a financial institution does not have centralized or clean data, it is difficult to implement new regtech solutions. It is somewhat like buying the latest Ferrari, but not having the proper gas to run it.

Today regtech remains in its infancy, with no unicorns or globally known brands, but the need for technology-enabled regulatory solutions in financial services is great enough that this is likely to change. But before that happens, we should expect to see a considerable number of failures in the regtech space, driven by the difficulties of working with incumbent financial institutions' procurement and partnership teams. At the same time, many regtech startups may be acquired by traditional technology and regulatory service providers hoping to add to their suite of products.

A particular area to watch is whether the same phenomenon that we observed in the fintech space, where large tech providers may dominate the market, will happen in the regtech space. A good example is mainland China. Many large tech firms like Baidu, Alibaba, and Tencent had to develop their own software as they could not find third-party solutions that were reliable, scalable, and delivered the user experience they wanted. Now these same tech firms are actually starting to offer these technologies to other financial institutions in the market.

For example, Ant Financial started offering some of its operational optimization, content generation, compliance, and risk management technology built for their Caifu Hao product to external fund managers. It was reported that 27 fund management companies that are using it were able to increase their operational efficiency by 70% while reducing their overall costs by 50%.[59]

Financial institutions have no choice but to change the way they look at regulatory compliance because the existing models are simply not sustainable. While the United States—at the time of writing—may be going through a period of deregulation under President Donald Trump, most other jurisdictions are enacting new regulations. This lack of uniformity is simply making compliance an ever more challenging task that requires use of some of the latest technology.

3.3   Challenges Faced by Fintechs

Fintech companies have achieved considerable success, but this does not mean that such businesses have not so far—and do not today—face serious obstacles, nor that their competitive success against large incumbent institutions is assured. This section explores some of the serious challenges faced by fintech firms. We will also consider how the challenges facing fintechs seeking to directly interface with customers (B2C fintechs) differ from those fintechs attempting to serve existing financial institutions (B2B fintechs).

3.3.1   Access to Talent

All fintechs seek to use agile operating models and unique technologies to gain a competitive edge. Achieving this 'edge' requires the right people with necessary skills to make a founder's vision a reality, whether that entails designing a new and more intuitive customer experience, or designing a machine learning-enabled regtech system.

---

[59] "Ant Financial to Share Full Suite of AI Capabilities with Asset Management Companies," *Ant Financial Services Group*, June 19, 2018, https://www.businesswire.com/news/home/20180619006514/en/Ant-Financial-Share-Full-Suite-AI-Capabilities.

Unfortunately, these skills are not easy to come by in the current job market, where there is a deficit of individuals with requisite technical skills, particularly in cutting edge areas like AI and data science. Education systems, mired in traditional curriculums, also often lag in teaching and training students to meet the needs of today's private sector. These topics also rarely comprise core sections of most university-level finance curriculums.

Finally, even when individuals with the right skills are available, fintechs must overcome significant competition to hire these individuals. Large technology companies and financial institutions with deep pockets are often actively pursuing the same talent, forcing emerging fintechs to rely on equity compensation, mission orientation, and an innovative culture to attract new hires.

> **Box 3.2   Are Universities Teaching Fintech?**
>
> Traditional universities are notorious for moving slowly and taking time to embrace change. However, most institutions are now recognizing a need to change or augment their curriculums to suit new student and workplace demands. Several US-based institutions have launched fintech courses in business schools. New York University's Stern School of Business, for example, has fintech as an area of interest as part of its Master of Business Administration program.[60] Also, a growing number of universities, including Singapore Management University and Imperial College London, are launching master's degrees and certificate courses entirely focused on fintech. These courses cover digital currencies, blockchain, robo-advisors, systematic trading, entrepreneurial finance, fintech risk management, and payments.
>
> Interestingly, some of the world's most prestigious universities decided to address the need for fintech skills via online programs. The University of Hong Kong, after launching the first fintech university course in Asia,[61] also launched Asia's first massive open online course (MOOC) on the subject, which examines areas such as cryptocurrencies, blockchain, artificial intelligence, and big data, but also looks at areas like regulation technology.[62] The advantage of the MOOC

(continued)

[60] "Full-Time MBA | FinTech," NYU Stern, accessed January 30, 2019, http://www.stern.nyu.edu/programs-admissions/full-time-mba/academics/areas-interest/fintech.

[61] The course offered in the Masters in Finance and MBA programs since 2015 is taught by co-author Henri Arslanian.

[62] "Asia's 1st FinTech MOOC – Introduction to FinTech," *Asian Institute of International Financial Law, The University of Hong Kong*, accessed January 5, 2019, https://www.law.hku.hk/aiifl/asias-first-fintech-online-course-www-hkufintech-com/.

Box 3.2   (continued)

is that the course is free, available to anyone around the world and can be completed from the comfort of one's home. Such courses have proven to be in high demand: the HKU MOOC quickly surpassed 30,000 registrations from over 180 countries only weeks after launching.[63]

Another successful example can be found at Oxford's Saïd Business School. The school's Fintech Programme also looks at how technology is shaping the different areas of financial services. However, unlike a MOOC, which is by nature more introductory, this online program is designed to equip students with the ability to identify opportunities for disruption in finance as well as to launch a fintech venture.[64]

It is expected that most universities will have fintech as part of their core curriculum in the coming years, although many believe that this is not enough and that business schools need to adapt faster. For example, while courses like accounting, corporate finance, or strategy are still very important, computer programming, design, or product management should perhaps be offered in tandem as they may be essential for any executive moving forward.

3.3.2   Regulatory Compliance

Regulatory regimes in many jurisdictions have become markedly more open to, and in some cases even supportive of, fintech innovators. For example, take the United Kingdom where in 2014 the Financial Conduct Authority created an initiative called Project Innovate to provide regulatory advice and guidance designed for new fintech innovators. The regulator has even created a 'sandbox' to allow both startups and incumbents to test new product ideas in a controlled environment.

Despite these changes, the regulatory barriers to entry remain particularly high, and while a growing number of regulators are providing guidance to fintech firms, they do not look kindly on firms who are lackadaisical toward their compliance responsibilities. Further complicating this issue is the fact that regulations and licensing requirements differ across jurisdictions, and sometimes even within countries. For example, non-bank lenders in the United States must be licensed at the state level by each state in which they want to operate. While overcoming these kinds of obligations is not impossible, they can significantly add to costs and draw out the runway to launch.

---

[63] "Introduction to FinTech, Provided by University of Hong Kong (HKUx)," *EdX*, accessed January 5, 2019, https://www.edx.org/course/introduction-to-fintech.
[64] Saïd Business School, University of Oxford, "Oxford Fintech Programme," *GetSmarter*, accessed January 5, 2019, https://www.getsmarter.com/courses/uk/said-business-school-oxford-university-fintech-online-short-course.

Box 3.3 How Do Regulators View Fintech?

Just like all the other actors in the financial services ecosystem, regulators have started their fintech journey too and in many regards have done an impressive job. Currently, we are seeing a growing number of initiatives aimed at better understanding the use of innovative technologies in the finance sector. For example, in Hong Kong, the Securities and Futures Commission (SFC) has established the Fintech Contact Point to enhance communication with companies involved in the development and application of fintech.[65] Likewise, in the United States, the Commodity Futures Trading Commission (CFTC) has launched LabCFTC to promote responsible fintech innovation and fair competition for the benefit of the American public.[66] These are avenues that allow startups to interact with regulators in a collaborative and open environment.

Regulators are also setting up regulatory sandboxes that allow fintechs and financial institutions to experiment with new technologies in a controlled environment. These sandboxes have been quite popular: since 2015, eight Asia-Pacific jurisdictions—Australia, mainland China, Hong Kong SAR, Indonesia, Malaysia, Singapore, South Korea, and Thailand—have implemented regulatory sandboxes.[67] Other known examples include the United Kingdom, Canada, and the United Arab Emirates. In March 2018, Arizona became the first US state to launch a fintech regulatory sandbox.[68]

Regulators are also looking at using these new technologies to manage supervision challenges more efficiently and effectively. The latter is called Supervisory Technology, and the area is still in its infancy.[69] However, we can already observe interesting initiatives such as the use of machine learning to detect potential investment adviser misconduct by the SEC.[70] The Monetary Authority of Singapore (MAS) is working on a data analytics system to scour through the 3000 suspicious transaction reports that financial institutions file each month on money laundering and terrorist financing risks.[71]

[65] "Securities and Futures Commission Fintech Contact Point," *Hong Kong Securities and Futures Commission*, September 29, 2017, https://www.sfc.hk/web/EN/sfc-fintech-contact-point/.

[66] "LabCFTC Overview," *U.S. Commodity Futures Trading Commission*, accessed January 5, 2019, https://www.cftc.gov/LabCFTC/Overview/index.htm.

[67] James Lloyd, "Regulatory 'Sandboxes' Facilitate Optimal Regulation in Asia Pacific," *EY Financial Services*, March 2018, https://www.ey.com/gl/en/industries/financial-services/fso-insights-regulatory-sandboxes-facilitate-optimal-regulation-in-asia-pacific.

[68] Aaron Stanley, "Arizona Becomes First U.S. State To Launch Regulatory Sandbox for Fintech," *Forbes* (Forbes, March 23, 2018), https://www.forbes.com/sites/astanley/2018/03/23/arizona-becomes-first-u-s-state-to-launch-regulatory-sandbox-for-fintech/.

[69] Dan Murphy and "RegTech: Opportunities for More Efficient and Effective Regulatory Supervision and Compliance" (Milken Institute, July 2018), https://assets1b.milkeninstitute.org/assets/Publication/Viewpoint/PDF/RegTech-Opportunities-White-Paper-FINAL-.pdf.

[70] Scott W. Bauguess, "The Role of Big Data, Machine Learning, and AI in Assessing Risks: A Regulatory Perspective," June 21, 2017, https://www.sec.gov/news/speech/bauguess-big-data-ai.

[71] Mr Ravi Menon, Managing Director, Monetary Authority of Singapore, "Singapore FinTech Journey 2.0," November 14, 2017, http://www.mas.gov.sg/News-and-Publications/Speeches-and-Monetary-Policy-Statements/Speeches/2017/Singapore-FinTech-Journey-2.aspx.

3.3.3   Customer Trust

The global financial crisis shook consumers' faith in their financial institutions, showing that even the largest and oldest brands in the industry could find themselves at the precipice of collapse. It is likely that the lingering distrust toward incumbent financial institutions that followed the crisis, particularly among millennials, contributed to consumers' interest in the rise of both fintech startups and crypto-assets like Bitcoin (as we will discuss later in this book).

However, this interest does not necessarily equate to customer trust. Consumers often continue to view incumbents as safer, and treat startups with skepticism even when they have secured all necessary regulatory approvals.

3.3.4   Scaling the Customer Base

While a number of celebrated fintech unicorns have been able to rapidly acquire a significant user base and broad geographic penetration in just a few years, this does not mean starting such fintech businesses is easy, let alone scaling them. However, the nature of this challenge differs significantly depending on if the target customers are end consumers (B2C) or large institutions (B2B).

The business model of many B2C fintech startups requires them to build an enormous customer base to achieve profitability. While it is tempting to imagine that simply building a great product should be enough to have the world beat a path to your door, this is rarely the case—particularly given the need to build customer trust. The marketing budget required to achieve this can be very large, with only a handful of startups having successfully deployed viral marketing campaigns that have reeled in masses of active users.[72]

Take digital bank Revolut as an example. To fuel its growth, acquire clients, and be able to offer products at highly competitive fees, the company has had to spend millions (around £8 million according to some reports)[73] and has not yet achieved profitability. This is only possible if the company has a lot of funding and patient investors. For robo-advisory firms, the cost of customer acquisition for a very low-margin product has proved to be particularly high, with Morningstar estimating a cost between US$300 and US$1000 to acquire each new client.[74]

B2B startups seeking to sell to large institutions, including incumbent banks, insurers, and asset managers, face a slightly different challenge. While these

---

[72] Huy Nguyen Trieu, "Fintech Start-Ups Beware: Customers Are Expensive," *Disruptive Finance*, January 3, 2016, http://www.disruptivefinance.co.uk/2016/01/03/fintech-start-ups-beware-customers-are-expensive/.

[73] Oscar Williams-Grut, "Hot Foreign Exchange App Revolut Burned through £7 Million Fuelling Its Growth Last Year," *Business Insider*, June 27, 2017, http://uk.businessinsider.com/fintech-revolut-2016-accounts-loss-revenue-2017-6?IR=T.

[74] Tina Wadhwa, "One of the Hottest Investment Styles Might Be 'Financially Unviable,'" *Business Insider*, July 14, 2016, https://www.businessinsider.com/robo-advisors-may-be-financially-unviable-2016-7?IR=T.

firms often only need to secure a handful of clients in order to achieve profitability, securing these clients can be extremely expensive and time-consuming. Institutional sales cycles of 12–18 months are common, and prospective clients perform extensive due diligence and often request extensive product customizations before committing to an agreement. Together these factors can place an enormous strain on a company's cash reserves—potentially putting them at risk of bankruptcy even when significant demand for their product exists.[75]

Box 3.4   Why Is It So Difficult to Sell to Financial Institutions?

Selling any type of services to any financial institution requires a lot of determination, patience, and a good sense of humor.

First, finding the right individuals inside the financial institution is a challenge. Unless someone works in that organization, knowing who the right decision-makers are is very difficult. Each bank has individuals from their innovation teams attending various fintech events, but these individuals rarely have any significant decision-making power or budget. To make matters more complicated, many individuals inside banks have titles like 'vice president' or 'director' that may sound impressive but are common in financial institutions.

Second, agreeing to conduct a proof-of-concept (PoC) is a challenge. A PoC is a short experimental project to try to demonstrate that a technology works. The problem is that many banks don't want to pay for PoCs. So a startup needs to decide whether it wants to take the risk of doing a PoC that will require an investment of time and energy. Also, once a PoC is successful, there is no guarantee that the bank will move forward with implementation. Unfortunately, many innovation teams have targets of doing only a certain number of PoCs a year and each represents a substantial opportunity cost for a startup.

If the PoC is successful, the next step is generally to do a pilot (with real staff or even clients), with the goal of bringing it to production (e.g. deploying the solution inside the organization).

But even if all the above is perfect, going through the procurement process and contract negotiation can be a nightmare. Banks have structured procurement processes that are made for large technology providers, not small startups. These include stringent tests from a broad range of teams from technology and operations to cybersecurity and compliance. Going through the contract negotiations process as well can be time-consuming and costly. Even when all the above is done, there needs to be a proper deployment of the solution which can take months as the bank has to mobilize the right internal resources.

One big issue for a large financial institution is to try to find a place for these new solutions inside the legacy systems of the bank. Many banks use mainframe systems that were put in place decades ago, making integrations with modern systems much more complex and expensive.

Perhaps the most significant challenge to successfully selling a solution to a large financial institution is the people factor. Without that one internal champion who is ready to risk his or her career and push a solution across the various layers of the bank, it is difficult for startups even to get a foot in the door.

---

[75] "The Top 20 Reasons Startups Fail" (CB Insights, February 2, 2018), https://www.cbinsights.com/research/startup-failure-reasons-top/.

3.3.5 Raising Capital

While the global pool of available venture capital has grown in recent years, competition for investment remains fierce for any startup, and fintechs are no exception. Adding further complexity, high regulatory requirements of the sector discussed earlier in this chapter increase the complexity of product launch.

In many other areas of digital services, startups can—in the words of Silicon Valley venture capitalist Guy Kawasaki—'ship then test'. In other words, businesses can launch an early stage product that may have many bugs and later channel user feedback to further refine the product. For most fintechs this is not possible; regulators will often require a product and its underlying operations to be vetted before a launch, and indeed, every revision of the product may incur new levels of regulatory scrutiny. This may prolong key milestones, like scoring paying customers or breaking even, further making the operating cost of launching a fintech startup—for every stage from marketing to cybersecurity—much higher than those of many other digital products.[76]

---

[76] The trimplement Team, "What Challenges Are Fintech Startups Facing Today," *Medium*, May 28, 2017, https://medium.com/trimplement/what-challenges-are-fintech-startups-facing-today-6e2efef8ecb4.

4

Incumbent Financial Institutions and Their Response to Fintechs

The challenges that fintechs face in their efforts to achieve scale raise an important question about the broader dynamics of the financial ecosystem. Given the significant obstacles that fintechs face, how have they succeeded in acquiring millions of users and billion-dollar valuations? Why haven't incumbent financial institutions been the ones leading the innovation within their own industry?

You might be inclined to think that financial institutions have simply chosen not to make investments in technology, relying on their scale or regulatory barriers to entry to protect their market share. But the numbers tell a very different story, as technology investment by incumbent banks is high and on the rise. In 2018, overall bank IT spending in North America grew by 4.9% to US$104 billion, while global spending increased 4.2% to a staggering US$261 billion.[1]

In other words, banks (these numbers are for banks only and would be significantly larger if insurance and other non-banks were included) spent almost four and a half times as much as all venture capital investment in fintech in 2018. So how can it be that fintechs, not incumbents, are leading the way on technology? The trouble is that while total spending on IT is large, more than two-thirds of that budget is typically dedicated to maintenance of aging and outdated systems and most large-scale spending to change internal IT systems is dedicated to meeting new compliance and regulatory requirements.[2] To

---

[1] Adrian D. Garcia, "Big Banks Spend Billions on Tech But Innovation Lags | Bankrate," *Bankrate* (Bankrate.com, July 27, 2018), https://www.bankrate.com/banking/jpm-big-banks-spend-billions-on-tech-but-theyre-still-laggards/.

[2] Citi GPS: Global Perspectives & Solutions, "The Bank of the Future – The ABCs of Digital Disruption in Finance," *Citibank*, March 2018, https://www.citibank.com/commercialbank/insights/assets/docs/2018/The-Bank-of-the-Future/124/.

© The Author(s) 2019
H. Arslanian, F. Fischer, *The Future of Finance*,
https://doi.org/10.1007/978-3-030-14533-0_4

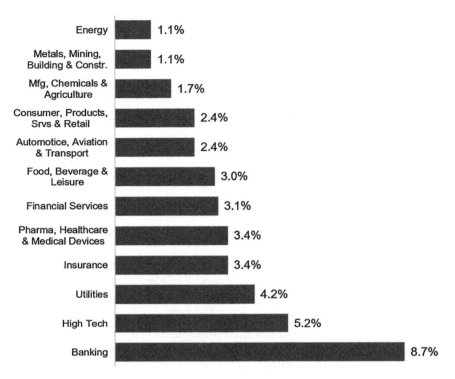

Fig. 4.1 Median IT expense as a percentage of revenue (2016); Bank's legacy IT systems contribute to their extremely high IT costs. Source(s): The Bank of the Future (Citigroup Inc., 2018), https://www.citibank.com/commercialbank/insights/assets/docs/2018/The-Bank-of-the-Future/, page 61

understand how this came to be the case, we need to look more deeply at the challenging set of barriers that financial institutions face when it comes to turning dollars into innovative products and improved digital experiences.

4.1   Impediments to Incumbent Innovation

The most significant impediment facing technological innovation in banks is ironically their long history of investing in new technology. In 1954, Bank of America took delivery of a Remington Rand UNIVAC-1, an early computer that used vacuum tubes and magnetic tape to process 12,000 numbers or letters per second.[3] In doing so, they became the first bank to employ a computer in the delivery of financial services. Investments like this, and the many that

---

[3] "Bank of America Revolutionizes Banking Industry from Bank of America," *About Bank of America*, August 12, 2014, https://about.bankofamerica.com/en-us/our-story/bank-of-america-revolutionizes-industry.html.

would follow—from automated tellers to online banking—created opportunities for financial institutions to improve efficiency and engage with customers through new channels. But being a first mover is a double-edged sword: as these early investments in technology aged, they led to the accumulation of 'technical debt', or put more simply, a pile of increasingly outdated information technology systems that remained central to the organization's operations.

While Bank of America has presumably phased out the Remington Rand UNIVAC-1, many 40- and 50-year-old 'legacy' systems continue to exist within large incumbent financial institutions, and while these systems are highly stable, they are also highly inflexible. Adding new technical features often requires patches to the legacy systems that can be time-consuming and expensive.

For example, many early bank systems were based on a programming language called COBOL (Common Business-Oriented Language) that was developed nearly 60 years ago. In the years following, COBOL has been gradually replaced in other industries by newer, more versatile languages such as Java, C, and Python.[4] Few university computer science programs today teach the language, and the average age of a COBOL programmer is over 45.[5] Despite this, COBOL continues to underpin the operations of financial institutions with 43% of banking systems built on it, and 95% of ATMs.[6]

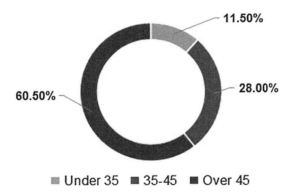

Fig. 4.2 Age distribution of COBOL programmers (as of 2018); The aging talent pool of specialists able to modify and maintain financial institutions' legacy mainframes limits incumbent innovation. Source(s): The Bank of the Future (Citigroup Inc., 2018), https://www.citibank.com/commercialbank/insights/assets/docs/2018/The-Bank-of-the-Future/, page 67

---

[4] Anna Irrera, "Banks Scramble to Fix Old Systems as IT 'Cowboys' Ride into Sunset," *Reuters*, April 11, 2017, https://www.reuters.com/article/us-usa-banks-cobol-idUSKBN17C0D8.

[5] Robert L. Mitchell, "The Cobol Brain Drain," *Computerworld*, May 21, 2012, https://www.computerworld.com/article/2504568/data-center/the-cobol-brain-drain.html.

[6] Chris Skinner, *Digital Human: The Fourth Revolution of Humanity Includes Everyone* (Marshall Cavendish International (Asia) Private Limited, 2018), page 77.

The result is that changes to bank systems are expensive, requiring specialized (and aging) programming talent to navigate a 'maze' of past updates and patches that have been made to the legacy systems over the decades. By contrast, most fintech startups' offerings are built in the cloud using modern code that allows them to implement changes to their systems much faster and at much lower cost.

Legacy technical debt is of course not the only reason that incumbent financial institutions have struggled to innovate. The culture of these organizations is often highly bureaucratic and risk averse, making it difficult for new ideas to flourish and challenging for the organization to attract and retain top technical talent. When combined with enormous investments needed to update incumbents' systems and processes to meet new regulatory requirements over the past decade, it becomes clear just how large a barrier banks face when it comes to keeping pace with the rapid advancement of technology.

This means that many processes within incumbent financial institutions that could theoretically be fully automated—and that in many cases have been fully automated by fintechs—remain largely manual. Take customer onboarding. Many banks still require new customers to arrive at a bank in person to present their identity documentation and signature—a highly anachronistic process in a world where recent studies suggest that facial recognition software can be 15–20 times better than humans at identifying an individual in a typical face-to-face interaction.[7] The result is a process that is both cost intensive and potentially less secure than one that a new organization could build from scratch. But incumbent financial institutions are not building from scratch, while startups have the luxury of operational and technical agility. Making changes to a core process like customer onboarding for incumbents is akin to turning around a supertanker.

Faced with these challenges, how have incumbent financial instructions sought to preserve their position? Well, as the adage goes, 'If you can't beat them, join them'. Financial institutions are increasingly looking to fintech startups and the ideas developed there as a path to improved offerings. While there are many different approaches, these incumbent-startup interactions can generally be categorized in three ways: building/replicating fintech capabilities, investing in fintech startups, and partnering with fintech startups.

---

[7] Brett King, *Bank 4.0: Banking Everywhere, Never at a Bank* (Marshall Cavendish International Asia Pte Ltd., 2018), page 80.

4.2   Incumbents Building/Replicating Fintech Offerings

While changing their core systems is extremely difficult and time-consuming for most incumbent financial institutions, there is little to prevent these organizations from employing modern programming tools and techniques in the creation of new 'standalone' offerings that can then be integrated in a limited way with core systems.

Perhaps the most successful example of this has been efforts by traditional wealth managers to emulate the offerings of fintech robo-advisors. In 2015, San Francisco–based bank and brokerage firm Charles Schwab launched a robo-advisor offering called Intelligent Portfolio that charged no fees aside from those associated with the financial products (typically low-fee exchange-traded funds) that users purchased.[8] Shortly after, Vanguard, one of the world's largest asset managers, deployed a similar offering called 'Vanguard Personal Advisor Services'.[9]

Able to leverage their established brand names, customer base, and sales channels, these services were able to grow much more rapidly than their fintech peers. As of the third quarter of 2018, fintech companies Wealthfront and Betterment had assets under management (AUM) of US$11.1 billion and US$14.1 billion, respectively, while Schwab Intelligent Portfolios had AUM of US$33.3 billion, and Vanguard Personal Advisor Services an impressive US$112 billion.[10] As a result, robo-advisory startups have found their valuations under significant pressure, with some apparently reduced to as little as one-third of their previous price.[11]

Of course, wealth managers are not the only institutions seeking to build their own fintech solutions. Examples of such projects abound, such as HSBC's launch of a payment tool called PayMe which rapidly reached a million users.[12] Incumbent efforts in this space typically seek to use fintech ideas

---

[8] "Schwab Intelligent Portfolios'," *Charles Schwab Intelligent Portfolios*, accessed January 5, 2019, https://intelligent.schwab.com/.

[9] Vanguard, "Vanguard Introduces Personal Advisor Services, Lowers Minimum to Investors With $50,000," *Vanguard*, May 5, 2015, https://pressroom.vanguard.com/news/Vanguard_Introduces_Personal_Advisor_Services_Lowers_Minimum.html.

[10] Brittney Grimes, "10 Largest Robo-Advisers by AUM," InvestmentNews, accessed January 30, 2019, https://www.investmentnews.com/gallery/20181107/FREE/110709999/PH/10-largest-robo-advisers-by-aum.

[11] Julie Verhage, "Wealthfront Valuation Said to Drop About a Third in New Funding," *Bloomberg*, March 24, 2018, https://www.bloomberg.com/news/articles/2018-03-23/wealthfront-valuation-said-to-drop-about-a-third-in-new-funding.

[12] "HSBC Payment App Users Surpass 1m," *The Standard*, July 18, 2018, http://www.thestandard.com.hk/breaking-news.php?id=110664&sid=2.

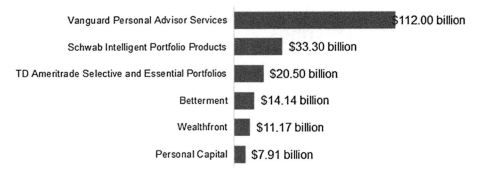

Fig. 4.3 Robo-advisor assets under management (Q3 2017) (US$); Incumbent asset managers have been more successful than fintech innovators at growing the assets under management of robo-advisor offerings. Source(s): Brittney Grimes, "10 Largest Robo-Advisers by AUM," InvestmentNews, accessed January 30, 2019, https://www.investmentnews.com/gallery/20181107/FREE/110709999/PH/10-largest-robo-advisers-by-aum

to both better serve their customers and improve their internal efficiency. For example, Bank of America has recently deployed a chatbot called Erica to help customers complete daily activities including making payments, checking balances, saving money, and paying down debt.[13] Another example is JPMorgan's COIN system that uses machine learning to automate redundant tasks like reviewing documents and commercial agreements—thus performing tasks in a matter of seconds that would take lawyers 360,000 hours.[14]

In some cases, efforts to replicate fintech offerings have driven impressive levels of collaboration between incumbent financial institutions. In response to the peer-to-peer payment app Venmo, over 90 incumbent US banks, including Bank of America, JPMorgan Chase, Wells Fargo, and Capital One, have partnered to offer a competing service call Zelle,[15] which according to some forecasts is set to overtake Venmo in terms of users in 2018.[16]

Even more ambitious undertakings include efforts to build entirely new banks from scratch designed to compete with emerging challenger banks. In

---

[13] Harriet Taylor, "Bank of America Launches AI Chatbot Erica – Here's What It Does," *CNBC*, October 24, 2016, https://www.cnbc.com/2016/10/24/bank-of-america-launches-ai-chatbot-erica%2D%2Dheres-what-it-does.html.

[14] Julie Verhage, "Wealthfront Valuation Said to Drop About a Third in New Funding," *Bloomberg*, March 24, 2018, https://www.bloomberg.com/news/articles/2018-03-23/wealthfront-valuation-said-to-drop-about-a-third-in-new-funding.

[15] "Get Started," *Zelle*, 2019, https://www.zellepay.com/get-started.

[16] Sarah Perez, "Zelle Forecast to Overtake Venmo This Year," *TechCrunch*, June 2018, https://techcrunch.com/2018/06/15/zelle-forecast-to-overtake-venmo-this-year/.

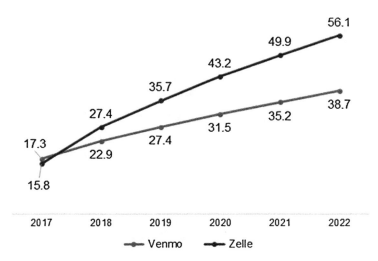

Fig. 4.4 Mobile P2P payments users by platform; Incumbent backed P2P payments service Zelle is on track to surpass Venmo according to some projections. Source(s): Sarah Perez, "Zelle Forecast to Overtake Venmo This Year," TechCrunch, June 2018, https://techcrunch.com/2018/06/15/zelle-forecast-to-overtake-venmo-this-year/

2016, Goldman Sachs launched its own digital consumer bank called Marcus. Marcus offers no-fee, fixed-rate personal loans, high-yield online savings accounts, and certificates of deposit to "help people achieve financial well-being".[17] It is operationally independent from its parent bank and boasts a lean structure. Moreover, giving Marcus a distinctly different brand could suggest a strategic effort to de-link this new offering from the legacy reputation and brand of its parent. Since Marcus started, it has attracted 1.5 million customers, made over $3 billion of loans, and gathered $22 billion in deposits.[18]

But the path to success is far from assured. In most cases, building a fintech offering in-house requires financial institutions to set up separate reporting lines and often requires them to establish separate physical office space where new ideas can flourish outside of the organization's dominant culture. Such spaces often also offer ancillary benefits such as fashionable office design and flexible working arrangements in order to attract technical talent who might not otherwise be interested in working with the institution. Most important though is clear and ongoing support from senior management—which is not

[17] "FAQs," *Marcus by Goldman Sachs*, 2018, https://www.marcus.com/us/en/faqs.
[18] Will Mathis, "Goldman Sachs Expects Marcus to Get 'Very Big, Very Profitable,'" *Bloomberg*, June 1, 2018, https://www.bloomberg.com/news/articles/2018-05-31/goldman-sachs-expects-marcus-to-get-very-big-very-profitable.

always easy to sustain. In May 2018, Deutsche Bank, having recently undergone a change in CEO, quietly decided to shelve a long-standing set of plans to build their own digital bank.[19] While this high-profile shift in strategy was announced, there have doubtlessly been many similar efforts by incumbent financial institutions abandoned long before they reached their intended users.

4.3   Incumbents Investing in Fintechs

In addition to building fintech-style capabilities in-house, many financial institutions have also chosen to both make investments in and directly acquire fintech startups. For example, in contrast to Charles Schwab and Betterment, who built robo-advisor capabilities internally, their peer organization and the world's largest asset manager, Blackrock, instead chose to acquire the San Francisco–based robo-advisory firm FutureAdvisor in 2015 and invest in European robo-advisory firm Scalable in 2017.[20]

Many financial institutions have chosen to set up corporate venture capital (CVC) funds as a vehicle to deploy these investments. From 2013 to 2017, Goldman Sachs and Citi have been the most active bulge bracket banks investing in fintech, with 37 and 25 major fintech investments, respectively.[21] Goldman's investments have largely focused on lending, while Citi has focused on databases and security.[22] In Europe, Banco Santander has made 23 equity investments into 19 fintech startups through its venture arm Santander InnoVentures,[23] whose portfolio includes unicorns such as Kabbage and Tradeshift.[24] Even typically conservative insurers have been active in deploying investments into insurtech firms through their venture arms.[25]

---

[19] "Deutsche Bank Plant Nun Doch Keine Digitalbank," *Reuters*, May 29, 2018, https://de.reuters.com/article/deutschland-deutsche-bank-idDEKCN1IT1Q8.

[20] Trevor Hunnicutt Simon Jessop, "BlackRock Takes Scalable Capital Stake in Europe 'Robo-Advisor' Push," *Reuters*, June 20, 2017, https://www.reuters.com/article/us-blackrock-scalablecapital/blackrock-takes-scalable-capital-stake-in-europe-robo-advisor-push-idUSKBN19A322.

[21] "JPMorgan Chase Competitive Strategy Teardown: How the Bank Stacks Up on Fintech and Innovation," *CB Insights Research*, January 11, 2018, https://www.cbinsights.com/research/jpmorgan-chase-competitive-strategy-teardown-expert-intelligence/.

[22] "Where Top US Banks Are Betting on Fintech," *CB Insights*, November 21, 2018, https://www.cbinsights.com/research/fintech-investments-top-us-banks/.

[23] "Https://www.cbinsights.com/research/europe-Bank-Fintech-Startup-Investments/," *CB Insights*, April 12, 2018, https://www.cbinsights.com/research/europe-bank-fintech-startup-investments/.

[24] "Portfolio Companies," *Santander Innoventures*, accessed January 6, 2019, http://santanderinnoventures.com/portfolio-companies/.

[25] "6 Charts Breaking Down How Insurers Are Investing in Tech Startups," September 14, 2016, https://www.cbinsights.com/research/insurance-corporate-venturing-2016/.

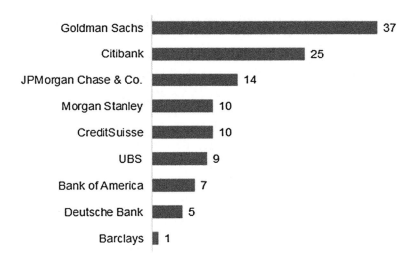

Fig. 4.5 Number of Fintech investments by institution (2013–2017); Many large banks have moved aggressively to invest in a wide range of emerging fintechs. Source(s): "JPMorgan Chase Competitive Strategy Teardown: How the Bank Stacks Up on Fintech and Innovation," CB Insights Research, January 11, 2018, https://www.cbinsights.com/research/jpmorgan-chase-competitive-strategy-teardown-expert-intelligence/

Of course, succeeding in the world of venture capital is no simple matter. There are many established fintech-focused venture capitalists with strong reputations and the established networks necessary to help them find the best emerging fintechs and invest in them quickly. As relative newcomers, financial institutions' corporate venture funds often fear their investments being dictated by 'adverse selection', or put another way, the risk of seeing only the startups that leading venture capitalists have chosen not to invest in.

Fortunately, the interests of fintech venture capital funds and the corporate venture capital funds of financial institutions are not identical. While venture capital funds are purely interested in the potential return on their investments, this is a secondary consideration for most CVCs. Their primary objective is typically strategic—providing access to insight, intellectual property, and to a potential partner.

On the other hand, taking an investment from an incumbent financial institution can be a double-edged sword for a startup. The fintech founder may worry that incumbents will use their minority investment to gather the necessary knowledge to construct a competing offering. At the same time, taking venture investment from one financial institution may deter other incumbents from investing in or partnering with the startup, out of concerns that it has become 'captive' to one of their competitors.

4.4   Incumbents Partnering with Fintechs

While significant investments in fintech and efforts to build out fintech capabilities remain the exception rather than the rule among incumbent financial institutions, it is a near universally stated view among these organizations that they are dedicated to cooperative partnerships with fintechs. In fact, as highlighted by the PwC 2017 Global FinTech Report, more than 82% of incumbent financial institutions expect to increase fintech partnerships in the next three to five years.[26]

One common example of a fintech and incumbent partnership has been in the small business lending space, where large incumbents have traditionally struggled to achieve profitability targets due to relatively high underwriting costs on smaller denomination loans. In response, several organizations have partnered with small business–focused fintech lenders with the goal of combining the incumbents' scale and low cost of capital with the streamlined customer onboarding and loan underwriting capabilities of the startup. In 2016, JPMorgan Chase announced a partnership with fintech lender On Deck Capital, with JPMorgan's CEO Jamie Dimon saying the partnership would allow them to do "the kind of stuff we don't want to do or can't do".[27] Also in 2016, European bank Santander announced a partnership with fintech lender Kabbage in the United Kingdom on similar grounds.[28]

Interesting examples of partnerships can be found in other subsectors of financial services as well. For example, in addition to making a number of investments in insurtech firms, German reinsurance company Munich Re has launched partnerships with a range of insurtech startups providing the underlying capital to back their offerings and bringing to bear their expertise in pricing and cross-jurisdictional operations.[29]

But young fintech companies are radically different animals from incumbent financial institutions, with completely different cultures and values. Attempts at partnership within the confines of the traditional incumbent organization often fail. For this reason, many incumbents have elected to set

[26] "Redrawing the Lines: FinTech's Growing Influence on Financial Services," *Pwc*, 2017, https://www.pwc.com/jg/en/publications/pwc-global-fintech-report-17.3.17-final.pdf.

[27] "Love and War - Banking and Fintech," The Economist, December 5, 2015, https://www.economist.com/finance-and-economics/2015/12/05/love-and-war.

[28] "Kabbage and Santander UK Partner to Accelerate SMB Growth," April 3, 2016, https://www.kabbage.com/blog/kabbage-santander-uk-partner-accelerate-smb-growth/.

[29] "Reinventing Insurance for the Digital Generation," *Munich RE*, January 16, 2017, https://www.munichre.com/topics-online/en/digitalisation/reinventing-insurance-digital-generation.html.

up internal innovation teams and labs with the objective to learn how to effectively collaborate with fintechs. Broadly speaking, these labs are a new kind of physical environment created by companies, with a mission to serve as a focal point for innovation programs, research, or design activities. These innovation labs or teams will scan the market for new technologies or start-ups, meet them, and potentially run proofs of concept to test their technology. The end goal is to be able to integrate some of these startups or their technology into existing systems.

Yet for all their popularity, such labs face a litany of problems. The creation of a lab is not the same as clear executive vision and deep commitment of resources to the transformation of an organization. A lab may be created simply for marketing and public relations reasons, or to point to when shareholders ask questions about the institution's strategy for addressing fintech disruptors. Labs created in this way are typically not granted a meaningful budget and have limited authority to challenge the entrenched interests of product owners and other mid-level executives across the organization. This is frustrating not only for the fintech startups who risk spending considerable time and resources on proofs of concept with no scope to scale across the organization, but also for the incumbent organizations' innovation teams who do not feel empowered. Given this, it is not surprising that innovation teams in incumbent financial institutions tend to see high rates of turnover.

Indeed, even when strong support and clear direction exist for innovation lab teams, their work can face significant resistance from within the institution. The aim of the lab is to develop capabilities that will give the institution a competitive advantage in the long term, but the immediate economic impact of many lab projects is often not measurable. This creates clear tension with many staff and executives responsible for 'business as usual' operations whose buy-in is essential to the project's success, but whose performance is measured on a quarterly or annual basis.

5

The Emergence of Techfin

Until recently, most of the analysis into the potential for competitive disruption in financial services revolved around new fintech entrants as the key catalyst for change to the structure of the financial ecosystem. But today, more and more attention is being given to a potentially much more disruptive set of new entrants: ones who bring vast sums of capital and unparalleled technical capabilities as well as enormous pre-existing user bases who engage with them via digital channels on a daily basis. These are, of course, the world's large technology companies. A growing number of financial executives fear that their entry into financial services as direct competitors is simply a matter of time.

5.1 The Case for Tech to Techfin

Large technology companies seem uniquely well positioned to disrupt financial services in a way that few fintechs or incumbent financial institutions are. Unlike newly minted fintechs, large technology companies do not need to acquire a customer base, as they already have one that is larger than not only any fintech but also any bank. Both Revolut's two million users[1] and JPMorgan's

---

[1] "About Revolut."

© The Author(s) 2019
H. Arslanian, F. Fischer, *The Future of Finance*,
https://doi.org/10.1007/978-3-030-14533-0_5

80 million customers are dwarfed in the face of Google's one billion Gmail users[2] or Facebook's two billion accounts.[3]

These firms have frequent contact with their users, years of data to support the personalization of offerings, and, most importantly for the purposes of financial services, significant user trust. While large technology companies have certainly not been free from scandals, users remain comfortable sharing highly sensitive data within these firms. Why would a new mother comfortable with sharing her baby photos on Facebook not be comfortable also using it as a payments channel for sending and receiving money? If a couple uses Amazon to buy all of their daily necessities, why wouldn't they also use it to buy insurance products?

In fact, according to a survey conducted by Bain & Co,[4] nearly 60% of bank customers in the United States are willing to try a financial product from tech firms they already use. Younger respondents were even more likely to consider a switch, with 73% of millennials saying they would test such products. This trend is similar over the world: Asian consumers, for example, are the most open to this type of service, and unsurprisingly, in both China and India, more than 80% of respondents are willing to purchase financial products from large technology firms.

5.2   China as a Template for the Growth of Techfin

Indeed, the potential for large technology companies to dominate the delivery of financial services to retail customers is not just an idea: it's a reality in a number of Asian markets. Most notable among them is China, where technology firms Tencent and Alibaba have successfully integrated extensive consumer payment, lending, and investment services into their digital offerings.

5.2.1   Alibaba's and Tencent's Transformation of Payments in China

In 2004, e-commerce giant Alibaba launched Alipay to facilitate online payments. Tencent entered the space later with the launch of their mobile-only messaging app called WeChat in 2011. Over the ensuing years, both apps,

---

[2] Frederic Lardinois, "Gmail Now Has More Than 1B Monthly Active Users," *TechCrunch*, February 1, 2016, https://techcrunch.com/2016/02/01/gmail-now-has-more-than-1b-monthly-active-users/.

[3] Brett King, *Bank 4.0: Banking Everywhere, Never at a Bank* (Marshall Cavendish International Asia Pte Ltd, 2018), page 136.

[4] Hugh Son, "Consumers Want Tech Firms to Take on the Banks," *Bloomberg*, November 20, 2017, https://www.bloomberg.com/news/articles/2017-11-20/banks-beware-most-customers-suspect-tech-can-do-your-job-better.

and the services they provide, have continually evolved and their user bases have grown rapidly, transforming the landscape of payments in China. WeChat now has over 1 billion users globally (approximately 70 million of whom are outside of China), with 800 million using WeChat Pay, while Alipay has over 620 million users.[5] An astounding 600 million payments are made each day using WeChat, and as of 2016, the two technology giants controlled 90%[6] of the 58.8 trillion yuan (approximately, US$8.8 trillion in 2016) Chinese consumers spent via their phones that year.[7,8]

These numbers dwarf those found in the West. Consider how the user numbers of WeChat and Alipay compare to the 25 million active users of the Bank of America mobile app[9] or the miniscule US$112 billion in mobile payment transactions that Forrester Research estimates are made by US consumers.

5.2.2 Alibaba's and Tencent's Expansion Beyond Payments

Having dominated the payments space, Alibaba and Tencent have sought to expand their suite of financial offerings to include an array of services such as loans, credit scoring, and wealth management.

Ant Financial, Alibaba's financial arm which includes Alipay, runs the world's biggest money market fund, called Yu'e Bao that had US$266 billion worth of assets under management as of March 2018.[10] This is about six times the size of JPMorgan's Prime Money Market Fund. Tencent also offers extensive wealth management products by providing direct access through apps to products from one of the country's largest mutual fund managers.[11]

---

[5] Stella Yifan Xie, "Jack Ma's Giant Financial Startup Is Shaking the Chinese Banking System," *WSJ Online*, July 29, 2018, https://www.wsj.com/articles/jack-mas-giant-financial-startup-is-shaking-the-chinese-banking-system-1532885367.

[6] Clay Chandler, "Tencent and Alibaba Are Engaged in a Massive Battle in China Play Video," *Fortune*, May 13, 2017, http://fortune.com/2017/05/13/tencent-alibaba-china/.

[7] Pengying, "China's Mobile Payment Volume Tops 81 Trln Yuan," *Xinhua*, February 19, 2018, http://www.xinhuanet.com/english/2018-02/19/c_136985149.htm.

[8] "2017 Mobile Payment Usage in China Report," *IPSOS*, August 2017, https://www.ipsos.com/sites/default/files/ct/publication/documents/2017-08/Mobile_payments_in_China-2017.pdf.

[9] "Bank of America Surpasses 1 Million Users on Erica | Bank of America," *Bank of America*, accessed January 6, 2019, https://newsroom.bankofamerica.com/press-releases/consumer-banking/bank-america-surpasses-1-million-users-erica.

[10] Yue Wang, "Ant Financial Said to Close $150B Funding Round," *Forbes* (Forbes, May 29, 2018), https://www.forbes.com/sites/ywang/2018/05/28/ant-financial-said-to-close-150-b-funding-round/.

[11] Maggie Zhang, "Tencent Gets a Licence to Sell Mutual Funds to WeChat's 1 Billion Users in China," *South China Morning Post*, 04 January 2018, https://www.scmp.com/business/companies/article/2126876/tencent-granted-licence-sell-mutual-funds.

Alibaba's and Tencent's agile technology capabilities and their ability to leverage their customers' payment data has allowed them to deploy and rapidly scale targeted offerings designed to both serve highly specific markets and create opportunities for later expansion. For example, MyBank, launched by Alibaba in 2015, is designed to provide inclusive and innovative financial solutions for individuals and small enterprises that were previously unbanked or underbanked. MyBank's executive chairman Eric Jing was quoted as saying that the product is 'for the little guys'.

MyBank's online-only business model and ability to process loans under three minutes without any human involvement[12] allows them to extend much smaller loans than would be economically feasible for a traditional bank.[13] By leveraging Alibaba's existing user base, and the data accumulated by Alipay on its customers, this neo-bank offering was able to grow much faster than its peers in the West. As of October 2017, MyBank had lent approximately US$65 billion and served over seven million small business owners.

One interesting consumer implication of the adoption of techfin in China is that Chinese consumers' financial lives are much more tightly intertwined with other aspects of their digital lives than even the most tech-savvy North American or European consumer. WeChat in particular has truly evolved from a messaging app or a mobile payment solution to a lifestyle platform for its users. As we can see from the chart below, WeChat users can transfer money to their contacts, pay bills, buy financial products, book hotels and taxis, and access many other services all on the same platform.

The app even plays an important role in connecting individuals during important holidays. During the 2018 Chinese New Year, 688 million WeChat users either sent or received digital red envelopes[14] (a Chinese tradition where friends, family, and colleagues gift each other red envelopes with money).

The broad range of services WeChat provides enables users to spend more time on the app than they would on any other platform. More than one-third of its users spend over four hours a day on the service—a massive amount, even when compared to other highly successful digital services such as Facebook, whose average user spends just 22 minutes a day on the platform.[15]

---

[12] Shu Zhang, "Alibaba-Backed Online Lender MYbank Owes Cost-Savings to Home-Made Tech," *U.S.*, February 1, 2018, https://www.reuters.com/article/us-china-banking-mybank-idUSKBN1FL3S6.

[13] Steven Millward, "Alibaba Launches Online Bank: 'It's for the Little Guys, Not the Rich'," *Tech in Asia*, June 25, 2015, https://www.techinasia.com/alibaba-launches-online-bank-mybank.

[14] Matthew Brennan, "Wechat Red Packets Data Report of 2018 New Year Eve," *China Channel*, February 18, 2018, https://chinachannel.co/2018-wechat-red-packets-data-report-new-year-eve/.

[15] Alex Gray, "Here's the Secret to How We Chat Attracts 1 Billion Monthly Users," *World Economic Forum*, March 21, 2018, https://www.weforum.org/agenda/2018/03/wechat-now-has-over-1-billion-monthly-users/.

5.2.3   Alibaba's and Tencent's International Expansion

Having conquered their home market, these Chinese techfins have begun to explore international expansion. WeChat now has over 70 million users outside of China (though many of these do not have access to the full suite of services available to users in China), and WeChat Pay is available today in 25 countries and 13 currencies with a primary focus on other ASEAN countries.[16]

For its part, Alibaba and its financial services–focused subsidiary Ant Financial have a combined shareholding of 62% of Indian e-commerce and payment giant Paytm,[17] which reportedly has over 100 million users and processes over one billion transactions per quarter (Fig. 5.1).[18]

For now, efforts of Alibaba and Tencent seem focused on Asia, but with Alipay terminals popping up in Honolulu[19] to serve Chinese tourists and WeChat advertisements now visible in the London Underground,[20] it seems plausible that the ambitions of these firms are global.

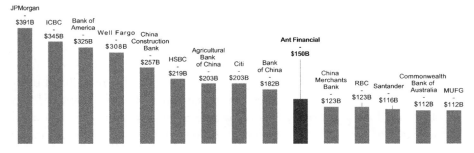

Fig. 5.1   Financial institutions by market capitalization (2018); Ant Financial is now one of the world's largest financial services firms. Source(s): "What The Largest Global Fintech Can Teach Us About What's Next In Financial Services," CB Insights Research, October 4, 2018, https://www.cbinsights.com/research/ant-financial-alipay-fintech/

---

[16] Emma Lee, "WeChat Pay Tries to Duplicate Domestic Success Overseas with Killer Recipe: Social Networking," *Technode*, March 1, 2018, https://technode.com/2018/03/01/wechat-pay-social-networking/.

[17] Madhav Chanchani, "Alibaba to Hike Stake in Paytm's Marketplace for $177 Million," *Economic Times*, March 3, 2017, https://economictimes.indiatimes.com/small-biz/money/alibaba-to-hike-stake-in-paytms-marketplace-for-177-million/articleshow/57428717.cms.

[18] "These Figures Show the Incredible Growth of Paytm as Payments Platform," *Business Today*, July 9, 2018, https://www.businesstoday.in/current/corporate/paytm-transactions-wallet-firm-upi-payments-bank-50-billion/story/280040.html.

[19] "Alipay Expands in-Store Mobile Payments to North American Retailers," *Mobile Payments Today*, January 17, 2017, https://www.mobilepaymentstoday.com/news/alipay-expands-in-store-mobile-payments-to-north-american-retailers/.

[20] "Website," accessed January 6, 2019, https://www.ft.com/content/2d0ba0da-cedf-11e7-9dbb-291a884dd8c6.

5.3   Early Techfin Developments Outside of China

While China is undoubtedly the global leader in terms of large technology firms making inroads into the realm of financial services, they are far from the only example. Large technology firms around the world are paying close attention to the path that Alibaba and Tencent have taken, looking to emulate their models.

Facebook, for example, may be seeking to take a page from WeChat's play-book by allowing its users to make payments via its Messenger app. This service is already available in the United States and the United Kingdom, with plans to expand into Europe and very likely India.[21] In Korea, the country's largest mobile messaging app platform, Kakao, has also explored the potential of this approach. In summer 2017, the firm launched a digital bank that within one week saw over one million account openings and over US$1 billion in deposits.[22]

A growing number of commentators have also begun to speculate on the potential entry of Amazon into the business of financial services. In fact, the firm has already made a significant foray into the small business lending space. Beginning in 2011, Amazon began extending loans of anywhere from US$1000 to $750,000 to third-party sellers on their platform to fund business growth.[23] Amazon has a unique data advantage in the extension of loans to sellers on their platform, as they are able to clearly gauge the historical performance of not just the firm seeking a loan but also its competitors, as well as broader factors such as seasonality of the industry.

As of mid-2017, the service had extended over US$3 billion in loans to over 20,000 companies, with $1 billion of those loans written in the preceding 12 months.[24] Moreover, users of the service appear satisfied, as over half ultimately secured a second loan from Amazon.

In addition to lending, Amazon has repeatedly explored opportunities to innovate in the area of payments through offerings like Amazon Pay, Amazon Cash, and most recently with Amazon Go, an offering that seeks to make

---

[21] Suprita Anupam, "Is Facebook Really Entering The P2P Payments Space In India?," June 15, 2018, https://inc42.com/buzz/messenger-is-facebook-really-entering-the-p2p-payments-space-in-india/.

[22] Brett King, *Bank 4.0: Banking Everywhere, Never at a Bank* (Marshall Cavendish International Asia Pte Ltd, 2018), page 180.

[23] Jeffrey Dastin, "Amazon Lent $1 Billion to Merchants to Boost Sales on Its Marketplace," *Reuters*, June 8, 2017, https://www.reuters.com/article/us-amazon-com-loans-idUSKBN18Z0DY.

[24] Ibid.

point of sale payments a completely seamless experience where individuals make purchases without needing to pay at a register.[25] The company has also made a number of fintech investments, primarily in fintech startups in emerging markets with the goal to give both merchants and consumers easier access to the Amazon platform.[26]

It can be tempting to imagine the entry of a firm like Amazon into financial services taking the form of a shocking announcement that the organization intends to build, or perhaps even buy a traditional bank. Indeed, in early 2017, rumors circulated that Amazon planned to buy Capital One, a US bank and credit card issuer. However, this kind of direct entry into financial services would be very difficult in many Western countries, particularly in the United States, where several laws including the Bank Holding Company Act of 1956 and the Gramm-Leach-Bliley Act of 1999 create significant barriers between banking and commerce.[27]

In practice though, this kind of aggressive entry into financial services may not serve the interests of would-be Western techfins. Companies like Apple, Amazon, Google, and Facebook are in the privileged position to pick and choose the aspects of the financial products, and the points on the financial value chain, that are most relevant to their organizations. This allows them to avoid the most onerous aspects of financial regulation and the challenging task of building new infrastructure from scratch, while at the same time establishing competencies and customer trust that leave them better positioned for a later push into the core products of incumbent financial institutions.

---

[25] "Everything You Need To Know About What Amazon Is Doing in Financial Services," *CB Insights*, 2018, https://www.cbinsights.com/research/report/amazon-across-financial-services-fintech/.

[26] Ibid.

[27] Kristin Broughton, "Amazon Buying Capital One? Fat Chance, but Fun to ponder Website," *American Banker*, February 17, 2017, https://www.americanbanker.com/news/amazon-buying-capital-one-fat-chance-but-fun-to-ponder.

6

The Changing Structure of the Financial Ecosystem

Brash new fintechs with extensive venture backing, banks seeking to reinvent themselves, and technology companies poised on the edge of becoming techfins: it's clear that the business of financial services is primed for rapid and transformative change. But how will that change play out, and what will the financial ecosystem of tomorrow look like? The answer is unlikely to be simple. It's improbable that a single class of competitor will emerge as the uncontested winner. Instead, it is likely that each of these types of organizations will emerge to play a unique role in an even more competitive landscape.

In earlier chapters of this section, we have considered how fintechs can partner with each other (such as in the case of N26 and TransferWise) and how incumbent financial institutions can partner with fintechs (such as in the case of JP Morgan Chase and OnDeck Capital). But what about partnerships between banks and techfins or techfins and fintechs?

6.1 Incumbent Collaboration with Techfins

We are already seeing many examples of collaboration between large technology firms and incumbent financial institutions. In some cases, this collaboration centers around technology firms' role as a key vendor to the financial institution. As we will discuss later in this text, cloud computing offerings from large technology companies are becoming increasingly central to the technology strategies of incumbent financial institutions, particularly where those institutions are seeking to deploy AI-enabled strategies.

© The Author(s) 2019
H. Arslanian, F. Fischer, *The Future of Finance*,
https://doi.org/10.1007/978-3-030-14533-0_6

In other cases, collaboration is driven by the ubiquitous proliferation of technology firms' physical devices. For example, many financial institutions have built 'skill packs' for Amazon's Echo smart speaker, allowing them to easily check balances or get updates on their portfolio via the device. Apple Pay could also be argued to be another example of such a partnership. Rather than attempting to disrupt the payment system outright, Apple's deployment of a mobile payment experience sought to leverage existing payments infrastructure and collaborate with banks on the sharing of fee revenue.

Finally, there are examples on the horizon of more ambitious partnerships, such as a 2018 partnership announced by Amazon, JPMorgan, and Berkshire Hathaway to cut healthcare costs and improve health services for their United States–based employees.[1] While the exact aims of their partnership are not yet clear, it may indicate an interest by these three players to experiment with the disruption of the sizable US health insurance market.

6.2   Fintech Collaboration with Techfins

While there are fewer immediate examples of collaboration between fintechs and large technology companies, the complementarity of these two groups is clear. Recall from our exploration of the challenges faced by fintechs that the ability to acquire customers and achieve distributional scale is a critical barrier to their success. The massive customer bases and deep pockets of technology firms place them in a unique position as a platform for the distribution of fintech firms' financial products, and indeed could serve as a point of distribution for incumbent financial institutions' products as well.

To imagine how this might work, think about how Amazon operates today. Amazon does not manufacture the millions of products that it sells. Instead, it acts as a platform for the sale and fulfillment of products that are (mostly) produced by third-party manufacturers. It also assists consumers in navigating this universe of products through customized recommendations and the curation of customer reviews. If we apply this platform model, we could imagine a techfin choosing to act as a platform for distribution of financial products built by other more heavily regulated entities and providing customers with recommendations to assist them in finding the products that are the best fit for their needs.

---

[1] Jeff Cox Angelica LaVito, "Amazon, Berkshire Hathaway, and JPMorgan Chase to Partner on US Employee Health Care," *CNBC* (CNBC, January 30, 2018), https://www.cnbc.com/2018/01/30/amazon-berkshire-hathaway-and-jpmorgan-chase-to-partner-on-us-employee-health-care.html.

Examples of this can already be found in China, such as Tencent's wealth management offerings that provide a platform for users to access over 100 products operated by a number of incumbent fund managers.[2] In doing so, WeChat is the key point of distribution for wealth management products without needing to build back-office asset management functions or hire specialized staff.

A growing number of commentators argue that the next frontier of competition between incumbents, fintechs, and potential techfins will be to build and control these platforms. Incumbent retail banks in North America and Europe are particularly concerned about the possibility of technology firms seizing this role as it would disintermediate the bank from its relationship with the end customer and control of pricing,[3] relegating it to the position of a commoditized utility. As a result, a growing number of banks are stating that evolving their organizations to become a platform for the distribution of their own and third-party financial services is a key institutional priority.[4,5]

It's far from clear how this race for platform dominance will evolve in the coming years; technology companies and incumbent financial institutions each bring a different set of strengths and weaknesses to the table. In either case, the results could be good news for fintechs as the development of platforms reduces the frictions of getting their products into the hands of customers. Also poised to win are customers themselves as platforms have a potential increase in scope of products available, offer valuable recommendations, and create greater competition on both price and customization.

---

[2] Zhang, "Tencent Gets a License to Sell Mutual Funds to WeChat's 1 Billion Users in China."

[3] Stefan van Woelderen Lei Pan, "Platforms: Bigger, Faster, Stronger," *ING Groep N.V.*, July 6, 2017, https://www.ingwb.com/insights/research/platforms-bigger,-faster,-stronger.

[4] "Purpose & Strategy," *ING Groep N.V.*, accessed January 6, 2019, https://www.ing.com/About-us/Purpose-strategy.htm.

[5] "BBVA Launches First BaaS Platform in the U.S.," *BBVA*, October 16, 2018, https://www.bbva.com/en/bbva-launches-first-baas-platform-in-the-u-s/.

7

Financial Innovation and Inclusion

New technology and fintech innovators are playing an important role in addressing the serious challenge of financial inclusion. The majority of the world's adult population, almost three billion adults, are unbanked,[1] meaning they have no access to a bank account or any other banking service.

While we might be tempted to think of this as a problem exclusive to developing countries, it is important to realize that this a serious issue faced by residents in developed nations as well. Twenty percent of households in cities like Miami and Detroit function without bank accounts.[2] In fact, it is estimated that in the United States, up to 130 million Americans are either unbanked or underbanked, living on the fringes of the financial system and relying on high cost offerings.[3]

7.1 Fintech as a Driver of Financial Inclusion

Over the past decade, fintech innovation has contributed to enormous progress in the pursuit of financial inclusion. Perhaps the most famous example of this is the success of mobile money transfer and banking service M-Pesa.

---

[1] "Financial Inclusion on the Rise, But Gaps Remain, Global Findex Database Shows," *World Bank*, April 19, 2018, http://www.worldbank.org/en/news/press-release/2018/04/19/financial-inclusion-on-the-rise-but-gaps-remain-global-findex-database-shows.

[2] "How FinTech Is Shaping the Future of Banking | Henri Arslanian | TEDxWanChai," *YouTube*, December 5, 2016, https://www.youtube.com/watch?v=pPkNtN8G7q8&t=682s.

[3] Brett King, p. 83.

© The Author(s) 2019
H. Arslanian, F. Fischer, *The Future of Finance*,
https://doi.org/10.1007/978-3-030-14533-0_7

M-Pesa was launched in 2007 by mobile network operator Safaricom, and allows users to "deposit, send, and withdraw funds using their mobile phones" without the need for a bank account.[4] The service has transformed the financial landscape of Kenya. In 2000, only 27% of the Kenyan population were banked, and today that number is 80%,[5] with estimates suggesting that at least 40% of Kenya's GDP is transmitted via M-Pesa.[6]

The advent of ubiquitous digital payments has dramatically reduced the need for Kenyans to use cash to conduct day-to-day transactions, but when cash is required, it can be withdrawn from a network of over 130,000[7] physical agents around the country. This is important given that research from Accenture and Standard Bank has shown that 70% of the currently unbanked population residing on the African continent need to spend more than an entire month's salary just to physically get to a bank branch.[8]

The service also positively impacts the lives of Kenyans by enabling residents in cities to cheaply send money back home to rural areas, saving them the risk of cash getting lost in transit.[9] Given this, it is perhaps not surprising that a 2016 MIT study shows that M-Pesa is responsible for lifting 2% of Kenyan households out of poverty.[10]

The initiative's success is being replicated in other countries. M-Pesa itself has expanded its services and now runs in ten countries with over 30 million users.[11] Other fintech innovators are also emerging such as bKash, a Bangladeshi mobile money service launched in 2011 that now serves more than 24 million individuals,[12] 15% of Bangladesh's population of 160 mil-

---

[4] "M -Money Channel Distribution Case – Kenya," *World Bank*, March 2009, http://documents.world-bank.org/curated/en/832831500443778267/pdf/117403-WP-KE-Tool-6-7-Case-Study-M-PESA-Kenya-Series-IFC-mobile-money-toolkit-PUBLIC.pdf.

[5] World Bank Group, "Global Findex Report" (World Bank, 2017), https://globalfindex.worldbank.org/sites/globalfindex/files/chapters/2017%20Findex%20full%20report_chapter2.pdf.

[6] More by This Author, "Yearly Mobile Money Deals close to Half GDP," *Daily Nation*, accessed January 6, 2019, https://www.nation.co.ke/business/Yearly-mobile-money-deals-close-GDP/996-4041666-dtaks6z/index.html.

[7] Saruni Maina, "Safaricom FY2017: Data and M-Pesa Were Safaricom's Biggest Earners," *Techweez*, May 10, 2017, https://techweez.com/2017/05/10/safaricom-fy-2017-data-m-pesa/.

[8] Brett King book, p. 79.

[9] T. S., "Why Does Kenya Lead the World in Mobile Money?," *The Economist*, March 2, 2015, https://www.economist.com/the-economist-explains/2015/03/02/why-does-kenya-lead-the-world-in-mobile-money.

[10] Rob Matheson, "Study: Mobile-Money Services Lift Kenyans out of Poverty," *MIT News*, December 8, 2016, http://news.mit.edu/2016/mobile-money-kenyans-out-poverty-1208.

[11] Michael Joseph, "M-Pesa: The Story of How the World's Leading Mobile Money Service Was Created in Kenya," *Vodafone*, March 6, 2017, https://www.vodafone.com/content/index/what/technology-blog/m-pesa-created.html#.

[12] "bKash in Bangladesh: 24 Million Customers Using Mobile Money," *Global Payments Summit*, 2018, https://globalpaymentsummit.com/bkash-bangladesh-24-million-customers-using-mobile-money/.

lion.[13] Moreover, according to an InterMedia Bangladesh Financial Inclusion Insights (FII) tracker survey, about 39% of Bangladeshis 'accessed mobile money' using bKash as of September 2016.[14]

In addition to these improvements to domestic payment networks, improvements in access to and reductions in the cost of cross-border transfers have also had an important impact on inclusion. Remittance payments from individuals working abroad to persons in emerging economies frequently face high fees, particularly to destinations in Africa. According to the World Bank's Migration and Remittance Factbook, the average remittance cost in sub-Saharan Africa can be as high as 19%.[15] Services such as WorldRemit and Azimo targeting cross-border payments that also reduce remittance costs could have a wide-scale and beneficial social impact in developing regions.

But the deployment of new technology in support of financial inclusion is more than just an opportunity to drive positive social impact; it is also a significant business opportunity and one that is increasingly catching the attention of both incumbent banks and the Chinese techfin giants. For example, in

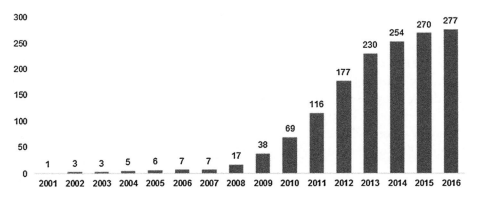

Fig. 7.1 Number of mobile money services operating worldwide; Building on the success of M-Pesa, the number of mobile money services globally has exploded since 2008. Source(s): "State of the Industry Report on Mobile Money" (GSMA, 2017), https://www.gsma.com/mobilefordevelopment/wp-content/uploads/2017/03/GSMA_State-of-the-Industry-Report-on-Mobile-Money_2016.pdf

[13] "Bangladesh Population," *Trading Economics*, accessed January 6, 2019, https://tradingeconomics.com/bangladesh/population.

[14] "Financial Inclusion Insights Bangladesh 2016 Annual Report (Wave 4 Tracker Survey)," *Finclusion*, September 2017, http://finclusion.org/uploads/file/Bangladesh%20Wave%204%20Report_20_Sept%20 2017.pdf.

[15] "Migration and Remittances Factbook 2016 Third Edition" (Global Knowledge Partnership on Migration and Development (KNOMAD), World Bank, n.d.).

2018, Standard Chartered announced the launch of a fully digital bank in Nigeria to be quickly followed by Ghana and Côte d'Ivoire.[16] Meanwhile, in April of the same year, Ant Financial, a subsidiary of Alibaba that, among other services, runs Alipay, announced its acquisition of a 10% stake in bKash[17] in an effort to push financial inclusion for Bangladesh's 'unbanked and underbanked' population.[18]

7.2   Government as an Enabler of Inclusive Fintech Solutions

National initiatives and government policy can play an important role in enabling fintech innovations to drive financial inclusion. For example, a case study by the International Finance Corporation shows that M-Pesa's success is spurred by regulatory support, particularly the Central Bank of Kenya working with Safaricom to give a green light for the service.[19]

Perhaps the most impactful government program over the last decade in support of financial inclusion has been India's Aadhaar initiative, with the goal to provide a digital identity to its entire population of over one billion people.

In 2009, the Indian government formed the Unique Identification Authority of India (UIDAI) with a mandate to establish a biometric system of identity to provide individuals with a 12-digit 'unique identification number' from the country's central government.[20] The rollout of the program has been massively successful with 1.2 billion Indian citizens enrolled,[21] amounting to roughly 90% of the country's population.

---

[16] "Standard Chartered Deepens Investments in Digital Solutions," The Guardian Nigeria Newspaper, December 10, 2018, https://guardian.ng/business-services/standard-chartered-deepens-investments-in-digital-solutions/.

[17] Xiao Liu, "Ant Financial to Acquire Stake in Bangladesh's bKash," Caixin Global, April 27, 2018, https://www.caixinglobal.com/2018-04-27/ant-financial-to-acquire-stake-in-bangladeshs-bkash-101240395.html.

[18] Ant Financial, "Ant Financial Invests in Bangladesh-Based bKash," Finextra, April 26, 2018, https://www.finextra.com/pressarticle/73644/ant-financial-invests-in-banladesh-based-bkash.

[19] The World Bank, "M-Money Channel Distribution Case – Kenya : Safaricom M-Pesa" (The World Bank, January 1, 2017), http://documents.worldbank.org/curated/en/832831500443778267/M-money-channel-distribution-case-Kenya-Safaricom-m-pesa.

[20] "Journey of Aadhaar," Software Freedom Law Center, India, May 21, 2016, https://sflc.in/journey-aadhaar.

[21] "Aadhaar Dashboard," Unique Identification Authority of India (UIDAI), Government of India, accessed January 13, 2019, https://uidai.gov.in/aadhaar_dashboard/index.php.

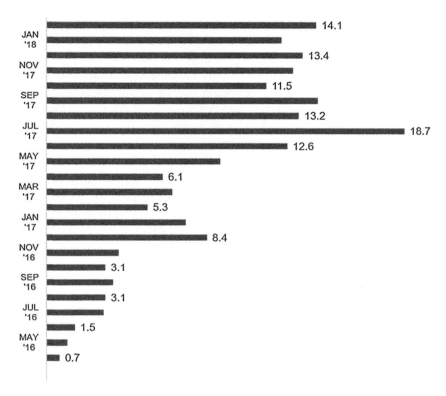

Fig. 7.2 Monthly number of successful Aadhaar e-KYC verifications; India's Aadhaar identity program has enabled faster and more accessible KYC, facilitating increased financial inclusion. Source(s): Ronald Abraham et al., "State of Aadhar Report 2017–18" (ID Insight, May 2018), https://stateofaadhaar.in/wp-content/uploads/State-of-Aadhaar-Report_2017-18.pdf

Through Aadhaar, various arms of the Indian government have encouraged the creation and use of online payment channels, customer and documentation verification processes, and other digital platforms.[22] These initiatives were supported through the development of the 'India Stack', an advanced 'open application programming interface (API)' with combined sets of software and four critical layers—the paperless layer, presenceless layer, cashless layer, and consent layer.

This system ensures digital verification through Aadhaar, with the specific goal of encouraging cashless, online payment systems that allow users to give their permission for a range of daily transactions.[23] For example, services like

---

[22] "What Is IndiaStack?," IndiaStack (blog), accessed January 13, 2019, http://indiastack.org/about/.

[23] Pavithra Babu, "What Is IndiaStack and How Is It Set to Change India?," Razorpay, accessed January 13, 2019, https://razorpay.com/blog/what-is-indiastack-and-how-is-it-set-to-change-india/.

how the 280-million-strong Paytm—India's leading mobile wallet—now allow users to choose whether they would like to share their Aadhaar card details for electronic 'know your customer' formalities.[24]

Inevitably, such a system has repeatedly raised questions around privacy.[25] In September 2018, a landmark decision by the country's Supreme Court deemed the Aadhaar Act valid, but ruled that private entities—including telecom firms, e-commerce businesses, and banks—are not required to obtain Aadhaar information in order to serve the customer. At the same time, India's top court also underlined the importance of strong data protection.[26]

Ultimately, by giving customers autonomy over where and how they choose to share their data, India is enfranchising their citizens to be participants in the process of financial inclusion. Moreover, the successes of the Aadhaar and India Stack initiatives provide an interesting template for governments around the world to closely examine as they seek to encourage increased financial inclusion of their own residents.

---

[24] Saikat Neogi, "Aadhar Verdict: eKYC Curbed; Instant Loan Approvals, MF and Insurance Sales Online Take a Hit," *The Financial Express*, October 1, 2018, https://www.financialexpress.com/money/aadhar-verdict-ekyc-curbed-instant-loan-approvals-mf-and-insurance-sales-online-take-a-hit/1332333/.

[25] Ibid.

[26] "What Supreme Court's Aadhaar Verdict Means for You: 10 Points," *Livemint*, September 26, 2018, https://www.livemint.com/Companies/cpSHu1fjQ1WvOP8vMi27aL/What-Supreme-Courts-Aadhaar-verdict-means-for-you-10-point.html.

Part III

The Fundamentals of Crypto-assets

Recent years have seen an explosion of popular and media attention on a surprising and fascinating topic: crypto-assets. Despite being steeped in complex mathematics and having been borne out of a community calling themselves cypherpunks, discussions of Bitcoin, blockchains, initial coin offerings (ICOs), and the very nature of money have become common fare for the nightly news and the family dinner table.

To assess the potential implications of this technology on financial services, we must first understand its fundamentals. In the following chapters, we will explore the underlying workings of Bitcoin and consider a taxonomy of the universe of different crypto-assets that have followed in its wake. We will also consider the evolving ecosystem of stakeholders that provide essential services to the crypto-asset economy as well as a number of the regulatory, organizational, and technical challenges that these assets face in their bit to reshape the financial system.

Discussion of this space often focuses on a few notable assets such as Bitcoin or uses the general term cryptocurrency. However, as we will discuss in the following chapters, this innovation ecosystem extends well beyond Bitcoin with a range of intended use cases extending beyond the notion of a 'digital currency'. As such, we use the word crypto-assets to encapsulate the spectrum of innovations happening in this space.[1]

---

[1] Other recent authors have also taken the same view by using the term "crypto-assets." Burniske, Chris, and Jack Tatar. *Crypto-assets: The Innovative Investor's Guide to Bitcoin and Beyond*. McGraw Hill Professional, 2017.

8

The Basics of Cryptography and Encryption

To properly understand the significant interest around crypto-assets and the claim that it holds the potential to transform the financial system, we must first understand a bit about the 'crypto' part of their name, that is, the technology that enables these assets to function.

While we do not intend to cover the technical specifics of cryptography and the different encryption techniques in this book (there are numerous online blogs and academic literature on the topic for those interested), it is still important to cover the basics as they matter to crypto-assets.[1] In the following chapter, we will explore the basics of cryptography and early attempts to use this technology to create novel digital payment systems.

8.1   Early Encryption

Cryptography, which comes from the ancient Greek words 'kryptos' (hidden secret) and 'graphein' (to write), is the practice and study of techniques for secure communications.[2]

Encryption is probably the most well-known use of cryptography and is defined as the process of encoding a message or information in such a way

---

[1] The co-authors thank Mr. Antony Lewis for his valuable help in reviewing certain parts of this chapter. Thank you, Antony!

[2] "Cryptography," *Wikipedia*, January 11, 2019, https://en.wikipedia.org/w/index.php?title=Cryptography&oldid=877811989.

that only authorized parties can access it and those who are not authorized cannot.[3]

Encryption techniques have been employed for centuries. Julius Caesar used basic encryption techniques to inform his generals of his plans. He would write messages using letters that were three letters after the letter they were supposed to represent.[4] For example, ABC would be written as DEF. More recently, Nazi Germany would encrypt messages using the Enigma machine, which was finally broken by Alan Turing and his team, thereby helping the Allies win the Second World War.[5]

There are numerous types of encryption. For example, one of the most basic types of encryption is called 'symmetric' encryption, which refers to encryption method in which both the sender and the receiver share the same key.

Let's use a simple example based on that of Julius Caesar. Imagine Alice and Bob want to send secret messages to each other. They meet before and agree that if Alice writes an 'a', it actually should be read as 'd' and that if she writes 'b', it should be read as an 'e', basically implementing a 'plus 3' rule for all communications between them. In this case, they are both using the same 'key' (in this case our 'plus 3' rule).

Of course, this method of encryption is not widely used these days as it could easily be 'broken' using today's technology (e.g. running numerous scenarios until one finds out the 'plus 3' rule). But there are also practical implications like key management (e.g. if Alice wants to also correspond secretly with other friends, she would probably have a separate 'key' for each so that Bob cannot read a secret message sent by Alice to others). While it's manageable when you only have Alice and Bob, this becomes complicated if you are communicating with many different parties. Also, Alice and Bob need to first find a way to communicate with each other that 'plus 3' is the magic key. How to do this secretly in the first place is challenging and creates a 'chicken and egg' problem. We are greatly simplifying things here, but you hopefully understand the challenges with symmetric encryption. It is important to mention that it was one of the main encryption methodologies known until 1976.[6]

---

[3] "Encryption," *Wikipedia*, January 12, 2019, https://en.wikipedia.org/w/index.php?title=Encryption&oldid=878014939.

[4] Chris Burniske and Jack Tatar, *Crypto-assets: The Innovative Investor's Guide to Bitcoin and Beyond* (McGraw Hill Professional, 2017).

[5] Ibid.

[6] "Cryptography," *Wikipedia*, January 11, 2019, https://en.wikipedia.org/w/index.php?title=Cryptography&oldid=877811989.

8.2   Asymmetric or Public Key Cryptography

In a groundbreaking 1976 paper, cryptographers Whitfield Diffie and Martin Hellman proposed the notion of asymmetric (commonly referred to as public key) cryptography in which two different but mathematically related keys are used—a public key and a private key. The public key is, as its name implies, public and available for anyone to see. The private key, however, is not meant to be seen by others. A public key is mathematically derived from a private key that anyone can then use to send you a message that only you will be able to decrypt as only you have the private key. If anyone intercepts the encrypted message, they will not be able to decrypt it as they don't have the private key.

However, for the above to work you need a mathematical algorithm that can generate a public key from the private key. But it is crucial that it is mathematically impossible to do the opposite (i.e. for someone to infer your private key by having your public key) and this is key (no pun intended!). Thankfully there are numerous algorithms that allow you to do that. One of the most widely used of such algorithms is called RSA (coined from the surnames of Rivest, Shamir, and Adleman, who first publicly described the algorithm in 1978).[7]

Bitcoin uses an algorithm called ECDSA (Elliptic Curve Digital Signature Algorithm) that also allows you to use your private key to generate a public key.[8] That public key allows you to then generate your Bitcoin address. It is impossible for anyone who has your public key to guess your private key, but more on this later.

8.3   Early Experiments with Cryptocurrencies

The cryptography developments in the 1970s started to change cryptography from being a mainly military-focused discipline to one that was exploring increasingly broader use cases.[9]

In 1985, David Chaum, an American computer scientist and cryptographer, revealed an electronic cash system that used cryptography to ensure anonymity to its users, which Chaum described in his article titled 'Security without

---

[7] "RSA (Cryptosystem)," *Wikipedia*, January 6, 2019, https://en.wikipedia.org/w/index.php?title=RSA_(cryptosystem)&oldid=877066365.

[8] Antony Lewis, *The Basics of Bitcoins and Blockchains: An Introduction to Cryptocurrencies and the Technology That Powers Them* (Mango Media, 2018).

[9] Jameson Lopp, "Bitcoin and the Rise of the Cypherpunks," *CoinDesk* (blog), April 9, 2016, https://www.coindesk.com/the-rise-of-the-cypherpunks.

identification: Transaction systems to make big brother obsolete'.[10] Four years later, Chaum founded Digicash, an electronic payment company which allowed its users to conduct online transactions in a completely secure and anonymous way by utilizing the latest developments of public and private key cryptography. While his company was ultimately unsuccessful, Chaum's work probably laid the foundation for blockchain and cryptocurrencies today. Interestingly, Chaum made a comeback in 2018 with a new project called Elixxir.[11]

The 1990s saw the rise of cypherpunk movements and welcomed the first formal steps toward the creation of cryptocurrencies. Chaum's work had greatly inspired three retired professionals—Eric Hughes, Timothy C. May, and John Gilmore—who were passionate about computer science, mathematics, and cryptography. Using Chaum's studies as a starting point, the trio began discussing these topics during regular meetings in San Francisco, which rapidly evolved into a full movement named Cypherpunks. The Cypherpunks, essentially advocating cyberspace freedom, also reached a broad audience of about 2000 people by 1997 through the 'Cypherpunks Mailing List'.[12] As described in 'A Cypherpunk's Manifesto',[13] published in March 1993 by Eric Hughes, the goal of the Cypherpunks was to give privacy and freedom back to individuals. To facilitate conversation between individuals and organizations, Hughes suggested creating systems allowing anonymous transactions to occur.

> We cannot expect governments, corporations, or other large, faceless organizations to grant us privacy out of their beneficence. It is to their advantage to speak of us, and we should expect that they will speak. (The Cypherpunk Manifesto)

As the years went by, the Cypherpunks developed several projects with features that can now be easily recognized as predecessors to Bitcoin and other cryptocurrencies. The two most notable examples are Hashcash,[14] proposed in 1997 by Adam Back, and B-money,[15] proposed in 1998 by Wei Dai. Hashcash

[10] David Chaum, "Security without Identification: Transaction Systems to Make Big Brother Obsolete," *Communications of the ACM* 28, no. 10 (October 1, 1985): 1030–44, https://doi.org/10.1145/4372.4373.
[11] Jimmy Aki, "ECash Founder David Chaum Makes Bold Promises with Elixxir Blockchain," Bitcoin Magazine, accessed January 13, 2019, https://bitcoinmagazine.com/articles/ecash-founder-david-chaum-makes-bold-promises-elixxir-blockchain/.
[12] Robert Manne, "The Cypherpunk Revolutionary: Julian Assange | The Monthly," The Monthly, March 2011, https://www.themonthly.com.au/issue/2011/february/1324596189/robert-manne/cypherpunk-revolutionary.
[13] Eric Hughes, "A Cypherpunk's Manifesto," Activism.net, March 1993, https://www.activism.net/cypherpunk/manifesto.html.
[14] Adam Back, "[ANNOUNCE] Hash Cash Postage Implementation," Hashcash.org, March 28, 1997, http://www.hashcash.org/papers/announce.txt.
[15] Wei Dai, "BMoney," November 6, 2018, http://www.weidai.com/.

was designed to reduce the impact of spam in emails by attaching a digital stamp to each email. The stamps essentially would require the spammer's computer's central processing unit (CPU) to do some work for the email to be successfully delivered, which as a result would make spam uneconomical as spammers need the ability to send huge volumes of emails at very little or no cost. B-money was an essay with two proposals for an anonymous and distributed "scheme for a group of untraceable digital pseudonyms to pay each other with money and to enforce contracts amongst themselves without outside help".[16] While these projects had limited success, they were both later referenced in the original Bitcoin white paper, which we will explore in detail in the following chapter.

---

[16] Wei Dai, "Wei Dai's Home Page," November 6, 2018, http://www.weidai.com/.

9

The Rise of Bitcoin

Context is critical to understanding the creation of Bitcoin. In 2008, the world was in the midst of the greatest financial crisis since the Great Depression. The prestigious 164-year-old investment bank Lehman Brothers filed for bankruptcy and American International Group (AIG), the biggest insurer in America, had to be bailed out with a US$85 billion loan by the New York Federal Reserve Bank.

As turmoil spread from the financial system into the broader economy, some lost their jobs and others their life's savings, triggering protests and a vilification of those working in the financial sector who were viewed as having created the crisis. A growing number of people began to wonder if the architecture of the financial system needed to be completely rethought.

In this chapter, we will consider how an anonymous white paper proposed a new technology called Bitcoin that imagined a different system for payment and the storage of value. We will consider the content of this white paper, and explore the underlying workings of the Bitcoin protocol as well as both the growth of and challenges facing the Bitcoin community.

9.1 The Bitcoin White Paper

On October 31, 2008, less than two months after the bankruptcy of Lehman Brothers, Satoshi Nakamoto revealed a white paper to the world titled 'Bitcoin: A Peer-to-Peer Electronic Cash System'. Interestingly, the domain

© The Author(s) 2019
H. Arslanian, F. Fischer, *The Future of Finance*,
https://doi.org/10.1007/978-3-030-14533-0_9

'bitcoin.org' was registered just a few weeks prior at anonymousspeech.com, a site that allows users to anonymously register domain names.[1]

Nakamoto introduced a system "based on cryptographic proof instead of trust, allowing any two willing parties to transact directly with each other without the need for a trusted third party".[2] This was revolutionary. The white paper set out, in nine simple pages, a vision of a purely peer-to-peer version of electronic cash that would allow online payments to be sent directly from one party to another without going through a financial institution. This is why Nakamoto's paper has become a sort of sacrosanct document in the crypto community.

The abstract of the white paper reads:

A purely peer-to-peer version of electronic cash would allow online payments to be sent directly from one party to another without going through a financial institution. Digital signatures provide part of the solution, but the main benefits are lost if a trusted third party is still required to prevent double-spending. We propose a solution to the double-spending problem using a peer-to-peer network. The network time stamps transactions by hashing them into an ongoing chain of hash-based proof-of-work, forming a record that cannot be changed without redoing the proof-of-work. The longest chain not only serves as proof of the sequence of events witnessed, but proof that it came from the largest pool of CPU power. As long as a majority of CPU power is controlled by nodes that are not cooperating to attack the network, they'll generate the longest chain and outpace attackers. The network itself requires minimal structure. Messages are broadcast on a best effort basis, and nodes can leave and rejoin the network at will, accepting the longest proof-of-work chain as proof of what happened while they were gone.[3]

Before discussing the innovations that Bitcoin brought forward, it is important to understand the problem that it was trying to solve: the reliance on financial institutions. Satoshi reaffirms that in the first line of the Bitcoin whitepaper when he mentions that "commerce on the Internet has come to

---

[1] "Bitcoin History: The Complete History of Bitcoin [Timeline]," accessed January 13, 2019, http://www.historyofbitcoin.org/.

[2] Satoshi Nakamoto, "Bitcoin: A Peer-to-Peer Electronic Cash System," http://Bitcoin.org/Bitcoin.pdf, May 2009, https://bitcoin.org/bitcoin.pdf.

[3] Ibid.

Box 9.1   Who Is Satoshi Nakamoto?

Satoshi Nakamoto is the author of the Bitcoin white paper. We still don't know who he, she, or they are.

Satoshi was active in various blogs and forums, including Bitcointalk, which he started and posted the first message under the pseudonym *satoshi*.[4] He remained active in the Bitcoin ecosystem until he suddenly stopped, saying that he had "to move on to other things".[5]

There have been numerous attempts to try to unearth the real Satoshi. Many have tried to analyze the time of his posts to guess where he was living (almost no posts between 5 a.m. and 11 a.m. GMT) or his style of language (use of British spelling of words like *optimise* or *colour*), but these can be easily misleading.[6] Some of the individuals who interacted with him online shared their experiences, saying that Satoshi was "weird, paranoid and bossy".[7]

Many of the individuals often mentioned as the possible Satoshi, like Hal Finney or Nick Szabo, were early crypto pioneers. Other individuals who have claimed to be Satoshi, like Australian computer scientist Dr. Craig Wright, have faced a lot of skepticism from the crypto community. Also, some tentative identifications by the media, including Newsweek that claimed to have located the real Satoshi, have been incorrect.[8] The reality is that we don't know and we may never know.

It is also important to remember that Satoshi holds a large number of Bitcoin, estimated to be around 1 million. At some of Bitcoin's higher valuations, the market capitalization of these coins would make Satoshi one of the richest individuals in the world.[9] Indeed a desire to ensure personal security may be one of the reasons Satoshi has chosen to remain anonymous.

Many believe that it would be better if Satoshi is never discovered. Any comments that Satoshi would make would have a very serious impact on Bitcoin and broader crypto community, which could go against the decentralized idea on which Bitcoin was built in the first place.

---

[4] "Bitcoin Forum," Bitcointalk.org, accessed January 13, 2019, https://bitcointalk.org/.

[5] Adrian Chen, "We Need to Know Who Satoshi Nakamoto Is," May 9, 2016, https://www.newyorker.com/business/currency/we-need-to-know-who-satoshi-nakamoto-is.

[6] Benjamin Wallace, "The Rise and Fall of Bitcoin," Wired, November 23, 2011, https://www.wired.com/2011/11/mf-bitcoin/.

[7] 1. Zoë Bernard, "Satoshi Nakamoto Was Weird, Paranoid, and Bossy, Says Early Bitcoin Developer Who Exchanged Hundreds of Emails with the Mysterious Crypto Creator," Business Insider Malaysia, May 30, 2018, https://www.businessinsider.my/satoshi-nakamoto-was-weird-and-bossy-says-bitcoin-developer-2018-5/.

[8] "Satoshi Nakamoto," Wikipedia, January 12, 2019, https://en.wikipedia.org/w/index.php?title=Satoshi_Nakamoto&oldid=878012844.

[9] Rob Wile, "Bitcoin's Mysterious Creator Appears to Be Sitting On a $5.8 Billion Fortune," Time, October 31, 2017, http://time.com/money/5002378/bitcoin-creator-nakamoto-billionaire/.

rely almost exclusively on financial institutions serving as trusted third parties to process electronic payments".[10]

This problem is inherent to digital assets. In the physical world, if Alice meets Bob in person and hands him a $5 bill, then Bob, upon inspecting it to ensure it is not counterfeit, becomes the holder of that $5 bill that was previously Alice's. It is truly peer-to-peer and Alice cannot possibly have spent that bill somewhere else or she would not have had it to give to Bob.

This is significantly more difficult in the digital world as any type of digital asset can be easily copied at zero or minimal cost. To use the example above, Bob would not be so willing to trust that $5 bill if Alice (and everyone else!) could easily print an unlimited amount. This is called the double-spend problem.

Satoshi acknowledged that the double-spend problem had been the main hurdle facing past efforts to create a digital peer-to-peer payment system. In the white paper, he mentions:

> We define an electronic coin as a chain of digital signatures. Each owner transfers the coin to the next by digitally signing a hash of the previous transaction and the public key of the next owner and adding these to the end of the coin. A payee can verify the signatures to verify the chain of ownership. The problem of course is the payee can't verify that one of the owners did not double-spend the coin.

The double-spend problem was one that the crypto community had been trying to solve for many years. To use an analogy as an example, when I send someone an email, an identical version of that email sits in both my outbox and the recipient's inbox. If others were copied to that email, that same email would exist in other locations as well. While this works very well for emails, it does not work if that email has some kind of monetary value. If one could 'create' an endless supply of money, then that money would be almost worthless.

The way that we have dealt with this issue is by relying on banks or other trusted central authorities to be those trusted intermediaries or bookkeepers, in exchange, of course, for a fee. Using such intermediaries, Alice can only send $5 if she has it in her account and when she sends it to Bob, she does not have it anymore to send it to someone else.

But these trusted central authorities have an outsized impact. Not only does their presence add a layer of cost to the system, but they also control who can

---

[10] Satoshi Nakamoto, "Bitcoin: A Peer-to-Peer Electronic Cash System," http://Bitcoin.org/Bitcoin.pdf, May 2009, https://bitcoin.org/bitcoin.pdf.

transact via their services and centralizes power in the hands of a few. Bitcoin looked to eliminate the necessity of trusted third parties through the revolutionary combination of a number of previously unconnected technologies.

9.2 The Technical Foundations of Bitcoin

Bitcoin's goal of eliminating the need for a trusted central party is built on the confluence of four concepts: cryptography, decentralization, immutability, and proof-of-work. We will discuss each of them in detail.[11]

9.2.1 The Role of Cryptography in Bitcoin

Let's go back to what Satoshi wrote in the white paper:

> We define an electronic coin as a chain of *digital signatures*. Each owner transfers the coin to the next by digitally signing a *hash* of the previous transaction and the *public key* of the next owner and adding these to the end of the coin. A payee can verify the signatures to verify the chain of ownership. The problem of course is the payee can't verify that one of the owners did not double-spend the coin.

Let's start with the public key. As we have seen earlier, your private key enables you to come up with a public key. Let's remember that this is a one-way street. While your private key enables you to come up with your public key, it is impossible to use the public key to deduce the private key. Our favorite analogy is the one used by blockchain commentator Don Tapscott in an interview that was (comically) subsequently picked up by the US talk show host John Oliver. Tapscott compares the process to chicken McNuggets, noting that it is easy to turn a chicken into a McNugget, but very difficult to turn the McNugget back into a chicken![12] This feature is critical to maintaining the security of Bitcoin transactions.

What is a digital signature? In the traditional world, one would sign a check or a receipt to make it valid. We all know that faking a signature made by

---

[11] For any reader interested in learning more in detail about how the Bitcoin blockchain works, we would recommend *The Basics of Bitcoins and Blockchains* by Antony Lewis, who explains in more detail how the Bitcoin blockchain works.

[12] William Suberg, "John Oliver Compares Bitcoin with Bitconnect, Ridicules Tapscott's 'Dumb' McNugget Metaphor," Cointelegraph, March 12, 2018, https://cointelegraph.com/news/john-oliver-compares-bitcoin-with-bitconnect-ridicules-tapscotts-dumb-mcnugget-metaphor.

hand is ridiculously easy, especially because you always use the same signature. It is frankly somewhat comical that we still ask for handwritten signatures these days.

In the crypto space, anyone who can see your public key can verify that the signature was created by the holder of the associated private key without the need to know the private key itself. To continue with our McNugget example, it would be like knowing that McNugget comes from a specific chicken, but without revealing the chicken's secret name. This is a comical analogy, but hopefully it serves the point.

In addition, as the signature is valid for a specific transaction, it cannot be copied and pasted on another piece of data without the signature being invalidated. So if one were to take the signature on the above McNugget and put it on a different McNugget by a different chicken, the signature would be invalid. This is not done by a subjective judgment call, but by pure mathematics. For anyone interested in learning more about digital signatures, there is a wealth of information easily accessible online.

Now moving on to the hash. As mentioned by Satoshi, it is the hash of the transaction that is signed, not the transaction itself. But what is a hash?

A hash is an algorithm used in cryptography that takes an input of any size and returns a fixed-length sequence of numbers. This is important as regardless of the length or the size of the data, you will get a fixed size hash. A hash can be generated from any piece of data, but the data cannot be generated from the hash. Basically it only works one way and you cannot guess the input by looking at the hash. Also, even if a very minor change is made in the data, the hash will be different.

The SHA-256 (Secure Hash Algorithm) is a good example of a hash function that is industry standard. Originally designed by the National Security Agency (NSA), it is used in various places in the Bitcoin network.

When it comes to Bitcoin transactions, you are in practice using your private key to sign the hash of the transaction (not the transaction itself), which enables you to have a small signature even if the underlying data behind the hash is huge. This is what proves ownership to others in the network as they know that it is the person with the right private key that signed the transaction. Once again, there are a number of articles and literature online on hashes and their history for anyone interested.

But while the above solves the ownership problem, it does not solve the double-spend issue. As Satoshi writes in his white paper:

> The problem of course is the payee can't verify that one of the owners did not double-spend the coin. A common solution is to introduce a trusted central authority, or mint, that checks every transaction for double-spending. After each

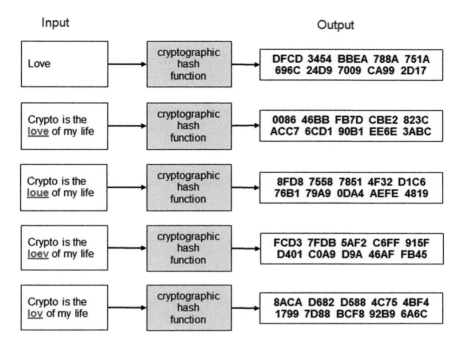

Fig. 9.1 How a hash function works; A hash function takes inputs of any size and creates a random output of uniform size and no relationship to the input; even very similar inputs have very different hash outputs. Source(s): 'File:Hash Function Long. Svg—Wikimedia Commons,' Wikimedia Commons, accessed January 30, 2019, https://commons.wikimedia.org/wiki/File:Hash_function_long.svg

transaction, the coin must be returned to the mint to issue a new coin, and only coins issued directly from the mint are trusted not to be double-spent. The problem with this solution is that the fate of the entire money system depends on the company running the mint, with every transaction having to go through them, just like a bank. We need a way for the payee to know that the previous owners did not sign any earlier transactions. For our purposes, the earliest transaction is the one that counts, so we don't care about later attempts to double-spend. The only way to confirm the absence of a transaction is to be aware of all transactions.[13]

As mentioned, the double-spend issue is dealt with in the traditional world by having banks and other trusted central authorities. But how can we have this in a decentralized world?

[13] Satoshi Nakamoto, "Bitcoin: A Peer-to-Peer Electronic Cash System," http://Bitcoin.org/Bitcoin.pdf, May 2009, https://bitcoin.org/bitcoin.pdf.

9.2.2   The Role of Decentralization in Bitcoin

While we could deal with the double-spend issue by having a network of bookkeepers, we would also need a 'master bookkeeper' or some type of gate-keeper (a good analogy are standard setters in the accounting profession today or the law societies for lawyers). However, this makes the system centralized.

So, the solution in the Bitcoin network is to allow anyone to be a book-keeper and to have the same set of books and records as anyone else. These bookkeepers are called nodes. All transactions are broadcast to the various nodes in the Bitcoin blockchain allowing anyone and everyone to see them and update their 'books'.

But then how can we be sure of the order of these transactions? While everyone can see all the transactions, we need to agree on a certain order of transactions. As Satoshi eloquently states:

> To accomplish this without a trusted party, transactions must be publicly announced, and we need a system for participants to agree on a single history of the order in which they were received.[14]

The Bitcoin network does this via blocks. If the Bitcoin network is one massive book, then each block is a page. For everyone to be 'on the same page' (no pun intended), the bookkeepers need to know what the last page is and how it reads. It would be like a big book club where nobody moves to the next page until everyone in the group has agreed on what the last page says or, for the Bitcoin blockchain, what each block says.

9.2.3   The Role of Immutability in Bitcoin

However, how can we ensure that nobody goes back and is able to change a page of the book? Satoshi suggests that each new page has to contain the hash of all the previous pages.

> The solution we propose begins with a timestamp server. A timestamp server works by taking a hash of a block of items to be time stamped and widely pub-lishing the hash (…). The timestamp proves that the data must have existed at the time, obviously, in order to get into the hash. Each timestamp includes the previous timestamp in its hash, forming a chain, with each additional time-stamp reinforcing the ones before it.

---

[14] Ibid.

As we have seen before, even if a single tiny detail is changed in any piece of data, its hash will be different. So, including the hash of all the previous pages in every single page makes it difficult to alter the record, since for someone to change a previous page, she will need to change every single page previous to that page. In the Bitcoin blockchain, a new block (or an official page of the book in our analogy) is created approximately every 10 minutes and added to the chain, ensuring that when any new piece of information is added to the blockchain, then it becomes immutable.

But if everyone will be using the same book and nobody will move forward until we have all agreed to the content of the last page, then who is going to decide what that last page will contain? We could have a 'master' editor or master bookkeeper but that would make the system centralized once again, defying the purpose of Bitcoin. That is when proof-of-work comes in.

9.2.4   The Role of Proof-of-Work in Bitcoin

The proof-of-work mechanism is really the secret sauce of the Bitcoin network. Satoshi sets it out as follows in the Bitcoin white paper:

> The proof-of-work involves scanning for a value that when hashed, such as with SHA-256, the hash begins with a number of zero bits. The average work required is exponential in the number of zero bits required and can be verified by executing a single hash. For our timestamp network, we implement the proof-of-work by incrementing a nonce in the block until a value is found that gives the block's hash the required zero bits. Once the CPU effort has been expended to make it satisfy the proof-of-work, the block cannot be changed without redoing the work. As later blocks are chained after it, the work to change the block would include redoing all the blocks after it.[15]

This process is what is commonly called 'mining'. It involves four separate pieces of data: a hash of the transactions on that block, the hash of the previous block, the time, and a number called the nonce. The nonce is a random number that is separate from the transactions that are set out on that block. So, a 'miner' will take these four variables and hope that the hash output will meet the necessary requirement of the number of starting zeros. That output is called the golden hash. The miner can start with a nonce of 0, then try a nonce of 1, then try a nonce of 2, and so on. The more nonces that a miner can

---

[15] Ibid.

test, the more chances the miner has to find the 'golden hash' that meets the requirements and will allow him to add that block to the Bitcoin blockchain.[16]

This means finding the right hash becomes purely a matter of chance. Anyone can in theory become a miner and find the next golden hash. The more different nonces a miner can test, the higher the chances she has of finding the golden hash and getting new Bitcoins as reward. The rate at which new nonces can be tested is called the hash rate which is broadly the number of times per second that a computer can run those four variables through a hash function and derive a new hash.[17]

To compensate these miners for their hard work, they are rewarded with Bitcoin. That transaction is called the coinbase transaction and is the first transaction of each block. At the time of writing the reward is 12.5 Bitcoin per block, but this reward gets halved each 210,000 blocks. For example, the next halving will happen in May 2020 where the reward will decrease to 6.25 coins.[18]

To continue with our bookkeeper analogy, the miner would be an auditor who will determine what is the correct last page of transactions (the block) to be used and the bookkeepers will use that to add their new transactions until the auditors confirm another page. But for an auditor to be able to determine that her page will become part of the official book, she would need to throw a pair of dice and whoever gets a double six would be able to add her page to the book. Of course, the odds of an auditor throwing two six-sided dice with the goal of eventually getting a double six are relatively good. When it comes to real Bitcoin mining, the odds are significantly smaller.

The purpose of this reward is to compensate miners, but also to create new Bitcoins. Today there are about 1800 new Bitcoins created every day (approximately 6 new blocks per hour * 12.5 Bitcoin per new block * 24 hours = 1800 new Bitcoins).

But this raises an issue. If the secret to getting new Bitcoins is to win at this game of chance, then why wouldn't I simply throw a large number of computers to the problem, increase the mining hash rate? While this may sound appealing, it would cause monetary inflation as it would dramatically increase the supply of Bitcoin. This is why Satoshi added a 'self-regulatory' rule in the

---

[16] Chris Burniske and Jack Tatar, Crypto-assets: The Innovative Investor's Guide to Bitcoin and Beyond (McGraw Hill Professional, 2017), p. 212.

[17] Chris Burniske and Jack Tatar, Crypto-assets: The Innovative Investor's Guide to Bitcoin and Beyond (McGraw Hill Professional, 2017), p. 212.

[18] "Bitcoin Block Reward Halving Countdown," accessed January 13, 2019, https://www.bitcoinblock-half.com/.

Bitcoin blockchain where if more computing power is added to the network, then the network makes it harder to find the golden hash by adding zeros to the hash that is required. This is called the 'difficulty'. This adjustment is done roughly every two weeks with a target of miners finding the golden hash in about 10 minutes.[19]

So approximately every 10 minutes, a new block is added to the chain. This is where the origin of the name blockchain comes from, but it is noteworthy that Satoshi never used the word 'blockchain' in the Bitcoin whitepaper (more on this later). As we can see, "The network is robust in its unstructured simplicity. Nodes work all at once with little coordination."[20]

In theory, anyone can connect to the Bitcoin network, download past blocks, keep track of new transaction, and try to crunch the data to find the golden hash. This is one of the key benefits of the Bitcoin network.[21] However, mining Bitcoin in the pursuit of a golden hash has now become extremely difficult. Simply plugging in your laptop and hoping to find the golden hash is extremely unlikely. The technology used for mining has evolved fairly quickly from CPUs in computers and graphical processing units (GPU) in graphic cards to application specific integrated circuits (ASIC). To put things in perspective, some of the best ASIC devices that are available on the market at the time of writing have hash rates of over 13 TH/s, allowing you to crunch data and output a hash 13 trillion times a second.[22] (Imagine throwing those dice at that speed!) Many of these mining operations are also located in places where there is cheap electricity as mining operations today consume a lot of energy.

9.3   The Growth of Bitcoin

The first documented purchase of goods through Bitcoin is dated May 2010. On May 22, Bitcoin enthusiast Laszlo Hanyecz posted online a receipt of his successful Bitcoin transaction: two pizzas for 10,000 Bitcoin, the equivalent of US$41 at the time.[23] By 2017, those 10,000 were worth millions, arguably

---

[19] Chris Burniske and Jack Tatar, *Crypto-assets: The Innovative Investor's Guide to Bitcoin and Beyond* (McGraw Hill Professional, 2017), p. 214.

[20] Satoshi Nakamoto, "Bitcoin: A Peer-to-Peer Electronic Cash System," http://Bitcoin.org/Bitcoin.pdf, May 2009, https://bitcoin.org/bitcoin.pdf.

[21] Chris Burniske and Jack Tatar, Crypto-assets: The Innovative Investor's Guide to Bitcoin and Beyond (McGraw Hill Professional, 2017), p. 212.

[22] https://www.techradar.com/news/best-asic-devices-for-bitcoin-mining-in-2018.

[23] "Laszlo Hanyecz," Bitcoin Wiki, accessed January 13, 2019, https://en.bitcoin.it/wiki/Laszlo_Hanyecz.

making it most expensive pizza order ever. May 22 is now celebrated by many in the global crypto community as 'Bitcoin Pizza Day'.

Over the last decade, Bitcoin steadily began gaining momentum, experiencing an important boom at the end of 2013[24] when its price rose to about US$1000. But just when things seemed to be taking off, the price started to fall. It continued to experience a steady decline and plummeted back to about US$200 over the next two years. Those were difficult times for the Bitcoin community due to many public events including the association with the Silk Road marketplace arrests, as well as the hack of a Bitcoin exchange called Mt. Gox.[25] However, the usage of Bitcoin increased during that time, with the number of confirmed daily Bitcoin transactions almost doubling every year, reaching over 100,000 by 2015.[26]

Box 9.2   What Is Silk Road and Its Connection to Bitcoin?

The 'Silk Road' marketplace, founded in 2011 and shut down by the FBI two years later, was an online platform founded by Ross Ulbricht.[27] The website essentially used Bitcoin for money laundering transactions, drug sales, and illegal activity. Designed as a free and open marketplace, Ulbricht's platform also used Tor, a network that ensures anonymity of its users' data. Bitcoin was the main form of currency facilitating these transactions and because it is a much harder form of payment to trace back to its ultimate owner (unlike, e.g. using a credit card). Eventually, the website was shut down after the FBI caught up with the network and its founder was sentenced to life in prison.

While the Bitcoin community had nothing to do with Silk Road (in the same sense that the Federal Reserve is not associated with crime because drug dealers use cash), this was seen as one of the main uses of Bitcoin by the media and to the general public and led to many having a negative initial outlook toward Bitcoin and other crypto-assets.

This being said, it is not wise to conduct illegal transactions using Bitcoin. While transactions can be difficult to trace back to their user, all transactions are recorded in the Bitcoin ledger (unlike in the case of cash). There are numerous examples in the media of academics (and of course, law enforcement) successfully identifying individuals who sent Bitcoin for such purposes.[28] Today these 'dark web' transactions for Bitcoin represent less than 1% of transactions (down from 30% in 2012, the early days of Bitcoin).[29]

---

[24] Kitco News, "2013: Year of the Bitcoin," Forbes, December 10, 2013, https://www.forbes.com/sites/kitconews/2013/12/10/2013-year-of-the-bitcoin/#2f0b622e303c.

[25] Kitco News, "2013: Year of the Bitcoin," Forbes, December 10, 2013, https://www.forbes.com/sites/kitconews/2013/12/10/2013-year-of-the-bitcoin/#2f0b622e303c.

[26] "Confirmed Transactions Per Day," Blockchain.com, accessed January 13, 2019, https://www.blockchain.com/charts/n-transactions.

[27] Jake Frankenfield, "Silk Road," Investopedia, October 26, 2016, https://www.investopedia.com/terms/s/silk-road.asp.

[28] Andy Greenberg, "Your Sloppy Bitcoin Drug Deals Will Haunt You for Years," Wired, January 26, 2018, https://www.wired.com/story/bitcoin-drug-deals-silk-road-blockchain/.

[29] Ibid.

Box 9.3   The Mt. Gox Scandal

Mt. Gox—a former Tokyo-based Bitcoin exchange that allowed people to trade Bitcoin for cash—started around 2010 and met its end four years later after it shut down, filed for bankruptcy protection, and eventually faced liquidation.

The exchange was originally built to trade Magic fantasy-based game cards, resulting in the abbreviation 'Mt. Gox' from the name 'Magic: The Gathering Online eXchange'.

By 2013, it was handling around 70% of the world's Bitcoin trading when it was hacked for US$473 million.[30] This breach was a massive setback for the momentum that was being gathered by Bitcoin. The hack not only had a negative impact on the price of Bitcoin, but arguably also had a far-reaching impact on the broader crypto ecosystem.

While there were many things that went wrong with Mt. Gox, it is safe to say that it was not built with top-class security and governance frameworks in mind. By 2014, Mt. Gox halted all withdrawals and ended up filing for bankruptcy protection.[31] The court proceedings on Mt. Gox are still ongoing at the time of writing.

But following these events, the tide started slowly turning in favor of Bitcoin and the broader crypto ecosystem.

In the early days of crypto-assets, the buyers, sellers, and users of these assets were a niche group of individuals. These individuals ranged from experienced cryptographers and geeks to developers and libertarians. The landscape started to change quickly in 2015 and 2016 as more and more individuals became interested in cryptocurrencies, from university students day trading in their dorm rooms to early adopters who chose to invest a portion of their diversified portfolio in this new asset class.

The year 2017 will be remembered as a game changing year for Bitcoin and the broader crypto ecosystem.[32] Bitcoin's price hit US$10,000 in November 2017—a new high that would have been unthinkable for many only a couple of years back. But the frenzy continued with Bitcoin's price reaching nearly US$20,000 toward the end of December 2017. Suddenly, Bitcoin was being discussed regularly on media platforms like Bloomberg and CNBC, which in turn generated mass amounts of global buzz in the crypto space.

---

[30] Robert McMillan Metz Cade, "The Rise and Fall of the World's Largest Bitcoin Exchange," Wired, November 6, 2013, https://www.wired.com/2013/11/mtgox/.

[31] Andrew Norry, "The History of the Mt. Gox Hack: Bitcoin's Biggest Heist," Blockonomi, November 19, 2018, https://blockonomi.com/mt-gox-hack/.

[32] Garrick Hileman, "State of Bitcoin and Blockchain 2016: Blockchain Hits Critical Mass," CoinDesk, January 28, 2016, https://www.coindesk.com/state-of-bitcoin-blockchain-2016.

Many retail and institutional investors also started paying attention to and becoming seriously involved into crypto-assets. People started discussing Bitcoin at the dinner table and at family gatherings. For example, US-based exchange Coinbase opened over 100,000 new accounts over the 2017 Thanksgiving holiday.[33] Demand was so high that many exchanges had to stop taking on new clients or were flooded with requests when they did. For example, the Hong Kong–based exchange Binance opened around 250,000 new accounts in just an hour after it reopened its platform in 2017.[34]

The price of Bitcoin and many other crypto-assets fell in 2018. Bitcoin closed the year at slightly over US$4000, far from the highs it saw in 2017. This revived the debate between Bitcoin believers and its skeptics. For example, Nobel laureate Nouriel Roubini gave a presentation at a US Senate Committee calling Bitcoin the 'mother of all scams'.[35]

Others have begun to take a more nuanced view: the International Monetary Fund's managing director Christine Lagarde mentioned that it could change how people save and invest.[36] Others have embraced cryptocurrencies more proactively: for example, several reputed global organizations started accepting Bitcoin. PwC's Hong Kong office accepted Bitcoin payment in 2017 for its advisory services.[37] Online travel booking platform, Expedia, allows users to book some hotels via Bitcoin, while Microsoft[38] allows users to buy content from Windows and Xbox stores through Bitcoin.

Many believe that we have passed the point of no return with not only Bitcoin but also broader crypto-assets and that they are here to stay. However, others believe that some of the challenges, as we will discuss below, are serious roadblocks and that we still have a long way to go before Bitcoin and other crypto-assets become mainstream.

---

[33] Evelyn Cheng, "Bitcoin Tops $8,700 to Record High as Coinbase Adds 100,000 Users," CNBC, November 26, 2017, https://www.cnbc.com/2017/11/25/bitcoin-tops-8700-to-record-high-as-coinbase-adds-100000-users.html.

[34] Gedalyah Reback, "Binance Claims 240,000 New Users in One Hour after Relaunching Service," Cointelligence, January 11, 2018, https://www.cointelligence.com/content/binance-claims-240000-new-users-in-one-hour-after-relaunching-service/.

[35] Kate Rooney, "Nouriel Roubini: Bitcoin Is 'Mother of All Scams,'" CNBC, October 11, 2018, https://www.cnbc.com/2018/10/11/roubini-bitcoin-is-mother-of-all-scams.html.

[36] Anthony Cuthbertson, "Bitcoin Just Got a Boost from the World's Leading Financial Authority," The Independent, April 17, 2018, https://www.independent.co.uk/life-style/gadgets-and-tech/news/bitcoin-price-latest-updates-imf-christine-lagarde-blogpost-cryptocurrency-invest-a8308491.html.

[37] PricewaterhouseCoopers, "PwC Accepts Payment in Bitcoin for Its Advisory Services," PwC, November 30, 2017, https://www.pwchk.com/en/press-room/press-releases/pr-301117.html.

[38] Sean Williams, "5 Brand-Name Businesses That Currently Accept Bitcoin – The Motley Fool," The Motley Fool, July 6, 2017, https://www.fool.com/investing/2017/07/06/5-brand-name-businesses-that-currently-accept-bitc.aspx.

9.4   Challenges Facing Bitcoin

Despite its many innovations, Bitcoin is not perfect. Some commentators compare Bitcoin to the automobile Model T's engine, designed by Ford Motor Company in 1908. While revolutionary at the time, it was relatively slow (about 40 miles per hour),[39] which is not much faster than a horse's running speed. Also, the engine was not very efficient and it was highly energy intensive. However, we've come a long way since then to today's Tesla electric cars. Many hope that crypto-assets will go through the same evolution.

Currently, Bitcoin faces many challenges. For example, its price is still volatile. While volatility is great for speculators and traders, it is not good for an asset that can be used as a store of value. People buy blue chip stocks or gold in part because of their stability. Many hope that as Bitcoin adoption increases and the number of institutional investors grows, volatility will decline, but that is not the case yet. The volatility is also an obstacle to having more widespread acceptance such as from merchants.

Another issue is legal, regulatory, and especially tax clarity. It is very difficult for an asset to gain mainstream acceptance if investors don't know what the tax impact will be for any gain or loss that they make. Also, one needs to have certainty on the legal and regulatory framework before putting her life savings in that asset. The good news (as will be discussed later in this chapter) is that lots of governments, regulators, and tax authorities are looking at addressing these issues but this does not happen overnight unfortunately.

Some of the challenges are also technical, for example, the scalability of Bitcoin. Currently the Bitcoin network can only process fewer than six or seven transactions per second. Just by way of comparison, Visa's network can process around 24,000 per second.[40] While there have been initiatives to solve this issue in the Bitcoin network with hard forks (e.g. Bitcoin Cash) or soft forks (e.g. Segregated Witness), this is still an outstanding issue. We will discuss forks later in the book.

Bitcoin also faces serious ecological challenges as mining takes an incredible amount of energy. As of 2018, the network is expected to consume about 2.55 gigawatts (GW) of electricity annually. In comparison, the entire country of Ireland on average consumes about 3.1 GW of electricity and estimates

---

[39] History.com Editors, "Ford Motor Company Unveils the Model T," HISTORY, November 13, 2009, https://www.history.com/this-day-in-history/ford-motor-company-unveils-the-model-t.

[40] Manny Trillo, "Visa Transactions Hit Peak on Dec. 23," Visa's Blog – Visa Viewpoints (blog), January 12, 2011, https://www.visa.com/blogarchives/us/2011/01/12/visa-transactions-hit-peak-on-dec-23/index.html.

show that in the past year, the amount of terawatt hours (TWh) used by the Bitcoin network annually may have increased by as much as 400%.[41]

The electricity consumption required by the proof-of-work mechanism is clearly not scalable in a sustainable way. While many other cryptocurrencies use methods that are not as energy intense as proof-of-work (e.g. proof-of-stake), it is still a problem for Bitcoin today.

Box 9.4   What Is Proof-of-Stake?

As discussed above, while proof-of-work is an ingenious way to operate the Bitcoin network, it is not energy efficient. There are numerous debates in the crypto community as to whether there could be other consensus mechanisms that could be used to validate and verify transactions. One of the most discussed is proof-of-stake.

However, it is important to understand that in addition to proof-of-work and proof-of-stake, there is a constant flow of new consensus mechanisms being developed (e.g. proof-of-weight, delegated proof-of-stake, proof of activity, byzantine fault tolerance). These go beyond the scope of this book, but it is important to understand that this is an area in constant flux.

As we have seen, under a proof-of-work system, miners compete to win a game of chance to have the opportunity to verify all the transactions in the next block. The winner is rewarded with a certain amount of Bitcoin, the block is shared with everyone, and miners then move to try to solve the next block.[42] In a proof-of-work mechanism, the more hashing power one has, the more chances she has of 'winning' at that game of chance and mining the next block.

Proof-of-stake differs entirely from proof-of-work as the right to mine the next block is determined not by winning at that game of chance, but rather by your share or 'stake' in that crypto asset. Forgers (the proof-of-stake equivalent of a miner) are chosen to build blocks based on their stake in a currency and the age of that stake within the blockchain's network. For instance, let's say you hold 100,000 of Crypto X, so you would be more likely to create the candidate block than someone with 1000 of Crypto X. Also, if you would be holding your stake for a year, you would have more chance to be chosen than someone who has been holding it only for one month.[43]

(continued)

---

[41] Patrick Thompson, "Bitcoin Mining's Electricity Bill: Is It Worth It?," Cointelegraph, June 2, 2018, https://cointelegraph.com/news/bitcoin-minings-electricity-bill-is-it-worth-it.

[42] Colin Harper, "Making Sense of Proof of Work vs. Proof of Stake," CoinCentral, January 24, 2018, https://coincentral.com/making-sense-of-proof-of-work-vs-proof-of-stake/.

[43] Ibid.

Box 9.4 (continued)

A good analogy of proof-of-stake is to imagine that someone's odds of winning the lottery increase based on the number of lottery tickets you buy and for how long you have been buying those lottery tickets.

Another important difference is that for some proof-of-stake currencies, all the coins are created at the launch of the currency and their number is fixed. Therefore, rather than receiving new coins as rewards (as is the case for Bitcoin miners, for example), forgers receive transaction fees.[44] To validate transactions and create blocks, a forger must first put their own coins (and reputation) at stake. If a forger validates a fraudulent transaction, they lose their holdings, as well as their future rights to participate as a forger. Forgers are therefore incentivized to validate only correct transactions.[45]

There is tremendous debate in the crypto community on the pros and cons of each consensus mechanism. While proof-of-stake has clear environmental benefits, in that it does not consume as much electricity as proof-of-work, many would argue that is less democratic than proof-of-work as it gives an advantage to those who already hold the currency and have held it for a long time. On the other hand, proof-of-work may itself be considered undemocratic due to the high level of capital required to be able to mine cryptocurrencies like Bitcoin.

Please note that there are always discussions in the crypto community about improving or amending either proof-of-work or proof-of-stake. For example, a delegated proof-of-stake model has been gathering some traction recently where a system of voters, witnesses, and delegates is used.[46] Once again, there are many articles online on the developments on this topic for anyone who might be interested.

---

[44] Shaan Ray, "The Difference Between Traditional and Delegated Proof of Stake," Hacker Noon, April 23, 2018, https://hackernoon.com/the-difference-between-traditional-and-delegated-proof-of-stake-36a3e3f25f7d. It is important to note that in few cases, new currency units can be created by inflating the coin supply, and can be used to reward forgers.

[45] Ibid.

[46] Ibid.

10

Blockchain As an Enabling Technology

Before giving further consideration to the emerging role that crypto-assets are playing in the financial ecosystem, it is important to take a moment to consider the broader impacts of the technical innovations encapsulated in the Bitcoin white paper. This chapter will consider how the broader application of this technology—typically called blockchain—is shifting the way in which the financial services community thinks about the potential architecture of the systems that enable financial transactions. We will consider the characteristics and challenges facing the application of blockchains and explore several potential use cases.

10.1 Defining the Characteristics of a Blockchain

To the surprise of many, the term 'blockchain' is not even mentioned once in Satoshi's white paper. The closest Satoshi comes to saying blockchain is via references to 'blocks are chained' or 'chains of blocks'.[1] However, the idea of having blocks and linking them in a chain using cryptographic functions is the basis of the Bitcoin network, and why the birth of blockchain is attributed to Satoshi as well.

---

[1] Chris Burniske and Jack Tatar, Crypto-assets: The Innovative Investor's Guide to Bitcoin and Beyond (McGraw Hill Professional, 2017).

© The Author(s) 2019
H. Arslanian, F. Fischer, *The Future of Finance*,
https://doi.org/10.1007/978-3-030-14533-0_10

> **Box 10.1   What Is the Difference Between Distributed Ledger Technology and Blockchain?**
>
> Distributed ledger technology (DLT) is simply a decentralized database that is managed by various participants.[2] Blockchain is simply a type of DLT with a specific set of features which consists of having blocks form a chain. Another way of looking at it is that DLT is the generic umbrella term and blockchain is a subcategory. For example, a car is a type of vehicle in the same way that blockchain is a type of DLT.[3]
>
> As a matter of fact, there are now numerous DLT networks out there that are not using blockchain (e.g. IOTA, Hashgraph).[4]

> **Box 10.2   Where Does the Name Blockchain Come from?**
>
> If Satoshi never used the term 'blockchain' in the Bitcoin white paper, then where did it come from?
>
> While some claim that the term 'block chain' (used separately) can be found in some cryptography mailing lists around 2008,[5] the term did not enter the mainstream until about 2015.
>
> According to some researchers, a couple of media articles in late 2015 catalyzed the use of the term 'blockchain'.[6] One was an article in *Bloomberg Markets* titled 'Blythe Masters Tells Banks the Blockchain Changes Everything'[7] featuring Masters who was a respected financial innovator having helped develop the credit default swaps markets. The other was the October 31, 2015, issue of *The Economist* titled 'The Trust Machine' which featured blockchain and used the term 'blockchain' throughout.[8] Google searches for the term 'blockchain' are reported to have risen over 70% in the days following those articles.[9] Since then, the term has been widely used.

[2] "What Is the Difference between DLT and Blockchain? | BBVA," BBVA, accessed January 13, 2019, https://www.bbva.com/en/difference-dlt-blockchain/.

[3] Max Thake, "What's the Difference between Blockchain and DLT?," *Nakamo.To* (blog), February 8, 2018, https://medium.com/nakamo-to/whats-the-difference-between-blockchain-and-dlt-e4b9312c75dd.

[4] Ibid.

[5] richbodo, "Usage of the Word 'Blockchain,'" *Richbodo* (blog), September 20, 2017, https://medium.com/@richbodo/common-use-of-the-word-blockchain-5b916cecef29.

[6] Chris Burniske and Jack Tatar, *Crypto-assets: The Innovative Investor's Guide to Bitcoin and Beyond* (McGraw Hill Professional, 2017).

[7] Edward Robinson and Matthew Leising, "Blythe Masters Tells Banks the Blockchain Changes Everything – Bloomberg," Bloomberg News, accessed January 13, 2019, https://www.bloomberg.com/news/features/2015-09-01/blythe-masters-tells-banks-the-blockchain-changes-everything.

[8] "The Trust Machine – The Promise of the Blockchain," *The Economist*, accessed January 13, 2019, https://www.economist.com/leaders/2015/10/31/the-trust-machine.

[9] *Crypto-assets*.

It is also important to clarify that there is no single blockchain. For example, the Bitcoin blockchain is completely different from the Ethereum blockchain or the NEO blockchain or the EOS blockchain (we will discuss these separately later). They may all achieve more or less the same goal, but each has its own rules, coding languages, purpose, and so on. A good analogy (for our older readers!) would be VHS and Betamax cassette formats or (for the slightly younger ones!) the HD DVD vs Blu-ray formats. Both allow you to watch a movie, but the way each operates is different. A somewhat more modern analogy could be the Apple iOS versus Google Android operating systems. Both allow you to use your smartphone in new and innovative ways, but each operates slightly differently. However, unlike operating systems or cassette formats, where there were often two or three competing systems, there are now dozens of blockchain networks. It may be that in the future, there will be only a handful that become widely adopted with large developer communities, applications, and users.

That said, there are a number of characteristics that most blockchains generally have[10]:

- *Decentralized and transparent:* There is no central database or central authority and each participant maintains a copy of the ledger. Users are able to check on any transaction that has taken place at any time on the blockchain. The degree of decentralization varies from blockchain to blockchain.
- *Consensus-driven:* All participants share and update the ledger after reaching a consensus and agreeing on the validity of transactions taking place. While true of most major blockchains, there are other various ways of reaching this consensus as we have seen previously.
- *Immutable:* Once data is added to the blockchain, it cannot be altered. This is done via the use of particular cryptographic techniques as we discussed earlier.

There are obviously always exceptions to the above, but being decentralized, consensus-driven, and immutable are characteristics that are common across most blockchains. The biggest fundamental difference between different blockchains are whether they are public or private.

---

[10] Michael J. Casey and Paul Vigna, "In Blockchain We Trust," MIT Technology Review, April 9, 2018, https://www.technologyreview.com/s/610781/in-blockchain-we-trust/.

> **Box 10.3   What Is the Difference Between Private and Public Blockchains?**
>
> If one wants to start a passionate debate between blockchain aficionados, bringing up the topic of private versus public blockchain is a sure bet.
>
> The main distinction between a public (also called permissionless) and private (also called permissioned) blockchain is who is allowed to participate in the network. A good analogy is the difference between the internet (open to many) and an intranet (set up by a company for its own use).
>
> A public blockchain network is completely open and anyone can join and participate. Anyone can become a 'bookkeeper', add blocks to the blockchain, and conduct transactions. Bitcoin, Ethereum, or Litecoin are good examples of public blockchain networks.
>
> A private blockchain network requires an invitation and places restrictions on who is allowed to participate wildly.[11] Hyperledger Fabric (Linux Foundation), Corda (R3), or Quorum (JP Morgan) are good examples of private blockchains.
>
> These private blockchains came about when certain businesses realized they liked the utility of Bitcoin's blockchain but were not comfortable (or in certain cases not allowed by law) to be as open with the information they wanted to place on a distributed ledger.[12]
>
> While we could go on for hours on the pros and cons of each (and there are many articles online for anyone interested), the reality is that there are uses for both public and private blockchains and they are both likely to co-exist for the foreseeable future, each with its own set of use cases.

10.2   Challenges

But blockchain technology is not a panacea that will solve all the world's problems. While it has many unique advantages, it also has some downsides:

- **Anonymity**: One of the things that makes public blockchains, such as the Bitcoin blockchain, so unique is that they allow anyone to join the system and conduct transactions. However, while every transaction is traceable, it is difficult to know who is behind a given movement of funds. While this may present a number of positive factors, including the elimination of unreasonable censorship, it can prove a challenge when it comes to complying with KYC, AML, and other transaction-monitoring requirements. This is why certain industries have instead opted to using private blockchains where the identity of participants is known.

---

[11] Praveen Jayachandran, "The Difference between Public and Private Blockchain," Blockchain Pulse: IBM Blockchain Blog, May 31, 2017, https://www.ibm.com/blogs/blockchain/2017/05/the-difference-between-public-and-private-blockchain/.

[12] Chris Burniske and Jack Tatar, *Crypto-assets: The Innovative Investor's Guide to Bitcoin and Beyond* (McGraw Hill Professional, 2017).

- **Quality of Information**: While the data on a blockchain is immutable, it does not necessarily mean that it is accurate. The same principle of 'garbage in, garbage out' applies as with any other database.
- **Interoperability**: The blockchain is still in its infancy and there are no established industry standards for its technology infrastructure. Most blockchains today operate in their standalone universe with little interoperability with other blockchains.
- **Mass Adoption**: Blockchain is still new and most people and enterprises are still in the early days of their learning curve. It is unlikely that any large enterprise will move their entire database on blockchain anytime soon. This adoption will take some time and there will be a day where people will be able to conduct transactions faster and more efficiently, for example, without knowing that the backend they are using is blockchain. A good analogy would be how people today turn on their Wi-Fi and surf the web without really knowing about the various internet protocols operating in the background.
- **Legal Uncertainty**: Current regulatory frameworks and requirements—particularly in highly regulated industries like financial services or healthcare—were not drafted with blockchain technology in mind. Basic legal concepts ranging from customer data protection to more recent developments in data privacy requirements like the 'right to be forgotten' require detailed review in a blockchain context.

While the above challenges are important, a lot of individuals and groups globally are working on addressing these issues. The blockchain ecosystem is growing at an astonishing pace and the interest in the space from large corporates and financial institutions has greatly increased in recent years.

From 2012 to 2017, blockchain firms have raised more than US$2.1 billion in traditional venture capital funding via 650 equity deals. Furthermore, over the same period, corporates invested nearly US$1.2 billion in more than 140 equity investments.[13] Also, many companies have established in-house capabilities to carry out 'proofs of concept' (a test or exercise of a technology in a controlled environment to verify concepts for real-world usage) to test how decentralized ledger technologies can be applied to their own businesses. However, although significant progress has been made, the blockchain is still in its early stages and corporates are far from taking advantage of the full potential of this technology.

The financial services industry has been actively involved in the blockchain space, usually by experimenting on permissioned and private blockchains via

---

[13] "Blockchain Investment Trends In Review," CB Insights Research, accessed January 13, 2019, https://www.cbinsights.com/research/report/blockchain-trends-opportunities/.

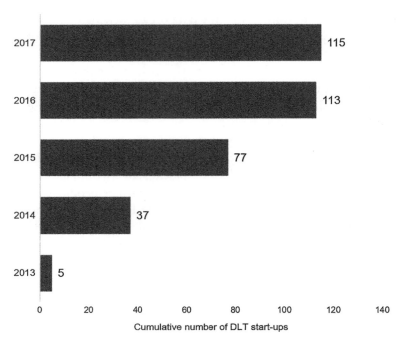

Note: Excludes cryptocurrency-focused firms, dApps (decentralised applications), and 'pure' consulting firms that do not provide development

Fig. 10.1 Cumulative number of enterprise DLT startups. Since 2013, we have seen a significant increase in the number of startups dedicated to the development of enterprise blockchain applications. Source(s): Garrick Hileman and Michel Rauchs, 'Global Blockchain Benchmarking Study' (University of Cambridge Judge Business School, 2017), https://www.jbs.cam.ac.uk/fileadmin/user_upload/research/centres/alternative-finance/downloads/2017-09-27-ccaf-globalbchain.pdf

various consortiums. Such consortiums allow financial institutions to experiment with blockchain while operating in private environments. There are various examples of such consortia, for example, Hyperledger Fabric (Linux Foundation),[14] Corda (R3),[15] Quorum (JPMorgan),[16] or the Ethereum Enterprise Alliance,[17] each consortium with its own particularities.

---

[14] Martin Valenta and Philipp Sandner, "Comparison of Ethereum, Hyperledger Fabric and Corda," *Frankfurt School Blockchain Center*, June 2017.

[15] "Corda | Training & Certification," Corda, accessed January 13, 2019, https://www.corda.net/develop/training.html.

[16] "Quorum | J.P. Morgan," J.P. Morgan Chase & Co., accessed January 13, 2019, https://www.jpmorgan.com/global/Quorum#section_1320553510217.

[17] Joe Ross, "Home," Enterprise Ethereum Alliance, accessed January 13, 2019, https://entethalliance.org/.

10.3   Use Cases of Blockchains

Given that the existing financial system is built on a complex network of trusted third parties and hub and spoke systems, it is no surprise that discussions of the potential use cases of blockchain have generated innumerable ideas. A few that are frequently cited include clearing and settlement,[18] trade finance,[19] KYC,[20] or cross-border payments.[21]

There are also numerous use cases specific to the insurance industry from smart contracts in episodic insurance to basic claim processing. For example, insurance group AXA has started to implement blockchain smart contracts to offer "direct and automatic compensation to policyholders whose flights are delayed".[22] If a policyholder purchases flight delay insurance on AXA's new platform 'fizzy', the transaction—or insurance contract—is recorded on the Ethereum blockchain. The smart contract is directly linked to global air traffic databases and so, if a delay of two or more hours is recorded in air traffic systems, policyholders will automatically receive their compensation.

In another example, a great deal of research has been done on how blockchain-based land registries can harness smart contract technology to not only establish land titles but also automatically transfer land ownership and hamper fraudulent transactions.[23] Using this technology could cut transaction time between land buyers and sellers substantially.[24]

Moreover, according to a report by the United Nations Development Programme, in a country like India where factors like corruption, lack of information, and inability to verify transactions have led to a loss of confidence in the system, this technology could be a real game-changer in enhanc-

---

[18] Chris Skinner, "Applying Blockchain to Clearing and Settlement – Chris Skinner's Blog," August 2016, https://thefinanser.com/2016/08/applying-blockchain-clearing-settlement.html/.

[19] Noelle Acheson, "How Blockchain Trade Finance Is Breaking Proof-of-Concept Gridlock," *CoinDesk* (blog), April 30, 2018, https://www.coindesk.com/blockchain-trade-finance-breaking-proof-concept-gridlock.

[20] Eamonn Maguire et al., "Could Blockchain Be the Foundation of a Viable KYC Utility?" (KPMG International, 2018).

[21] Ravishankar Achanta, "Cross-Border Money Transfer Using Blockchain – Enabled by Big Data" (Infosys, 2018).

[22] "AXA Goes Blockchain with Fizzy | AXA," AXA, September 13, 2017, https://www.axa.com/en/newsroom/news/axa-goes-blockchain-with-fizzy%23xtor%3DCS3-9-%5BShared_Article%5D-%5Baxa_goes_blockchain_with_fizzy%5D.

[23] "Establishing a Chain of Title – Leveraging Blockchain for the Real Estate Industry," Dentons Rodyk, November 20, 2017, https://dentons.rodyk.com/en/insights/alerts/2017/november/21/establishing-a-chain-of-title-leveraging-blockchain-for-the-real-estate-industry.

[24] Molly Jane Zuckerman, "Swedish Government Land Registry Soon To Conduct First Blockchain Property Transaction," Cointelegraph, March 7, 2018, https://cointelegraph.com/news/swedish-government-land-registry-soon-to-conduct-first-blockchain-property-transaction.

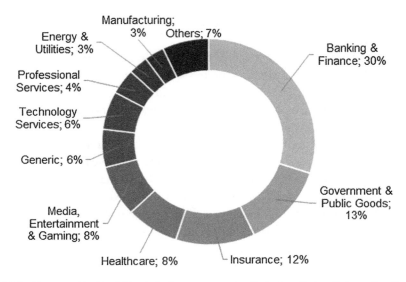

Fig. 10.2 Frequently cited blockchain use cases by industry. Potential applications of blockchain technology span almost every industry, but banking and finance remain the area of greatest focus. Source(s): https://www.jbs.cam.ac.uk/fileadmin/user_upload/research/centres/alternative-finance/downloads/2017-09-27-ccaf-globalbchain.pdf

ing the reliability of land recognition.[25] Sweden's land-ownership authority, the Lantmäteriet, may also soon make use of this technology to conduct their first blockchain technology property transaction.[26]

Even institutions like central banks have given the application of blockchain serious consideration. Several experiments have been conducted around the use of blockchain in the development of next-generation real-time gross settlement (RTGS) systems, where payments are processed individually, immediately, and with finality throughout the day in 'real time' between the central bank and the various clearing banks of the national payment system.

Particularly notable examples of such projects include the Bank of Canada (Project Jasper)[27] and the Monetary Authority of Singapore (Project Ubin).[28]

---

[25] Alexandru Oprunenco and Chami Akmeemana, "Using Blockchain to Make Land Registry More Reliable in India," United Nations Development Programme, May 1, 2018, http://www.undp.org/content/undp/en/home/blog/2018/Using-blockchain-to-make-land-registry-more-reliable-in-India.html.

[26] Shefali Anand, "A Pioneer in Real Estate Blockchain Emerges in Europe," *Wall Street Journal*, March 6, 2018, sec. Markets, https://www.wsj.com/articles/a-pioneer-in-real-estate-blockchain-emerges-in-europe-1520337601.

[27] "Fintech Experiments and Projects," Bank of Canada, accessed January 13, 2019, https://www.bankof-canada.ca/research/digital-currencies-and-fintech/fintech-experiments-and-projects/.

[28] "Project Ubin," Singapore Financial Centre | Monetary Authority of Singapore, accessed January 13, 2019, http://www.mas.gov.sg/singapore-financial-centre/smart-financial-centre/project-ubin.aspx.

These two projects provided strong evidence that it was possible to use a distributed ledger system to deliver instant settlement. However, in the case of Canada, the bank concluded that "a standalone DLT wholesale system is unlikely to match the efficiency and net benefits of a centralized system".[29]

The Bank of Canada has continued its experimentation with blockchain systems in spite of these results, including a direct collaboration with the Monetary Authority of Singapore,[30] but the results raise a critical point. It is not sufficient for a blockchain-based solution to be possible; it must be better than the existing centralized solution—indeed it must be sufficiently better so as to justify the non-trivial costs of transitioning away from an existing system and developing a new one.

As excitement about the potential of blockchain continues to grow and pressure increases for firms to demonstrate their engagement with the technology, there is a risk that organizations may be pursuing pilots and proofs of concept that are unlikely to deliver long-term value or scale to production. In fact, a November 2017 report published by Deloitte found that out of a total of 26,000 blockchain projects launched in 2016 (that had made contributions to the public code repository Github), only 8% remained active.[31] While the promise of blockchain technology may be large, long-term success will require participants to avoid innovation theatre and focus activities on use cases with strong potential to develop into production implementations of the technology.

---

[29] "Canada Says No To Blockchain For Now," *PYMNTS.Com* (blog), May 29, 2017, https://www.pymnts.com/news/b2b-payments/2017/bank-canada-interbank-payment-system-blockchain/.

[30] Darshini Dalal, Stanley Yong, and Antony Lewis, "Project Ubin: SGD on Distributed Ledger" (Deloitte; Monetary Authority of Singapore, 2017).

[31] Jesus Leal Trujillo, Steve Fromhart, and Val Srinivas, "The Evolution of Blockchain Technology," Deloitte Insights, November 6, 2017, https://www2.deloitte.com/insights/us/en/industry/financial-services/evolution-of-blockchain-github-platform.html.

11

The Proliferation of Crypto-assets

While Bitcoin claimed the title of the world's first crypto-asset, it was certainly not the last. In this chapter, we will explore how the success of Bitcoin, and a desire to deliver new types of services on public blockchains, led to an explosion in the number and valuation of crypto-assets in the years following its launch. We will provide a brief overview of the state of crypto-assets at the time of writing, consider the various ways in which new assets come into existence, and dedicate particular attention to the sale of new crypto-assets commonly called an initial coin offering.

11.1 The Emergence of New Crypto-assets

It should not be surprising that as the level of awareness and interest in Bitcoin rose, so did the desire to experiment with the creation of new systems that employed many of the core innovations of Bitcoin (in particular its unique combination of cryptography and decentralization) to deliver new value propositions.

Early crypto-assets, sometimes called 'alt-coins', included Litecoin (launched in 2011), which sought to deliver faster speed of settlement, and Ethereum (launched in 2015), which sought to expand on the functionality of so-called smart contracts introduced by Bitcoin where conditional, self-executing transactions could be immutably agreed upon by users. Other assets

© The Author(s) 2019
H. Arslanian, F. Fischer, *The Future of Finance*,
https://doi.org/10.1007/978-3-030-14533-0_11

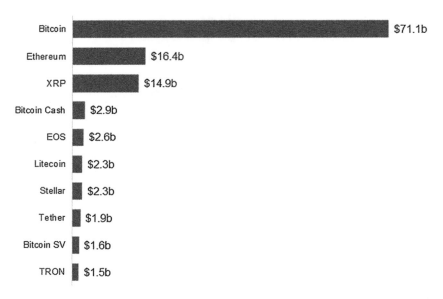

Fig. 11.1 Top ten Cryptocurrencies and utility tokens by market cap (January 1, 2019). While the total number of crypto-assets has proliferated, Bitcoin has consistently retained the highest market capitalization. Source(s): 'Top 100 Cryptocurrencies by Market Capitalization,' CoinMarketCap, accessed January 31, 2019, https://coinmarket-cap.com/

sought to perform a specific function, such as Namecoin, which aimed to create a decentralized system for internet domain names. There are even early coins created simply as a joke, such as Dogecoin, whose logo bears the likeness of the eponymous Doge, a Shiba Inu dog popularized by an internet meme.

By 2019, over 2000 such crypto-assets had been created, using a wide variety of underlying technical protocols and pursuing a wide range of (sometimes competing) aims. But how exactly did these assets come into existence?

One of the fascinating ways in which crypto-assets differ from more traditional financial instruments is that anyone can create them (whether or not this is legal to do so is another question to be discussed later in this and subsequent chapters). All that is needed is a bit of technical know-how and a community of people who believe the crypto-asset that you have created has some value, or could have. The key question is how you get the crypto-asset—which we will generically refer to here as a token—into the hands of that community.

Box 11.1   What Is Ethereum?

Ethereum and its currency, Ether (ETH), have become a very important element of the global crypto ecosystem. Ethereum wants to be a decentralized world computer where every node runs a copy of the Ethereum virtual machine (EVM).[1]

Ethereum was invented in 2013 by Vitalik Buterin. Born in Russia but raised in Canada, Buterin attended the University of Waterloo before dropping out when he received the Thiel Fellowship, allowing him to focus on Ethereum. Ethereum was formally announced to the public in early 2014 at a Bitcoin conference in Miami and funded via a pre-sale of Ether in the summer of 2014, which raised around US$18 million (at an original price of 2000 ETH for 1 BTC—when BTC was worth around US$500). The platform finally went live in the summer of 2015.[2]

While the Ethereum platform is similar to Bitcoin in many ways, most notably that it is blockchain-based and permissionless, there are also some important technical differences. For example, while there is a new block on the Bitcoin blockchain every 10 minutes, there is a new block on the Ethereum blockchain every 14 to 15 seconds. Also, while Bitcoin has a concept of transaction fees to compensate miners for each block, Ethereum uses a concept of 'gas' which is the fee you need to pay to perform a particular transaction, which varies depending on the nature of the transaction. Also, while both Bitcoin and Ethereum currently use proof-of-work, the Ethereum network is expected to move to a proof-of-stake approach in the foreseeable future.[3] But one of the most important distinctions is that the Ethereum network can also run smart contracts[4] and decentralized applications (dApps).[5]

Generally speaking, smart contracts are self-executing contracts with the terms of the agreement written directly in the line of code.[6] In the Ethereum context, a good example is the ERC-20 smart contract standard which provides a common set of features for how that contract will function in the Ethereum ecosystem.[7] A good analogy would be a regulatory handbook with templates that a lawyer can use to draft a contract. The ERC-20 standard has been used by the vast majority of companies doing an initial coin offering (ICO) and has contributed greatly to the growth of the Ethereum network and ETH in recent years.

The Ethereum community is generally seen as strong and continuously works on enhancing its functionalities, from scalability to new smart contract standards.

---

[1] Alyssa Hertig, "What Is Ethereum? – CoinDesk Guides," CoinDesk (blog), accessed January 13, 2019, https://www.coindesk.com/information/what-is-ethereum.

[2] Chris Burniske and Jack Tatar, Crypto-assets: The Innovative Investor's Guide to Bitcoin and Beyond (McGraw Hill Professional, 2017). Page 56.

[3] Alyssa Hertig, "Ethereum's Big Switch: The New Roadmap to Proof-of-Stake," CoinDesk (blog), May 5, 2017, https://www.coindesk.com/ethereums-big-switch-the-new-roadmap-to-proof-of-stake.

[4] Alyssa Hertig, "How Do Ethereum Smart Contracts Work?," CoinDesk (blog), accessed January 13, 2019, https://www.coindesk.com/information/ethereum-smart-contracts-work.

[5] Alyssa Hertig, "What Is a Decentralized Application?," CoinDesk (blog), accessed January 13, 2019, https://www.coindesk.com/information/what-is-a-decentralized-application-dapp.

[6] Jake Frankenfield, "Smart Contracts," Investopedia, April 18, 2017, https://www.investopedia.com/terms/s/smart-contracts.asp.

[7] "ERC-20," Wikipedia, December 19, 2018, https://en.wikipedia.org/w/index.php?title=ERC-20&oldid=874510987.

11.2 Mechanisms for Distributing New Crypto-assets

The enormous diversity of crypto-assets has driven a highly diverse set of approaches to the distribution of new tokens to the community of individuals and organizations interested in holding or using those tokens. We will explore three primary methods at a high level: mining, forking, and sale.

11.2.1 The Creation of New Tokens Via Mining

We have already discussed one process for the distribution of new tokens in our examination of Bitcoin, where new Bitcoins are added to the system via a process called mining. As discussed in Chap. 8, 'miners' provide the processing power necessary to maintain consensus within the Bitcoin blockchain by attempting to guess the correct answer to a challenging mathematical puzzle. Each time a miner correctly solves this puzzle, they are awarded with a predefined number of newly created Bitcoins. In the case of the Bitcoin network, the protocol specifies a fixed upper limit of 21 million Bitcoins that can be mined. In theory, when this number is reached in the year 2140, Bitcoin miners will only be rewarded through fees paid by users to have their transaction added to the next block. However, it is important to know that this is a specific protocol design choice of the Bitcoin protocol—other crypto-assets have chosen not to specify a fixed cap for the number of new tokens that can be mined and instead only defined the rate at which new tokens will be created by miners.

11.2.2 The Creation of New Tokens Via a Hard Fork

The world of crypto-assets is full of colorful disagreements, and disagreements around a particular crypto-asset can manifest themselves in an interesting way called a 'hard fork' (see Box 11.2 for a distinction between hard and soft forks). For example, the Bitcoin community has seen a vigorous set of debates around how the protocol could be improved, with many arguments focused on questions of how transaction-processing speed could be increased, a discussion commonly referred to as the 'block size debate'.

While the technical details of this debate are outside the scope of this book, it is enough to know that a portion of the Bitcoin community favored increasing the number of transactions in each block on the Bitcoin blockchain to

Box 11.2   What Is the Difference Between a Soft Fork and a Hard Fork?

An easy rule of thumb to remember is that a soft fork is when the protocol rules are to become stricter and a hard fork is when the protocol rules are to become more relaxed.[8]

A soft fork is a change of protocol when tighter rules are introduced. For example, if previously all blocks had a block size of 5 MB, then the introduction of a block size limit of 1 MB would be a soft fork. The blocks created in a soft fork can still work with the older version as they are backwards compatible.[9] Because of that, only miners have to update their software, while nodes can stay part of the network without updating.[10] Segregated Witness (SegWit) is an example of a soft fork that took place on the Bitcoin blockchain in the summer of 2017.[11]

A hard fork is a change of protocol where the rules are relaxed so that previously invalid blocks can now become valid. For example, if previously all blocks had a block size of 5 MB, then the introduction of a block size limit of 10 MB would be a hard fork. Since a hard fork makes invalid blocks valid, all network participants, namely miners as well as the nodes (our bookkeepers), have to update their systems. Otherwise, they would reject newly valid blocks and therefore be isolated from the network.[12] Bitcoin Cash and Ethereum Classic are examples of hard forks that have been successful so far.

Let's try to use an imperfect but hopefully useful analogy with bookkeepers and auditors. Imagine that today, bookkeepers (nodes) have ledgers that have transactions amounting to $5 a page and that their auditors (miners) are able to audit up to $5 of transactions at a time. Now imagine that the auditors decide that they will only audit up to $1 at a time. So the 'audit' rules have become stricter (soft fork). In this case, even if the auditors (miners) audit only $1 of transaction at a time, these would still fit in the bookkeepers' $5 per page format. The change in audit rules does not impact the bookkeepers. This would be the equivalent of a soft fork.

Now imagine that bookkeepers (nodes) have ledgers that have transactions that amount to $5 a page and that their auditors (miners) are able to audit up to $5 of transactions at a time. But one day, the auditors (miners) decide that they

(*continued*)

---

[8] Antony Lewis, The Basics of Bitcoins and Blockchains: An Introduction to Cryptocurrencies and the Technology That Powers Them (Mango Media, 2018). Page 289.

[9] John Light, "The Differences between a Hard Fork, a Soft Fork, and a Chain Split, and What They Mean for The…," Medium (blog), September 25, 2017, https://medium.com/@lightcoin/the-differences-between-a-hard-fork-a-soft-fork-and-a-chain-split-and-what-they-mean-for-the-769273f358c9.

[10] Jackie Liu, "Blockchain Research: What the Fork? What Happens When the (Block)chain Splits?," Blockchain Research Technical University of Munich, July 31, 2017, https://www.blockchain.tum.de/en/news-single-view/?tx_ttnews%5Btt_news%5D=9&cHash=6d77c31a3e4a8161867eef483b96cdb4.

[11] Noelle Acheson, "What Is SegWit?," CoinDesk (blog), accessed January 13, 2019, https://www.coindesk.com/information/what-is-segwit.

[12] Jackie Liu, "Blockchain Research: What the Fork? What Happens When the (Block)chain Splits?," Blockchain Research Technical University of Munich, July 31, 2017, https://www.blockchain.tum.de/en/news-single-view/?tx_ttnews%5Btt_news%5D=9&cHash=6d77c31a3e4a8161867eef483b96cdb4.

Box 11.2 (continued)

want to audit up to $10 at a time. So the 'audit' rules have become more relaxed (hard fork). In this case, if the auditors (miners) audit $10 of transactions at a time, these will not fit in the old $5 pages of the bookkeepers (nodes). They can decide to upgrade their books so that they can keep up to $10 of transactions per page. Or they may decide that they don't agree with this change and that they will only work with auditors that want to stick with the old rules of $5 of transactions per page. This is a hard fork scenario.

It is important to note that the above hard and soft forks are different from cases where the code of a cryptocurrency is taken, amended, and then launched as a new cryptocurrency. For example, Litecoin is an example of a cryptocurrency that is based on Bitcoin but with certain amendments (e.g. 84 million coins instead of BTC's 21 million, blocks every 2.5 minutes vs. BTC's 10 minutes, Scrypto algorithm vs. BTC's SHA-256, etc.). It is not a fork as it is simply launched on a new blockchain as a Day 1 coin.

increase transaction-processing speed, while another larger group favored keeping the block size and transaction processing unchanged. In August 2017, with the debate at an impasse, one group of miners chose to implement an altered version of the Bitcoin protocol, while a larger group chose to maintain the existing system creating a 'hard fork'.

This hard fork split the Bitcoin blockchain in two, one operating on the original protocol, which continued to be called Bitcoin, and a second using larger blocks that became called Bitcoin Cash. Owners of single unit of Bitcoin at the time of the hard fork found were now in possession of two tokens, a unit of Bitcoin and a unit of Bitcoin Cash. In this way, a completely new crypto-asset came into existence as an offshoot of an existing token and was immediately held by a broad group of people. New units of Bitcoin Cash will continue to be added via the activities of miners.

11.2.3   The Distribution of New Tokens Via Sale

A third way to facilitate the distribution of tokens is to create a protocol where some or all of the tokens have already been created (sometimes it is said the tokens have been 'minted') prior to the launch of the protocol itself or there is a mechanism for how such tokens will be created. These tokens are then sold, or in some cases given away, to individuals interested in the protocol.

The sale of these tokens can be used to fund further development of the protocol and broader ecosystem around the crypto-asset and is often called an ICO (more on that below). The initial number of tokens might be further expanded by mining. Alternately, the protocol might be designed in such a way that no mining takes place. In such cases, the total available supply is created at the birth of the currency and a portion of that released in the market with the remainder generally kept in reserve by the issuing entity. A good example of this is Ripple, a San Francisco–based company that issued 100 billion Ripple tokens (called XRP) of which around 40 billion are in circulation. The rest is controlled by Ripple, who can release up to 1 billion XRP a month. The only way to acquire XRP is via an existing crypto exchange.

11.3   A Closer Look at ICOs

Initial coin offerings represent a new approach to financing the development of a new service offering and warrant some exploration. The first significant ICOs were for Mastercoin in 2013,[13] followed shortly thereafter by Ethereum, which raised US$15 million; however, significant ICO activity didn't take off until early 2017 with a succession of big ticket ICOs including Filecoin, Tezos, and Block.one, which raised $257 million, $230 million, and $185 million respectively.[14] A PwC report estimates that over US$7 billion was raised in 2017 by over 500 ICOs and double that amount was raised in the first half of 2018 alone.[15] With such eye-popping valuations it is no surprise that ICOs caught the attention of the financial press and captured the imagination of the average investor.

11.3.1   Technical Structure of an ICO

From a technical perspective, the launch of a new token in an ICO need not be complicated. A number of existing crypto protocols including Ethereum, NEO, EOS, Stellar, Cardano, and many others specifically look to enable innovators to create new crypto-assets that 'piggyback' on their existing protocols and ecosystem of stakeholders.

---

[13] Laura Shin, "Here's The Man Who Created ICOs and This Is The New Token He's Backing," Forbes, September 21, 2017, https://www.forbes.com/sites/laurashin/2017/09/21/heres-the-man-who-created-icos-and-this-is-the-new-token-hes-backing/#6b4878d81183.

[14] Block.one would then go on to raise around US$4 billion. Kate Rooney, "A Blockchain Start-up Just Raised $4 Billion, without a Live Product," CNBC, May 31, 2018, https://www.cnbc.com/2018/05/31/a-blockchain-start-up-just-raised-4-billion-without-a-live-product.html.

[15] Daniel Diemers et al., "Initial Coin Offering – A Strategic Perspective" (Strategy& | PwC, June 28, 2018).

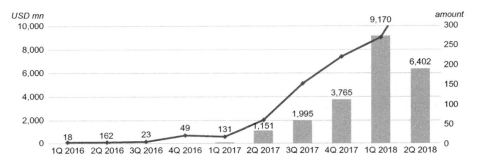

Fig. 11.2 Quarterly ICO number and volume. ICOs have radically increased both the number of crypto-assets in circulation and the total market capitalization of crypto-assets. Source(s): 'CoinDesk ICO Tracker—CoinDesk,' Coindesk, accessed January 31, 2019, https://www.coindesk.com/ico-tracker

For example, the majority of ICOs that took place in 2017 used a technical standard on the Ethereum blockchain called ERC20 (Ethereum Request for Comment). ERC20 provides a suite of open source standards for the creation of a new token. One way to imagine why such a system would be useful is to think of a mall in the physical world where everyone is welcome to come and open a shop. Everything about that shop is standardized including the dimensions, the positioning of the electricity sockets, the security system, and how customers can pay for goods and services. If you have a business idea, all you need to do is show up and launch it at the mall.

Box 11.3   What Are the Most Popular Cryptocurrencies and Tokens?

As mentioned earlier, there are at the time of writing over 2000 different types of cryptocurrencies and tokens, each with different features and particularities. Examples of crypto-assets that are regularly mentioned in the media, along with data valid at the time of writing, include:

- **Bitcoin Cash (BCH)**: Bitcoin Cash is the result of a Bitcoin hard fork in August 2017. Bitcoin Cash aims to solve scalability problems of Bitcoin with an increased block size of 8 MB, as compared to Bitcoin's 1 MB, which provides faster and cheaper transactions. It is intended to be used as a payment system and many of its supporters believe that it more closely resembles the ideology of what Satoshi wanted to accomplish. It uses a proof-of-work consensus mechanism and, similar to Bitcoin, has a total supply of 21 million BCH, of which around 80% are in circulation. At the time of writing, a further split of BCH was taking place between two camps, called Bitcoin ABC and Bitcoin SV, with divergent views on the type of upgrades that needed to be made to the network.

(continued)

Box 11.3 (continued)

- **Cardano (ADA)**: Cardano can be seen as a competitor to Ethereum's platform as it allows its users to develop smart contracts on its own platform. It is a layered blockchain with a first settlement layer combined with a computational layer (whereas Ethereum has them both combined). It uses proof-of-stake and has a total supply of 45 billion ADA of which around 60% are in circulation.
- **Dash (DASH)**: Dash (combination of 'Digital' and 'Cash') was launched in 2014 under the name Xcoin and then Darkcoin before settling on its current name. It is intended to be used as a payment system. Dash is unique as it is a decentralized autonomous organization where a network of masternodes vote on improvements to the network. It also has a privacy option allowing you to send DASH anonymously using what is called a PrivateSend option.[16] It uses proof-of-work (with an additional proof-of-service performed by the masternodes) and has a total supply of around 18 million with approximately 45% in circulation.[17]
- **IOTA (IOT)**: IOTA is unique as it does not use blockchain but rather a different distributed ledger technology called Tangle, where each new transaction is verified by two random nodes that have previously requested a transaction. There are no transaction fees, and as the network gets bigger,[18] the faster transactions can be confirmed. IOTA's focus is to be the transaction settlement and data layer for the internet of things. It has a total supply of 2.8 billion IOTA that are all in circulation.[19]
- **Litecoin (LTC)**: Litecoin shares many features with the Bitcoin and is often considered as the 'Silver' to 'Bitcoin's Gold', mainly because of its larger supply (84 million Litecoins) and speed to generate blocks (4× faster than Bitcoin). Similar to Bitcoin Cash, it is intended to be used as a payments system. It uses proof-of-work and has a total supply of around 84 million LTC of which approximately 70% are in circulation.
- **Monero (XMR)**: Monero is a private cryptocurrency that hides the sender, amount, and receiver in each transaction by using a combination of privacy technologies including ring signatures, ring confidential transactions (RingCT), and stealth addresses. It also does not have a hard block size limit; instead the block size can increase or decrease over time based on demand.[20] It has

(continued)

---

[16] Steven Buchko, "Off to the Races: Crypto's Top 4 Privacy Coins," CoinCentral, January 31, 2018, https://coincentral.com/top-privacy-cryptocurrency-race/.

[17] "Understanding Masternodes," Dash, accessed January 13, 2019, https://docs.dash.org/en/latest/masternodes/understanding.html.

[18] Ibid.

[19] "The Next Generation of Distributed Ledger Technology," IOTA, accessed January 13, 2019, https://www.iota.org/.

[20] "Monero FAQ," The Monero Project, accessed January 13, 2019, https://getmonero.org/get-started/faq/index.html.

Box 11.3 (continued)

become the go-to cryptocurrency for dark web transactions.[21] It uses proof-of-work and it has an initial total supply of around 18 million XMR with around 85% in circulation.[22]

- **NEO (NEO):** NEO is often referred to as the Chinese Ethereum due to the origins of its founding team. It uses a type of proof-of-stake mechanism called Byzantine Fault Tolerance that can support up to 10,000 transactions per second. Similar to Ethereum, it allows users to build smart contracts and uses a 'gas' system to pay for transaction fees. It has a total supply of 100 million NEO of which approximately 65% are in circulation.[23]

- **Ripple (XRP):** Ripple is a payment protocol that functions similarly to a payment system, a remittance network, and a currency exchange. One of its main uses is for inter-bank transactions. It uses a consensus mechanism called Ripple Protocol Consensus Algorithm which is different from the more widely used proof-of-work or proof-of-stake mechanisms. It has a total supply of 100 billion XRP of which around 40% are in circulation.

- **Stellar (XLM):** Stellar aims to be a platform that connects banks, payment systems, and people. It uses its own Stellar consensus protocol and currency called Lumens and wants to allow people (especially in emerging markets) to make payments with traditional currencies while using the efficiency of a cryptocurrency network to lower costs and speed up processing.[24] It had an initial total supply of 100 billion Lumens with a built-in 1% inflation rate where new Lumens are added to the network at a rate of 1% each year.[25]

- **ZCash (ZEC):** ZCash uses a form of zero-knowledge proof called zk-SNARKs and provides a privacy option. Zcash has a public blockchain to show transactions, but hides the amount, sender, and recipient addresses from all. It does this by encrypting the transaction metadata rather than making it publicly available, as Bitcoin does.[26] There is the possibility to provide a viewing key to disclose all transactions for a given address.[27] Unlike other projects, ZCash is run by a private for-profit company and 10% of the monetary base will go to the founders. It has a total supply of 21 million ZEC of which approximately 25% are issued.

---

[21] Steven Buchko, "Off to the Races: Crypto's Top 4 Privacy Coins," CoinCentral, January 31, 2018, https://coincentral.com/top-privacy-cryptocurrency-race/.

[22] "MoneroXMR – A Privacy-Focused Code Fork of Bytecoin," Messari, accessed January 13, 2019, https://messari.io/asset/monero.

[23] "NEO – An Open Network for Smart Economy," NEO, accessed January 13, 2019, https://neo.org/.

[24] Michael J. Casey and Paul Vigna, "Mt. Gox, Ripple Founder Unveils Stellar, a New Digital Currency Project," WSJ (blog), July 31, 2014, https://blogs.wsj.com/moneybeat/2014/07/31/mt-gox-ripple-founder-unveils-stellar-a-new-digital-currency-project/.

[25] "Lumens FAQ," Stellar (blog), accessed January 13, 2019, https://www.stellar.org/lumens/.

[26] "What Are Zk-SNARKs?," Zcash, accessed January 13, 2019, https://z.cash/technology/zksnarks/.

[27] Paige Peterson, "Selective Disclosure & Shielded Viewing Keys," Zcash (blog), January 22, 2018, https://z.cash/blog/viewing-keys-selective-disclosure/.

11.3.2   The Regulatory Treatment of ICOs

While media commentators frequently compare ICOs with IPOs—the initial public offering of a company's equity on an exchange—they differ in several fundamental ways.[28] Most importantly, the regulatory treatment of IPOs is tightly defined by regulatory frameworks, with prescribed steps that must be taken and approvals that must be secured before a listing can take place. These rules are well understood by the investment banks, exchanges, and law firms that guide firms through the IPO process and are tightly enforced by the regulator.

By contrast ICOs, particularly those that took place before 2018, sometimes seemed to be happening in a 'Wild West' environment with little clarity in terms of whose regulatory purview that they sat under and with many founding teams of new crypto-assets seeking only minimal legal input into their multimillion-dollar token sales. This regulatory gray zone means that token holders often do not benefit from the same transparency or protections that an investor in an IPO does. While prospective shareholders have well-defined rights and are able to review highly transparent filings in the lead up to an IPO, there is significant variance in the rights and transparency afforded to prospective token holders in an ICO. Several other significant differences between ICOs and IPOs are listed below (Table 11.1).

Table 11.1 Differences between an ICO and an IPO

ICO	IPO
No specific regulatory framework	Specific and well-defined regulatory framework
Generally early-stage company	Minimum track record and revenue requirements
Funds generally raised for specific purpose	Funds raised for company's long-term development
Limited rights given to token holders	Shareholders have very well-defined and regulated rights
Generally no economic exposure to issuing entity	Provides economic exposure to issuing company
Varied levels of transparency	Prescribed and well-defined levels of transparency

While frequently compared, the characteristics of an ICO differ significantly from those of an IPO
Source(s): PricewaterhouseCoopers, 'Introduction to Token Sales (ICO) Best Practices' (PwC), accessed January 13, 2019, https://www.pwchk.com/en/industries/financial-services/publications/introduction-to-token-sales-ico-best-practices.html

[28] PricewaterhouseCoopers, "Introduction to Token Sales (ICO) Best Practices" (PwC), accessed January 13, 2019, https://www.pwchk.com/en/industries/financial-services/publications/introduction-to-token-sales-ico-best-practices.html.

Unsurprisingly, regulators have been unwilling to allow this uncertainty to persist indefinitely. Most notably, in 2018, the SEC launched a number of enforcement actions against firms that had been involved in ICOs including Airfox, a Boston-based startup that raised approximately $15 million and Paragon, which raised $12 million, stating that their token sale constituted an unlicensed securities issuance.[29] Put another way, this enforcement action argued that the tokens that were issued constituted de facto securities and that as such the issuance was subject to strict regulations similar to those surrounding an IPO. Another notable case saw SEC charges settled out of court by boxer Floyd Mayweather and music producer Khaled Khaled, known as DJ Khaled, for having failed to disclose payments related to their promotion of an ICO.[30]

Box 11.4   When Is a Token a Security?

Every jurisdiction has generally well-defined rules around what is considered a security. In some cases, the definition of what constitutes a security is set out in legislation and in other cases, it is decided by the courts. Let's examine the legal treatment of this question in two jurisdictions: Hong Kong and the United States.

For example, in Hong Kong, where digital tokens offered in an ICO represent equity or ownership interests in a corporation, these tokens may be regarded as 'shares'. For example, token holders may be given shareholders' rights, such as the right to receive dividends and the right to participate in the distribution of the corporation's surplus assets upon winding up.

Where digital tokens are used to create or to acknowledge a debt or liability owed by the issuer, they may be considered as a 'debenture'. For example, an issuer may repay token holders the principal of their investment on a fixed date or upon redemption, with interest paid to token holders. If token proceeds are managed collectively by the ICO scheme operator to invest in projects with an aim to enable token holders to participate in a share of the returns provided by the project, the digital tokens may be regarded as an interest in a 'collective investment scheme' (CIS).

In Hong Kong, shares, debentures, and interests in a CIS are all regarded as 'securities'. Where an ICO involves an offer to the Hong Kong public to acquire 'securities' or participate in a CIS, registration or authorization requirements under the law may be triggered unless an exemption applies.[31]

(continued)

---

[29] "Two Celebrities Charged with Unlawfully Touting Coin Offerings," Securities and Exchange Commission, November 29, 2018, https://www.sec.gov/news/press-release/2018-268.
[30] Ibid.
[31] "Statement on Initial Coin Offerings," Securities & Futures Commission of Hong Kong, September 5, 2017, https://www.sfc.hk/web/EN/news-and-announcements/policy-statements-and-announcements/statement-on-initial-coin-offerings.html.

Box 11.4   (continued)

In the United States, the question of what is, and is not, a security regulated by the Securities and Exchange Commission is determined by the 'Howey Test', a legal framework that emerged from the 1946 case, *SEC v. W. J. Howey Co.*

The case revolved around a complex set of real estate transactions related to a tract of Florida orange groves. The owner of these groves, the eponymous Mr. Howey, allowed individuals to purchase parcels of land and then lease the land back to him under a service arrangement where the maintenance of the land and sale of its produce would be fully managed while the owner themselves would have no right of entry to the land. While purchasers could make other leasing arrangements, the sales materials advertised the significant profits and superior quality of his services. Most purchasers of land under this agreement were not farmers, and in many cases not Florida residents, but rather professionals with little to no agricultural experience.

The SEC filed an injunction against Howey's corporations arguing that this leaseback arrangement constituted an investment contract and was thus a security. The case was ultimately decided by the US Supreme Court, in which the author of the majority opinion, Justice Frank Murphy, established one of the court's earliest tests to ascertain if a given arrangement constitutes and 'investment contract' for the purposes of the Securities Act. Justice Murphy wrote that

[a]n investment contract for purposes of the Securities Act means a contract, transaction or scheme whereby a person invests his money in a common enterprise and is led to expect profits solely from the efforts of the promoter or a third party, it being immaterial whether the shares in the enterprise are evidenced by formal certificates or by nominal interests in the physical assets employed in the enterprise.

In other words, the Howey test says that an investment contract is a security if it is

1. an investment of money
2. in a common enterprise
3. with an expectation of profits
4. solely on the efforts of others

This test has become a very important consideration in the minds of both entrepreneurs and investors as they consider whether the sale of their tokens would meet all four of these criteria and thus require registration with the SEC in order to be legally sold in the United States.

In spite of this enforcement action, much of the regulation around ICOs remains unclear and regulatory treatment of these instruments varies widely depending on each jurisdiction. Some jurisdictions such as China[32]

---

[32] "China Bans Initial Coin Offerings," BBC News, September 5, 2017, sec. Business, https://www.bbc.com/news/business-41157249.

and Korea[33] have taken the hardline position of banning ICOs entirely. Other countries, such as Switzerland, Singapore, Hong Kong, Gibraltar, and Malta, have sought to provide various levels of regulatory clarity. Further regulatory clarity is expected in the short and medium term from regulators around the world, not only in terms of ICOs, but crypto-assets more broadly as well.

11.3.3   Advantages and Challenges of ICOs

In spite of the fluid regulatory environment for the sale of tokens, they represent an interesting new model for the raising of funds to develop a new product or service. Successful ICOs can theoretically enable the rapid 'bootstrapping' of a team to develop an idea while at the same time taking the initial steps toward forming a community of users for the offering. Ideally, they can also democratize aspects of the fundraising process, giving entrepreneurs the ability to raise funding even if they don't have connectivity to venture capital networks and giving small investors equal access to early-stage investments that could have the potential to make a big impact.

In practice though, there are also serious challenges. While the initial vision of the ICO was of a democratized funding process involving the broader public, the role of established venture capitalists and large funds in the ICO ecosystem has grown significantly, with these players often gaining access to significantly discounted 'pre-sales' of tokens.[34]

The lack of regulations to enforce transparency also create challenges for investors. In May 2017, a *Wall Street Journal* investigation of 1450 token sales found 271 projects (which had collectively raised over US$1 billion) with "red flags that include plagiarized investor documents, promises of guaranteed returns and missing or fake executive teams".[35]

In some instances these red flags might be indicative of scams such as PlexCoin, whose founders, according to the SEC's Cyber Unit, promised to give investors a 13-fold return on their investment within one month, but in fact intended to use the funds raised to supplement their own expenses

---

[33] Reuters, "South Korea Bans All New Cryptocurrency Sales," CNBC, September 29, 2017, https://www.cnbc.com/2017/09/28/south-korea-bans-all-new-cryptocurrency-sales.html.

[34] Brady Dale, "Even Investors with Access Want ICO Presale Reform," CoinDesk (blog), November 19, 2017, https://www.coindesk.com/ico-presales-boost-vc-3iq-multicoin.

[35] Shane Shifflett and Coulter Jones, "Buyer Beware: Hundreds of Bitcoin Wannabes Show Hallmarks of Fraud," *Wall Street Journal*, May 17, 2018, sec. Markets, https://www.wsj.com/articles/buyer-beware-hundreds-of-bitcoin-wannabes-show-hallmarks-of-fraud-1526573115.

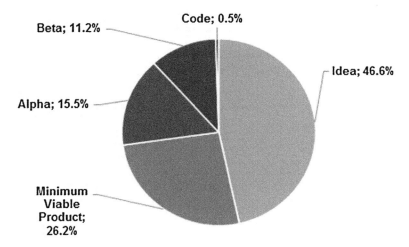

Fig. 11.3 Level of startup maturity at time of ICO. Many ICOs have raised significant funding with little more than an idea. Source(s): Mikhail Mironov and Steven Campbell, 'ICO Market Research Q1 2018,' *ICORATING*, 2018, page 23

including 'home decor projects'.[36] In other instances, actors, including founders, have conspired to actively manipulate their price of tokens in so-called pump and dump schemes.[37]

In other instances, the excitement surrounding crypto-assets may have allowed projects with minimal prospects for success to raise significant funds. In some cases, the team might have lacked the necessary technical expertise to deploy their vision, while in others, they might have lacked an addressable market of sufficient size or a sufficient understanding of the complexity of the market that they were seeking to disrupt. Moreover, unlike startups funded by venture capitalists, where funding is doled out in stages to incent continued performance by the founding team, ICOs tend to raise all of their funding at the beginning of the project's life cycle, reducing the ability of investors to discipline founding teams that exhibit poor performance.

These are likely some of the contributing reasons why, as of July 2018, over 800 crypto-asset projects that had either conducted an ICO or aimed to do so were inactive with near zero valuations.[38]

---

[36] Matt Levine, "SEC Halts a Silly Initial Coin Offering," Bloomberg Opinion, December 5, 2017, https://www.bloomberg.com/opinion/articles/2017-12-05/sec-halts-a-silly-initial-coin-offering.

[37] Eugene Kim, "SEC Warns on ICO Scams, 'Pump and Dump' Schemes," CNBC, August 28, 2017, https://www.cnbc.com/2017/08/28/sec-warns-on-ico-scams-pump-and-dump-schemes.html.

[38] Arjun Kharpal, "Over 800 Cryptocurrencies Are Now Dead as Bitcoin Feels Pressure," CNBC, July 2, 2018, https://www.cnbc.com/2018/07/02/over-800-cryptocurrencies-are-now-dead-as-bitcoin-feels-pressure.html.

Despite some of these many initial hurdles, ICOs may represent an interesting new capital raising mechanism for many blockchain-based companies. As the ICO landscape continues its evolution and becomes more institutionalized and regulated, it will be exciting to see what kind of innovative business models it enables.

12

A High-Level Taxonomy of Crypto-assets

The creation of Bitcoin and subsequent proliferation of crypto-assets have established a financial environment where new digital networks for the exchange of value can be rapidly deployed at relatively low cost. This creates potential opportunities for the establishment of new asset classes, improvements to the liquidity and transparency of existing markets, and the formation of new communities. However, these low barriers to entry mean that the universe of crypto-assets is in constant flux, making it extraordinarily difficult to keep track of the assets within it or to understand how such assets should be valued.

No universally accepted system exists for the categorization of these assets, with many different taxonomies in use. In this chapter, we consider several of the dimensions for the categorization of crypto-assets and present a framework for understanding key differences between crypto-assets based on their intended usage and then examine each high-level crypto-asset category.

12.1   Establishing a Taxonomy of Crypto-assets

The diversity of crypto-asset projects currently being pursued by innovators, combined with the relative newness of this ecosystem, makes the accurate categorization of crypto-assets a challenging task. No useful and sufficiently detailed framework is likely to either establish clean mutually exclusive categories or be collectively exhaustive in categorizing the full universe of tokens.

Several conceivable approaches exist for categorization. The simplest would likely be to categorize crypto-assets based on easily measurable factors such as

© The Author(s) 2019
H. Arslanian, F. Fischer, *The Future of Finance*,
https://doi.org/10.1007/978-3-030-14533-0_12

the specifications of their underlying technical protocols, the size of their active user communities, or their market capitalization. However, while definitive, such categorizations provide little value for those wishing to understand the appropriate legal treatment of a given token or consider the appropriate valuation methodology.

A more complex approach might be to use an existing industry classification system and assign tokens to categories based on the industry that they most closely align to. In such a system, a token designed to support traceability of supply chain provenance would be categorized separately from one designed to establish a network for the monetization of artistic content.

Another way of thinking about the categorization of assets would be to consider the rationale that a token holder would have for possessing a given token and categorizing crypto-assets accordingly. For example, tokens intended to be redeemed in exchange for access to cloud computing services would be categorized differently from those representing loyalty rewards or those serving as speculative investments into a newly created business.

The taxonomy we have chosen to introduce in this chapter draws on multiple sources to present a simplified taxonomy of crypto-assets based primarily on the intended usage and functionalities of the token. In this structure, we first consider whether a token is fungible; in other words, is a given token of the crypto-asset functionally identical to and interchangeable with any other token of the crypto-asset. For example, in the same way that a given US dollar, or a given share of General Electric common stock, is interchangeable with any other, one unit of Bitcoin is identical in its characteristics, usefulness, and valuation. Within the category of fungible tokens, we define three high-level subcategories: tokens intended to be used to facilitate payments (often called cryptocurrencies); tokens intended to serve as investments in financial assets/securities (investment tokens); and tokens intended to be redeemed for a consumable service (utility tokens).

Within the category of non-fungible tokens, each of which may have a unique set of properties, we define two broad subcategories. Tradeable tokens are 'alienable' and can be transferred to a new owner, and non-tradable tokens are inalienable and thus not transferable between owners.

In the pages that follow, we will provide a brief explanation of each of these token categories while providing existing or theoretical examples of each. However, it is important to bear in mind that the universe of crypto-assets is at a nascent stage. If these assets are to gain large-scale adoption, each of these categories is likely need to expand and change, and new dimensions of categorization will need to be considered.

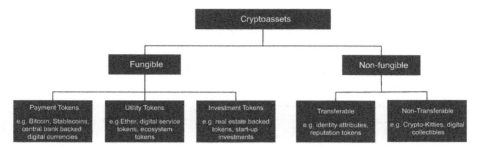

Fig. 12.1 Proposed taxonomy of crypto-assets. Our proposed taxonomy of crypto-assets used in this text classifies tokens based on fungibility and intended usage

12.2 Payment Tokens

A payment token is a crypto-asset whose features are intended to serve as a medium of exchange, a store of value, and a unit for account for a broad array of transactions. In other words, they are cryptographic tokens that use block-chain technology to secure transactions and to control the creation of monetary units. They aim to serve a function similar to that of traditional fiat currencies and their associated payment networks (e.g. debit/credit networks, PayPal, Venmo, remittance networks). For this reason, it is common to hear these assets referred to as 'cryptocurrencies'. However, given the confusion created by frequent conflation of 'cryptocurrencies' with the broader set of crypto-assets and with the strict legal definitions of what constitutes a currency in many jurisdictions, we have chosen to instead use the more generic term of payment tokens. By far the best known example of such an asset is Bitcoin.

For purposes of our classification, we also include stable coins, discussed later in this chapter, as payment tokens. While some stable coins are highly centralized their purpose to facilitate crypto-asset liquidity makes them most suitable for this category.

12.2.1 Characteristics of a Payment Token

While the structure of each payment token is different, they tend to share several general characteristics[1]:

---

[1] Ricky Cove, "Breaking down Bitcoin and Cryptocurrencies: Key Characteristics," Market Realist, November 21, 2017, https://marketrealist.com/2017/11/breaking-down-bitcoin-and-cryptocurrencies-key-characteristics.

- **Irreversible**: Once a transaction has been executed, it is impossible to reverse as no central authority exists to override past transactions. Transactions can only be functionally reversed through a second, mutually agreed upon, transaction between counterparties that mirrors the first transaction. In this way, systems very much resemble the use of physical cash.
- **Pseudo-anonymous or anonymous**: The majority of payment tokens operating today provide some level of anonymity to users (another similarity with the use of physical cash). In the case of Bitcoin and many similar systems, users have pseudo-anonymity, meaning that while transactions are public and traceable, the counterparties in a payment transaction are identified only by a unique string of numbers and letters (their public key) making it difficult to identify the beneficial owner of any given token. In other cases, such as the crypto-asset 'Z-Cash' and 'Monero', additional features have been added in an effort to create 'true' anonymity in which data on the transaction history itself is hidden.
- **Global and always available**: You can transfer or receive cryptocurrencies 24 hours a day, 7 days a week, 365 days a year. Crypto markets don't sleep.
- **Cryptographically Secure**: Blockchain networks use a combination of public and private key cryptography. These are secure and unbreakable based on the technology available today. However, as we will discuss in Chap. 13, there is still a risk that the holder of the token's private keys will be stolen, allowing a malicious actor to steal her funds.
- **Fast**: While some payment tokens, such as Bitcoin, have slower processing times than domestic payment systems (e.g. debit and credit card networks), they offer significantly faster processing times for most cross-border transactions.
- **Inexpensive**: Transferring cryptocurrencies is (almost) free depending on how each blockchain is designed and what type of transaction fees or gas it charges. However, the fees may increase significantly during times of high demand of the network.

12.2.2 Challenges Facing Payment Tokens

Despite their unique characteristics, crypto-payment tokens have faced challenges in achieving consumer adoption. As we noted in our broader assessment of fintech payment innovators, many consumers in advanced economies do not have a strong appetite to change their current payment methods. Crypto-assets aiming to serve as widely accepted payment vehicles face all of these challenges, as well as a few unique issues that are worth noting:

- **Poor Usability**: Despite some improvements, sending and receiving crypto-assets is still not a very user-friendly process and the use of public keys and crypto wallets is difficult to understand for the average person. Usability improvements are likely to continue, as is public understanding of crypto-assets, but this is unlikely to occur overnight. Even in the case of transformative technologies like the internet, broader public adoption is a process that occurs over many years, if not decades.
- **High Volatility**: Crypto-assets exhibit high volatility when compared to fiat currencies. While this may be desirable for speculators and traders, it creates serious challenges for both consumers and merchants seeking to use the asset as a unit of account and a means of exchange.
- **Irreversibility**: While the irreversibility of crypto-asset transactions may be desirable in some instances, it is also a source of customer concern. If you lose your bank PIN or make a wrong transaction, you can always call the bank to get help. If you lose the private keys or transfer to an incorrect crypto address, those crypto-assets are gone forever. There is no universal helpline for crypto-assets!

12.2.3   Regulation of Payment Tokens

As with most areas of the emerging crypto-asset ecosystem, the use of tokens for the purpose of payments lacks regulatory clarity and regulatory treatment of these instruments often varies significantly from jurisdiction to jurisdiction. In spite of this, there is a growing consensus among regulatory authorities that supports the view of the Financial Action Task Force (an intergovernmental organization founded in 1989 to combat money laundering) that crypto-asset-based payment service providers should be subject to the same obligations as their non-crypto peers.[2]

In most jurisdictions, this would mean that any organization facilitating the exchange of payment tokens would be bound to observe a host of AML, KYC, and combating terrorist financing (CTF) regulations. Moreover, many jurisdictions that have issued rulings or guidance on the matter have specified that the exchange of crypto-based payment tokens for fiat should be subject to all AML requirements.

These regulations are an important step in creating a smoother interface between payment token users and incumbent financial institutions. Many banks

---

[2] Barbara Stettner, "Cryptocurrency AML Risk Considerations – Allen & Overy," Allen & Overy, accessed January 13, 2019, http://www.allenovery.com/publications/en-gb/lrrfs/cross-border/Pages/Cryptocurrency-AML-risk-considerations.aspx.

have serious concerns about their ability to effectively enforce AML, KYC, and CTF regulations on businesses in the crypto-asset ecosystem, particularly exchanges (more on these later) who facilitate the trading of crypto for fiat.

The concerns of incumbent banks stem from a perceived higher level of difficulty complying with identification and monitoring requirements (particularly given the anonymity offered by many crypto-payment tokens). Also relevant is a perceived increased risk that the payment tokens being exchanged for fiat have been used in financial crime, such as the trafficking of illicit goods on a marketplace such as Silk Road, or have been illegitimately acquired via hacking, identity theft, ransomware, or some other illegal method.[3]

As a result, many financial institutions will categorically refuse to provide banking services to organizations facilitating the use of payment tokens, even if regulators have clearly stated that the use of these instruments is technically legal, on the grounds that they may inadvertently facilitate the violation of AML, KYC, or CTF regulations, placing them at risk of a significant fine.[4]

However, given that global money laundering transactions are estimated to total US$1–2 trillion a year,[5] many estimated times the total market capitalization of all crypto-assets, it is clear that crypto transactions are at worst a drop in the bucket of total global money laundering. Moreover, Danske Bank, which recently put aside US$2.7 billion for fines related to facilitating over US$200 billion in suspicious transactions through their Estonian branch over a nine-year period,[6,7] serves as an instructive lesson that facilitating any sort of payment comes at a risk of fines.

12.2.4   Stable Coins

These impediments to exchanging payment tokens for fiat money have created demand among some stakeholders in the crypto-asset ecosystem for a unique form of payment token that is commonly called a 'stable coin'.

---

[3] Ibid.

[4] Ibid.

[5] "UNODC Estimates That Criminals May Have Laundered US$ 1.6 Trillion in 2009," UNODC, October 25, 2011, https://www.unodc.org/unodc/en/press/releases/2011/October/unodc-estimates-that-criminals-may-have-laundered-usdollar-1.6-trillion-in-2009.html.

[6] Frances Schwartzkopff, "Danske Bank Puts €2.4bn aside for Money-Laundering Case," Independent.ie, accessed January 24, 2019, https://www.independent.ie/business/world/danske-bank-puts-2-4bn-aside-for-moneylaundering-case-37592181.html.

[7] Juliette Garside, "Is Money-Laundering Scandal at Danske Bank the Largest in History?," *The Guardian*, September 21, 2018, sec. Business, https://www.theguardian.com/business/2018/sep/21/is-money-laundering-scandal-at-danske-bank-the-largest-in-history.

The purpose of these instruments is to provide a crypto-payment token whose value is linked to that of a reference asset outside the crypto-asset ecosystem, such as US dollars or gold. Typically, the stable coin token will be backed, in whole or in part, by its reference asset with a promise from the issuer that it can be redeemed for that asset at any time.

An imperfect analogy would be the early forms of paper notes issued by a bank or central bank that were backed by gold. These notes often promised to pay the bearer the equivalent in gold when presented to a bank. Carrying a piece of paper that was accepted as being worth a specified amount in gold was more practical than carrying the gold itself. At any time, the bearer could go to a bank, present that piece of paper, and receive the gold equivalent instead. The same is true for stable coins.

One of the main purposes of these instruments is to provide a stand-in for a low volatility asset, enabling crypto traders to move away from volatile crypto-assets into a stable coin without the need to leave the crypto ecosystem. This is not dissimilar to a trader of traditional stocks or bonds who might respond to significant market volatility by liquidating a portion of her holdings to be kept in treasuries until markets stabilize. Given the high volatility of crypto-assets and the difficulties many stakeholders face in accessing fiat money via traditional financial institutions (discussed earlier in this chapter), the stable coin can serve as a desirable 'safe-haven' asset.[8]

Furthermore, many payment tokens such as Bitcoin are not currently suitable for day-to-day purchases given their high volatility. Stable coins help address this problem, making it easier for individuals to pay for goods denominated in a fiat currency using crypto-assets and to make cross-border transfers without fear of volatility.

The most prominent example of this is a crypto token called 'Tether', which aims to maintain a constant value of one US dollar. According to company documents, Tether does this by backing each unit of their payment token with a bank deposit of one dollar for each of the 2.1 billion units of Tether as of December 2018.[9]

Obviously, confidence in the redeemability of a stable coin is central to its usefulness. In the case of Tether, the token has been the object of intense conjecture, plagued by allegations that the asset is not fully backed by

---

[8] https://www.blockchain.com/ru/static/pdf/StablecoinsReportFinal.pdf.
[9] "Tether," accessed January 13, 2019, https://tether.to/.

Name	Price	Market Cap	Market Cap (%)	Volume (24h)	Velocity of Money (%)	Volume (%)
Tether (USDT)	$1.00	$1,774,299,364.15	78.34%	$2,204,901,634.72	124.27%	96.52%
Paxos Standard Token (PAX)	$1.01	$107,400,948.54	4.74%	$39,546,774.30	36.82%	1.73%
TrueUSD (TUSD)	$1.01	$174,193,464.74	7.69%	$27,097,371.95	15.56%	1.19%
Gemini Dollar (GUSD)	$1.01	$11,049,010.22	0.49%	$7,375,036.84	66.75%	0.32%
Dai (DAI)	$1.02	$68,911,842.66	3.04%	$4,086,861.22	5.93%	0.18%
USD Coin (USDC)	$1.00	$127,871,637.67	5.65%	$1,087,015.21	0.85%	0.05%
bitUSD (BITUSD)	$1.01	$10,688,635.83	0.47%	$165,425.33	1.55%	0.01%
nUSD (NUSD)	$1.00	$1,498,086.52	0.07%	$92,283.96	6.16%	0.00%
		$2,264,863,980.10	100.00%	$2,284,352,403.52	6.16%	100.00%

Fig. 12.2 Top stable coins by US dollar market capitalization (2019). Recent years have seen a proliferation of stable coins using a variety of reference assets and technical approaches. Source(s): 'Stablecoin Index,' accessed January 31, 2019, https://stablecoinindex.com/marketcap

reserves and that its reserves have been used to manipulate the price of Bitcoin.[10] There are numerous other such stable coins backed by US dollars in the market today (e.g. True USD, Paxos, Gemini), and they all operate in somewhat similar ways. If the role of these assets continues to grow, increased transparency and a consistent and credible auditing and assurance framework will likely be required to ensure investor confidence.

It should be noted that not all stable coin tokens choose to use a fiat currency as their reference asset, with some choosing instead to use a physical commodity, most frequently gold. Stable coins of this type are less common than those pegged to fiat currency and add a level of complication to our taxonomy. This is because they may serve a dual function, straddling the categories of payment instrument and investment instrument. As a result, unlike other payment tokens, they may be considered a security by regulatory agencies.

There is also a subset of stable coins that take a more decentralized approach, which does not involve directly holding fiat currencies. While a detailed exploration of these approaches, and their strengths and weaknesses, is beyond the scope of this book, it provides evidence of the strong demand for stable coin assets and the active ongoing experimentation.

---

[10] Matt Robinson and Tom Schoenberg, "Bitcoin-Rigging Criminal Probe Focused on Tie to Tether," *Bloomberg News*, November 20, 2018, https://www.bloomberg.com/news/articles/2018-11-20/bitcoin-rigging-criminal-probe-is-said-to-focus-on-tie-to-tether.

Box 12.1   Are Stable Tokens a Security?

There is an ongoing debate as to whether tokens backed by liquid assets (e.g. US dollars) should be securities. A good example is Tether which tracks the value of the US dollar. In theory, each Tether is backed 1:1 with reserves of US dollars and the price should always be US$1 or very close to US$1.[11]

Each of these stable coins has different features and related risks, which complicates how they are characterized. For example, the structure that they adopt could be based on market consensus alone, be asset backed, operate as structured products or money market funds, reflect debt instruments or stored value facilities, or use third-party price stabilization activities. Some can even be decentralized.

Extreme care is required in using stable coins. While they can serve a valuable purpose, some may be considered securities in certain jurisdictions and many are likely to be subject to some level of regulation. In certain jurisdictions, price stabilization activity could also constitute unlawful asset price manipulation. Customers may also be confused as to which assets they hold (fiat vs. stable coin), particularly if the names are similar. This being said, stable coins have a role to play in the broader crypto ecosystem and their usage is likely to increase in the coming years.[12]

12.3   Utility Tokens

Utility tokens are crypto-assets designed to be consumed and to provide their user with some specific utility. For example, a consumer token could be used to access a service, offered by a certain blockchain. That might be the usage of cloud storage, it could be a loyalty token redeemable for a physical good such as a coffee, or it might provide access to a specific piece of content such as an online multiplayer video game. These assets can theoretically enable a range of benefits for consumers, allowing them greater flexibility in coordination with the exchange of consumption rights.[13]

Perhaps the most well-known example of a utility token in use today is Ether, the native token of the Ethereum blockchain. As we discussed in greater detail earlier in this book, Ethereum seeks to provide a decentralized and shared world computer where anyone can use Ether tokens, sometimes referred to as 'gas', to run segments of code called smart contracts. Other blockchains such as NEO and Ethereum Classic exhibit similar characteristics.

---

[11] "Tether – FAQs," accessed January 13, 2019, https://tether.to/faqs/.

[12] Mark Austen et al., "ASIFMA Best Practices for Digital Asset Exchanges" (ASIFMA, June 2018), https://www.lw.com/thoughtLeadership/ASIFMA-best-practices-digital-asset-exchanges.

[13] "Global Digital Finance Code of Conduct: Taxonomy for Cryptographic Assets" (Global Digital Finance, October 2018), https://www.gdf.io/wp-content/uploads/2018/10/0003_GDF_Taxonomy-for-Cryptographic-Assets_Web-151018.pdf.

Utility tokens encompass a vast array of potential use cases and should arguably be regulated under whatever consumer protection regulation governs the goods, services, or media being consumed by the user. Unfortunately, while regulatory statements to date have largely held this to be true for platforms that *currently* provide access to consumable goods, services, or media, things can be a little bit more complicated for those platforms who only plan to do so, but are not yet operational.

The reason for this is best explained through the analogy of a private club. Imagine a consumer token that is used to pay membership dues in a private club that provides access to a range of facilities including a golf course, restaurant, and steam room. The token provides access to the club, but does not confer rights to a portion of the club's income or a claim on the club's assets. Clearly the token is not a security, right? Well, it turns out that, at least in some jurisdictions, especially in the United States, that depends on whether the club has already been built.

In the landmark 1961 case of *California Silver Hills Country Club v. Sobieski*, a California judge ruled that the use of a membership plan to finance the construction of a new, for-profit country club constituted a solicitation of risk capital and thus required registration as a security issuance. The judge noted that only by a member risking capital alongside other members could the benefits of club membership be created. Interestingly, the conclusion of this case differs from the previously discussed Howey test because even though members of the prospective club do not stand to profit directly from the success of that club, the fundraising scheme is still considered a securities issuance.[14]

The challenge this poses in the United States to issuing a consumer token is clear. While selling such a token for an existing service likely does not constitute a securities sale, the selling of such a token to fund the creation of a prospective service may well be a securities issuance and therefore subject to much more extensive regulatory scrutiny.

Efforts to clarify the regulatory landscape for utility tokens in the United States and abroad are underway, but in many jurisdictions, there is no clear timeline to the delivery of regulatory guidance. It should therefore be expected that treatment will differ from region to region, and that in many jurisdictions, regulatory uncertainty regarding utility tokens will persist for the foreseeable future.

---

[14] June Lin, "Is a Country Club Membership a Security? | Primerus," Primerus, accessed January 13, 2019, http://www.primerus.com/business-law-news/is-a-country-club-membership-a-security.htm.

12.4   Investment Tokens

Crypto-investment tokens are instruments whose primary function is to serve as a financial investment for the holder of the token and thus are considered securities (or in some cases commodities) under most regulatory regimes. These can include both instances where pre-existing physical assets or legal rights (such as a bond or a share of stock) are 'tokenized' on a blockchain, and instances where new investment opportunities are created that are native to the crypto-asset ecosystem (including a significant number of ICOs). We will explore both in the following section.

12.4.1   Tokenization of New Investment Instruments

In addition to facilitating payment or providing a utility function, crypto-assets can act as investment instruments for the formation of capital around a new venture. For example, a promising startup seeking funding from investors might choose to sell equity in the form of an investment token. In theory, this could enable the firm to involve fewer intermediaries in the raising of capital, give early stage investors access to improved liquidity, streamline corporate actions like dividends, and could even democratize access to investments in the startup, allowing average people to purchase small stakes, where once only venture capitalists or the very wealthy could make investments.

This is a compelling narrative, but unfortunately, implementing it is a good deal more complicated. In most jurisdictions, before a security can be sold to the general public, it needs to be registered with the relevant regulatory authorities. This process is typically lengthy, costly, and complex, but is designed to protect small-time investors saving for their retirement. Regulators are concerned that average people who lack specialized training in investments, and lacking sufficient funds to endure a significant financial loss without experiencing financial hardship, may be persuaded by promises of vast returns to invest in high risk or poorly conceived ventures.

Fortunately, for those wishing to raise capital via the sale of a newly created investment tokens, 'private placement' exceptions exist in most jurisdictions. These allow securities to be sold without the same onerous registration requirements placed on securities issuances to some types of investors and the general public, if certain requirements are met.

The most common of such requirements is ensuring that the security is issued only to 'accredited investors', also sometimes called 'professional investors'. These are individuals deemed sufficiently sophisticated and wealthy enough to understand and evaluate the risks of their investments and to endure the consequences if the investment fails to meet expectations. Requirements to be considered an accredited investor differ from jurisdiction to jurisdiction, in some cases being determined by income and in others by liquid net worth, but if the token offering limits marketing only to such individuals, it will likely be exempt from registration, or subject to much less onerous requirements.

Based on these exemptions, many crypto companies have decided to offer their tokens only to such professional/accredited investors, even if they themselves do not consider the token a security. Given existing regulatory uncertainty, this limits their exposure to regulatory action in the event that regulator comes to a different conclusion. This strategy was particularly common in the United States, where the SEC chairman stated publicly that the commission viewed most ICOs as securities.[15] For example, mobile messenger app Telegram initially planned to market their token offering to the general public, but subsequently abandoned this plan, choosing instead to secure funding exclusively from private placements.[16]

While such an approach solves some problems, it also opens new ones. For example, most token ecosystems require a critical mass of users to be sustainable. If funds are raised from a broad community of retail investors, it could create a natural base from which to build user engagement. By contrast, building such an ecosystem with only professional investors and not end users can be a challenge. Restrictions on public ownership may also limit the value of a token to accredited investors, limiting the range of potential buyers for the tokens in secondary markets.

12.4.2   Tokenization of Pre-existing Investment Instruments

In addition to facilitating the creation of tokens that act as new investment instruments, blockchain technology enables the 'tokenization' of existing investment instruments. This is another way of saying that legal rights to the underlying instrument are represented by an entry in the distributed ledger of a blockchain network. This allows the asset to be freely traded between network participants via updates to the distributed ledger, and in some cases features such as the distribution of dividends and voting rights might also be handled via

[15] Kate Rooney, "SEC Chairman Clayton Says Agency Won't Change Definition of a Security," *CNBC*, June 6, 2018, https://www.cnbc.com/2018/06/06/sec-chairman-clayton-says-agency-wont-change-definition-of-a-security.html.

[16] Jon Russell and Mike Butcher, "Telegram's Billion-Dollar ICO Has Become a Mess," TechCrunch, May 2018, http://social.techcrunch.com/2018/05/03/telegrams-billion-dollar-ico-has-become-a-mess/.

the blockchain. In all other ways, the instrument continues to have the same properties as it would if it were traded on a more traditional centralized exchange or through a peer-to-peer 'over-the-counter' (OTC) arrangement.

Theoretically there is no limit to the assets that could be tokenized, including financial instruments such as equities, bonds, and derivatives or commodities like gold, silver, wheat, or even orange juice. In practice though, these instruments are already actively traded on long-standing exchanges around the world, making it difficult for blockchain-based solutions to displace their network effects (at least in the near term).

Where blockchain can potentially be more disruptive is in assets where existing markets are informal, disconnected, or inefficient. While gold and oil are highly standardized products that are actively traded and have global prices, markets for less standardized assets like fine art or diamonds are not. As a result, these assets can suffer from an 'illiquidity discount' where the price of the asset is negatively affected by their inability to be easily bought and sold. Advocates argue that tokenization of these assets would facilitate improved liquidity by increasing asset transparency and reducing the cost of price discovery.[17]

For example, one could tokenize the shares of a holding company that owns a piece of real estate, an asset that has traditionally suffered from significant illiquidity. Instruments for doing this already exist in traditional markets, most notably real estate investment trusts (REIT) that offer investors exposure to fractional assets; however, these organizational forms are expensive to establish and are typically only used for very large properties. If blockchain networks for fractional ownership of tokenized real estate could be deployed cheaply and at sufficient scale, it could enable the sale of fractional ownership in a much smaller asset, such as a personal home.[18] A recent example of real estate tokenization in action is the Aspen Digital Security Token, which enables investors to own an indirect equity stake in the St. Regis Aspen Resort in Colorado.[19]

Tokenization may also serve a purpose in the case of particular kinds of funds. Accredited and institutional investors will often allocate money to venture capital and private equity funds in addition to their more traditional allocations of capital to stocks and bonds. The underlying assets that these private equity and venture capital funds invest in are highly illiquid, so the fund will typically

---

[17] "Global Digital Finance Code of Conduct: Taxonomy for Cryptographic Assets" (Global Digital Finance, October 2018), https://www.gdf.io/wp-content/uploads/2018/10/0003_GDF_Taxonomy-for-Cryptographic-Assets_Web-151018.pdf.

[18] Helen Zhao, "Own Shares of Brooklyn Building with Tokens Blockchain Real Estate," March 19, 2018, https://www.cnbc.com/2018/03/19/own-shares-of-brooklyn-building-with-tokens-blockchain-real-estate.html.

[19] "The Aspen Digital Security Token," Indiegogo Token Sales, accessed January 13, 2019, https://blockchain.indiegogo.com/projects/aspen/.

require allocations to be 'locked in', often for years at a time. Sales of the end investors' capital are possible today in so-called secondary markets, which lack liquidity and transactions often require extensive paperwork.

Having marketplaces of tokenized secondary sales may make it easier for investors to buy and sell such fund units. It may also allow individuals holding large allocations of private stock (e.g. the founding team of a fast-growing startup) to more efficiently realize sales of that stock prior to an initial public offering (IPO). Indeed, NASDAQ has already piloted such an offering in its NASDAQ Private Market service which enables the issuance and transfer of the shares of privately held companies.[20]

Additionally, tokenization of physical assets can also enable fungibility for assets that are not fungible in the physical world. For example, in the physical world an expensive painting generally can only have one owner, but when tokenized, ownership can be distributed more easily among many individuals. For example, in June 2018, fractional ownership of Andy Warhol's painting '14 Small Electric Chairs' was sold using a blockchain platform that allowed buyers to each own a fraction of the painting.[21]

It is important, however, to temper our excitement for such solutions. The tokenization of an existing investment instrument on a blockchain will not in and of itself automatically create more liquidity or investor interest. There are many traditional marketplaces that have not been successful in delivering those improvements. Instead, arguments in favor of such systems rely on uncertain assumptions that tokenizing the asset on a blockchain would expand the pool of possible investors, for example, by creating greater asset transparency, greater connectivity across regions, or resolving specific issues of mistrust between buyers and sellers. It is also important to remember that the successful design of any such token would be highly complex, in some cases requiring embedded features such as disclosure requirements, transfer or ownership restrictions, corporate actions, and so on.

While these barriers are significant, interest remains. A growing number of major players in the capital markets are experimenting with blockchain, with NASDAQ's head of Blockchain Product Management, Jon Toll, saying that they are 'all in' on using blockchain to enable their transactions and to support external marketplaces that are moving into blockchain-based solutions.[22]

---

[20] Brandon Tepper, "Building on the Blockchain: Nasdaq's Vision of Innovation" (Nasdaq, March 2016), https://business.nasdaq.com/Docs/Blockchain%20Report%20March%202016_tcm5044-26461.pdf.

[21] Molly Jane Zuckerman, "Andy Warhol Painting to Be Sold via Blockchain in 'World's First' Crypto Art Auction," Cointelegraph, June 7, 2018, https://cointelegraph.com/news/andy-warhol-painting-to-be-sold-via-blockchain-in-world-s-first-crypto-art-auction.

[22] Jordan French, "Nasdaq Exec: Exchange Is 'All-In' on Using Blockchain Technology," *TheStreet*, April 23, 2018, https://www.thestreet.com/investing/nasdaq-all-in-on-blockchain-technology-14551134.

> **Box 12.2   How Are Crypto-assets Valued?**
>
> The highly varied nature of crypto-assets creates challenges for their valuation, with the unique characteristics of each token informing the appropriate valuation technique. While an entire book could be written on the methodologies and challenges of valuing crypto-assets, we present here a generalized high-level framework:
>
> - Payment tokens are typically priced by the traditional metrics of supply and demand used in the valuation of currencies. For example, given there are only a limited number of Bitcoin in circulation and if there is more demand, then the price of a Bitcoin should increase.
> - Investment tokens can be valued using traditional financial techniques. The specific technique will differ depending on the underlying asset or financial instrument represented by the token. For example, the appropriate valuation technique or a piece of real estate would differ from that of a bar of gold or a share of equity.
> - Utility tokens are probably the most complicated to price today as there are no established frameworks to do so. There are a number of individuals who have started to develop frameworks to value the economics of utility tokens.[23] These are generally a mix of traditional valuation methods that try to integrate the network effects of platforms and the particularities of blockchain technology. If the popularity of consumer tokens accelerates, the valuation methodologies for these assets are likely to evolve significantly.

12.5   Non-fungible Tradable Tokens

Non-fungible tradable crypto-assets are tokens that are unique and not fungible. These tokens use the properties of blockchain technology to facilitate more transparent and enforceable scarcity of a digital asset by allowing that scarcity to be easily verified and its ownership transferable.[24] For example, a Bitcoin is equivalent to any other Bitcoin. But a non-fungible tradable token is unique and can be mathematically proven so by using blockchain technology.

A good example has been the buzz created by a system of non-fungible tradable tokens called CryptoKitties, built on the Ethereum blockchain. The game allows users to buy and 'breed' virtual cats, with unique sets of properties. When launched, they became so popular that they represented 25% of traffic on the Ethereum network and resulted in a slowing down of the network.[25]

---

[23] Chris Burniske and Jack Tatar, *Crypto-assets: The Innovative Investor's Guide to Bitcoin and Beyond* (McGraw Hill Professional, 2017).

[24] Phil Glazer, "An Overview of Non-Fungible Tokens," Hacker Noon, April 1, 2018, https://hacker-noon.com/an-overview-of-non-fungible-tokens-5f140c32a70a.

[25] "CryptoKitties Cripple Ethereum Blockchain," December 5, 2017, sec. Technology, https://www.bbc.com/news/technology-42237162.

In many ways, CryptoKitties is no different than other traditional physical or digital card sets such as 'Magic the Gathering' cards, 'Pokémon' cards, or even baseball cards. In each case, the cards provide value to their owner, but are also tradable with other card collectors. Unfortunately, in traditional centralized systems, the issuer of the cards may be tempted to debase the cards' value. For example, they might do this by selling many copies of a highly prized card, thereby making it less rare and less valuable, or by unilaterally changing the rules of the game to undermine the value of existing cards and generate demand for new cards now on sale.

CryptoKitties seeks to solve this problem by using blockchain to create firm limitations on the issuance of each cards and establishing the provable uniqueness of each kitty using a non-fungible token protocol called ERC-721.[26] In the words of the game maker's marketing materials, "CryptoKitties is a game centered around breedable, collectible, and oh-so-adorable creatures we call CryptoKitties! Each cat is one-of-a-kind and 100% owned by you; it cannot be replicated, taken away, or destroyed".[27]

Each kitty has a unique visual appearance determined by its immutable 'genes' which are stored in a smart contract on the Ethereum blockchain. Players can 'breed' their cats to create new kitties whose physical appearance (phenotype) is determined by their parents' combined genes (genotype). The founding team notes that they are seeking to create "an exciting, self-sustaining community where users can create new collectibles and trade them".[28]

In theory, such non-fungible tokens can be created for any type of digital collectible and at the time of writing, there were numerous projects using non-fungible tradable tokens.

One example is Decentraland, which has a finite, traversable, 3D virtual space called LAND, a non-fungible digital asset maintained in an Ethereum smart contract. LAND is divided into parcels that are identified by Cartesian coordinates (x, y). These 10 m-by-10 m parcels are permanently owned by members of the community and are purchased using MANA, Decentraland's cryptocurrency token. This gives users full control over the environments and applications that they create, which can range from anything like static 3D scenes to more interactive applications or games. Each LAND token includes

---

[26] "ERC-721," accessed January 13, 2019, http://erc721.org/.

[27] CryptoKitties, "CryptoKitties | Collect and Breed Digital Cats!," CryptoKitties, accessed January 13, 2019, https://www.cryptokitties.co.

[28] "CryptoKitties: Collectible and Breedable Cats Empowered by Blockchain Technology," White Paper (CryptoKitties, n.d.).

a record of its attributes, its owner, and a reference to a content description file or parcel manifest that describes and encodes the content the owner wishes to serve on her land.[29]

Non-fungible tradable tokens have a broad range of potential applications related to gaming, art, and media. While we are still in the early days of experimentation with such tokens, there is significant room for innovation.

12.6   Non-fungible Non-tradable Digital Assets

The final category in our taxonomy of crypto-assets are non-fungible non-tradable tokens. You might be wondering why such a token would exist given that the entire point of a blockchain is to facilitate the transfer of assets between users.

The answer is that in some cases the immutability of all blockchains provides value, but the ability to transfer a token would render it meaningless. Take for example a token designed to provide a proof of reputation. Such a token might aggregate reviews of a small business that could be proven to come from real users of that business. Such a token could help overcome prospective customers' concerns about fake reviews, but obviously it would not be credible if a business with a poor reputation could simply purchase a reputation token from a business with a good reputation.

One example of such a project currently under development is the Decentralized Reputation System (DREP). DREP aims to create a "decentralized reputation ecosystem comprising of a public chain, a reputation-based protocol and the tools for Internet platforms to leverage its power". In doing so, it hopes to solve a host of problems that plague reputation-based online systems today, such as the proliferation of fake reviews.[30]

Another potential use case for non-fungible, non-transferable tokens is identity. Blockchain-based tokens could enable a user to more effectively prove their identity attributes—for example their age, country of residence, or that they hold a given certification—within an online environment. In theory, such a system could give users improved control over their personal data, and allow them greater discretion in the identity attributes that they choose to share with counterparties.

---

[29] "Decentraland," accessed January 13, 2019, https://decentraland.org/.
[30] "Decentralized Reputation System," White Paper (DREP Foundation, n.d.).

One example of such a system under development today is Sovrin. Sovrin is a nonprofit foundation dedicated to the establishment of a new online identity system, that, in the words of the founding team, "bring[s] the trust, personal control, and ease-of-use of analog IDs—like driver's licenses and ID cards—to the Internet". The system is designed to be 'self-sovereign' in that "the individual identity holder can access and use their credentials on the Sovrin Network whenever and however they please".[31]

These non-fungible, non-tradable tokens have the potential to fulfill a range of exciting use cases; however, the many projects in this space are currently at a nascent stage. Only time will tell which projects (if any) will be successful in scaling and achieving broad-based adoption.

---

[31] "Home," Sovrin, accessed January 13, 2019, https://sovrin.org/.

13

The Crypto-asset Ecosystem

Blockchain technology enables a significant reduction in the number of inter-mediaries in the financial ecosystem. It enables counterparties to engage in direct peer-to-peer transactions. However, this does not remove the need for a number of specialized players to exist in order for crypto-assets to fulfill some of their more complex and ambitious goals. As with any other financial system, crypto-assets require an ecosystem to flourish. In this chapter, we will explore a number of critical aspects of that emerging ecosystem.

Our simplified view of the crypto-asset ecosystem has six key stakeholders: issuers; miners; investors/users; platforms, wallets, and custodians; advisory and consumer services; and governments/policymakers/regulators. In Chap. 10, we covered the relationship between issuers and miners, and in Chaps. 11 and 12, we focused extensively on the relationships between the issuers and inves-tors/users, as well as on the relationships between issuers and governments/policymakers/regulators.

Therefore, in this chapter, we will explore the role played by platforms (pri-marily exchanges), followed by wallets and custodians, before briefly consid-ering the nascent but rapidly evolving world of advisory and consumer services for the crypto-asset ecosystem.

13.1 Crypto-asset Exchanges

Any asset class, including crypto-assets, needs a marketplace where they can be bought and sold. Equities are sold on stock exchanges like the New York Stock Exchange or the London Stock Exchange and the crypto-asset ecosystem

© The Author(s) 2019
H. Arslanian, F. Fischer, *The Future of Finance*,
https://doi.org/10.1007/978-3-030-14533-0_13

has its equivalent service providers. These exchanges come in many shapes and sizes, but can be broadly separated into two categories: centralized exchanges and decentralized exchanges.

13.1.1   Centralized Crypto-asset Exchanges

Centralized exchanges operate in a way that is not dissimilar to the operations of an international stock exchange. They match buyers and sellers of crypto-assets, acting as the middleman for all trades without revealing the identity of the buyer or seller. In many cases, they may also serve as the custodian of the assets, a role that will be discussed further later in this chapter.

There are two main types of centralized exchanges: fiat-to-crypto and crypto-to-crypto. A fiat-to-crypto exchange allows a user to deposit fiat funds in their account (e.g. USD, EUR, JPY) and convert that into the desired crypto-asset (Fig. 13.1).

By contrast, a crypto-to-crypto exchange does not touch fiat currencies and only facilitates the exchange of one crypto-asset for another. In order to use such a service, a user must send a crypto-asset to the exchange, typically Bitcoin or Ether (which she may have gotten from a fiat-to-crypto exchange or potentially from mining), and use that crypto-asset to buy other crypto-assets.

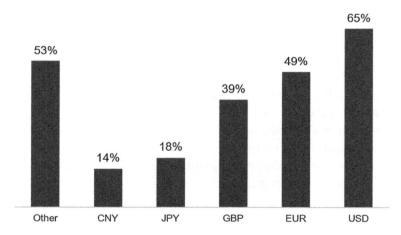

Fig. 13.1 Percentage of crypto exchanges supporting national currencies. US dollars are the most frequently supported currency on fiat-to-crypto exchanges, but options exist for a wide array of other currencies. Source(s): Garrick Hileman and Michel Rauchs, 'Global Cryptocurrency Benchmarking Study' (Cambridge Centre for Alternative Finance, 2017), https://www.jbs.cam.ac.uk/fileadmin/user_upload/research/centres/alternative-finance/downloads/2017-04-20-global-cryptocurrency-benchmarking-study.pdf, page 32

To date, specific regulations for crypto exchanges are limited, which may pose a number of risks for users. A report released by the New York Attorney General in September 2018 on crypto exchanges found that many crypto exchanges lacked sufficient internal controls with regard to conflicts of interest, market manipulation, and protection of customer funds.[1]

In an attempt to address these issues, a number of industry-led initiatives are underway aimed at establishing best practices for crypto exchanges. For example, the Asia Securities Industry & Financial Markets Association (ASIFMA), an independent Asia-focused trade association, published a report with best practices that crypto exchanges could adopt. It covers listing and regulatory recommendations, as well as suggestions for KYC/AML and custodial practices.[2] This is a good example of how best practices from the traditional financial services industry are increasingly being transferred into the crypto-asset ecosystem. This is also an area in constant flux so it is likely that by the time this book is published, there will be more regulatory clarity on crypto exchanges.

Box 13.1   Do Crypto Exchanges Need KYC?

Some levels of KYC procedures to ensure customer identification have become standard practice across fiat-to-crypto exchanges, especially for those that are looking to build a long-term institutional-grade business. However, there are still some crypto-to-crypto exchanges or decentralized exchanges that operate without any formal KYC mechanisms.

Although there may not be today any strict regulatory requirements that require crypto-to-crypto exchanges to conduct such KYC procedures, it is likely that such exchanges will eventually voluntarily choose to adopt such practices, in part to attract large institutional investors as such large clients need to be comfortable with the level of compliance of their counterparties.

Compliance with AML and CTF requirements is an area of intense focus for the broader financial services industry and there are serious concerns that crypto-assets could be used to facilitate new vectors of illicit financial flows for several reasons:

- Crypto-assets may allow greater anonymity than traditional noncash payment methods.
- The global reach of crypto-assets means that responsibility for AML/CTF compliance and supervision/enforcement may be unclear.
- Components of a crypto-asset system may be located in jurisdictions that do not have adequate AML/CTF controls.[3]

(continued)

---

[1] Barbara D. Underwood, "Virtual Markets Integrity Initiative" (Office of the New York State Attorney General, September 18, 2018).
[2] "ASIFMA Best Practices For Digital Asset Exchanges" (Asia Securities Industry and Financial Markets Association (ASIFMA), June 2018).
[3] "ASIFMA Best Practices For Digital Asset Exchanges" (Asia Securities Industry and Financial Markets Association (ASIFMA), June 2018). Page 19.

Box 13.1 (continued)

For this reason, there is growing pressure on crypto exchanges to develop and maintain an adequate AML/CTF framework, policies, and procedures with recent developments at the FATF being a good example of such global pressure.[4] Several jurisdictions around the world, including the United States, Japan, and Australia, have also introduced mandatory registration and compliance obligations for crypto exchanges, which include detailed AML/CTF obligations. More recently, arrests have been made and exchanges that did not conduct KYC and were suspected of money laundering (e.g. BTC-e) have been shut down.[5]

Even in countries which have not moved to ban digital asset exchanges or introduce specific legislation to regulate such exchanges, financial services, tax and data privacy regulators, and law enforcement agencies have sometimes sought to access customer and transaction records to carry out regulatory functions.[6] While some more libertarian-inclined advocates for crypto-assets may strongly disagree with identification requirements, arguing that they invalidate the very purpose of crypto-assets, the reality is that facilitating financial crime has negative impacts on society at large and on the popular opinion of crypto-assets. Furthermore, putting in place such measures are likely to help crypto-assets become more mainstream.

13.1.2 Decentralized Crypto-asset Exchanges

Decentralized crypto exchanges operate somewhat differently from their centralized counterparts. Instead of acting as a middleman, trading takes place directly between buyers and sellers. The decentralized exchange simply exists to facilitate the direct connection between the buyer and seller. Such exchanges may provide advantages in terms of lower fees or facilitate a greater degree of anonymity; however, they may also suffer from lower levels of liquidity and may be more complex to use, particularly for the average retail investor.

---

[4] "Regulation of Virtual Assets," Financial Action Task Force (FATF), October 19, 2018, http://www.fatf-gafi.org/publications/fatfrecommendations/documents/regulation-virtual-assets.html.
[5] Justin Scheck and Bradley Hope, "The Man Who Solved Bitcoin's Most Notorious Heist," Wall Street Journal, August 10, 2018, sec. Markets, https://www.wsj.com/articles/the-man-who-solved-bitcoins-most-notorious-heist-1533917805.
[6] "ASIFMA Best Practices for Digital Asset Exchanges" (Asia Securities Industry and Financial Markets Association (ASIFMA), June 2018). Page 19.

Box 13.2   What Is the Role of Crypto OTC Brokers?

It is important to mention the role played by OTC brokers in the crypto-asset ecosystem. Each trade that a buyer and seller conducts on an exchange is shown to the world (although the identity of the buyer and seller is typically only known to the exchange). This can present a challenge to anyone seeking to conduct a very large transaction, as that large transaction may move the markets.

For this reason, individuals or institutions seeking to conduct large transactions (often called block trades) will often use an OTC desk. These are brokers that are regularly in touch with large institutional investors and can match a buyer and a seller (in exchange for a fee of course) or simply buy it from a seller (placing it on their own balance sheet) with the objective of reselling it at a higher price in the near future.

13.2   Crypto-asset Custodians and Wallets

Once a party has purchased a crypto-asset, she will require a facility to safely store that asset. In the case of crypto-assets, this generally refers to the storage of the private keys—the string of digits that allow its holder to prove that she is the owner of that crypto-asset. The immutability of transactions conducted on the blockchain, means that if the holder of an asset loses control of her private keys, there will be no way to repudiate or reverse the loss of those assets.

This is different from traditional equity markets. The average investor is not particularly worried that the shares in her retirement savings account will be stolen. By contrast, investors and crypto-assets must be cognizant about the vulnerability of their investments to hacking, and must determine if they wish to hand over these assets to a custodian or store them themselves in a 'wallet'.

13.2.1   Crypto-asset Custodians

Many centralized exchanges provide custodianship services for their clients. This offers customers of the exchange a high level of convenience, reducing frictions around the purchase and sale of those assets. However, a number of high-profile incidents have highlighted the risk of hacking faced by centralized exchanges. While many of today's exchanges have learned from these events and instituted improved security measures, as well as in some cases some basic levels of insurance, significant risks remain.

This presents a challenge for large institutional investors, such as family offices and hedge funds, who have shown increased interest in making investments in crypto-assets. These institutions are subject to strict fiduciary requirements and regulatory oversight, and they may in some cases wish to deploy millions of dollars. Therefore, they must be certain that those investments can be kept safe. One interesting recent development is the entry of Fidelity Investments, an asset manager responsible for over US$7.2 trillion in client money, into the crypto-custodianship space. In October 2018, Fidelity announced the launch of a separate company called Fidelity Digital Asset Services, to handle custodianship for a range of crypto-assets and to support the execution of trades on multiple exchanges for hedge funds and family offices.[9]

13.2.2   Crypto-asset Wallets

Those who are not comfortable with entrusting their crypto-assets to a third party may choose to instead transfer them to a personal 'wallet'. A crypto-asset wallet enables an individual to manage the secure storage of her private

---

[7] "5 High Profile Cryptocurrency Hacks – (Updated)," Blockgeeks, accessed January 13, 2019, https://blockgeeks.com/guides/cryptocurrency-hacks/.

[8] Nikhilesh De, "Numbers or Not, Coincheck Isn't Mt. Gox," CoinDesk (blog), January 26, 2018, https://www.coindesk.com/numbers-not-coincheck-isnt-another-mt-gox.

[9] Kate Rooney, "Fidelity Launches Trade Execution and Custody for Cryptocurrencies," CNBC, October 15, 2018, https://www.cnbc.com/2018/10/15/fidelity-launches-trade-execution-and-custody-for-cryptocurrencies.html.

Table 13.1 Characteristics of 'Hot' and 'Cold' crypto-asset storage mechanisms

Type of wallet	Characteristics
Hot wallets/hot storage	• Connected to the internet • Can be accessed through the internet or is on a platform that has internet access • Pros: Faster to move assets in and out as connected to the internet. Useful for conducting transactions on a frequent basis • Cons: Higher risk of hack due to existing internet connection
Cold wallet/cold storage	• Not connected to the internet • Not accessible unless gaining physically access to the wallet • Pros: Significantly lower risk of hack as not connected to the internet • Cons: Requires more time to conduct a transaction as requires reconnecting to the internet

'Hot' and 'cold' crypto-asset wallets have distinct characteristics, each with their own advantages and disadvantages

keys, and is comparable to storing money into a personal vault rather than at a bank. There are numerous types of wallets, but they largely can be separated into two types: hot and cold wallets.[10] The basic details of each type are covered in Table 13.1.

13.3 Advisory and Consumer Services for the Crypto-asset Ecosystem

Advisory and consumer services include a large number of organizations dedicated to enabling the smooth functioning of the broader crypto-asset ecosystem. This might include trade or advocacy organizations, such as Coin Centre or the Wall Street Blockchain Alliance, as well as specialized media outlets such as CoinDesk or CoinTelegraph. We are already beginning to see a growing number of law firms and consulting firms with dedicated crypto-asset offerings as well as research firms focused on providing high-quality insights and analysis about emerging blockchain projects. In time, we might even see the emergence of rating agencies dedicated to tracking the probability of failure for a given token and specialized auditors dedicated to evaluating the details of smart contract or attesting to the reserves of a stable coin.

While many of these actors may not use blockchain in their daily activities, their ability to provide specialized services will be critical to both those entrepreneurs seeking to build out crypto-asset projects with broad-based adoption and the prospective users of and investors in these projects.

---

[10] Stellabelle, "Cold Wallet Vs. Hot Wallet: What's The Difference?," Medium (blog), April 9, 2017, https://medium.com/@stellabelle/cold-wallet-vs-hot-wallet-whats-the-difference-a00d872aa6b1.

Part IV

The Fundamentals of Artificial Intelligence

Human beings have long been fascinated by the notion of a machine that can think. While the term artificial intelligence (AI) was first coined by American computer scientist John McCarthy in 1956, at the first academic conference on the subject,[1] our obsession with the idea of AI goes back centuries. In the 1770s, royal courts across Europe were entranced by a device called 'the Turk', a chess-playing machine that was able to defeat many human opponents, including notable historical figures such as Napoleon and Benjamin Franklin.[2]

Ultimately, the Turk was revealed to be an elaborate hoax, wherein a human chess master was concealed inside the machine, but this and many other disappointments have not stopped us from pouring our hopes and fears into the idea of a machine that can think. Public interest in AI has increased enormously in recent years, as has excitement about its potential to improve our lives in domains ranging from medicine to transportation, and of course, financial services. But at the same time, our technological advances in this space have also driven uncertainty and mistrust. There are growing concerns from individuals and policymakers alike that AI has the potential to deeply disrupt labor markets in coming years. Pundits have resurfaced old fears that artificial intelligence will render humans obsolete, for example, Tesla CEO Elon Musk, who called AI "a fundamental risk to the existence of human civilization."[3]

---

[1] Chris Smith et al., "The History of Artificial Intelligence," *University of Washington*, December 2006, 27.

[2] "The Turk," in *Wikipedia*, January 17, 2019, https://en.wikipedia.org/w/index.php?title=The_Turk&oldid=878918745.

[3] "Musk Says A.I. Is a 'Fundamental Risk to the Existence of Human Civilization,'" *CNBC*, July 16, 2017, https://www.cnbc.com/2017/07/16/musk-says-a-i-is-a-fundamental-risk-to-the-existence-of-human-civilization.html.

In the following chapters, we will seek to understand the nature and workings of artificial intelligence, the actors driving its development, the inputs necessary to the successful deployment of artificial intelligence, and the implications of all these things for the financial services ecosystem. In this chapter, we will seek to answer the surprisingly tricky question of how to define artificial intelligence before conducting a high-level exploration of both the analytical techniques used to enable AI and the specific capabilities that those techniques enable. Then, in Chap. 15, we will consider the ways that financial institutions today are deploying AI across several subsectors of the industry, as well as some of the most significant impediments that exist for the success of these deployments.

14

Understanding Artificial Intelligence and Its Capabilities

There are few topics that inspire as much excitement, fear, and confusion as artificial intelligence. Outspoken pundits argue that it will bring about everything from a utopian world of leisure to the end of human civilization, and yet even the very definition of the term is plagued with uncertainty. In this chapter, we will seek to clarify some of the confusion surrounding artificial intelligence and do away with some of the myths. We will advance a definition of AI and explore some high-level AI techniques and their resulting capabilities, before concluding with a few thoughts on the implications of AI on the business sector at large.

14.1 The Surprisingly Tricky Problem of Defining AI

What is artificial intelligence? It is a simple question, but the answer is elusive. The simplest computer can execute logic in the form of computation, but at what point does this constitute AI? To understand what constitutes *artificial intelligence*, we must first be able to define what constitutes *intelligence*, a question that has confounded philosophers for centuries.

This confusion is well illustrated by the so-called Chinese room thought experiment introduced by American philosopher John Searle.[1] Imagine for a

---

[1] David Cole, "The Chinese Room Argument," in *The Stanford Encyclopedia of Philosophy*, ed. Edward N. Zalta, Spring 2019 (Metaphysics Research Lab, Stanford University, 2019), https://plato.stanford.edu/archives/spr2019/entries/chinese-room/.

© The Author(s) 2019
H. Arslanian, F. Fischer, *The Future of Finance*,
https://doi.org/10.1007/978-3-030-14533-0_14

moment that you are in a locked room. Cards with sentences written in English are passed through a slot in the wall on one side of the room and you are expected to pass their translation in Chinese characters through a slot in the wall on the other side of the room. The trouble is that you only speak English. Fortunately, the room is filled with books containing rules and lookup tables that enable you to accurately translate English into Chinese characters. This means you can translate the cards, but does it mean that you really understand the language?

Attempting to reconcile the philosophic fuzzy notion of intelligence with the cold practicality of computer science has been a tricky business. The result has been something called the 'AI effect', wherein observers tend to 'move the goal posts' on what constitutes 'real' artificial intelligence. Whereas once, defeating a grand master chess or translating a foreign language might have been considered a sign of intelligence, today the ubiquity of computers who can perform those functions makes those capabilities easy to reject as not true thinking.

We can start to put some clarity around the idea of AI by dividing it into two high-level categories: broad AI, sometimes also called 'general AI' or 'strong AI', and narrow AI, sometimes called 'weak AI'. General AI is the stuff of science fiction, the idea of a machine that fuses a human being's ability to perform a wide variety of tasks, conduct highly generalized reasoning, apply common sense, and solve problems creatively with a computer's ability to apply rapid computation to vast stores of data. While an exciting, and to some frightening, idea, most experts expect broad AI to remain the exclusive purview of films and novels for at least the next few decades.

By contrast, narrow AI is capable of effectively addressing a highly specific problem, such as playing chess at a high level, or recognizing if there is a cat in a photo. Significant advancements have been made in this realm over the past 50 years, with particularly notable advancements having taken place over the course of the past decade. Given that this text is intended to serve as a practical companion for readers interested in the impact of new technologies on financial services, we will not conduct further explorations of theoretical applications of broad AI, and instead confine our discussion exclusively to narrow AI and its applications.

However, simply focusing our discussion on narrow AI does not fully solve the problem of how to properly define AI. It may surprise some readers to know that although AI is a frequently used term in the media, and that we will use it extensively in this text, the term does not refer to a specific technology or field of study, but rather is an umbrella term that encompasses many different approaches (e.g. machine learning, neural networks, etc.) seeking to achieve a wide array of specific goals (e.g. identifying a face in a photo, translating a language etc.).

With that in mind and for the purposes of this book, we will define AI as a set of technologies capable of adaptive predictive power against a well-defined problem and exhibiting some degree of autonomous learning and improvement in the solving of that problem. This may not be a perfect definition, but as this text is designed for students and practitioners of financial services and not computer science, it should suffice to allow us to focus on the much more relevant question of why this technology matters.

14.2 Why Artificial Intelligence Matters

To put it simply, AI matters because it is the only tool at our disposal that will enable us to detect patterns, derive insights, and drive actions from the truly staggering quantities of data that are being created every day. Even with the most powerful traditional computing techniques, no human or group of humans could effectively analyze these streams of data.

This is in part due to their sheer scale, but much more important is the fact that so much of the data now being created is raw and unstructured. Structured data is highly organized. It can be codified, placed in spreadsheets, sorted, and searched. Records of transactions, income statements, and historical temperature are all examples of structured data. They can be easily analyzed with computing techniques that (while a good deal more powerful today) have been around for decades.

Unstructured data is the opposite. It has no predefined model or organization. The individual data points have no clear and well-defined relationship with each other, and so can't be sorted in a neat spreadsheet or organized in by pivot table. The millions of random photos taken each day, the hours of recorded conversations between stockbrokers, and the countless emails fired back and forth between corporate servers are all examples of unstructured data.

Traditional approaches to computing are only able to use unstructured data effectively if it has first been refined or processed by human beings into structured data, significantly increasing the cost of analyzing the data and decreasing the speed of reaction to it. More importantly, this manual structuring of the data necessarily robs it of its richness, placing it into a predefined framework rather than enabling unexpected patterns and insights to emerge.

AI is all about applying machines rather than humans to the process of interpreting unstructured data. It aims to accelerate the process and scale it to accommodate the enormous quantities of data involved, while also enabling the identification of new and emerging patterns that a human might not have thought to look for. It is only able to do this because unlike more traditional approaches to computing which are static, AI learns from experience using past and present data.

This idea of learning is an essential component of what defines AI, in that successive iterations or 'loops' of data applied to the model 'train' it to improve its performance. There are many techniques for this kind of learning. For example, the technique of 'supervised learning' provides the model being trained with data that has been structured and labeled by humans and where a clear objective has been outlined. By contrast, unsupervised learning training data does not include labels or instructions, and sometimes does not even provide a goal, instead allowing the model to identify its own structures, patterns, and groupings within the data. A third method called reinforcement learning scores the performance of variations in a model against an objective to determine which model works best for a given data set. While the details of which learning models are the best fit to a given problem is beyond the scope of this text, one thing remains true across each methodology is that significant quantities of data and iterations of learning are required for the resulting models to perform effectively.

All of this is important because the lion's share of today's explosion of data is unstructured. While detailed measurements are tricky, some estimates suggest that unstructured data is growing at a stunning compounded annual growth rate of almost 40%, resulting in a world where 90% of usable data is unstructured.[2]

In other words, if artificial intelligence provides businesses the means to obtain insights from unstructured data quickly, accurately, and inexpensively, harnessing that AI is the difference between making decisions based on the 'tip of the iceberg' or the entire picture. With that in mind, it is no surprise that AI is at the top of executive agendas across many industries, including financial services.

14.3 Selected AI Techniques

It may be useful to readers to have a passing familiarity with some of the most commonly used AI techniques. Here we will explore three such techniques: machine learning, neural networks (including deep learning), and genetic and evolutionary algorithms.

---

[2] Tracy Kambies et al., "Analyzing Dark Data for Hidden Opportunities," Deloitte Insights, February 7, 2017, https://www2.deloitte.com/insights/us/en/focus/tech-trends/2017/dark-data-analyzing-unstructured-data.html.

14.3.1   Machine Learning

Much like AI itself, the term machine learning, which was coined in 1959 by Arthur Samuel, is the subject of many definitional arguments and incorporates under its banner a range of techniques. For example, several variants of machine learning exist using supervised, unsupervised, and reinforcement learning, each of which is suited to different tasks.

At its most basic level, machine learning parses existing data, 'learns' insights from it, and then makes a prediction based on that learning. Of course, this is not learning, in the sense that a human being learns. Instead, we can think of the way that the 'line of best fit' in a simple regression model might improve each time a new data point is added. When the line of best fit is recalculated with this new data, it could be said to have 'learned', in that it is now a more accurate model for predicting the next data point. The mathematical details behind a machine learning model are much more complex, but the process of learning is effectively the same.

In practice, machine learning models are often trained by splitting a dataset into two pieces, with one half of the data used to train the algorithm, and a second half used to test the performance of the algorithm. With a few exceptions, as the size of the dataset available to be used for training and evaluation of the model increases, so does the accuracy and granularity of the model's outputs.

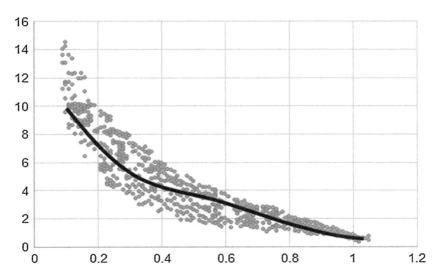

Fig. 14.1   An illustrative scatter plot and 'Line of Best Fit' produced by a linear regression model. Machine learning models do not learn in the sense that a human learns; they merely update their predictions in response to new data in much the same way as any statistical model

14.3.2　Neural Networks and Deep Learning

AI implementations using a neural network structure borrow on insights from the human brain. The basic unit of the human nervous system is the neuron, a simple cell capable of transmitting an electrical signal in response to stimuli. Neurons in the human brain are connected to each other via junctions called synapses. The process of an individual learning is a shifting of the strength of the connections at those synapse points. A neural network seeks to replicate aspects of this densely interconnected system of neurons, as well as the process of learning through adjusting the strength of their connections to one another, all within the digital world.

A typical neural network might have anything from a few dozen to thousands, or even millions, of artificial neurons. Each of these artificial neurons falls into one of three categories. The first are input units, which are designed to receive various data inputs such as any of the types of structured or unstructured data discussed earlier in this chapter. The second are output units which provide the results, such as predictions or decisions. The final types of neurons are called hidden units. They typically make up most of the neurons in a neural network and provide the layers of connectivity between the input units and the output units.

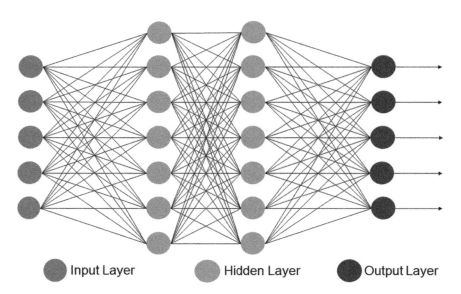

Fig. 14.2 An illustrative example of a neural network topology. Neural networks 'learn' by reweighting the connections between artificial 'neurons'

The learning process of this network also resembles that of the human brain. In the brain, neurons are connected to one another in a complex network, and the strength of those connections is increased or decreased in response to external stimuli. In a computational neural network, training data flows through the system adjusting the strength, or 'weighting', of connections between input units and the hidden units they are connected to, as well as between the hidden units themselves, and finally between the hidden units and the output units.

There are many different approaches to using training data to reweight the connections between neurons, and many different topologies for the layers of connections between input units, hidden units, and output units. These different topologies and learning approaches make up the many different subsets of neural networks including deep learning models and convolutional neural networks.

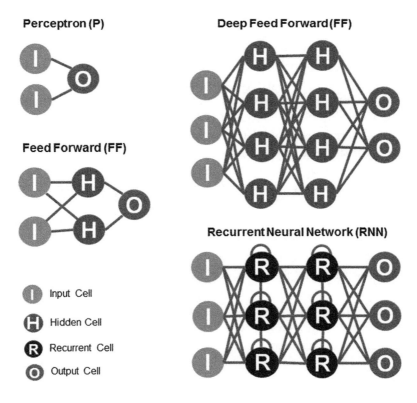

Perceptron is a single layer neural network and a multi-layer perceptron is called Neural Networks.

Fig. 14.3 Examples of neural networks. Many subcategories of neural network topologies and learning techniques exist, each with its own set of possible use cases

14.3.3   Genetic and Evolutionary Algorithms

The final AI approach that we will consider are genetic and evolutionary algorithms. This approach applies the principles of evolution found in nature to the process of training an AI model by incorporating features such as Darwinian natural selection and the randomness of mutations.

Under this process, a population of different possible models is created and then winnowed down through natural selection, with only those that produce the best results surviving. A new generation of algorithms is then created alongside the surviving ones through 'mutations' which introduce randomized changes to portions of the code of the surviving models. The natural selection process can then be run again and again to produce a truly best of breed algorithm.

14.3.4   Limitations of These Techniques

While powerful, the techniques discussed above have several limitations. First, as the number of neurons and the layers of neurons increase, so too does the granularity of the resulting model. However, as a model's complexity increases, so do the resources required to operate it. For this reason, it is important when designing such a model to consider the trade-off between marginal improvement in predictive results and the increased costs in terms of resources—electricity, human talent, and so on—to achieve that complexity.

Second, as the complexity of the model increases, it may become more and more difficult to obtain an understanding of why a given input to a model has resulted in a given output (at least in a way that is interpretable to humans). In other words, some complex neural networks, such as deep learning models, may be 'black boxes', a feature that we will discuss later in the book, and that may raise issues for some financial regulators.

Finally, any AI model is only as good as the data that is used to train it. If that data is inaccurate or if the sampling of the training data contains biases, the outputs of the model will be inaccurate or have biases. As we will discuss in later chapters, both issues of accuracy and issues of bias are of critical concern to financial institutions.

14.4   Selected Capabilities of AI

Having explored the techniques used to build AI models, let's take a moment to consider how those techniques are being used to create capabilities that achieve practical and specific goals. In the pages that follow, we will explore two such capabilities: natural language processing and machine vision.

These are by no means the only applications of AI currently in use, but they are important ones, and have improved significantly in recent years. Moreover, as you will see in the following chapter, both of these tools are key ingredients to many of the deployments of AI being conducted by financial institutions today.

14.4.1 Machine Vision

Machine vision is the sub-branch of artificial intelligence concerned about the analysis and interpretation of images and videos. While modern digital photos contain some degree of structured data in the form of embedded metadata about where and when they were taken, the photo itself remains an unstructured data element that traditional approaches to computing struggle to interpret.

Machine vision seeks to analyze the pixels of a photo to identify groupings and patterns of data, such as what the human eye would consider shapes, to convert this unstructured data into a structured form that it can interpret. Using training data, these groupings can then be associated with the objects that they represent, enabling the system to recognize that a combination of groupings it has identified matches what a human would call a cat.

Given sufficient training data, machine vision models can meet a wide range of use cases. For example, this technique enables 'optical character recognition' where pictures of text are converted to machine readable and searchable text. It also enables a range of facial recognition techniques such as the iPhone X's Face ID system and Alipay's Smile to Pay feature. Moving forward, machine vision will be one part of a suite of technologies that contribute to the ongoing improvement of autonomous driving systems.

14.4.2 Natural Language Processing

Natural language processing (NLP) is the branch of artificial intelligence focused on enabling computers to interpret and process both spoken and written human language. It does this by combining the power of various AI models, including machine learning and deep learning, with the principles of linguistic structure, to break sentences down into their elemental pieces and identify semantic relationships.[3]

---

[3] "What Is Natural Language Processing?", SAS, accessed January 24, 2019, https://www.sas.com/en_us/insights/analytics/what-is-natural-language-processing-nlp.html.

This is an extremely challenging task for machines for many reasons. Each language, and indeed many regional variations on language, use unique sets of grammar and syntax, not to mention slang and abbreviations. Written inputs will contain grammatical errors, misspellings, and missing punctuation, while spoken inputs will need to be distinguished from background noise and conversations before the challenging work of navigating accents or understanding the implications of tonal shifts like sarcasm can begin.

In recent years, our capabilities in this space have evolved considerably, particularly for English language systems. For example, as of 2017, Google's voice-based NLP system boasts a work accuracy level of 95%, meeting or exceeding the threshold of human accuracy.[4]

The potential applications for this technology are obvious, having been experienced firsthand by anyone who has ever spoken to an Amazon's Alexa or had a conversation with Apple's Siri digital assistant. As the quality of this technology continues to improve, more and more organizations are exploring opportunities to apply it in order to rapidly respond to customer questions or review and analyze a large number of documents.

Interestingly, this last example provides a compelling illustration of how AI applications can be combined to increase their power. Consider the hundreds of boxes of paper-based evidence that might be involved in a large-scale corporate lawsuit. Using optical character recognition capabilities of machine vision, those documents could be converted to digital text and then subjected to natural language processes to better identify all references to a particular project.

14.5   High-Level Implications of AI for Business

In this chapter, we have covered many complex topics, including the nature of intelligence, high-level approaches for designing AI models, and a cursory exploration of a few of the ways these models are being deployed in the real world. From this there are two critical conclusions that warrant reinforcing.

The first is that despite the sometimes sensational media coverage surrounding AI, none of these models are poised to revolt against humanity anytime soon. The AI models being developed today are not the broad AI of science fiction. Instead they are narrow systems that must be trained to address highly specific problems based on large datasets, but are able to apply massive computational power to those problems.

---

[4] April Glaser, "Google's Ability to Understand Language Is Nearly Equivalent to Humans," Recode, May 31, 2017, https://www.recode.net/2017/5/31/15720118/google-understand-language-speech-equivalent-humans-code-conference-mary-meeker.

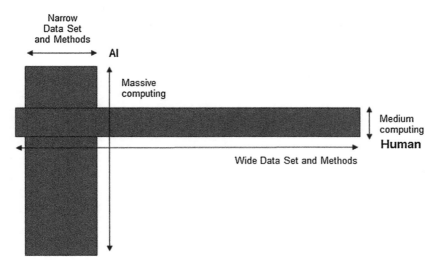

Fig. 14.4   Illustrative comparative capabilities of current AI models and human beings. AI models and humans have highly complementary skill sets

AI is moving the threshold of our ability to apply that massive computational power to new (highly specified) unstructured datasets, but it is still no match for the human brain when it comes to the ability to ingest a vast array of datasets and use an equally wide array of analytical methods. For this reason, the true power of AI is where the complementary strengths of humans and machines are deployed together to augment our collective ability to solve the problems of business and society more broadly.

The second critical insight is the centrality of data to the deployment of any AI model. Useful AI models can only be developed where a sufficient breadth and depth of training data of high-quality unbiased training data exists. As we will see in the following chapters, competition to acquire these datasets is becoming a key strategic priority in every sector of the economy, and financial services is no exception.

15

Applications of Artificial Intelligence in Financial Services

Having explored the definition of artificial intelligence, the core capabilities that it offers, and the dynamics of its evolution, we will now turn our attention to the application of artificial intelligence in financial services. Unlike some large technology companies, very few financial services firms are directly involved in pushing the boundaries of what artificial intelligence can do. Instead, most financial institutions are focused on the deployment of existing artificial intelligence techniques and capabilities against key strategic problems, and in the areas of competitive opportunity.

In other words, most work being done today by financial institutions is in the deployment of existing AI technology against the specific needs of the financial institution. For that reason, our analysis in this chapter will not focus on the technological specifics of the AI approaches being used by financial institutions, but instead on how those AI capabilities are enabling financial institutions to better achieve their goals.

In the pages that follow, we will explore some specific examples of how different areas of financial services, namely, lending, insurance, wealth management, and payments, are using AI as part of a broader strategy to achieve business goals. However, before doing so, we should first consider the general set of opportunities that artificial intelligence represents for financial institutions. At the conclusion of this chapter, we will also conduct a high-level exploration of the serious hurdles that many incumbent financial institutions face in the implementation of these technologies.

© The Author(s) 2019
H. Arslanian, F. Fischer, *The Future of Finance*,
https://doi.org/10.1007/978-3-030-14533-0_15

15.1   Key Artificial Intelligence Opportunities for Financial Institutions

There are a variety of dimensions along which a financial institution might use AI technology to meet its aims. In the following pages, we will consider four categories of strategies that are particularly relevant to financial institutions today: automation, customization, improved decision-making, and new value propositions.

15.1.1   AI-Enabled Automation

The deployment of artificial intelligence technology against the goal of automation allows a financial institution to improve the speed and efficiency with which a process can be completed by reducing or altogether eliminating human intervention in the process. This can significantly reduce operational costs and may at the same time improve users' experiences.

In some cases, automation can be enabled with relatively unsophisticated technology such as 'robotic process automation' (RPA), wherein the way the process is conducted is substantially unchanged and a suite of relatively 'dumb' tools allow the process to be automated so long as inputs do not deviate from expectations. For more complex processes with more varied inputs, sophisticated techniques such as machine vision and advanced pattern recognition systems with self-learning capabilities can be deployed, potentially completely transforming the structure and the required inputs of the process itself.

The ability to deploy automation in financial services is particularly important given the strong focus on cost cutting that exists within many institutions as a result of the sustained period of low profitability following the 2008 financial crisis. At the same time, the ability of a growing number of fintech firms to deliver 'straight through processing' experiences that significantly speed traditional processing times for everything from filing an insurance claim to onboarding a new banking customer, have increased the competitive pressure on incumbent institutions to streamline their own processes and deliver improved customer experiences.

A focus on AI technologies that enable automation is likely to be most valuable for financial institutions that service a very large number of customers with relatively low profitability per customer because it can enable them to more aggressively compete on margin or to squeeze incrementally more value out of each of their many accounts. It may also be of relevance to institutions for whom compliance constitutes a significant share of their labor costs given that automation can enable them to streamline these operations and increase focus on their core business activities.

While automation is certainly not the most exciting example of how AI can be deployed in financial services, it is a strategy that can have far-reaching consequences. More than any other strategy that we discuss in this book, automation has the potential to have implications on the operational structure and talent needs of the organization, potentially leading to significant reductions in the headcount of specific functions of the organization.

15.1.2 AI-Enabled Improved Decision-Making

Artificial intelligence technologies give financial institutions the capability to incorporate much broader and less structured sets of data into their analytics processes, theoretically enabling significantly improved foresight. Given that the core function of a financial institution is the effective management of risk, the ability to better understand how an uncertain situation will evolve constitutes a significant advantage whether that financial institution is writing a loan, insuring a car, or placing bets on the market's next move.

AI-enabled strategies focused on improved decision-making are likely to be particularly relevant for organizations that compete on performance metrics that are easily measurable, such as investment returns compared to the market. They may also be useful in businesses where products are highly commoditized, such as consumer lending, if they can enable users to expand services into customer or product segments that would have been deemed too risky under less mature decision-making models.

15.1.3 AI-Enabled Customization

In financial services, as in many other industries, there has traditionally been a trade-off between customization and cost. It is possible to receive highly customized financial products and services, particularly in the realms of wealth management and wholesale banking. Unfortunately, these services are only accessible to those able to pay higher fees, or to particularly large and important clients. This is because customization has traditionally required the attention of highly specialized human capital, and thus the cost of delivering a customized product has scaled in proportion to the degree of customization. Artificial intelligence technology enables financial institutions to break this tradeoff, theoretically enabling the deployment of fully personalized financial products services at zero marginal cost once a system is in place.

A focus on AI technologies that enable customization is likely to be most valuable for financial institutions where customer acquisition or retention can be significantly improved by offering more complex financial products and services that would have previously required human input to interpret the client's needs. In many cases, this will allow institutions that are currently focused on serving mass-market clientele to borrow some of the differentiation techniques of high-end institutions to improve the outcomes and experiences of their customers (or alternately, for those more high-end institutions to expand down-market using similar techniques).

15.1.4   AI-Enabled New Value Propositions

A final AI-enabled strategy that financial institutions can deploy is the creation of new value propositions. A financial institution may find that it is in possession of a unique set of data streams that place it in an advantageous position either to deploy monetizable insights such as more detailed macroeconomic reports or to build out suites of AI-enabled services that support the automation, customization, and decision-making aims of other financial institutions.

By its very nature, opportunities in this space are diverse with significant variation occurring across subsectors and even depending on the specific data profiles of individual firms. That said, these strategies may be particularly relevant for institutions whose existing lines of business are under significant margin pressure and where new value propositions may be able to offset these negative impacts on performance. They can also help where there is a growing threat of losing clients to new entrants and where the delivery of a set of ancillary products and services around commoditized core offerings may help meet customer retention goals.

15.2   Specific Applications of AI in Subsectors of Financial Services

In the following pages, we will consider how AI-enabled strategies for automation, improved decision-making, customization, and the creation of new value propositions are being deployed by financial institutions today. While almost every corner of the financial system is exploring how AI might be used, we will confine our analysis to four key areas: lending, wealth/asset management, insurance, and payments.

15.2.1 Key Applications of Artificial Intelligence in Lending

The application of AI-enabled strategies in lending to date has primarily focused on the improvement of retail consumer and small business loans across several dimensions.

Automation techniques have been used to significantly reduce the cost of processing loan applications and to improve the speed with which loans can be deployed. Technologies such as natural language processing and machine vision are now being used to support the verification of a prospective client's documentation, accelerate the KYC process, and reduce fraud.[1] These same technologies are also being applied to support the unique needs of loans to small and mid-sized businesses where it can enable the rapid ingestion of nonstandard documents such as company financials, and remove the need for manual processing and analysis of the data in these documents.

AI can also support efforts to improve decision-making around lending activities by allowing the ingestion and modeling of a universe of alternative data sources. The underwriting models built from this data can potentially reduce the number of nonperforming loans, for example, by including more forward-looking indicators about a prospective borrower's ability to repay. They can also increase a lender's pool of potential customers by using alternative data signals to assess creditworthiness in cases where traditional credit scoring metrics are not available—such as in the case of new immigrants who may lack an established or easily accessible credit score, or in emerging markets where credit agency data may be spotty or nonexistent.[2]

The alternative factors that feed such models can include a range of sources, such as bill payments, data on shopping behaviors, and social media posts. In some cases, financial institutions will even develop whole new sources of data to feed into the underwriting process such as the case of Chinese lender Ping An, who will initiate video calls with some prospective borrowers and use AI-enabled micro-gesture facial recognition technology to evaluate the truthfulness of their responses to questions about how they intended to use the loan.[3]

---

[1] Khari Johnson, "Inscribe Raises $3 Million to Automate Document Fraud Detection," VentureBeat (blog), December 12, 2018, https://venturebeat.com/2018/12/12/inscribe-raises-3-million-to-automate-document-fraud-detection/.

[2] Brian Browdie, "Can Alternative Data Determine a Borrower's Ability to Repay?," American Banker, February 24, 2015, https://www.americanbanker.com/news/can-alternative-data-determine-a-borrowers-ability-to-repay.

[3] Oliver Ralph, Dan Weinland, and Martin Arnold, "Chinese Banks Start Scanning Borrowers' Facial Movements," Financial Times, October 29, 2018, https://www.ft.com/content/4c3ac2d4-d865-11e8-ab8e-6be0dcf18713.

In small and medium-sized lending operations, direct integration with a prospective borrower's IT systems, such as their enterprise resource planning, accounting, or supply chain management systems, can enable real-time data flows that feed predictive models to enable more accurate decision-making and could ultimately be used to enable proactive anticipation of customers lending needs and the offering of more customized lending products. For example, global banking giant HSBC has partnered with digital invoicing platform Tradeshift on the provision of supply-chain lending[4] and accounting software provider QuickBooks has established a financing arm called QuickBooks Capital aimed at writing loans to QuickBooks users.[5]

There are even examples of lenders building new businesses on the back of the strategic AI investments. For example, UK-based lender OakNorth built a specialized cloud-based platform designed to ingest a wide variety of data and use machine learning to drive ongoing iterative improvements in the quality of their underwriting model. Having done this, OakNorth has now launched a service called AcornMachine that licenses the use of this platform to lenders outside of the United Kingdom in order to provide them with easy access to the same AI-enabled tool-set.[6]

15.2.2 Key Applications of Artificial Intelligence in Wealth and Asset Management

AI techniques have also found fertile ground in the world of wealth management and asset management. As was the case in lending, natural language processing and machine vision can support faster client onboarding. These techniques are also being used by an array of specialized regtech firms to automate and streamline aspects of the compliance process.[7] Such automated

---

[4] Oscar Williams-Grut, "HSBC Partners with Tradeshift as Banks Increasingly See Fintech as Friends Not Foe," Business Insider, March 30, 2017, https://www.businessinsider.com/hsbc-partners-with-fintech-tradeshift-on-financing-product-2017-3.

[5] "Small Business Loans," Intuit, QuickBooks, accessed January 13, 2019, https://quickbooks.intuit.com/features/loans/.

[6] Lawrence Wintermeyer, "The Rise of the Unicorn Challenger Bank You've Never Heard of – OakNorth," Forbes, November 17, 2017, https://www.forbes.com/sites/lawrencewintermeyer/2017/11/17/the-rise-of-the-unicorn-challenger-bank-youve-never-heard-of-oaknorth/.

[7] April J. Rudin, "The Regtech Revolution: Compliance and Wealth Management in 2017," CFA Institute – Enterprising Investor (blog), January 12, 2017, https://blogs.cfainstitute.org/investor/2017/01/12/the-regtech-revolution-compliance-and-wealth-management-in-2017/.

solutions can significantly reduce the cost of monitoring changes in regulatory regimes across hundreds of jurisdictions in dozens of languages.[8]

However, automation for wealth and investment managers is not limited to rote customer management and compliance processes; efforts are underway to automate large portions of the quantitative modeling processes that are central to a fund manager's investment decisions. Take, for example, Boston-based Kensho's signature platform, named Warren for legendary investor Warren Buffet, which uses a range of AI techniques to respond to financial questions posed in natural language. A 2018 Forbes article on the platform claimed that Warren could "find answers to more than 65 million question combinations in an instant by scanning more than 90,000 actions such as drug approvals, economic reports, monetary policy changes, and political events". By automating the quantitative analysis process, offerings like Kensho have the potential to shift the talent requirements of fund managers away from individuals who can quickly execute quantitative analysis, and toward individuals skilled in asking the right questions and working in partnership with AI.[9]

In addition to automating analysis that informs investment decisions, many fund managers are seeking to use AI-enabled strategies to improve the quality of those investment decisions themselves. Broadly speaking, they are doing this in two ways. The first is by using sophisticated machine learning and deep learning combined with unique data sources to build 'active' portfolios aimed a beating the market. For example, in spring of 2018, Two Sigma, a New York–based hedge fund with US$50 billion in assets under management, hired a senior staff research scientist from Alphabet Inc.'s Google to lead an expansion of their AI efforts.[10]

While investments in hedge funds such as Two Sigma are typically restricted to large-scale investors and charge high fees, the second application of AI to enhance investment decision-making seeks to use AI to deliver active investing return characteristics on more accessible low-fee passive investing products. This technique builds on the growing popularity of 'smart beta' exchange

---

[8] Owen Kraft, "How Natural Language Processing Is Changing Financial Risk and Compliance and Why You Should Care," Captech Consulting, Inc. (blog), July 20, 2018, http://www.captechconsulting.com/blogs/how-natural-language-processing-is-changing-financial-risk-and-compliance.

[9] Antoine Gara, "Wall Street Tech Spree: With Kensho Acquisition S&P Global Makes Largest A.I. Deal in History," Forbes, March 6, 2018, https://www.forbes.com/sites/antoinegara/2018/03/06/wall-street-tech-spree-with-kensho-acquisition-sp-global-makes-largest-a-i-deal-in-history/.

[10] Kristy Westgard, "Two Sigma Hires Google Scientist Mike Schuster for AI Expansion," Bloomberg News, April 16, 2018, https://www.bloomberg.com/news/articles/2018-04-16/two-sigma-hires-google-scientist-mike-schuster-for-ai-expansion.

traded funds (ETF) which look to deliver excess returns by weighting certain investment factors, such as firm size or industry category, rather than simply tracking an index like the S&P 500.

A growing number of these products are using artificial intelligence techniques to select factors from a wide range of alternative data sources and to inform the real-time rebalancing of those factors as the underlying algorithm learns and responds to new data. Examples of this approach include the Aberdeen Global Artificial Intelligence Equity fund which uses machine learning to time and weight its investments,[11] and BlackRock's China A-Share Opportunities Private Fund 1 which uses machine learning to assess a mix of fundamentals, market sentiment, and macroeconomic policies in the Chinese market and will use a range of alternative data sources including satellite imagery and machine readable news.[12]

Of course, customization is also a focus for wealth managers with even the earliest robo-advisors focused on delivering asset advice and allocation that is tailored to the risk profile, pre-existing investments, and demographics of each investor. Today, a growing range of services focuses on delivering tools to provide even more customized portfolios, such as Clarity AI, which helps allocate investors' funds according to a range of social impact investing factors,[13] or Motif, which helps investors weigh their portfolio against an array of thematic groupings such as cybersecurity, renewable energy, or even water scarcity.[14] However, it is important to note that while the term 'robo-advisor' tends to conjure up the idea of an anthropomorphized AI making investment allocation decisions on your behalf, many of these systems (at least to date) are built on conventional data analysis frameworks and do not include some of the more advanced techniques necessary to be included in our definition of AI such as a self-learning component.

Finally, while examples of asset managers building out whole new value propositions on the back of AI are difficult to find, there is reason to believe that moving forward we will see more organizations focused on using AI to enhance their ancillary technology-as-a-service businesses. Of particular note is fund management giant BlackRock's Aladdin platform. Aladdin, which

[11] Darius McDermott, "Aberdeen Launches AI Smart Beta Venture," FTAdvisor – Financial Times, August 30, 2018, https://www.ftadviser.com/investments/2018/09/05/aberdeen-launches-ai-smart-beta-venture/.

[12] Samuel Shen and John Ruwitch, "Satellites and Blogs: BlackRock to Raise Game in China Stock Picking," Reuters, July 25, 2018, https://www.reuters.com/article/us-china-blackrock-fund-idUSK-BN1KE16U.

[13] "Clarity | Bringing Societal Impact to Markets," accessed January 13, 2019, https://clarity.ai/.

[14] "Motif Thematic Portfolios," Motif (blog), accessed January 13, 2019, https://www.motif.com/products/thematic-portfolios.

stands for Asset Liability and Debt and Derivatives Investment Network, is effectively an operating system for asset managers and is currently used across the insurance and asset management industry, including by some of BlackRock's key competitors such as Schroders, the United Kingdom's largest listed fund manager.[15]

While the degree of AI-enabled insights delivered by this platform today are not clear, BlackRock's Chief Engineer Jody Kochansky notes that "the building blocks of artificial intelligence today—applied mathematics and data science— are embedded deep within Aladdin and are being applied in new, innovative ways across the platform".[16] Given BlackRock CEO Larry Fink's stated view that Aladdin should account for 30% of revenues by 2022 (compared to 7% in 2017) and growing competitive pressure from similar services in this space such as SimCorp's Dimension platform, it is likely that we will see increased efforts to differentiate products on the basis of AI-enabled offerings.[17,18]

15.2.3 Key Applications of Artificial Intelligence in Insurance

AI-enabled strategies are also being deployed across the insurance industry. For example, an array of automation techniques is being deployed in the area of claims processes to reduce costs and improve the customer experience. Leading Chinese insurer Ping An uses machine vision, and a range of other AI techniques, to enable its 'Smart Fast Claim' process which automatically assesses automobile damage and estimates repair costs based on images uploaded by the policyholder. Ping An expects this system to improve overall claims processing efficiency by over 40% while also significantly reducing both claims leakage (another way of saying the risk of paying out more than necessary in claims expenditures) and customer disputes.[19]

---

[15] Attracta Mooney, "BlackRock Bets on Aladdin as Genie of Growth," Financial Times, May 18, 2017, https://www.ft.com/content/eda44658-3592-11e7-99bd-13beb0903fa3.

[16] Jody Kochansky, "The Promise of Artificial Intelligence and What It Means to BlackRock," BlackRock Blog (blog), March 8, 2018, https://www.blackrockblog.com/2018/03/08/artificial-intelligence-black-rock/.

[17] Attracta Mooney, "BlackRock Bets on Aladdin as Genie of Growth," Financial Times, May 18, 2017, https://www.ft.com/content/eda44658-3592-11e7-99bd-13beb0903fa3.

[18] James Comtois, "BlackRock Puts More of Its Future in Tech," Pensions & Investments, April 3, 2017, https://www.pionline.com/article/20170403/PRINT/304039990/blackrock-puts-more-of-its-future-in-tech.

[19] Ping an Insurance (Group) Company of China, "Ping An Financial OneConnect Unveils 'Smart Insurance Cloud' to Over 100 Insurance Companies," PRNewswire, September 6, 2017, https://www.prnewswire.com/news-releases/ping-an-financial-oneconnect-unveils-smart-insurance-cloud-to-over-100-insurance-companies-300514482.html.

In North America and Europe, insurers are pursuing similar strategies such as Ageas, who has partnered with the insurtech firm Tractable to use deep learning algorithms to deliver faster and more accurate damage assessments for both home and automotive claims.[20]

AI techniques are also being leveraged to help automate fraud investigations, a serious source of cost for the property and casualty insurance sector. AI-enabled analytics are well positioned to identify complex and emergent patterns of potentially fraudulent activity, such as similar claims filed by connected individuals or overlapping networks of doctors and lawyers that may be involved in facilitating fraud. Such systems can use visual representation to significantly accelerate investigations that might have taken human agents weeks to conduct alone. This frees up investigators to focus on the more complex aspects of their investigations that can only be handled by humans.[21]

Chatbots are also playing an important role in the automation and streamlining of insurance processes, particularly when it comes to customer onboarding. San Francisco–based insurtech Lemonade uses a chatbot called Maya to support customer inquiries, and as of June 2018, 19% of all customer support requests are handled by the bot, which has a customer satisfaction score of 4.53 out of 5.[22]

US incumbent insurer Allstate has also developed a chatbot, but rather that being designed to speak with the end customer, ABIE (which stands for Allstate Business Insurance Expert) was designed to support Allstate's personal lines insurance agents in their efforts to expand the sale of commercial insurance policies. The system uses natural language processing to understand the context of an agent's questions and provides detailed support for the quoting and issuance of Allstate's business insurance products.[23]

In addition to delivering more streamlined and accurate processes through AI-enabled automation, insurers are also using AI techniques to improve their decision-making in the underwriting process. One way of doing this is

[20] Teresa Alameda, "What Is Computer Vision and How Is It Changing the World of Auto Insurance," BBVA (blog), August 31, 2017, https://www.bbva.com/en/computer-vision-changing-world-auto-insurance/.

[21] Steven Melendez, "Insurers Turn to Artificial Intelligence in War on Fraud," Fast Company, June 26, 2018, https://www.fastcompany.com/40585373/to-combat-fraud-insurers-turn-to-artificial-intelligence.

[22] Shai Wininger, "We Suck, Sometimes," Lemonade (blog), June 21, 2018, https://www.lemonade.com/blog/lemonade-transparency-review/.

[23] "Allstate's Intelligent Agent Reduces Call Center Traffic and Provides Help During Quoting Process," KMWorld, December 30, 2015, http://www.kmworld.com/Articles/Editorial/Features/Allstates-Intelligent-Agent-Reduces-Call-Center-Traffic%2D%2Dand-Provides-Help-During-Quoting-Process-108263.aspx.

by getting better insights from available data. For example, in December 2017, QBE, Australia's largest international insurer, partnered with London-based insurtech Cytora to improve commercial underwriting accuracy through the application of machine learning on a mix of public and internal data sources.[24]

Insurers are also seeking new data points that would allow them to improve underwriting, such as the use of machine vision to identify and track new risk factors with significant predictive power. In 2016, US insurer State Farm conducted a data science competition where participants were asked to use visual input data from a dashboard camera to create a predictive framework for behavior connected with distracted driving.[25]

Finally, efforts to customize offerings and efforts to deploy new value propositions using AI-enabled strategies are often tightly interlinked in the realm of insurance. For example, Bay Area–based insurtech Zendrive captures detailed data on an individual driver's behavior and detects patterns associated with dangerous activities such as aggressive driving or phone use while driving. However, while earlier versions of this kind of telematics technology were primarily used to calibrate personalized insurance pricing, Zendrive instead focuses on delivering ongoing driver coaching with the goal of achieving risk reduction through incremental improvements in driver performance. In this way, the service aligns insurers and customers around the shared goal of accident avoidance, while also providing a new value proposition to the customer in the form of coaching (assuming the customer values that feedback).[26]

Comparable examples can also be found in commercial insurance sector as well. For example, US insurer RFM Global has developed a platform called 'RiskMark' that analyzes the 700 data points collected from each of its engineers' more than 100,000 sites annually. This data includes detailed photographs and engineering notes and is analyzed to provide the client with useful insights on the likely location of and severity of potential losses. This provides value to both RFM Global and their clients, by supporting the policyholder's more effective allocation of their scarce risk-improvement capital.[27]

---

[24] Sandra Villanueva, "QBE Partners with Cytora to Leverage Artificial Intelligence and Open Source Data," QBE Europe Facebook, December 6, 2017, https://qbeeurope.com/news-and-events/press-releases/qbe-partners-with-cytora-to-leverage-artificial-intelligence-and-open-source-data/.

[25] "State Farm Distracted Driver Detection," Kaggle, accessed January 13, 2019, https://kaggle.com/c/state-farm-distracted-driver-detection.

[26] "Zendrive," Zendrive, accessed January 13, 2019, http://zendrive.com.

[27] "Predictive Analytics," FM Global, accessed January 13, 2019, https://www.fmglobal.com/products-and-services/services/predictive-analytics.

15.2.4   Key Applications of Artificial Intelligence in Payments

Payments may seem like a surprising sector for the application of AI-enabled strategies; however, as we discuss at multiple points in this text, compliance with increasingly stringent anti-money laundering and financial crime regulations is a growing challenge for financial institutions involved in the facilitation of payments. The deployment of machine learning against this challenge can enable more sophisticated algorithms that learn to recognize suspicious behavior and automate the process of identifying, scoring, triaging, and resolving alerts. This reduces the number of false positive alerts, providing more customers with 'straight-through' processing of their transactions and allowing payment service providers to deploy specialized human resources only against complex problems.[28]

In November 2018, HSBC, one of the world's largest global banks, announced a partnership with Google Cloud for the development of just such a platform, with the objective of using machine learning to improve efforts to spot criminal financial activity among its 38 million customers.[29]

A similar set of techniques can be deployed to improve fraud detection processes. In 2018, Citibank announced a partnership with Feedzai, a fintech that had previously received a strategic investment from its Citi Venture arm, to improve real-time detection and response to payment fraud.[30] Feedzai claims to be able to use machine learning to deliver an improvement of over 61% over more traditional models with no significant increase in false positives.[31]

Interesting efforts are also underway to build new businesses at the intersection of AI techniques and payments. The most obvious of these is using aggregated streams of payments data to train AI-enabled models that can provide unique and differentiated insights. A particularly interesting example of this can be seen in a data partnership between Mastercard and Google, wherein a stockpile of payments data purchased by Google allowed a trial

---

[28] "Leveraging Machine Learning Within Anti-Money Laundering Transaction Monitoring" (Accenture, 2017), https://www.accenture.com/_acnmedia/PDF-61/Accenture-Leveraging-Machine-Learning-Anti-Money-Laundering-Transaction-Monitoring.pdf.

[29] Trond Vagen, "HSBC Set to Launch Cloud-Based AML System next Year, Says Senior…," Reuters, November 28, 2018, https://www.reuters.com/article/bc-finreg-hsbc-data-cloud-aml-idUSKCN1NX1KU.

[30] Citi, "Citi Searches for Fraud in Real-Time Transactions with Feedzai Machine Learning Tech," Finextra Research, December 19, 2018, https://www.finextra.com/pressarticle/76809/citi-searches-for-fraud-in-real-time-transactions-with-feedzai-machine-learning-tech.

[31] "WHITE PAPER: Machine Learning | Modern Payment Fraud Prevention at Big Data Scale" (Feedzai, 2013).

subset of their advertisers to better track when their online advertising lead to sales at physical locations within the United States.[32]

Given that Google reportedly paid millions of dollars for this data, it represents an interesting potential revenue source for payment services providers, particularly as payments margins come under increased pressure. However, although double-blind encryption tools were used to prevent disclosure of individual's personally identifying data, many cardholders and privacy rights organizations considered the arrangement problematic, raising questions about the future of these types of arrangements.[33]

15.3   Key Challenges to the Deployment of Artificial Intelligence in Financial Institutions

While the potential of AI-enabled strategies in financial services is clearly large, the impediments to the successful delivery of these projects are not trivial. In the following pages, we will consider four key hurdles that must be overcome by any financial institution seeking to effectively deploy AI-enabled strategies: obstacles to the effective use of data; constraints imposed by the existing technology architecture of the firm; the challenges of transforming the organization's use of human talent; and finally, the constraints imposed by regulators and regulatory uncertainty.

15.3.1   Data Challenges to Deploying of AI in Financial Institutions

As we discussed in Chap. 14, data is an essential input to the development of any useful application of AI. Unfortunately, while financial institutions are in possession of large quantities of data on their customers and the broader financial markets, the effective application of this data within an AI model can be extremely challenging.

There are several reasons for this, chief among them being the fact that data within financial institutions is often heavily fragmented across a range of

---

[32] Mark Bergen and Jennifer Surane, "Google and Mastercard Cut a Secret Ad Deal to Track Retail Sales," Bloomberg News, August 30, 2018, https://www.bloomberg.com/news/articles/2018-08-30/google-and-mastercard-cut-a-secret-ad-deal-to-track-retail-sales.

[33] Ibid.

Cost of AI systems — 50%
Shortage of specialist skills to operate / maintain the technology — 38%
Cyber security concerns — 32%
Integrating humans and technology — 26%
Senior management board buy-in — 25%
Shortage of analytical skills — 25%
Data privacy concerns — 23%
Risks of malfunctioning technology — 15%
Identifying and mitigating all material legal risks — 12%
Customer buy-in — 10%
Regulatory constraints — 9%
Ethical concerns — 7%
Other — 2%

Based on responses from 355 senior executives working for financial institutions globally

Fig. 15.1 Toughest obstacles facing my organization in the introduction of AI in new areas. Financial executives perceive a range of impediments to the implementation of AI, chief among them cost and the challenge of accessing the right talent. Source(s): David Budworth, "Ghosts in the Machine: Revisited" (Baker McKenzie, Thought Leadership, 2018), http://www.euromoneythoughtleadership.com/ghosts2

product-specific systems, making it difficult to form (to give one example) a single view of a customer. This is particularly true in organizations that have grown via mergers and acquisitions, often leading to multiple legacy technology stacks that are extremely difficult to build integrations between.

Financial institutions also tend to suffer from serious data quality issues created by a range of factors including human input errors and incomplete or inconsistent data ontology standards across the organization. In some cases, it is still a problem that data processes have not yet been fully digitized, and that paper-based data intake forms must be made machine readable before AI solutions can be effectively deployed. Together these challenges make the implementation of AI-based projects significantly more expensive, limiting the degree to which developers can experiment with AI-enabled strategies that might deliver value, and requiring them to instead focus on projects where there is a high degree of confidence that the expensive undertaking of data digitization, consolidation, and sanitization will be justified.

Unfortunately, financial institutions' data challenges are also not limited to their internal data. AI-enabled systems provide their greatest value when the data supporting them is both broad and deep. While financial institutions' datasets boast significant depth, the integration of third-party data can often deliver significant advantages by providing breadth. This is particularly true for strategies that seek to improve decision-making through the integration of nontraditional data sets and to customize strategies where nonfinancial personal data can support the design of more personalized products and services.

So long as this continues to be the case, incumbent financial institutions will be at a significant disadvantage to fintechs and (potentially) large technology companies whose more modern data methodologies enable them to rapidly iterate experimental AI-enabled financial services strategies and more quickly deploy successful experiments at scale.

Some incumbent financial institutions are currently in the process of modernizing their internal data architecture through the development of improved data ontologies, the development of new APIs to streamline third party data ingestion, and the creation of centralized data lakes that reduce frictions to the deployment of AI techniques like machine learning. However, such projects are not a simple undertaking, as they require significant investment and sustained executive sponsorship over the many years they often require to be completed.

15.3.2 Technology Challenges to Deploying of AI in Financial Institutions

Implementing the target data architecture described above will require significant changes to the complex 'spaghetti' of legacy technology systems that form the core of most incumbent financial institution's operations. While many financial institutions are demonstrably skilled in making 'bolt on' additions to these systems, the deployment of truly impactful AI strategies will typically require much more in-depth changes.

The successful implementation of a majority of AI techniques requires a flexible technology environment that enables easy access to significant quantities of both processing power and storage. That can be difficult to deploy in an on-premises mainframe system and is much better suited to deployment in a public or private cloud environment. AI strategies are therefore more easily implemented in organizations that have already commenced a migration of their technology to a cloud-based architecture, with those aspects of the organization that have already made the transition much better suited to be candidates for AI experimentation.

15.3.3 Talent Challenges to Deploying of AI in Financial Institutions

Human talent is critical to the successful implementation of AI within any environment, and within incumbent financial institutions talent-related challenges manifest themselves in several ways.

First, in order to be successful, AI-enabled strategies must integrate with and support the broader strategic goals of the organization. For this to happen, senior decision-makers must have a strong vision of the future of their organization and the role that a range of technologies, including AI, will play in achieving that vision. Moreover, they must be willing to make what are often long-term investments in laying a foundation for experimentation with AI strategies whose ultimate value might remain uncertain for multiple quarters (with the exception of some automation strategies, where potential value is more easily measured). While there are doubtlessly leaders within incumbent financial organizations who combine this vision with the authority to invest, the risk averse and bureaucratic corporate culture that pervades many established financial institutions means that these individuals are not as common as might be hoped.

Even if a promising and ambitious AI project receives executive approval, its implementation can face talent challenges. Individuals with skills and experience in the deployment of AI strategies are in extremely high demand and are frequently courted by suitors from a range of industries, most notably large technology companies. For many individuals with these skills, a large financial services company may not be their preferred employer. This is partially due to issues of cultural mismatch, but more critically is related to the previously discussed limitations imposed by legacy data structure and technology systems. These limitations can make leading AI projects a frustrating experience, and as a result many financial institutions both struggle to acquire top AI talent and to retain that talent once acquired. While it is possible to develop some AI skill sets internally, this is a long-term investment and may place limitations on the types of AI strategies that an organization can explore.

Finally, even when a project can secure the necessary executive sponsorship and necessary talent to deliver it, the project may still face significant resistance from staff whose roles and responsibilities will be transformed by the AI strategy. Even if the objective of the strategy being deployed is to augment the capabilities of existing talent, the system may face opposition from individuals who view the project as a 'first step' to their replacement, or who are generally resistant to any changes in their role description. Moreover, in circumstances where existing activities are being automated but there is a strong desire not to reduce headcount, the redeployment of staff can present a significant challenge and impose large retraining costs.

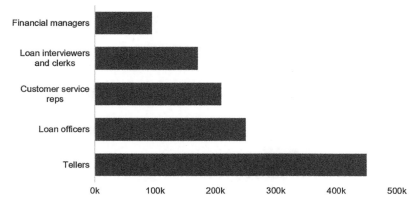

Fig. 15.2 Estimated number of banking and lending roles replaced by AI by 2030. Implementation has the potential to create significant disruptions to the financial services workforce, particularly for lower-skilled individuals. Source(s): Penny Crosman, "How Artificial Intelligence Is Reshaping Jobs in Banking | American Banker," *American Banker*, May 7, 2018, https://www.americanbanker.com/news/how-artificial-intelligence-is-reshaping-jobs-in-banking

15.3.4   Regulatory Challenges to Deploying of AI in Financial Institutions

Innovation of any kind in the domain of financial services is accompanied by an increased risk of regulatory scrutiny and action. It is no surprise then, given the general confusion and concern surrounding the topic of artificial intelligence, that the potential application of AI in financial services has prompted both considerable regulatory attention and ongoing regulatory uncertainty.

While a full assessment of the current disposition of global regulators toward AI-enabled strategies is beyond the scope of this chapter, there are a few critical issues that are germane to cover at a high level.

Significant concerns exist around how institutions should work to ensure that AI-enabled systems do not manifest unwanted biases, either through their independent learning processes or through the unintended transference of biases from their programmers. This is particularly relevant in jurisdictions like the United States where strict laws exist to ensure that minority groups are not discriminated against by financial decision-making systems. However, it is also broadly relevant to all financial institutions, given the reputational and brand damage that revelations of biased decision-making can impose.

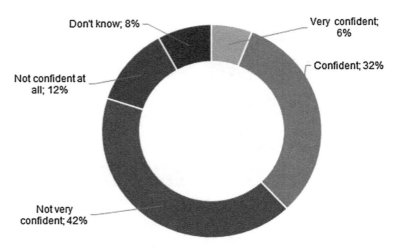

Based on responses from 355 senior executives working for financial institutions globally

Fig. 15.3 Confidence that my organization understands all material and legal risks associated with new financial technologies. Financial services executives lack confidence that they fully understand the legal and regulatory requirements associated with the use of AI. Source(s): David Budworth, "Ghosts in the Machine: Revisited" (Baker McKenzie, Thought Leadership, 2018), http://www.euromoneythoughtleadership.com/ghosts2

Another area of concern is the auditability and interpretability of some AI-enabled systems. Some AI techniques, such as deep learning, create models that are highly effective at achieving a goal, but the workings of the underlying model are so complex that not even the model's creator is able to interpret the reasoning behind a given output. While very few AI systems being implemented in financial services today lack interpretability, regulators are likely to have concerns about these so-called black boxes.

While non-interpretable systems obviously require both cautious implementation and ongoing supervision, it is worth noting that the interpretability requirements of a system may vary from use case to use case. Take for example machine vision, which is often supported by deep learning making it impossible to know how the system has concluded that a photo contains a cat. Given that the model's decision can be easily validated by a human as correct or incorrect, it may not matter that we are not able to articulate why the model was right or wrong in a given case. This topic is discussed in greater detail in Chap. 19.

In addition to these frequently discussed areas of regulatory uncertainty, there are several less commonly discussed issues that still present serious impediments to the deployment of AI-enabled strategies. The treatment of personal data as an input to these models is under increasing scrutiny, both in terms of the globally fragmented regulations that govern the use of data, as well as the uncertain liability frameworks surrounding new partnerships for the exchange of data.

Also relevant are questions of how consumer financial protection will evolve in response to the increased use of AI to enable product customization and product recommendations. Existing frameworks for ensuring that consumers receive suitable product recommendations are largely predicated on an assumption that the agent making recommendations will be human and may need to be reconsidered in light of AI-enabled systems seeking to act directly as product brokers or individuals' fiduciary representatives.

Part V

Future Trends in Fintech, Crypto, and AI

Predicting the future is a tricky business, and that seems to be particularly true when we try to make long-term predictions about technology. Roy Amara, an American researcher and president of the Institute for the Future, is best known for coining what is now known as 'Amara's law', which states that "we tend to overestimate the effect of a technology in the short run and underestimate the effect in the long run."[1]

Popular reactions to a range of new technologies, including personal computers and the internet, have all been impacted by this phenomenon, creating the well-known Gartner hype cycle, where observers initially expect rapid and disruptive change, then dismiss the technology, only to find it a ubiquitous part of their lives a decade later.

At the same time, we can fall victim to a narrow focus on specific technologies that ignore the complex interrelationships between various technologies and the innovations they enable. For example, few could have predicted how the confluence of increased computational power, inexpensive storage, and broadband connectivity would have led to the central role that cloud computing now plays in the technologies we use every day.

Financial Times columnist Tim Hardford tells a particularly amusing anecdote of how Hollywood's attempts to predict the future have gone astray due to just this sort of thinking. Hardford reflects on the iconic 1982 film *Blade Runner*, which takes place in the 'futuristic' world of 2019 and where the main character Rick Deckard drives a flying car and interacts with an organic robot named Rachel who is so advanced that she is effectively indistinguishable

---

[1] Roy Amara, "Roy Amara 1925–2007 American Futurologist," Oxford Reference, October 31, 2006, http://www.oxfordreference.com/view/10.1093/acref/9780191826719.001.0001/q-oro-ed4-00018679.

from a human. Yet, when Deckard wishes to contact Rachel in this version of 2019, how does he do so? He reaches into his pocket for some coins and goes looking for a payphone![2]

In the chapters that follow, we will do our best to avoid these pitfalls and provide you with a considered outlook on emerging fintech, crypto, and AI trends that recognize the perils of overenthusiasm and seek to place those developments in a broader strategic and technological context. In Chap. 17, we will consider how the continued evolution of fintech might drive significant changes in the organizational and competitive structure of the broader financial ecosystem and the implications that could have for a range of stakeholders, including incumbents, fintechs, technology companies, and regulators. In Chap. 18, we will consider the outlook for crypto-assets; the broader outlook for the application of blockchain technology and the potential impact of several assets currently in development; and various scenarios for the evolution of regulators' outlook on these assets. Finally, in Chap. 19, we will explore the future of artificial intelligence in financial services, considering how institutions might use this emerging technology as a means to establish a sustainable competitive advantage, as well as the potential impacts of a broader democratization of artificial intelligence tools on the talent needs of financial institutions.

It is critical to note that while the chapters prior to this section were retrospective and could therefore draw on established data sources and observations of past performance, the chapters that follow are speculative and predictive in nature. While they draw on the best of our collective knowledge and those of a broader network of experts, they are inherently subject to error and will inevitably be proven wrong on at least a few counts.

---

[2] Tim Harford, "What We Get Wrong About Technology," FT Magazine, July 8, 2017, http://timharford.com/2017/08/what-we-get-wrong-about-technology/.

16

Fintech and the Future of the Financial Ecosystem

The world is changing fast for executives at incumbent financial institutions. Fintech startups that were once dismissed as irrelevant now play an important role in shaping the pace and direction of innovation, forcing incumbents' labs and corporate venture funds to compete for the opportunity to partner with them. At the same time, the threat that the largest technology companies in the Western world will decide to compete for a piece of the financial services pie feels ever more inevitable. Whereas a few short years ago, the world's largest financial institutions might have seemed unassailable, today it is clear to most that their existing business models will need to be transformed to remain economically viable.[1]

But to think about this transformation as simply a competition between incumbent financial institutions and fintech new entrants, or even a *battle royale* that includes techfins, is to miss a central aspect of the change that is currently underway. It is the view of the authors of this book, as well as a growing number of commentators, that the very structure of the financial ecosystem is shifting. This shift will impact not just whom you purchase your financial products from, but also the way in which those products are designed, built, bought, and delivered.

In this chapter, we will consider the changing shape of the financial ecosystem at three interconnected levels—the platformization of the customer experience, the shifting market dynamics that platformization will create for the sale of financial products, and the much-needed 'renovation' of the back-office

---

[1] Jacques Bughin et al., "Why Digital Strategies Fail," McKinsey, January 2018, https://www.mckinsey.com/business-functions/digital-mckinsey/our-insights/why-digital-strategies-fail.

© The Author(s) 2019
H. Arslanian, F. Fischer, *The Future of Finance*,
https://doi.org/10.1007/978-3-030-14533-0_16

systems and interinstitutional infrastructure that keeps the whole ecosystem running. In each case, we will also seek to address some of the governance and societal challenges that the financial ecosystem will need to address as it navigates this unprecedented transformation.

16.1   The Changing Shape of the Financial Ecosystem

Not too long ago the path to success in banking was simple—open more branches. The expansion of the branch network enabled incumbent banks to acquire new deposits as well as new consumers for its loans and other products. But the branch wasn't just a place to deliver in-person services; it was an opportunity to deepen relationships with consumers, to gather information on those same people, and to cross-sell products that would make that relationship even more deeply entrenched.

Today the story is very different, and customers are shifting away from branches in favor of digital channels. A recent study in the United Kingdom predicts that consumer visits to retail bank branches will decline by 36% in the five years between 2017 and 2022, with the average customer ultimately visiting a branch only four times a year. For younger consumers, the drop is expected to be even more precipitous, with the average British millennial expected to visit a bank only twice a year by 2022.[2]

16.1.1   The Shift from In-person to Digital Channels

A key driver of the shift away from branches is that customers no longer need them to fulfill most of their financial needs. The advent of the ATM enabled customers to conduct financial transactions outside of the operating hours of their bank, and subsequent channel innovations such as telephone banking, online banking, and mobile banking have freed customers from the need to conduct their banking in a specific physical place.

As we look to the future, new and more engaging channels of customer interaction are in development. Many financial institutions are also focused on building out their interactions via the emerging voice channel. In recent years, a growing number of financial institutions have developed integrations with 'smart speaker' devices such as Amazon Echo or Google Home to enable their

---

[2] Jim Marous, "Banking Needs a Customer Experience Wake-Up Call," The Financial Brand, February 6, 2017, https://thefinancialbrand.com/63654/banking-customer-experience-research-survey/.

customers to perform routine tasks, such as balance inquiries, via these devices. At the same time, the sophistication of mobile devices and their suite of sensors has the potential to further transform this experience, creating the opportunity for more frequent and proactive interactions with customers based on factors such as their location, proximity to others, and even the weather, though few institutions have taken advantage of these capabilities to date.

Future battles for customer engagement will clearly take place in the digital world, not the physical one. In fact, North America–based TD Bank has set a near-term goal for itself of having 90% of all transactions completed on a self-serve basis.[3]

Unfortunately for incumbents, that shift leaves them with an expensive network of real estate and human capital that does not produce the value it once did. In response, a pruning of branch networks is already underway. In the 12 months leading up to June 2017, more than 1700 branches closed across the United States and from 2012 to 2017, both Capital One and CitiGroup, large US banks, reduced their branch network by over 30%.[4]

Of course, simply closing branches is not enough. Incumbents also need to establish themselves as leaders in delivering financial products and services in

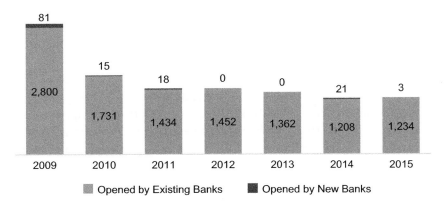

Fig. 16.1 Gross new bank branch openings in the United States. New branch openings are on the decline as customers shift to digital channels. Source(s): "Wiley: Bankruption Companion Site Content," Wiley, November 2016, https://www.wiley.com/WileyCDA/Section/id-829480.html

[3] Doug Alexander, "TD Aims for 90% of Transactions to Be Self-Serve in Digital Push," Bloomberg News, October 11, 2018, https://www.bloomberg.com/news/articles/2018-10-11/td-aims-for-90-of-transactions-to-be-self-serve-in-digital-push.

[4] Rachel Louise Ensign, Christina Rexrode, and Coulter Jones, "Banks Shutter 1,700 Branches in Fastest Decline on Record," Wall Street Journal, February 5, 2018, sec. Markets, https://www.wsj.com/articles/banks-double-down-on-branch-cutbacks-1517826601.

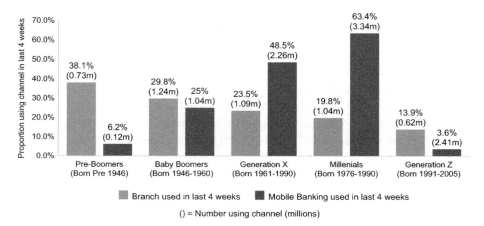

Fig. 16.2 Financial services channel usage in the past four weeks by age group. Younger individuals tend to prefer mobile rather than branch-based financial interactions. Source(s): "Big Decline in Usage of Bank Branches," Roy Morgan, November 30, 2018, http://www.roymorgan.com/findings/7817-big-decline-in-usage-of-bank-branches-201811300632

the digital world, something this is proving more of a challenge. A 2018 study by Capgemini shows that globally only half of customers are satisfied with their current banking experiences,[5] while a report from the same year by J.D. Power and Associates showed that in the United States, satisfaction was particularly low with digital-only customers.[6]

Incumbent financial institutions are clearly struggling to succeed in the transition to the digital world, but ask yourself, what would success look like? Will the customer of tomorrow be satisfied with a shift that simply moves the existing banking structure—be it run by an existing incumbent, a fintech, or a techfin—to a digital environment? Or will they require something more?

16.1.2   Larger Shifts in the Financial Ecosystem on the Horizon

The current structure of the financial services ecosystem has been in place for so many decades that it can be difficult to imagine any other structure is possible. Part of the reason for that is that even though customers are frequently dissatisfied with their primary financial institution, they are shockingly loyal. In fact, in

---

[5] IANS, "Globally, Just Half of Retail Bank Customers Happy with Services: Report," Business Standard India, September 21, 2018, https://www.business-standard.com/article/finance/globally-just-half-of-retail-bank-customers-happy-with-services-report-118092100610_1.html.

[6] "2018 U.S. Retail Banking Satisfaction Study," J.D. Power, April 26, 2018, https://www.jdpower.com/business/press-releases/jd-power-2018-us-retail-banking-satisfaction-study.

the United Kingdom, the average 17-year tenure of an individual's relationship with their bank significantly outstrips the average 11-year length of a marriage![7]

In spite of this loyalty, it would be difficult to argue that the current structure of the financial ecosystem has done a good job of serving clients' efforts to maintain financial health or meet financial goals. While most customers' financial activity rests with a single firm, the product-centric nature of those firms often makes it difficult for customers to obtain a single view of their financial health. Advice remains expensive or conflicted, and in many cases, the fee structure of banks can even reward the institution when its clients mismanage their spending. Take for example the mismatch of bank/client incentives as overdraft fees have continued to ratchet up over the past decade.[8]

Given this, it is perhaps unsurprising that while many bankers will rhapsodize about their relationship as a 'trusted advisor' to their clients, most retail banking customers feel the cornerstone of their relationship with their banks is built on basic transactions, rather than trusted advice.[9]

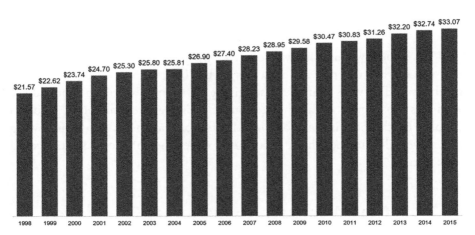

Fig. 16.3 Average overdraft fees in the United States. The fee structure of many financial institutions creates a mismatch between their interests and those of their customers. Source(s): "Average Overdraft Fee | Increase in Average Overdraft Fees, over Time in the United States," Wiley, 2016, https://media.wiley.com/assets/7349/04/web-Accounts-Average_Overdraft_Fee_US.png

[7] Patrick Collinson, "Switching Banks: Why Are We More Loyal to Our Bank than to a Partner?," The Guardian, September 7, 2013, sec. Money, https://www.theguardian.com/money/2013/sep/07/switching-banks-seven-day.

[8] "Average Overdraft Fee | Increase in Average Overdraft Fees, over Time in the United States," Wiley, 2016, https://media.wiley.com/assets/7349/04/web-Accounts-Average_Overdraft_Fee_US.png.

[9] "Banking Relationship in 2015 (U.S.)," Wiley, 2016, https://media.wiley.com/assets/7350/52/web-Trust-Banking_Relationship_In_2015_US.png.

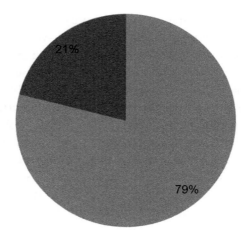

Fig. 16.4 Banking consumers categorization of their relationship with their primary financial institution. Few American consumers view advice as a cornerstone of their relationship with their primary financial institution. Source(s): "Banking Relationship in 2015 (U.S.)," Wiley, 2016, https://media.wiley.com/assets/7350/52/web-Trust-Banking_Relationship_In_2015_US.png

What if there was another way of structuring the financial ecosystem? One that placed the customer at the center of her interactions with the financial products and services that they use, giving consumers access to more advice with less bias and a broader selection of more tailored financial products enabled by the best innovations in AI, crypto, and more. In the following pages, we will imagine what the customer experience of such a system could look like.

16.2   A New Approach to Customer Experience

Take a moment to think about how you shop for physical rather than financial products. Chances are you don't do all your shopping from a single retailer, particularly if you are doing that shopping online. Instead, you likely do much of your online shopping via a platform that provides connectivity between you and many merchants, all competing within the ecosystem of the platform for your business. The platform in turn provides value to both you and the merchants. You get the opportunity to compare prices, read user-generated reviews, and perhaps even get personalized recommendations based on your past shopping behavior. Merchants get access to a large number of potential customers, and might also benefit from integrated payment services, web development tools, or fulfillment/delivery services for their products.

16.2.1   Open Banking and the 'Platformization' of the Customer Experience

So why can't financial services work the same way? Imagine a world where rather than getting to choose between the five credit card products offered by your primary financial institution, you could instead choose between 5000 credit cards from a range of financial institutions, and better yet, get advice on which one will deliver to best value to you based on your purchasing patterns and preferences.

Some areas of financial services already function in this way, at least to some degree. For example, most wealth managers will provide you with the opportunity to choose between funds assembled by many different institutions (although they get a commission from the sale of those products). However, for the core banking activities of most individuals and small businesses, there is no easy way of viewing the universe of financial products, and the only way of gaining access to a third-party product is to sign up as a client to that firm, further fragmenting an already fragmented customer experience.

That's where the concept of platform-based financial services comes in; the idea that the provider of the customer experience shouldn't necessarily be the producer of all, or even most, of that customer's financial products. A financial platform could focus on providing a customer-centric experience, curating a diverse ecosystem of products from many different financial institutions, and using the customer's data to provide highly personalized financial recommendations about the products best suited for them.

Such an idea might seem far-fetched, because after all, why would any bank want to participate in such a system? Incumbent financial institutions today control a large portion of the financial value chain, from customer interaction to the underlying 'raw materials' (such as deposits) that they use to produce financial products (such as loans). Why would they want to give up that level on control?

In the long run, they may not have a choice, due in large part to a shifting regulatory landscape that increasingly supports the notion of 'open banking'. Open banking is a generic term for regulations that oblige financial institutions to provide secure channels for customers to share their financial data with third parties, and in some cases requires the financial institution to provide third parties with the ability to move customer funds. While the exact structure of these regulations differs from jurisdiction to jurisdiction, implementations are underway or being actively considered in the European Union, the United Kingdom, Canada, Japan, and Australia. It may also be the case

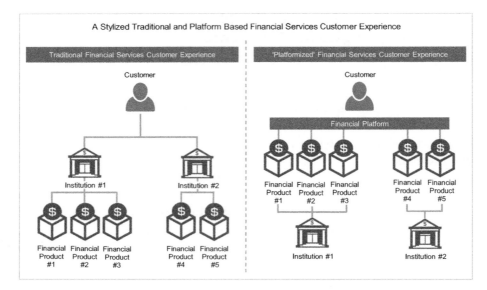

Fig. 16.5 A stylized traditional and platform-based financial services customer experience. The 'platformization' of financial services significantly alters the customer's experience

that the Dodd Frank Act of 2010 obliges American financial institutions to deliver some version of open banking to their customers. (A July 2018 Treasury Department report on financial innovation seems to provide support for this notion, but when, how, and even if open banking will be implemented in the United States remains uncertain.[10])

While open banking in no way requires financial institutions to sell their products on third-party platforms, it does create a significant risk to their control over the customer relationship. In particular, it makes it much easier for the customer to use a financial institution's products without interacting with the financial institution itself. This in turn creates an opportunity for the entry of a new platform that provides them access to third-party financial products without asking individuals to give up the products they already have, since the platform can leverage open data to tie information about an individual's current products together with any new products they acquire.

---

[10] "A Financial System That Creates Economic Opportunities Nonbank Financials, Fintech, and Innovation" (U.S. Department of the Treasury, July 2018), https://home.treasury.gov/sites/default/files/2018-08/A-Financial-System-that-Creates-Economic-Opportunities%2D%2D-Nonbank-Financials-Fintech-and-Innovation.pdf.

16.2.2   Who Will Own the Financial Platform of the Future?

Who is in the best position to create such a platform? Well, a successful platform would need to be able to create cutting edge customer-centric experiences in a digital environment. It would also need to bring together, curate, and manage a diverse set of ecosystem partners whose products it would distribute. It would need to have the ability to provide valuable automated advice and product recommendations to customers. Finally, it would need to be able to navigate the regulations surrounding the brokering of a range of financial products, but interestingly would not necessarily need to navigate the more onerous regulations around holding deposits or manufacturing financial products, unless it specifically chooses to offer those products directly.

The description is a remarkably good match to today's large technology companies. In other words, Amazon, Apple, Google, or Facebook don't need to 'become a bank' to disrupt financial services; they need only become a platform for the distribution of financial services. Indeed, doing so would likely disrupt the financial system significantly more than if they were to build their own neo-bank that attempted to replicate the structure of current incumbents. Such an evolution would not be quite similar to the path that Chinese technology firms like Alibaba and Tencent have taken to dominate the Chinese market for consumer financial services. At the same time, fintech neo-banks such as Revolut, Monzo, and N26 will have the opportunity to use this regulation to improve their insights about their customers and expand their partnerships with other fintech and incumbent manufacturers of financial products.

In response, some incumbent financial institutions are looking to beat technology firms to the prospective punch, by building platforms of their own. For example, in 2018, while speaking at Europe's largest fintech conference, the CEO of Dutch bank ING declared that the openness of digital platforms to third parties was especially relevant to the bank of the future and that "if you truly want to empower customers, you have to provide them with the most relevant offering—even if some of the products and services are not your own".[11] Many more incumbent financial institutions are likely working on such initiatives, though few have released details at this time.

Incumbent financial institutions do have some advantages; if they can move quickly, they can take advantage of the fact that they are already the trusted source of financial services for most individuals, and have a superior

---

[11] "'Being Open Is the Way' – Ralph Hamers," ING, June 7, 2018, https://www.ing.com/Newsroom/All-news/Being-open-is-the-way-Ralph-Hamers.htm.

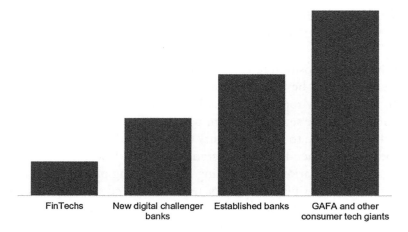

FinTechs   New digital challenger   Established banks   GAFA and other
                    banks   consumer tech giants

Fig. 16.6 Biggest perceived threat to banks post PSD2 (open banking). European banks view large technology companies as their most significant threat following the implementation of open banking regulation. Source(s): *The Bank of the Future* (Citigroup Inc., 2018), https://www.citibank.com/commercialbank/insights/assets/docs/2018/The-Bank-of-the-Future, page 56

understanding of the nuances of the regulatory landscape. But these advantages will fade, and in the meantime, incumbents seeking to become financial platforms will face an uphill battle to deploy new technology (a challenge given their legacy mainframe structure and fragmented data architecture), while also needing to fundamentally reorganize their operating model for a new way of doing business.

16.2.3   Broader Challenges of a Platform Model of Customer Experience

If the dominant model for the distribution of financial products and services to retail and small business customers becomes financial platforms, then there are a few issues that will need to be addressed no matter by whom those platforms are run.

First, our experiences with platforms in other sectors suggest that platforms exhibit significant returns to scale because of network effects. As the platform becomes larger and attracts more users, it becomes more valuable to those users, creating a self-reinforcing cycle.[12] These network effects mean a sector

---

[12] Howard Shelanski, Samantha Knox, and Arif Dhilla, "Network Effects and Efficiencies in Multisided Markets" (Organisation for Economic Co-operation and Development, June 21, 2017), https://one.oecd.org/document/DAF/COMP/WD(2017)40/FINAL/en/pdf.

dominated by platforms tends to have a lower number of competing firms than a sector exhibiting more traditional corporate structures. This could mean that as platforms become a more common model for the distribution of retail and small business financial products, the number of institutions with direct customer relationships could shrink. This in turn could attract the attention of antitrust regulators as it has for digital media and retail sales platforms such as Google and Amazon's European operations.[13]

A shift to platform distribution will also increase the urgency of addressing issues around customer data protection. The platform approach to financial services has the potential to significantly improve customers access to advice, product recommendations, and as we will discuss later in this chapter, product customization. However, all these benefits are contingent upon use of the customer's financial and nonfinancial data, raising questions about how customers can control the sharing of their data, understand the implications of the ways in which their data is being used, and ensure that their personal data is secure. This means that to ensure that customers benefit from open banking regulation and the shift toward a platform economy in financial services, significant improvements may need to be made to the digital identity tools that customers have at their disposal.[14]

Finally, it will be critical for customers to have transparency into the business models of the platforms that they use and for consumer protection regulators to ensure that their statutes adapt to the changing structure of the financial system. There are many possible business models for a financial customer experience platform; it could charge a commission for all products sold, it could charge a flat subscription fee to users, or it might also monetize the data it gathers on customers through either advertisements or the sale of data to third parties. It will be critical for customers to understand how the business model of a platform impacts the products they see and the recommendations that they receive, as well as any conflicts of interest that the platform may have. For example, if the platform receives a commission for each product sold, could the seller of a financial product pay the platform a higher commission to have their product recommended to more people even if some other product is a better fit?

---

[13] Adam Satariano, "Amazon Dominates as a Merchant and Platform. Europe Sees Reason to Worry," The New York Times, November 1, 2018, sec. Technology, https://www.nytimes.com/2018/09/19/technology/amazon-europe-margrethe-vestager.html.

[14] Rohan Pinto, "The Role Of Verified Digital Identities In The Open Banking Ecosystem," Forbes, December 11, 2018, https://www.forbes.com/sites/forbestechcouncil/2018/12/11/the-role-of-verified-digital-identities-in-the-open-banking-ecosystem/.

Of course, none of these changes will happen overnight, as shifts in customer behavior happen over a period of years. After all, despite the first ATM being installed at a Barclays Bank branch in London in 1967, tellers are still hard at work in branches around the world.[15] However, as the world becomes more digital, the pace of change accelerates, making it important for the private and the public sectors to consider how both customer trust and consumer protections can remain strong as the dominant model of customer experiences changes.

16.3   New Market Dynamics for Competing Financial Products

If customers' financial experiences and the distribution of financial products come to be managed by digital platforms, rather than vertically integrated financial institutions selling the products that they make, this will obviously mean sizable changes for those building and selling financial products.

Where once financial institutions customers had been relatively captive audiences, those same individuals will now be able to compare products from many different financial institutions. In many product categories, this will mean that simply having a product that is 'pretty competitive' will no longer be enough to ensure strong performance. With customers facing no frictions to using products from a range of different institutions, there will be only two ways for a product to be successful: being the best price or by being a uniquely good fit to the individual or organization selecting the product.

This is likely to drive the market for many financial products and service toward a 'superstars and long tails' market structure, where 'winners-take-all' dynamics around a given product category combine with an expansion of niche product variety to create a world with a few big winners and many small but agile niche players. MIT professors Erik Brynjolfsson, Yu (Jeffrey) Hu, and Michael D. Smith have observed these dynamics in a number of industries that have undergone rapid digitization including the music industry and retail industry.[16]

On one side of this dynamic are volume players, able to use scale to provide highly commoditized financial products at extremely low margins. An example of this today can be found in the market for exchange traded funds (ETF).

---

[15] Kevin Peachey, "Can a 'Bank in a Box' Replace a Branch?," BBC News, April 28, 2017, sec. Business, https://www.bbc.com/news/business-39709920.

[16] Erik Brynjolfsson, Hu (Jeffrey) Yu, and Michael D. Smith, "Long Tails Versus Superstars: The Effect of IT on Product Variety and Sales Concentration Patterns" (MIT Center for Digital Business, September 2010), http://ebusiness.mit.edu/erik/Long%20Tails%20Versus%20Superstars.pdf.

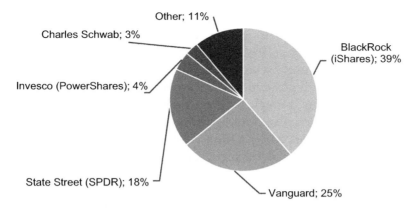

Fig. 16.7   Market share of the five largest issuers of US market listed ETF assets (2017). In markets for commoditized products, such as ETFs, scale players can use low margins to acquire a dominant share of the market. Source(s): Trefis Team Great Speculations, "Five Largest ETF Providers Manage Almost 90% Of The $3 Trillion U.S. ETF Industry," Forbes, August 24, 2017, https://www.forbes.com/sites/greatspeculations/2017/08/24/five-largest-etf-providers-manage-almost-90-of-the-3-trillion-u-s-etf-industry/#320c41 973ead

As the assets under management of an ETF grow, the fixed costs of running that fund can be spread out across a larger and larger number of customers, reducing the management costs associated with a given unit of the ETF. These dynamics have allowed large-scale players like BlackRock and Vanguard to charge extremely low fees for their funds, which have in turn attracted a greater share of the ETF market. This creates a virtuous circle that enables them to charge progressively lower fees. The result is that over 70% of ETF assets globally are now managed by the three largest players.[17]

Those product manufacturers unable or uninterested in competing on price will instead need to identify ways of competing based on the uniqueness of their products, potentially by delivering new features, nonfinancial benefits, or development of highly customized products that are specifically tailored to the needs of specific subsets of customers. For these players, access to customer data, presumably obtained from the platform, would become an essential resource to facilitating customization. Understanding the intricacies of the platform's recommendation algorithms would also be critical for these niche players, in much the same way that optimizing Amazon and Google rankings are critical to online retailers today.

---

[17]Trefis Team, "Five Largest ETF Providers Manage Almost 90% Of The $3 Trillion U.S. ETF Industry," Forbes, August 24, 2017, https://www.forbes.com/sites/greatspeculations/2017/08/24/five-largest-etf-providers-manage-almost-90-of-the-3-trillion-u-s-etf-industry/.

These 'superstars and long tails' dynamics are likely to reward players with existing scale who are able to leverage that scale to establish dominance in certain product categories. At the same time, it has the potential to reward agile firms, such as fintechs who can rapidly deploy and iterate on new product offerings. Less well positioned are many of today's mid-sized banks, who have succeeded to date through a broad competence in many product categories. These organizations risk finding themselves squeezed on both sides, by trying to find customers in a platform ecosystem for their products that are neither competitively priced nor sufficiently tailored to be successful.

16.4   Renovating the Back Office and Shared Financial Infrastructure

The potential changes that we have proposed so far in this chapter are transformative, both for the competitive dynamics of the financial ecosystem and for the day-to-day experiences of consumers of financial services. However, it is critical to remember that the financial system can only achieve its full potential in serving the needs of its customers if the parts of the business that those customers don't see, such as the complex back-office processing, compliance functions, and shared financial infrastructure are brought into the twenty-first century as well.

16.4.1   Outsourcing the Back Office

It is no secret that the technology that keeps the wheels of incumbent financial institutions turning is a mess. As we have discussed at numerous points earlier in this book, the legacy technology systems of today's financial institutions are frequently decades old and composed of a near impossible to navigate series of patches, updates, and one-off integrations that have been layered into the system over the years.

These systems are expensive, restrict organizational agility, and impose an increasingly antiquated product-centric structure of the organizations that use them, all of which limit the strategic options of incumbents as the financial ecosystem evolves. Whether a given incumbent wishes to evolve into a 'superstar' selling high-scale/low-margin products on third-party platforms, serve the 'long tail' by becoming an agile producer of niche financial products on third-party platforms, or wants to become a customer-centric platform, migration away from their legacy systems will be critical to achieving those goals.

A growing number of large financial institutions are looking to the cloud, rather than a more traditional replacement of on-premises IT, as a means of escaping the costs and limitations of their legacy systems. This brings an opportunity for increased efficiency, as well as the 'elasticity' to quickly scale up and down their use of those resources. More importantly, when existing applications are re-engineered for the cloud environment, they can enable improvements in the agility of incumbent players, theoretically allowing them to innovate and deploy product interactions much more rapidly.[18]

As incumbents re-engineer themselves for the cloud, they will also lower barriers to integration with third parties via standardized and secured data exchange tools called application program interfaces (API). This significantly reduces the cost and complexity associated with integrating service providers, such as regtechs, into an incumbent financial institution's operations.

Over the next few years, we may see the proliferation of many specialty providers of financial services solutions in areas like compliance, customer onboarding, risk assessment, and more. These services will tempt incumbents who are moving to the cloud, and whose capabilities in these areas are lacking, to simply outsource these aspects of their businesses and focus instead on their core competencies. Over time, such a shift might see a move from today's 'jack of all trade' institutions—who perform most of their back-office activities internally—to much more specialized financial institutions who outsource most of their back-office activities and retain only those aspects that they believe provide them with a competitive advantage.

16.4.2   The Much-Needed Modernization of Financial Infrastructure

Across much of the Western world, critical infrastructure is aging toward the point of replacement, and the financial infrastructure that connects institutions is no exception. National clearing houses that enable domestic payments, services like SWIFT and the system of correspondent banks that enable global payments, securities clearing houses, and more all provide critical services that keep the modern economy up and running. However, like the incumbent financial institutions they serve, these infrastructure providers make use of aging technology and maintain business standards for their users that enshrine processing times of a day or more, where real-time transactions are possible.

---

[18] Citi, "Bank of the Future – The ABCs of Digital Disruption in Finance" (Citi Global Perspectives & Solutions (Citi GPS), March 2018), https://www.citibank.com/commercialbank/insights/assets/docs/2018/The-Bank-of-the-Future/124/.

At the same time, these critical components of the financial ecosystem are increasingly vulnerable to threats from malicious actors. For example, hackers compromised the security of the SWIFT system via the Bank of Bangladesh in 2016 and Taiwan's Far Eastern Bank in 2017, diverting millions of dollars.[19] Such attacks can be damaging to the faith in financial systems, but also risk being a starting point for financial crises. A recent working paper by the Brookings Institution, a public policy think tank, argues that "an attack on critical financial infrastructure—such as a payment or wholesale funding system—could hit at precisely the place and time that the infrastructure is most economically and technologically fragile".[20]

In addition, these compelling arguments in favor of replacing existing financial infrastructure, we should also consider the opportunities that could be enabled by the integration of cutting edge new technologies into these systems. Various artificial intelligence techniques have the potential to significantly improve our ability to identify fraudulent activities, financial crimes, and prohibited behaviors such as insider trading in real time. For example, in October 2018, Western Union, IBM, and Europol announced efforts to construct a shared financial data hub dedicated to applying machine learning to payment flows with the aim of detecting human trafficking activity and preventing it before it occurs.[21]

Unfortunately, technology is only a small part of the challenge of replacing these systems and building out new ones. Whether new infrastructure is built in the cloud, on a blockchain, or using AI, there is no way of getting around the problem that the system will only work if it has a critical mass of users who agree to use it and can agree on how to use it. Successfully delivering the coordination and alignment of vision needed to drive the continued evolution of financial infrastructure in the years to come will be a key challenge for the financial ecosystem.

---

[19] Erica Borghard, "Protecting Financial Institutions Against Cyber Threats: A National Security Issue," Carnegie Endowment for International Peace (blog), September 24, 2018, https://carnegieendowment.org/2018/09/24/protecting-financial-institutions-against-cyber-threats-national-security-issue-pub-77324.

[20] Jason Healey et al., "The Future of Financial Stability and Cyber Risk," The Brookings Institution (blog), October 10, 2018, https://www.brookings.edu/research/the-future-of-financial-stability-and-cyber-risk/.

[21] Thomson Reuters Foundation, "IBM Wants to Use AI to Stop Human Trafficking Before It Occurs," Global Citizen, October 19, 2018, https://www.globalcitizen.org/en/content/data-human-trafficking/.

17

The Continuing Evolution of Crypto-assets

At the time of writing, the crypto-assets ecosystem could be thought to be facing serious headwinds. No longer buoyed by the record-high valuations of 2017, the community faces a growing number of disappointing and abandoned ICO projects and a drop in overall crypto-asset prices. Yet despite these challenges, a growing number of highly established stakeholders, including large financial institutions, large technology firms, and even central banks, are accelerating their experimentation and investments in this field.

In this chapter, we will consider some of the trends that we believe are likely to shape the evolution of the crypto-asset ecosystem in the years to come. We will first consider how regulators around the world may adapt their outlook toward crypto-assets in the coming years. Following that, we will explore the growing role that incumbent financial institutions are playing in the facilitation of their client's investments in crypto-assets. From there, we will consider the possible disruptive entry of a large technology player into the payments business through the deployment of a stable coin. Finally, we will consider how a central bank could 'beat them to the punch' with the creation of a central bank back digital currency.

17.1 Regulators Provide Improved Clarity on Crypto-assets

It is sometimes said that the world of crypto-assets moves at a 'dog years' pace with each year in the crypto world the equivalent of seven years in the traditional financial system. This rapid evolution has posed a serious challenge for

© The Author(s) 2019
H. Arslanian, F. Fischer, *The Future of Finance*,
https://doi.org/10.1007/978-3-030-14533-0_17

regulators seeking to provide proper guidance for this industry, while also fulfilling their varied responsibilities for systemic stability and consumer protection.

Regulators know the decentralized nature of crypto-assets means they cannot simply stop the emergence of these asset classes, much in the same way that it would not be feasible to 'stop' the internet. However, their disposition toward, and classification of, the various instruments and stakeholders in the crypto-asset ecosystem will have a powerful impact on the evolving structure of the industry. They must walk a challenging line: on the one hand they do not wish to stifle innovations that could drive growth and improve the efficiency and accessibility of the financial system, while on the other hand they must ensure that the best interests of the public are protected. Most difficult of all, regulators cannot simply sit on the sidelines indefinitely waiting to see how crypto-assets evolve, as some financial incumbents have; they must decide and act.

In more and more jurisdictions, we are seeing this action from regulators, clarifying their disposition toward crypto-assets, and in the months and years to come, we expect this trend to continue. While the regulatory landscape is complex and highly varied, we can generally categorize responses into three broad approaches: (1) positive, (2) neutral, and (3) negative. In the pages that follow, we will briefly explore each of these.

17.1.1   A Positive Disposition to Crypto-assets

Some jurisdictions have taken the view that by clearly articulating the requirements for issuing and dealing in crypto-assets, while at the same time expressing a welcoming disposition toward these instruments, they can both achieve their regulatory aims and attract new businesses and innovators to their country's broader financial ecosystem. Switzerland, where the Financial Market Supervisory Authority (FINMA) has adopted an active hands-on approach to crypto-assets, is an example of such an approach. In early 2018, FINMA published its initial coin offering guideline[1] while the canton of Zug, a hub for crypto activity that is often referred to as 'the Crypto Valley', announced that residents can even pay for government services using cryptocurrencies.[2]

---

[1] FINMA, "FINMA Publishes ICO Guidelines," Swiss Financial Market Supervisory Authority FINMA, February 16, 2018, https://www.finma.ch/en/news/2018/02/20180216-mm-ico-wegleitung/.

[2] Michael del Castillo, "For Blockchain Startups, Switzerland's 'Crypto Valley' Is No New York," CoinDesk (blog), October 31, 2016, https://www.coindesk.com/blockchain-innovation-switzerland-crypto-valley-new-york.

Gibraltar, Malta, and Bermuda also provide similar illustrations of such an approach where the government and regulator have taken a proactive approach to crypto-assets, in part to reinforce their position as financial hubs.[3] In the coming years, it will be interesting to see how these efforts evolve.

17.1.2   A Neutral Approach to Crypto-assets

A majority of jurisdictions have taken a neutral stance to crypto-assets, neither explicitly welcoming nor prohibiting dealing in these instruments, and instead trying to fit them into existing regulatory frameworks. In many cases, the focus of these jurisdictions has been on ensuring public protection while also adopting a wait-and-see stance as the crypto ecosystem and its technology evolves.

Hong Kong and Singapore are great examples of jurisdictions taking a neutral view. In November 2018, the key regulators in Hong Kong issued a framework allowing crypto funds and crypto exchanges to fit within existing regulatory frameworks for similar non-crypto institutions,[4] building on earlier statements which had provided clarifications on when a crypto-asset could be classified as an investment or a utility token. In a similar vein, Singapore's primary financial regulator, the Monetary Authority of Singapore, has issued a Frequently Asked Questions page where it provides clarity on the distinction between investment and utility tokens.[5]

Other jurisdictions such as the United States have also been substantially neutral, though some would argue with a stronger leaning toward a negative disposition than the previously cited examples. Part of this may be a result of

---

[3] Paddy Baker, "Gibraltar Stock Exchange Confirms Move into Security Tokens," Crypto Briefing (blog), July 11, 2018, https://cryptobriefing.com/gibraltar-stock-exchange-security-tokens/; Viren Vaghela and Andrea Tan, "How Malta Became a Hub of the Cryptocurrency World," Bloomberg News, April 23, 2018, https://www.bloomberg.com/news/articles/2018-04-23/how-malta-became-a-hub-of-the-cryptocurrency-world-quicktake.

[4] "SFC Sets out New Regulatory Approach for Virtual Assets," Securities & Futures Commission of Hong Kong, November 1, 2018, https://www.sfc.hk/edistributionWeb/gateway/EN/news-and-announcements/news/doc?refNo=18PR126.

[5] "A Guide to Digital Token Offerings" (Monetary Authority of Singapore, November 14, 2017), http://www.mas.gov.sg/~/media/MAS/Regulations%20and%20Financial%20Stability/Regulations%20Guidance%20and%20Licensing/Securities%20Futures%20and%20Fund%20Management/Regulations%20Guidance%20and%20Licensing/Guidelines/A%20Guide%20to%20Digital%20Token%20Offerings%20%2014%20Nov%202017.pdf.

the complex and multilayered regulatory structure of the country. For example, crypto payment tokens can be considered commodities and are regulated by the country's Commodity Futures Trading Commission (CFTC). However, an investment token offering would be regulated by the Securities and Exchange Commission (SEC). Further complicating this issue, both federal and state level regulations may apply to some crypto-assets. For example, New York State requires a specific license, often called a 'Bitlicence', for certain crypto activities. Overall, many US regulatory agencies have made a variety of statements on their approach to crypto-assets, creating an overlapping patchwork of regulation that, at least for now, can create confusion and uncertainty.

17.1.3   A Negative Approach to Crypto-assets

A third group of countries have taken a more negative disposition toward the crypto ecosystem. This was seen particularly in response to the growth of ICOs, which several countries including China, South Korea, India, and Russia viewed as a major risk to the retail public and sought to place restrictions on.

China provides a particularly strong example of this view. The country undoubtedly has an active and sophisticated blockchain ecosystem, and indeed some would argue it boasts among the world's deepest expertise on blockchain technologies. However, this technology may also be viewed as a threat to the Chinese government's tight control of the national economy, particularly currency and capital flows. Moreover, in early 2017, as the ICO craze began to take off in China, people from all backgrounds and age groups began to actively invest in ICOs, with over US$400 million invested in the first half of the year. This sounded alarm bells for the country's authorities, who in September 2017 announced a ban on all ICOs, which remains in force at the time of writing of this book.

17.1.4   The Future of Crypto-asset Regulation

Over the coming months and years, we should expect many more regulators globally to clarify regulatory and policy frameworks for the crypto ecosystem. In many cases, this will be driven by certain global requirements. For example,

Box 17.1   What About Taxes on Crypto-assets?

Taxes and death are inevitable and so it should be no surprise that taxes are finding their way into the crypto-asset ecosystem. While many crypto-related enterprises and individuals are keen to be transparent and declare their crypto holdings, others have tried to remain under the radar, causing tax authorities to begin looking for such individuals.

For example, in late 2017, a federal court judge ordered San Francisco–based crypto exchange Coinbase to comply with a summons that required it to identify 14,355 accounts, which have accounted for nearly nine million transactions. This action was taken in response to a discovery by the IRS that only 802 people[6] across the US had declared Bitcoin-related losses or gains in their 2015 electronic tax filings.

Unfortunately, even for those wishing to comply, the details of tax treatment for crypto-assets remains complex and uncertain. While many established accounting and tax advisors are keen to help their crypto clients, the absence of rules and guidance on the topic has been a major hurdle. While some tax authorities, such as the U.S. Internal Revenue Service (IRS), have issued guidance, these insights have been limited and at a very high level.[7] If holdings of crypto-assets continue to grow in size and breadth, further clarification and guidance from these authorities will be essential.

the Financial Action Task Force has indicated that it would require its member countries to impose AML and licensing requirements on crypto exchanges.[8]

In other cases, it may be a policy decision where the government determines that the crypto-asset ecosystem provides an opportunity for them to take a leadership role in an emerging area of financial services, as has been the case in countries like Gibraltar, Malta, and Bermuda.

A final area of regulation that should not be overlooked is that of self-regulatory initiatives that emerge from within the crypto-asset ecosystem in an effort to address gaps resulting from the inaction of regulators and shape the future or regulatory policy. There are a growing number of examples of such initiatives, such as a best practices document focused on crypto exchanges produced by the Asia Securities Industry and Financial Markets Association (ASIFMA).[9] Other notable initiatives include a best practices guide for ICOs

---

[6] Jeff John Roberts, "Only 802 People Told the IRS About Bitcoin, Coinbase Lawsuit Shows," Fortune, March 19, 2017, http://fortune.com/2017/03/19/irs-bitcoin-lawsuit/.

[7] "Notice 2014–21 | IRS Virtual Currency Guidance" (Internal Revenue Service, April 14, 2014), https://www.irs.gov/irb/2014-16_IRB#NOT-2014-21.

[8] "Regulation of Virtual Assets," Financial Action Task Force (FATF), October 19, 2018, http://www.fatf-gafi.org/publications/fatfrecommendations/documents/regulation-virtual-assets.html.

[9] Manesh Samtani, "ASIFMA Publishes Best Practices Guide for Crypto Exchanges," Regulation Asia (blog), June 21, 2018, https://www.regulationasia.com/asifma-publishes-best-practices-guide-for-crypto-exchanges/.

from the FinTech Association of Hong Kong[10] and a voluntary code of conduct for multiple types of crypto-asset tokens proposed by Global Digital Finance,[11] a global crypto-asset industry body. Provided a continued rapid pace of evolution in the crypto-asset ecosystem we should expect to see such initiative to continue to emerge, particularly in jurisdictions where regulatory disposition remains uncertain.

17.2   Financial Incumbents as Facilitators of Crypto Investments

For years, observers have speculated about how, or when, incumbent financial institutions might make their entry into the crypto-asset ecosystem. After all, while they may lack the technical agility and fiery rhetoric of early entrants to the space, their entry could offer a level of institutional credibility that has long been elusive and at the same time open the door to a 'wave' of institutional capital.

After all, institutional investors such as sovereign wealth funds, pension funds, collectively control trillions of dollars around the world, a sum of money that makes the total crypto-asset market capitalization of around US$100 billion (at the time of writing), seem trivial in comparison. The flow of even a fraction of these funds into crypto-assets would obviously have massive impact on the value of crypto-assets and the interest in new crypto-asset projects.

17.2.1   Institutional Investors and Crypto-assets

While institutional investment to date has been limited, it would not be the first time that these organizations have expanded the remit of their investments as they have become more educated on an emerging asset class. For example, over the past 20 years, the success of alternative funds has given many institutional investors an appetite for exposure to absolute return strategies, short selling, and illiquid instruments such as distressed debt. While many of these players have either not wanted to make such investments directly, or lacked the in-house expertise to do so, they were able to access these instruments via investments in specialized hedge and private equity funds. If large institutional investors choose to seek exposure to crypto-assets, they are likely to use a similar strategy.

---

[10] "Fintech Association of Hong Kong," Fintech Association of Hong Kong, accessed January 16, 2019, https://ftahk.org/.
[11] "Home," Global Digital Finance (GDF), accessed January 16, 2019, https://www.gdf.io/.

If interest in crypto-assets by institutional investors begins to manifest, we should expect to see an increasing number of crypto funds. That is, funds setup specifically to invest in crypto-assets. There are over 300 crypto funds at the time of writing, ranging from those who invest only in ICO tokens to those who offer passive exposure to the crypto ecosystem's largest assets by market capitalization.[12] Over the coming years, it would not be surprising to see the number and diversity of such funds expand significantly. Not only could some of the established names in the fund management industry potentially launch their own crypto funds, but some of the existing large crypto players may continue to expand their offerings with the goal of capturing that small percentage of a diversified portfolio that investors may want to allocate to crypto-assets.

Family offices, including some of the largest in the world, are among the most aggressive institutional investors in crypto-assets. These organizations have been able to take advantage of their ability to make decisions faster (as there are rarely more than a handful of decision-makers) and the freedom offered by having only proprietary capital (i.e. they have no capital from external investors). While many may have expected hedge funds to be active in the crypto space, they have been careful in doing so without raising new funds, fearing that their existing investors may not be comfortable with allocations to this new asset class. Further, the continued lack of traditional players providing services like institutional grade custodianship, fund administration, trading systems, and auditing has been a concern, at least until recently. These are some of the reasons why many of the large crypto hedge funds launched in 2017 and 2018 were actually launched by former traditional hedge funds managers who setup a new fund and targeted investors who would like to get exposure to crypto-assets managed by a team of experienced hedge fund managers.

17.2.2   Incumbent Financial Institutions as Crypto-asset Service Providers

Given this demand, another type of market participant worth keeping an eye on are service providers. The demand for institutional grade service providers for crypto-assets, has seen a number of established financial institutions enter

---

[12] Josiah Wilmoth, "Major Milestone: There Are Now More than 300 Cryptocurrency Funds," CCN, July 27, 2018, https://www.ccn.com/major-milestone-there-are-now-more-than-300-cryptocurrency-funds/.

the space since late 2017, including Goldman Sachs,[13] Nomura Bank,[14] and Fidelity Investments,[15] with many more expected to follow. The drivers behind these announcements are numerous, but include demand from their existing clients like hedge funds or family offices and the potential for new sources of revenue such as structured products and market making.

Incumbent financial institutions are likely to use one of three strategies as they seek to offer crypto-asset servicing. The first option is to build their own crypto offering in-house. Fidelity did this by setting up a new entity focused on crypto-assets called Fidelity Digital Assets.[16]

The second approach is to partner with existing crypto players. This is the approach used by Nomura who has partnered with a French crypto custody and security company called Ledger. A final option is to simply invest in crypto-focused players. This is the approach that Goldman Sachs has taken by investing in firms like Bitgo and Circle.

Another investor group to watch are retail investors, given that the tools available for these investors are still not particularly user-friendly. For example, storing crypto-assets in a cold wallet is a complex process, particularly when you compare it to using a traditional online broker. It seems likely that someone, potentially an institutional player, will endeavor to make these processes simpler, particularly if retail investor interest in these assets continues to grow.

The most significant inflows from retail investors could be in response to an institution offering a passive style product such as a Bitcoin ETF or a mutual fund tracking crypto-assets. No such product has received regulatory approval at the time of writing, and as recently as July 2018, the U.S. SEC denied a second request to list an ETF.[17] However, there is no reason to believe that such a product could not be approved at some time in the future.

[13] Jennifer Surane, "Goldman to Add Crypto Contracts Without Trading Bitcoins," Bloomberg News, May 2, 2018, https://www.bloomberg.com/news/articles/2018-05-02/goldman-is-said-to-add-crypto-contracts-without-trading-bitcoins.

[14] Marie Huillet, "Japan: Nomura Bank Announces Crypto Custody Solution For Institutional Investors," Cointelegraph, May 16, 2018, https://cointelegraph.com/news/japan-nomura-bank-announces-crypto-custody-solution-for-institutional-investors.

[15] Kate Rooney, "Fidelity Launches Trade Execution and Custody for Cryptocurrencies," CNBC, October 15, 2018, https://www.cnbc.com/2018/10/15/fidelity-launches-trade-execution-and-custody-for-cryptocurrencies.html.

[16] Ian Allison, "Fidelity Looking to Expand Digital Asset Trading Beyond Bitcoin and Ether," CoinDesk (blog), November 29, 2018, https://www.coindesk.com/fidelity-looking-to-expand-digital-asset-trading-beyond-bitcoin-and-ether.

[17] Benjamin Bain, "Winklevoss-Backed Bid for Bitcoin-ETF Rejected by Regulators," Bloomberg News, July 26, 2018, https://www.bloomberg.com/news/articles/2018-07-26/sec-rejects-winklevoss-twins-request-to-launch-bitcoin-etf.

17.3   Large Tech Firms' Forays into Crypto

When it comes to crypto offerings to the retail market, it is also worth keeping an eye on the large tech players. The first signs of this have been messaging apps. Japanese tech giant Rakuten launched its own crypto token[18] and acquired a crypto exchange.[19] Japanese messaging app Line has also launched its own crypto token[20] and the 200 million user strong messaging app Telegram recently conducted a private placement for its own utility token that raised over US$1.5 billion.[21]

It would not be surprising to see other large tech firms launch their own crypto payment tokens as well. For example, Facebook today has more than two billion users. The social media network is widely available throughout the world and most would agree that, despite the recent scandals over their treatment of customer data, a large portion of users trust Facebook. So, what if Facebook launched its own payment token? Such a token could be exchanged between users, as well as spent within the network's own ecosystem, for example to pay for advertising. While such an idea felt far-fetched to many, media reports in December 2018 indicate that Facebook is in fact working on its own payment token, specifically a stable coin that can be used on its WhatsApp messaging platform.[22]

This begs the question, what if merchants in the real world, for example a supermarket, accepted Facebook's payment token? Would that token be a currency?

Let's take a step back and think about what a currency's purpose is: providing a medium of exchange, a unit of account, and a store of value. Over the course of human history, the physical form of such currency has changed greatly, but the important constant has been that people themselves defined what characteristics mediums of exchange must hold.

---

[18] Annaliese Milano, "E-Commerce Giant Rakuten Is Launching Its Own Crypto," CoinDesk (blog), February 27, 2018, https://www.coindesk.com/e-commerce-giant-rakuten-launching-cryptocurrency.

[19] Wolfie Zhao, "Rakuten Is About to Buy a Bitcoin Exchange for $2.4 Million," CoinDesk (blog), August 31, 2018, https://www.coindesk.com/rakuten-seeks-to-acquire-bitcoin-exchange-in-2-4-million-deal.

[20] Wolfie Zhao, "Messaging Giant LINE Is Launching Its Own Cryptocurrency," CoinDesk (blog), August 31, 2018, https://www.coindesk.com/messaging-giant-line-is-launching-its-own-cryptocurrency.

[21] Jon Russell and Mike Butcher, "Telegram's Billion-Dollar ICO Has Become a Mess," TechCrunch (blog), accessed January 16, 2019, http://social.techcrunch.com/2018/05/03/telegrams-billion-dollar-ico-has-become-a-mess/.

[22] Sarah Frier and Julie Verhage, "Facebook Is Developing a Cryptocurrency for WhatsApp Transfers, Sources Say," Bloomberg News, December 21, 2018, https://www.bloomberg.com/news/articles/2018-12-21/facebook-is-said-to-develop-stablecoin-for-whatsapp-transfers.

For example, in 1100 BC China began using duplicate models of tools as a means of exchange instead of actual tools. Eventually, these 'duplicates' were shaped into the round circles we know today as coins. In 600 BC, Lydia—now Western Turkey—created the first actual, tangible coins out of silver and gold.[23] The Micronesian island in the north Pacific known as 'Yap' used a fascinating kind of 'coin', large rocks with holes in the middle that can be up to four meters tall. Interestingly, even the heaviest rocks are used as collateral of exchange, though they are never actually carried around or moved.[24] The point here is that the act of defining currencies lies in the hands and eyes of the beholders.

Today, paper bills don't have any more value than any other piece of paper. While there was a time where many currencies were backed by gold, most stopped doing so during the last century and the United States stopped in the 1970s. These paper bills still do have an accepted value because most people and governments around the world agree that that paper notes may be used to buy goods or pay for services and to pay government taxes. Alternatively, people say that paper money is a good metric to price the value of material things and these notes may be stored while retaining their value for future purchases. These beliefs can only occur if a substantial portion of the population agrees to link a certain currency with the mentioned characteristics. That sense of mutual understanding is, in fact, what gives any currency its value.

Imagine now: a Bangladeshi migrant worker in the Gulf region sends Facebook coins via Facebook Messenger to his family, who can then sell them for hard currency on their favorite exchange (or Facebook's exchange) or perhaps even use those Facebook coins to buy goods and services back home. Indeed, one could even imagine Facebook telling its advertisers that to pay for ads, they must pay in Facebook coins. There are benefits to both. The worker can save on the costly cross-border remittance fees involved in sending fiat currencies, and Facebook can become an integral part of the lives of its users.

Facebook is of course not the only large multinational with the required brand recognition, global reach, and vibrant ecosystem who could decide to launch a crypto payment token. Take Amazon. The credit card and bank fees that a firm like Amazon and merchants using Amazon's platform must pay is not negligible. Now imagine the potential cost savings if everyone in that

---

[23] Andrew Beattie, "The History Of Money: From Barter To Banknotes," Investopedia, December 29, 2015, https://www.investopedia.com/articles/07/roots_of_money.asp.

[24] Ben Bohane, "Yap: Island of Stone Money, Micronesian Song and Just a Trickle of Tourists," ABC News, March 30, 2016, https://www.abc.net.au/news/2016-03-30/yap-balances-traditional-micronesian-values-with-tourism-push/7285664.

online marketplace could use a hypothetical Amazon Coin. The coin could be used to make all manner of payments and some individuals might even be willing to use such coins in transactions that have nothing to do with Amazon or its online marketplace.

These are radical and unlikely scenarios that would have tremendous practical difficulties. Organizations like Facebook and Amazon are not experts in the management of monetary policy, and it may well not be socially desirable for people's core payment mechanism and de facto currency to be controlled by a publicly traded private corporation. In spite of this, a survey conducted by LendEDU concluded that over half of 1000 online shoppers would be willing to try an Amazon-created cryptocurrency.[25]

17.4   Central Bank–Backed Digital Currencies

An alternative to a payment token issued by a large technology company that would avoid some of the challenges related to the broad-based adoption of such an asset would be a digital payment token issued by a central bank. In many ways, such a token would be identical to a stable coin whose reference asset is the currency issued by that central bank. But unlike a stable coin, this token would be issued and fully backed by the central bank (like a traditional fiat currency), and as such, it would be much easier for most users to have faith in its stability.

We have already discussed that many central banks have tested the use of blockchain for their next generation real-time gross settlement (RTGS) systems. In these pilots, the central bank effectively creates a digital token on a blockchain that is equivalent to the currency issued by the central bank. However, in these pilots, the use of the payment token is exclusively limited to chartered banks for their clearing operations with the central bank. These assets are often referred to as a 'wholesale central bank digital currency'. While interesting, the primary purpose of these crypto-assets is to facilitate more efficient central bank clearing operations.[26]

Potentially much more transformative would be the issuance of such a token that would be available for use by the average citizen. A 'retail central bank digital currency' would be effectively the equivalent of a bank note, but

---

[25] Mike Brown, "Should Amazon Get Into Virtual Currency & Other Products?," LendEDU (blog), February 27, 2018, https://lendedu.com/blog/amazon-virtual-currency-banking-insurance/.

[26] Morten Linnemann Bech and Rodney Garratt, "Central Bank Cryptocurrencies," BIS Quarterly Review, September 17, 2017, https://www.bis.org/publ/qtrpdf/r_qt1709f.htm.

available in digital form. Moreover, it could be transferable from person to person without a commercial bank or payment service provider as an intermediary. There are many benefits for the issuing central bank as well. It could provide a real-time picture of the economic activity facilitated by this digital currency, potentially providing more accurate and timely economic data than available today. It could also enable other new capabilities for the central bank, ranging from more effective capital controls to improved tools to detect and prevent money laundering.

Perhaps the best-known conceptual exploration of a retail central bank digital currency is Fedcoin. In 2014 and again in 2016, JP Koning published papers in which he proposed the idea of 'Fedcoin', which sought to combine the benefits of using Bitcoin with the stability that a central bank can offer.

As he writes in his 2016 paper:

> Bitcoin's creator envisioned an anonymous payments system without any central points of control. The removal of all central points of control over a currency has the effect of sacrificing price stability, since the absence of an independent entity to 'back' the bitcoins in circulation means that their price cannot be managed during periods of fluctuating demand. This price volatility in turn cripples any appeal bitcoins might have to a broader audience. Fedcoin is one solution to the volatility problem. It reintroduces one central point of control to the monetary system by granting a central bank the ability to set the supply of tokens on a Fedcoin blockchain. This allows the central bank to guarantee the one-to-one equivalence between digital Fedcoin tokens and physical banknotes. Even though Fedcoin restores the 'backing' point of control over currency, other decentralized features of Bitcoin, such as permissionless validation, may continue to be implemented, the result being that Fedcoin could inherit some of the features of coins and banknotes that Bitcoin has managed to digitally replicate. These include a degree of anonymity, censorship resistance and reusability of tokens.[27]

While the paper received support in some quarters, the concept was also widely criticized. For example, a paper from the Federal Reserve Bank of St. Louis said that the call for a "Fedcoin or any other central bank cryptocurrency is somewhat naive. Once we remove the decentralized nature of a cryptocurrency, not much is left of it".[28]

---

[27] JP Koning, "Fedcoin: A Central Bank-Issued Cryptocurrency" (R3, November 15, 2016), https://static1. squarespace.com/static/55f73743e4b051cfcc0b02cf/t/58c7f80c2e69cf24220d335e/1489500174018/R3+Report-+Fedcoin.pdf.

[28] Aleksander Berentsen and Fabian Schar, "The Case for Central Bank Electronic Money and the Non-Case for Central Bank Cryptocurrencies," Federal Reserve Bank of St. Louis Second Quarter 2018, Vol. 100, No. 2 (February 28, 2018), https://doi.org/10.20955/r.2018.97-106.

The paper further argued that "the distinguishing characteristic of crypto-currencies is the decentralized nature of transaction handling, which enables users to remain anonymous". The issue of anonymity is a key point here. A central bank does not require a distributed ledger in order to provide individuals with access to digital payment tokens that are the functional equivalent of physical cash or to enable peer-to-peer transfers of those tokens. That functionality could be offered by a centralized system operated directly by the central bank. In its simplest form, the central bank could do this by permitting citizens to open retail accounts directly with the central and enabling transfers between those accounts.

When we think about retail central bank digital currencies, two types of anonymity are important: counterparty anonymity (i.e. not revealing your identity to the recipient) and third-party anonymity (i.e. not revealing your identity to anyone not involved directly in that transaction). For example, a person sending Bitcoin to a public address does not need not reveal her true identity to the recipient—meaning these transactions offer counterparty anonymity. She also need not reveal her true identity to other members of the Bitcoin community—meaning the transaction also offers third-party anonymity.[29] Policymakers are likely to have serious concerns about enabling any means of payment that provides third-party anonymity, as it could be used to enable tax evasion, money laundering, or the facilitation of other forms of financial crime.

Of course, it is the case that physical cash is a system maintained by governments that offers third-party anonymity. If one person gives another one a US$100 bill, nobody can trace that transaction and the central bank will not even know that that transaction has taken place. However, as the Bank of International Settlements notes in a widely cited paper, in the event a central bank cryptocurrency is created, "the provision of anonymity becomes a conscious decision" whereas "the anonymity properties of cash are likely to have emerged out of convenience or historical happenstance rather than intent".[30]

Concerns also exist that a retail central bank digital currency could play a role in further destabilizing the financial system during a period of financial crisis. A 2017 publication by the Bank of International Settlements cites Marilyne Tolle of the Bank of England in noting "bank runs might occur more quickly if the public were able to easily convert commercial bank money into risk-free central bank liabilities".[31]

---

[29] Morten Linnemann Bech and Rodney Garratt, "Central Bank Cryptocurrencies," BIS Quarterly Review, September 17, 2017, https://www.bis.org/publ/qtrpdf/r_qt1709f.htm, page 64.
[30] *Central Bank Cryptocurrencies.*
[31] Ibid.

At the same time, there may be significant benefits to the issuance of digital payment tokens by the central bank. For example, a recent paper from the Bank of Canada showed that introducing a central bank digital currency could lead to an increase of up to 0.64% in consumption for Canada and up to 1.6% for the United States.[32] However, it should be noted that these results would likely be the case for any retail central bank digital currency implementation, including centralized implementations that would not provide third-party anonymity.

Today, a retail central bank digital currency remains a largely theoretical concept. In December 2017, the Venezuelan government, amid an ongoing period of economic crisis and high inflation, announced its intent to issue a digital currency called the Petro that would be backed by the country's oil reserves. However, at the time of writing, the Petro does not appear to be in active usage and some allege that the entire project is a scam.[33]

That said, serious explorations of retail central bank digital currencies are underway. Since 2015, the Bank of England has been actively conducting research into the implications of a retail central bank digital currency on the macro-economy and the financial system, as well as considering the technical implementation challenges that such a project would entail.[34] The People's Bank of China is even more advanced, having accumulated dozens of block-chain patents[35] and discussed the idea of a crypto renminbi, where there is counterparty anonymity but overall third-party transparency to the central bank.[36] The IMF also helped with the momentum in this space by publishing a paper in November 2017 encouraging countries to experiment with central bank–backed currencies.[37]

Further study is likely needed before any central bank takes serious steps toward the implementation of a retail central bank official currency, but their implementation would have a transformative effect on any economy. This is one area to watch in the coming years as many would argue that it is a question of when, not if, a central bank will launch its own cryptocurrency.

---

[32] S. Mohammad Davoodalhosseini, "Central Bank Digital Currency and Monetary Policy" (Funds Management and Banking Department, Bank of Canada, July 2018), https://www.bankofcanada.ca/wp-content/uploads/2018/07/swp2018-36.pdf, page 9.

[33] Katia Moskvitch, "Inside the Bluster and Lies of Petro, Venezuela's Cryptocurrency Scam," Wired UK, August 22, 2018, https://www.wired.co.uk/article/venezuela-petro-cryptocurrency-bolivar-scam.

[34] "Digital Currencies," Bank of England, December 3, 2018, http://www.bankofengland.co.uk/research/digital-currencies.

[35] "China's Plan to Sideline Bitcoin," *Bloomberg News*, December 13, 2018, https://www.bloomberg.com/news/articles/2018-12-13/china-s-plan-to-sideline-bitcoin.

[36] Wolfie Zhao, "PBoC's Yao: Chinese Digital Currency Should Be Crypto-Inspired," CoinDesk (blog), March 7, 2018, https://www.coindesk.com/pbocs-yao-qian-state-digital-currency-can-still-be-cryptocurrency.

[37] Christine Lagarde, "Winds of Change: The Case for New Digital Currency," (November 14, 2018), https://www.imf.org/en/News/Articles/2018/11/13/sp111418-winds-of-change-the-case-for-new-digital-currency.

18

Future Trends in Artificial Intelligence

With the development of AI capabilities a top priority for many financial institutions, there is little doubt that in coming years we will continue to see changes in the operational structure and competitive dynamics of financial services as a result of the progressively more sophisticated AI-enabled strategies.[1]

Unfortunately, predicting the future with any degree of accuracy is challenging, and predictions about AI have had a tendency to make their predictors look particularly silly. We will kick off this chapter with a brief exploration of why accurate AI forecasts prove so elusive before considering how barriers to accessing AI capabilities are falling away as new service offerings and plug-and-play toolsets 'democratize' AI. From there, we will consider possible developmental paths for some of the most interesting AI trends in financial services and discuss the use of data to drive superior returns in asset management, as well as the evolution of automated personalization and advice into 'self-driving' finance and the development of AI-as-a-service tools by financial institutions for financial institutions. Finally, we will provide a brief overview of the AI issues we believe are likely to be at the top of financial regulators' agendas in the years to come.

---

[1] Bryan Yurcan, "The Top Tech Priorities for Banks in 2018," American Banker, December 19, 2017, https://www.americanbanker.com/news/ai-development-top-of-2018-list-for-many-banks.

© The Author(s) 2019
H. Arslanian, F. Fischer, *The Future of Finance*,
https://doi.org/10.1007/978-3-030-14533-0_18

18.1   The Perils of Predicting AI Developments

One does not need to look very far to find predictions of AI's dire impacts on the future of society, with some even arguing that the advent of strong AI poses a risk to the very survival of humanity. Inventor Elon Musk is much cited for having called AI far "more dangerous than nukes",[2] while acclaimed physicist Steven Hawking warned that the advent of true AI could be the "worst event in the history of our civilization".[3]

Of course, these predictions pertain to the theoretical development of strong AI, which, as we discussed in Chap. 14, bears almost no resemblance to the narrow AI being developed and employed by scientists and engineers today. But even this much more limited vision of AI generates plenty of sensational headlines, with many pundits proclaiming that the technology will eliminate millions of jobs in the coming decades and lead to widespread social unrest. For example, a 2017 report by MarketWatch argues that AI-enabled robots will replace more than half of jobs within the next two decades.[4]

Rodeny Brooks, former director of the MIT Computer Science and Artificial Intelligence Laboratory, provides an important counterpoint to these narratives in his now famous article 'The Seven Deadly Sins of Predicting AI'. Brooks observes that many long-term predictions for AI and robotics have very little supporting evidence. For example, the MarketWatch report mentioned above argues that the number of grounds and maintenance workers in the United States will be reduced from one million to only 50,000 in the next 10 to 20 years, yet the number of robots currently working in that field (or even being piloted for deployment) is effectively zero. Of course, the prediction could still come true—a lot can happen in 20 years—but the evidence that we have to make such a conclusion is largely based on conjecture, and when it comes to AI, our skills in that department (already spotty over such a long time frame) may be particularly inaccurate.[5]

---

[2] Catherine Clifford, "Elon Musk at SXSW: A.I. Is More Dangerous than Nuclear Weapons," CNBC, March 13, 2018, https://www.cnbc.com/2018/03/13/elon-musk-at-sxsw-a-i-is-more-dangerous-than-nuclear-weapons.html.

[3] Arjun Kharpal, "Stephen Hawking Says AI Could Be 'Worst Event' in Civilization," CNBC, November 6, 2017, https://www.cnbc.com/2017/11/06/stephen-hawking-ai-could-be-worst-event-in-civilization.html.

[4] Sue Chang, "This Chart Spells out in Black and White Just How Many Jobs Will Be Lost to Robots," MarketWatch, September 2, 2017, https://www.marketwatch.com/story/this-chart-spells-out-in-black-and-white-just-how-many-jobs-will-be-lost-to-robots-2017-05-31.

[5] Rodney Brooks, "[FoR&AI] The Seven Deadly Sins of Predicting the Future of AI" RODNEY BROOKS | Robots, AI, and Other Stuff (blog), September 7, 2017, https://rodneybrooks.com/the-seven-deadly-sins-of-predicting-the-future-of-ai/.

Brooks argues that several of our human cognitive biases lead us to both make these predictions about AI and find them credible. Perhaps the most notable of these biases is that we tend to think of machine 'intelligence' as being of the same nature as human intelligence, when in fact it is not true intelligence, or at least is intelligence of a wholly different character than that of human beings. As a result, we tend to conflate the ability of a computer to perform a task expertly with the broader level of competence that we associate with the level of intelligence necessary to perform that task.

To borrow an example from Brooks, a human able to identify that a photo contains a picture of people playing Frisbee in the park might be expected to be able to answer a question such as "At what time of day do most people play Frisbee?", "About how large is a Frisbee", or "Do people eat Frisbees?", but a narrow AI system designed for machine vision will not be able to provide any of this context unless expressly trained to do so.

Moreover, our intuition regarding what is easy and what is difficult do not translate well into the world of the computer. We might consider mastery of the games of chess or the game of Go to be extremely difficult, but computers today can now defeat any human player at those games. By contrast, while we would expect a school-aged child to be able to summarize a passage of text, even the most advanced AI systems for doing so remain much 'sloppier and less coherent' than the work of an average human.[6]

Finally, the task of predicting the future impact of AI is challenging because of the irregular pace of progress in AI research. While it can be tempting to subscribe to the argument that technologies of every kind are advancing exponentially, the truth is more complex. The science of AI is advancing 'along a step function' with intermittent periods of rapid progress, marked by long 'AI winters' that make the pace of development much harder to predict over the long term.[7]

For these reasons, this chapter will not attempt to predict the future capabilities of AI, but instead will confine its focus on how the continued evolution of the AI ecosystem and efforts by providers of financial services to build out defensible competitive advantages using AI will transform the broader financial services environment.

---

[6] Will Knight, "A New AI Algorithm Summarizes Text Amazingly Well," MIT Technology Review (blog), May 12, 2017, https://www.technologyreview.com/s/607828/an-algorithm-summarizes-lengthy-text-surprisingly-well/.

[7] Filip Pieniewski, "The AI Winter Is Well on Its Way," VentureBeat (blog), June 4, 2018, https://venturebeat.com/2018/06/04/the-ai-winter-is-well-on-its-way/.

18.2   The Democratization of Artificial Intelligence

Where once organizations seeking to implement AI techniques in their businesses needed to acquire specialized talent and conduct extensive internal R&D, barriers to implementing AI are falling rapidly. This shift is driven in part by the proliferation of third-party 'as-a-service' providers of AI capabilities. Also playing a role is the advent of new tools that significantly reduce the level of technological specialization needed to build rudimentary AI applications. While this trend is often referred to as the democratization of AI, it may be more accurate to characterize it as a marked increase in the accessibility of AI.

Today a range of AI tools are easily available to even the smallest organizations. For example, Google Cloud provides a simple API integration to their 'Cloud Natural Language' service that provide firms with access to insights from unstructured text via natural language processing.[8] Similarly, Google Cloud's 'Cloud Vision' service provides access to advance machine vision algorithms.[9]

More specific to the world of financial services, Bay Area-based firm Ayasdi uses machine learning to create human interpretable visualizations that support improved risk analysis, and accelerate the completion of a range of complex regulatory processes. For example, several of Ayasdi's banking clients have used this offering to streamline the completion of the Federal Reserve's Comprehensive Capital Analysis and Review (CCAR) process, more commonly known as stress testing.[10]

In the event that nobody is offering the right AI-as-a-service model to fit your needs, it is also becoming easier to develop your own. The growth of robust sets of open-source code repositories such as Google's TensorFlow, Microsoft's Azure Machine Learning, and Amazon's SageMaker have commoditized access to machine learning algorithms (though not the data to train them—more on that later) making it relatively easy to develop new solutions by assembling a range of plug-and-play components.[11]

---

[8] "Cloud Natural Language | Cloud Natural Language API," Google Cloud, accessed January 16, 2019, https://cloud.google.com/natural-language/.

[9] "Vision API - Image Content Analysis | Cloud Vision API," Google Cloud, accessed January 16, 2019, https://cloud.google.com/vision/.

[10] Jonathan Symonds, "Modeling the Future of Regulatory Risk," Ayasdi (blog), June 21, 2017, https://www.ayasdi.com/blog/artificial-intelligence/modeling-the-future-of-regulatory-risk/.

[11] Barry Libert and Megan Beck, "The Machine Learning Race Is Really a Data Race," MIT Sloan Management Review (blog), December 14, 2018, https://sloanreview.mit.edu/article/the-machine-learning-race-is-really-a-data-race/.

Even if you don't have the skills to do that, there is a small army of folks who do, and using data science crowdsourcing tools like Kaggle, you can invite them to participate in a competition to crowdsource the best system for your business's specific needs.[12]

Efforts are even underway to provide access to AI tools for those with very limited or nonexistent programming skills. For example, IBM's Watson Analytics offers business users the ability to upload spreadsheet data, integrate alternative data such as social media feeds into that dataset, and then conduct basic queries using natural language rather than code.[13] AT&T Labs is working on an even more ambitious undertaking, building an in-house platform with AI 'widgets' for functions like machine vision or sentiment analysis that can be assembled into working AI applications.[14]

In many ways, these developments parallel those that helped personal computing devices achieve the ubiquity that that now enjoy. Prior to the advent of the graphical user interface, computers required their users to navigate a command line interface and have specialized knowledge of computer languages. The point and click interface pioneered by Apple in 1983[15] set the stage for a world where a user with no specialized skills could intuitively teach themselves to use new programs. In a similar vein, developing a personal or small business website once required users to learn specialized web development languages, but today a range of services exist to help users quickly assemble professional websites that include a range of features such as the ability to engage in e-commerce.

While these 'widget' approaches will presumably produce outputs that are less sophisticated and robust than those built from scratch by experts, they have the advantage of significantly reducing the cost of AI experimentation. Moreover, it places new tools in the hands of a diverse community of individuals with highly specialized knowledge about their business unit and its issues, giving them the power to solve problems the AI experts might not have even known existed. For example, Uber's deployment of an internal machine learning as a service platform called Michelangelo enabled their teams to

---

[12] "Kaggle: Your Home for Data Science," Kaggle, accessed January 16, 2019, https://www.kaggle.com/.

[13] Sean Captain, "A New Point-and-Click Revolution Brings AI To The Masses," Fast Company, March 24, 2017, https://www.fastcompany.com/3062951/a-new-point-and-click-revolution-brings-ai-to-the-masses.

[14] H. James Wilson and Paul R. Daugherty, "What Changes When AI Is So Accessible That Everyone Can Use It?," Harvard Business Review, January 30, 2018, https://hbr.org/2018/01/what-changes-when-ai-is-so-accessible-that-everyone-can-use-it.

[15] Andrew Pollack, "Apple's Lisa Makes a Debut," The New York Times, January 19, 1983, sec. Business Day, https://www.nytimes.com/1983/01/19/business/apple-s-lisa-makes-a-debut.html.

rapidly deploy new solutions and directly enabled significant improvements across the business, such as more accurate estimated time to delivery for their UberEats, offering improved dispatch routing and better demand forecasting.[16]

These developments stand to significantly improve the accessibility of AI tools and to transform the talent requirements of firms seeking to deploy AI. However, it is important that we not confuse that with the true democratization of AI. Access to talent will continue to matter, particularly for those seeking to push the boundaries of existing techniques. Moreover, as we will discuss in additional detail in the coming pages, access to data will also continue to confer market power, particularly where useful data is available only to select parties, or where data can be obtained at a massive scale.

18.3   AI Trends in Financial Services

What can we expect to be the most impactful implementations of AI-enabled strategies by financial institutions in the coming years? With a few possible exceptions, financial institutions are not leading the development of new AI techniques, nor are many likely to begin making such investments at scale in the foreseeable future. That means that competing financial institutions will largely be working from a toolkit of models that, while diverse and sophisticated, are ultimately commoditized.

Given this, how can financial institutions deploy AI in a way that provides differentiated and defensible source of returns? The answer is that the data which is used to train those commoditized models can make a vast difference in the relative effectiveness of their outputs. In the pages that follow, we will consider a range of ways to use data to gain a competitive advantage, giving attention to both attempts to establish differentiated datasets and the cultivation of 'virtuous data cycles' that enables an institution to develop a sustainable advantage in the scale of data at their disposal.

18.3.1   Alternative Data and 'Quantamental' Asset Management

Hedge fund and other active fund managers—in other words, those fund managers trying to beat, rather than match investor benchmarks like the S&P 500—are finding it more and more difficult to generate alpha (excess returns

---

[16] Jeremy Hermann and Mike Del Balso, "Meet Michelangelo: Uber's Machine Learning Platform," Uber Engineering Blog, September 5, 2017, https://eng.uber.com/michelangelo/.

over the benchmark). Investors are responding by shifting funds out of these products into lower fee passive investments (funds that track a benchmark index), placing active managers under pressure to find new ways of differentiating themselves and generating reliable alpha.[17]

AI sits at the cornerstone of one of the most powerful and popular strategies for responding to this dilemma. The power of AI tools to deliver actionable real-time insights from unstructured data has triggered something of a gold rush for alternative data that can provide useful signals about an asset's future performance. Examples of such data include geo-location data taken from cell phones, extensive scrapings from the internet and social media, and even satellite imagery of everything from a factory in a frontier economy to your local grocery store. Combined with the right model, that data can provide insights about future market movements, giving fund managers a crucial edge over their competitors (Fig. 18.1).

Purely quantitative, or 'quant' funds, who select investments on the basis of algorithmic or systematically programmed investment strategies, have been experimenting with these techniques for years, using AI to sift through vast reams of data to identify and react in real time. More recently, fundamental investors (who seek to make longer term investments based on the intrinsic

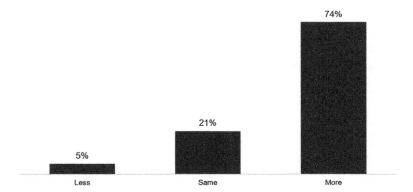

Fig. 18.1 Planned spending on alternative data—hedge funds 2018. Hedge funds and asset managers alike are expanding their investments into alternative data sources. Source: John Detrixhe, "Selling Data to Feed Hedge Fund Computers Is One of the Hottest Areas of Finance Right Now," Quartz, September 20, 2017, https://qz.com/1082389/quant-hedge-funds-are-gorging-on-alternative-data-in-pursuit-of-an-investing-edge/

---

[17] Mark Gilbert, "The Hedge Fund King and a Technological Arms Race," Bloomberg Opinion, December 27, 2018, https://www.bloomberg.com/opinion/articles/2018-12-27/man-group-ceo-luke-ellis-hedge-fund-king-in-technology-arms-race.

value of a security) are exploring how they might apply these same tools to their own strategies. This has led to a new style of investing that merges fundamental and quantitative techniques that is often referred to as 'quantamental'.[18]

While the strategies of pure quant funds often revolve around algorithms executing trades in real time with limited human supervision, quantamental techniques are much more focused on creating a symbiotic relationship between the fund manager and their AI tools and seek to combine the complementary strengths of each. In this way, they are comparable to teams of human chess experts and modern chess computers, who together consistently beat both human grandmasters and the world's most advanced chess programs.[19]

AI can facilitate the rapid ingestion and analysis of data and selectively surface key insights that support the evolution of fund manager's assessment of a company's fundamentals. For example, analysis by the *Financial Times* points out that fund managers could have avoided being surprised by a Q2 2017 earnings release by sportswear retailer Under Armor if they had been notified of a range of forward-looking indicators such as a drop in the number of job postings on the company website, declining internal ratings of the company on recruitment sites, and a decline in the average price of the brand's products sold on its website.[20]

This same data intensive analysis can be turned on money managers themselves and, when combined with the dispassionate and rational nature of a computer, used to improve human performance. Essentia Analytics provides fund managers with the tools to analyze their own historical trading activity, helping them to identify foibles, such as a tendency to abandon poorly performing investment positions too early (or too late), and then provides coaching on how to improve.[21] In fact, the system will even nudge traders who may be settling back into old patterns with a personalized email 'from their future selves' that reminds them to avoid these behaviors.

[18] Robin Wigglesworth, "The Rise of 'quantamental' Investing: Where Man and Machine Meet," Financial Times, November 21, 2018, https://www.ft.com/content/f1276122-ec19-11e8-8180-9cf212677a57.

[19] Chris Baraniuk, "The Cyborg Chess Players That Can't be Beaten," BBC News, December 4, 2015, http://www.bbc.com/future/story/20151201-the-cyborg-chess-players-that-cant-be-beaten.

[20] "Asset Management's Fight for 'alternative Data' Analysts Heats up," Financial Times, accessed January 17, 2019, https://www.ft.com/content/2f454550-02c8-11e8-9650-9c0ad2d7c5b5.

[21] Jeremy Kahn, "Traders Emulate pro Athletes to Improve Their Game, Hiring Coaches and Metrics Analysts," The Washington Post, March 22, 2014, https://www.washingtonpost.com/business/traders-emulate-pro-athletes-to-improve-their-game-hiring-coaches-and-metrics-analysts/2014/03/20/3152baf4-ad3a-11e3-9627-c65021d6d572_story.html.

There is good reason to expect exploration of the quantamental approach to accelerate in coming years. While the core idea of this strategy is not new (Bank of America Merrill Lynch has been practicing a more analog version of these techniques called 'alpha surprise' since 1986[22]), the explosion in both the accessibility of AI and the ability of AI techniques to chew through reams of unstructured data makes the approach much more powerful. Wall Street consultancy the Tabb Group estimates that the market for alternative data, which as of 2016 had US$200 million in sales, will double in the next four years, and a survey of hedge funds by Greenwich Associates showed that 74% planned to increase spending on alternative data in 2018.[23]

Ironically, the growing popularity of quantamental strategies may be a threat to the strategies' very profitability. That's because when strategies are based on publicly available data, the scope for generating alpha may be short-lived, as competing firms pile in, replicating the approaches. In the words of a report by Greenwich Associates, "alternative data will only be alternative for so long, eventually [it will become] a core part of any portfolio manager's toolkit".[24]

Some fund managers may seek to lock-in a data advantage by establishing exclusive arrangements with providers of alternative data. For example, you could imagine a situation where a hedge fund acquired exclusive access to geo-location data from multiple mobile network operators, giving them an edge in predicting the performance of various retailers. While exclusive access to this data would obviously be desirable, the legal ramifications of trading on it are murky. As of the time of writing, regulatory clarity on this issue remains limited, and no major legal cases on the subject have been tried. However, numerous commentators argue that such arrangements have the potential to be viewed as trading on the basis of material nonpublic information, and thus risk being in violation of insider trading statutes in the United States and many other jurisdictions.[25]

---

[22] William Watts, "The next Frontier in Investing Is 'quantamental' Stock Picking," MarketWatch, October 29, 2018, https://www.marketwatch.com/story/the-next-frontier-in-investing-is-quantamental-stock-picking-2018-10-03.

[23] John Detrixhe, "Selling Data to Feed Hedge Fund Computers Is One of the Hottest Areas of Finance Right Now," Quartz, September 20, 2017, https://qz.com/1082389/quant-hedge-funds-are-gorging-on-alternative-data-in-pursuit-of-an-investing-edge/.

[24] http://www.dnb.com/content/dam/english/dnb-solutions/alternative-data-for-alpha-final.pdf.

[25] "Hedge Funds See a Gold Rush in Data Mining," Financial Times, August 28, 2017, https://www.ft.com/content/d86ad460-8802-11e7-bf50-e1c239b45787.

18.3.2   AI-As-a-Service by and for Financial Institutions

Fortunately, acquiring exclusive datasets is not the only way for financial institutions to build a defensible value proposition around AI. Deploying strategies to acquire a differentiated scale of data flows can also help entrench a set of strategic advantages via what is often referred to as the 'virtuous cycle' of AI products, or the 'AI flywheel effect'. This describes a process wherein data enables improvements to AI products, which deepens the engagement of existing customers and attracts new ones, thereby creating more data that can be used to continue the cycle (Fig. 18.2).

This notion has been at the heart of many large technology companies for years where the aim of deploying a product is often not the generation of revenue, but rather the collection of data. This is worlds away from the thinking of many traditional financial institutions who tend to view the gathering and maintenance of data as a necessary means to achieving their ultimate end of selling financial products to their customers and who tend to think of their data as a stock to be analyzed rather that a flow to be augmented.

There are however a growing number of financial institutions beginning to think differently about the role of data and AI in their organizations. As we discussed in Chap. 16, Chinese financial institution Ping An has developed a number of AI applications to improve their operations. For example, they use micro-gesture facial recognition technology in video chat loan interviews to

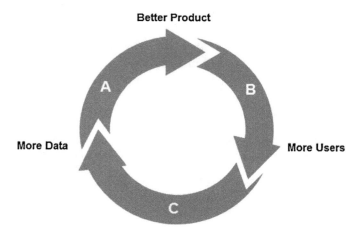

Fig. 18.2   The AI 'flywheel' effect. The role of data in improving AI applications makes it possible to realize a 'flywheel' effect where acquiring valuable data becomes a self-reinforcing cycle

assess the likelihood of borrower default[26] and have developed a system to expedite the processing of low-value auto insurance claims that employs machine vision.

Traditionally you would expect a financial institution that had developed such capabilities to guard them closely and attempt to use them to get a competitive advantage over their peers, but Ping An has taken a different route. Rather than keeping these technologies proprietary, Ping An has made them, and dozens of other capabilities, available on an as-a-service basis under an offering called OneConnect.[27] The service is now used by numerous smaller Chinese banks and insurance providers seeking to rapidly update their technological capabilities in order to compete with the likes of WeChat and Ant Financial.

The benefits of this strategy are twofold. On the one hand, Ping An is able to take a set of IT projects that it already invested in and is able to turn those cost centers into profit centers. More importantly, by flowing the loan adjudications and insurance claims of other institutions through their own system, Ping An expands the volume and diversity of the training data these models are exposed to (where users consent to the sharing of such data). This creates an opportunity for Ping An to kickstart the AI flywheel; as more data flow through OneConnect's models, the quality of those models relative to the internal systems of other financial institutions increases. This creates a strong rationale for those institutions to abandon their internal systems and adopt OneConnect's models, bringing still more data that further improves those offerings. Over time, this process has the potential to entrench a set of capability advantages on the basis of the scale of that data—something that is presumably reflected in the US$3 billion valuation OneConnect is expected (at time of writing) to fetch in a planned spinoff from Ping An.[28]

Looking forward, it is possible that we will see more organizations building out these kinds of offerings. Indeed, many of the examples of AI being used to create new value propositions that we considered in Chap. 16 could be structured in this way. In many regards, financial institutions are much better

---

[26] Oliver Ralph, Martin Arnold, and Don Weinland, "Chinese Banks Start Scanning Borrowers' Facial Movements," Financial Times, October 28, 2018, https://www.ft.com/content/4c3ac2d4-d865-11e8-ab8e-6be0dcf18713.

[27] Jessica Tan, "From Ping An to Platform: Technology Innovation for Growth," (November 20, 2017), http://www.pingan.com/app_upload/images/info/upload/68a59877-41d3-4fff-a1d3-5f01172bfcdb1.pdf.

[28] "Ping An Starts Work on Up to $3 Billion OneConnect IPO," Bloomberg News, March 28, 2018, https://www.bloomberg.com/news/articles/2018-03-28/ping-an-is-said-to-start-work-on-up-to-3-billion-oneconnect-ipo.

positioned to succeed in the deployment of these offerings than large technology firms. Their current operations provide them with the flows of data needed to develop these systems and 'kickstart' the AI flywheel. Short of actually getting into a given business area, it would be quite difficult for a large technology firm to build out a specialized offering of this kind.

The potential for these kinds of 'AI-as-a-service' offerings to transform the landscape of financial services is significant. As we have addressed numerous times in this book, incumbent financial institutions around the world are struggling to update their internal systems, and this task is particularly challenging for smaller regional and community banks given the significant costs involved. It is not that difficult to imagine large financial institutions in the United States or Western Europe seeking to build out offerings similar to OneConnect with the objective of simultaneously improving their own systems and developing a profitable new line of business. Such offerings could find many interested customers, ranging from Germany's sparkassen banks to thousands of US community banks, all of whom which have strong relationships with their customers, but increasingly out-of-date IT systems.

18.3.3   AI-Enabled 'Self-driving' Finance

Having considered how future trends in the application of AI to financial services will impact the way trading decisions are made and the way financial operations will be structured, it is important that we conclude by considering how AI might be used to shape customer experiences and deliver new forms of value to users in the years to come.

Historically, there have been two key points of differentiation for a financial offering—price and the ease with which it could be delivered. In other words, if the price of the product seemed good and it could be obtained by the customer with relatively little hassle, the offering was competitive. However, the differentiation power of both factors is beginning to erode. Aggregation tools and comparison sites are lowering the cost of price discovery for customers, making it easy to find the rock bottom lowest price, and as we discussed in Chap. 17, the 'platformization' of financial services would continue this trend, making differentiation on price a race to the bottom that only the largest scale players can win.

At the same time, our discussion of fintech and AI trends shows how operational excellence is becoming available on an as-a-service basis, both through small specialized firms such as regtechs and larger offerings like Ping An's OneConnect. This means that the ability to quickly onboard customers, adjudicate claims, or deploy basic digital services is likely to become less and less of a differentiator in the sales of financial products.

In response, financial institutions will need to find new ways of differentiating themselves in the eyes of their customers. In Chap. 17, we showed how the shift to a platform-based model of financial services would force sub-scale producers of financial products to become more focused on niche and customized products. Here we will consider how the owners of customer experiences, most likely platforms, will differentiate themselves in the years to come.

We know that financial platforms would provide the ability to compare products from many different financial institutions and would likely use AI to provide basic recommendations akin to Amazon's personalized 'Recommended for you' purchasing suggestions. Unfortunately, all of these new options and suggestions may not actually benefit customers. While it might seem counterintuitive, more choices aren't always better for the customer, particularly in financial services where products are highly complex. A 2003 study by Iyengar, Huberman, and Jiang found that employee participation rates in 401(k) plans declined as more fund options were added to the plan, likely because employees chose to not engage than be forced to pick from a vast menu of plans.[29]

This means that to successfully engage customers, a platform cannot simply expand the options available to that customer. They must also find ways to help customers navigate those options and improve their financial outcomes, ideally with as little hassle for the customer as possible. These twin goals—of improved outcomes and minimized aggravation—are at the heart of a new strategy often called autonomous, or self-driving, finance.

Self-driving finance is the notion the best way that customer experience owners in financial services can provide value to individuals and small businesses is by automating and optimizing the management of routine aspects of their financial affairs to help them better meet their financial goals. For example, a self-driving finance agent might facilitate the process of moving some of a customer's savings tagged for a vacation in three months into a short-term low-risk investment or might optimize the repayment or consolidation of an individual's debt.

Offering this kind of continuous, low-friction optimization has the potential to significantly improve customers' outcomes. For example, it would offer the opportunity to improve returns on short-term savings, in much the same way treasury management services provided by private bankers do for

---

[29] Sheena S. Iyengar, Wei Jiang, and Gur Huberman, "How Much Choice Is Too Much?: Contributions to 401(k) Retirement Plans" (Pension Research Council, The Wharton School, University of Pennsylvania, 2003), https://pdfs.semanticscholar.org/04f0/7b37fc9deb167e56c729e1f35e052998ba4a.pdf.

high-net-worth individuals. It would also help customers avoid some common and costly mistakes. Take the example of an individual looking to pay off debt held on multiple credit cards. The fastest way of doing this is to prioritize paying off the balance of the highest interest card, but a study in the United Kingdom suggests that only about 10% of individuals in this situation follow that strategy, with many choosing instead to spread their payments more or less evenly across their cards.[30] A customer relying on a 'self-driving' financial agent would not need to worry about making these kinds of mistakes.

In addition to these basic solutions, a self-driving agent could use an individual's personal data to identify savings opportunities and even provide behavioral coaching and nudges to help an individual develop better financial habits and meet their financial goals. This is increasingly referred to as financial health. In the same way that we exercise for our physical health and meditate for our mental health, we can use technology for our financial health. For example, an existing personal financial management service called Clarity Money searches through customers' transaction data to identify subscriptions that a customer may no longer be using and automates the process of cancelling that subscription.[31] Meanwhile, in South Africa, a newly created offering called Discover Bank (built by an insurance company also called Discover who is responsible for building the 'Vitality' offering discussed in Chap. 3) tracks customer behavior and provides rewards for healthy financial decisions.[32] While neither of these services appear to use AI to any significant degree, it is easy to imagine how such offerings could be expanded and enhanced through the application of AI tools that enable deeper and more timely insights drawn from large quantities of customers' unstructured personal data.

For small business, the benefits of such a system could be even more significant. Consider that some of the most common challenges facing such businesses are the management of cash flow and access the capital necessary to grow. This is no surprise given that most small businesses lack the scale necessary for specialized accounting and treasury functions within their organization. Simply because someone has the necessary skills to run a successful chain of flower shops or small metal galvanization plant does not mean that they

---

[30] Christopher Ingraham, "Most People Are Paying off Their Credit Card Debt All Wrong—Are You?," Washington Post, January 2, 2018, https://www.washingtonpost.com/news/wonk/wp/2018/01/02/most-people-are-paying-off-their-credit-card-debt-all-wrong-are-you/.

[31] "Clarity Money - Champion of Your Money," Clarity Money, accessed January 17, 2019, https://claritymoney.com/.

[32] Brian Browdie, "Health Platform Vitality Gets into Banking," Digital Insurance, January 2, 2019, https://www.dig-in.com/news/the-bank-that-watches-your-every-move-the-rise-of-behavioral-banks.

will also have the necessary skills to meet all their company's financial needs. A self-driving finance agent for these businesses could combine a detailed understanding of the historical seasonality of a business with forward-looking indicators to see a cash flow crunch or expansion opportunity on the horizon and secure a revolving line of credit on favorable terms long before it is needed. At the same time, through access to the company's books, it would have detailed knowledge of when and where retained earnings will be needed for operational outlays, allowing it to optimize the allocation of those funds to short-term low-risk investments.

The potential benefits of a self-driving finance agent are clear, but who is best positioned to deliver these kinds of offerings? To unlock the full potential of self-driving finance requires the combination of personal and financial data at the individual customer level and the ability to deploy technology against that data in a way that creates value. While financial institutions have the individual's financial data, open banking regulations are making it easier for that data to be pulled out of the institution by third parties and large technology companies have a massive head start both in terms of their flows of personal data and their expertise in applying AI to that data. For small businesses, the situation is even starker with the firm's provider of accounting software often in a much better position than their bank to leverage the firm's detailed operational data.

18.4 Responsible Regulation of AI in Financial Services

As the centrality of AI to financial services value proposition grows, so too will regulators' interest in this topic as they seek to ensure that consumer interests are protected, and that the application of this technology does not threaten the safety and soundness of the financial system. Already regulators around the world have launched efforts to better understand the ways in which AI is being used today and to articulate principles for future deployment of the technology. For example, the Financial Stability Board, an international coordination body for financial service regulators, has published the results of several reports on their detailed exploration of this topic[33] and the Monetary Authority of Singapore has launched a set of fairness, ethics, accountability,

---

[33] "Artificial Intelligence and Machine Learning in Financial Services" (Financial Stability Board, November 1, 2017), http://www.fsb.org/2017/11/artificial-intelligence-and-machine-learning-in-financial-service/.

and transparency (FEAT) principles for in the use of artificial intelligence in financial services.[34]

As this conversation evolves, it will be important to ensure that dialogue is nuanced and does not treat all applications of artificial intelligence to financial services as the same. Many applications of AI will require little or no changes to existing regulatory frameworks, while in others, the core regulatory principles will remain relevant and only the frameworks for applying the regulation will need to be updated. While in a few instances genuinely new policies may be required, these are likely to be the minority of cases.

For example, a prudential regulator's concerns about an AI-as-a-service offering may have much more to do with the way such offerings alter the operational structure of financial markets—potentially creating new concentration or contagion risks—than they do with the actual use of AI. Regulators already have well-honed tools for assessing and addressing such risks, and wherever possible should continue to use and refine those tools rather than building policies from the ground up simply because there is AI involved.

In the same vein, the actions of self-driving finance agents will need to be consistent with the same principles of suitability, best efforts, and, in some cases, fiduciary duty that would be applied to a human performing the same role. The fact that AI can perform that task at a lower cost while incorporating insights from a mountain of unstructured data that no human could navigate should have no impact on our expectations for the ways in which the customer's interests will be protected.

Of course, in some cases, the application of AI models to a business area will demand updates to regulatory standards and practices to ensure that the principles underlying those regulations continue to be met. For example, it is well known that the use of advanced adjudication models increases the risk that the model may unintentionally discriminate against minorities and a range of marginalized groups in ways that are neither legal nor ethical. This can occur both because of the internalization of a developer's conscious/unconscious biases, for example, through their selection of data inputs, or through biases learned by the model itself. In either case, the development of strong internal governance and review protocols and well-understood external regulatory and compliance practices may be necessary to ensure that these models do not have damaging social effects.

---

[34] "MAS Introduces New FEAT Principles to Promote Responsible Use of AI and Data Analytics," Monetary Authority of Singapore (MAS), November 12, 2018, http://www.mas.gov.sg/News-and-Publications/Media-Releases/2018/MAS-introduces-new-FEAT-Principles-to-promote-responsible-use-of-AI-and-data-analytics.aspx.

Finally, there will be instances that will raise new and interesting questions that require thoughtful regulatory response. The most obvious example of this is the frequently discussed issue of 'explainability': if a model is sufficiently complex that even its creators cannot explain the reasoning behind any given decision, should that model be used? Nuanced thinking will be essential to answering such questions, as there will rarely be a single answer. For example, why something needs to be explained shapes the type of requirements or solutions that should be put in place. Some models may only need to provide a customer or user a broad rationale for a decision, while others may need to provide full transparency to regulators. In some instances, it may even be sufficient for a set of 'guard rails' or 'circuit breakers' to be put in place to ensure that a model remains within a reasonable set of bounds.

Ultimately, proper regulation of the increased use of AI in financial services will require close attention and continuous examination. Even more importantly, to ensure that the application of this technology serves the needs of financial institutions, their customers, and society at large, the process of putting these regulations in place and periodically refreshing them must be a multi-stakeholder effort, bringing together the insights of financial institutions, academics, consumer advocacy groups, and more.

Part VI

Artificial Intelligence Meets Crypto-assets

Our exploration of current trends in the preceding section clearly illustrates the potential for rapid and foundational change in the financial sector over the years to come. Moreover, it highlights the two technologies likely to play a starring role in that transformation given how tightly interwoven the developments of crypto-assets and AI could be with the future developments of fintech and the broader financial system.

So as this book approaches its conclusion, it seems appropriate to ask the obvious question: What relationship will these two technologies have to each other? If crypto and AI continue to grow and develop, taking more central roles in our future financial system, what could be the potential impact of their interaction?

The production deployment of these technologies in financial services is at a nascent stage and it may be years before we fully appreciate their individual impact, let alone how they might intersect. Having said that, it should not, and has not, stopped us from imagining a few possibilities of how it *might* happen.

19

Selected Scenarios for a Crypto-AI World

We don't have a crystal ball to tell us how the future will unfold, but we can tell ourselves a few stories about how AI and crypto might interact to transform financial services. These scenarios may seem crazy or wild and potentially (if not probably!) turn out to be completely wrong, but it is worth discussing and reflecting on them.

In this chapter, we will explore a number of scenarios for how AI and crypto might come together to reshape the financial ecosystem and our broader economy. We will imagine a shift away from today's system of accounting to one characterized by real-time intelligent auditing on a blockchain. We will explore a possible world where AI-enabled blockchains take on a life of their own as 'distributed autonomous organizations' (DAO), redefining our notion of digital platforms in the process. We will imagine a society where blockchain and AI come together to help individuals regain control of their personal identity data not only via AI agents, but also via marketplaces that could enable the democratization of AI. We will discuss how AI may accelerate the adoption of crypto-assets, and finally, we will explore a world in which blockchains form the rails for AI-enabled systems to interact with and pay each other, ushering in a new era of machine-to-machine payments.

19.1   Real-time Auditing

The first scenario we will explore in the combination of AI and crypto is their ability to deliver radical improvements to real-time auditing. To understand the implications of the shift that these two technologies could deliver, let's first examine how an audit works today.

© The Author(s) 2019
H. Arslanian, F. Fischer, *The Future of Finance*,
https://doi.org/10.1007/978-3-030-14533-0_19

The current framework for auditing an organization is effectively looking in a rear-view mirror. For example, a small business owner may give her basic financial information (e.g. receipts, invoices, expenses) to her accountant who will then structure this data into a financial report, including documents such as the balance sheet and the income statement, in accordance with the generally accepted accounting standards. An external auditor may then need to be hired, to review the financial reports in accordance with standards laid out by relevant government bodies and express an opinion as to whether the information presented reflects the true and fair financial position of the organization at a given date.[1]

This is a well-established process, the framework for which dates back hundreds of years to the creation of the double-entry bookkeeping system in fifteenth-century Italy[2]; however, it has serious limitations. Perhaps most notably it is not practical for the auditor to review every transaction done by the organization or check every figure in the financial report, as that would be a never-ending, and perhaps impossible, task. Instead, the audits are based on selective sampling and testing only.

As a result, auditors today may miss some irregularities. This is deemed to be acceptable because the prime purpose of the audit is to identify signs of potential material fraud and to form an opinion on the credibility of the information in the financial report taken as a whole. Moreover, as auditors only visit a company periodically during a defined timeframe and auditing techniques are only designed to look retroactively, the process is only able to identify fraud that has occurred, not to prevent it from happening in the first place.

While the complexity of an audit varies in step with the size of an organization, these same processes are followed for almost every company, small or large, and while broadly effective, scandals in recent years have shown that the system is far from perfect. In the future, we can imagine how AI and blockchain technology might be combined in order to increase the efficiency of the auditing process, while also improving its effectiveness at identifying and responding to fraud in real time.

The combination of AI and blockchain in this scenario will follow a pattern repeated in most other scenarios in this chapter. Blockchain will serve as a trusted and immutable record, able to provide a single source of truth that is

---

[1] PricewaterhouseCoopers, "What Is an Audit?," PwC, accessed January 17, 2019, https://www.pwc.com/m1/en/services/assurance/what-is-an-audit.html.

[2] Tim Harford, "Is This the Most Influential Work in the History of Capitalism?," BBC News, October 23, 2017, sec. Business, https://www.bbc.com/news/business-41582244.

updated in near real-time across one or more organizations. AI will provide the analytic engine to process the data being added to that ledger in real time, applying its pattern recognition and independent learning capabilities to extract useful insights, and automate reactions to those insights.

First, let's imagine a next generation accounting system. Every transaction is directly and instantaneously reflected in the company's financials making the notion of year-end closing obsolete. Amortization is done on a real-time basis and even the most granular changes, such as the signing of a new contract or the replacement of a tool in a factory, are recognized by the system. A corporate-wide 'internet-of-things' could be harnessed to automate the collection and filing of this data, with both structured financial data and related unstructured data filed together in the system.

With such a system in place, structured and unstructured data related to every transaction could be analyzed by an AI-based system for errors, irregularities, and potentially fraudulent behavior. Using a combination of supervised and unsupervised learning techniques, we can imagine that as more and more data flowed though such a system, it would become increasingly accurate at identifying potential issues and either logging them for review, or directly redressing them.

Strictly speaking, such a system could be built on a centralized, rather than a decentralized, blockchain architecture; however, by adding blockchain into the mix, immutability can be incorporated into this system. By involving one or more third-party validators, responsible for the verification of new transactions and the maintenance of the immutability of the ledger, we would establish a provable assurance that each transaction, no matter how minor, has not been changed in any way since its initial entry.

In this way, we can imagine that the combination of credibly immutable record of a firm's transactions and an AI's analysis of those transactions— effectively an audit—would be available on demand at any time. Such a system would be of benefit to regulators, tax authorities, and most of all to the management of the company itself, as management would have access to far more granular analytics of their real-time performance, and the ability to make critical business decisions on the basis of those insights. This could allow for better capital allocation and value maximization as well as the ability to pivot faster. We would move to a continuous real-time pricing of the company making concepts like quarterly reporting or year-end audit obsolete.

Of course, there would be numerous challenges to establishing such a system. The central importance of the audit process to ensuring investor trust in corporate behavior is central to our current financial system, and thus should not be changed quickly or without a close review of the ramifications.

More importantly, we should not prematurely overstate the faith that we place in such as system. The strength of the system's immutability would be contingent on the consensus and validation mechanism put in place. If the incentives of the validators (effectively the ledger's miners) are such that they might be tempted to collude in the modification of a company's ledger, then the immutability and accuracy of the data cannot be taken for granted. Even more challenging than this would be addressing the so-called 'garbage in, garbage out' challenge. Even if the data in the ledger can be trusted to be immutable, this is no guarantee that the data initially entered was accurate and untampered with.

This would impact the role of auditors and large audit firms as well. Instead of the armies of young auditors with accounting backgrounds that the large audit firms have today, they would need fewer but more qualified staff that are knowledgeable across smart contract coding or data science with their roles more focused on reviewing the frameworks than doing the manual reviews and number crunching they often still do today.

19.2   Artificially Intelligent Distributed Autonomous Corporations

As we have seen in our discussions throughout this book, digital platforms like Amazon, Facebook, and Alibaba are among the most successful business models being deployed today. They enable the creation of lean, technology-focused organizations that can bring together millions, and in some cases billions, of users. These platforms perform a range of functions, connecting buyers and sellers, and often, enabling the creation and distribution of new types of user-generated content. Even more important, they become a magnet for data, enabling them to develop AI tools to automate processes and personalize users' experiences, in the process kicking off a self-reinforcing 'AI-flywheel'.

Unfortunately, these platforms are not without their challenges, as the self-reinforcing nature of their growth through network effects creates a tendency toward these organizations acquiring excess market power—a problem that is aggravated by the fact that interests of the platform's users are not always well aligned with those of the platform's owners.

But what if this didn't need to be the case? What if rather than being centralized digital entities with agency costs between owners and users, platform business models were decentralized entities where the owners and users of the platform were the same? In theory, blockchain technology provides the capabilities to deploy just such an entity, sometimes called a distributed autonomous organization (DAO) or distributed autonomous corporation (DAC), via the encoding of a system of business rules agreed upon by a community of users in smart contracts. Instead of having senior management make decisions, these would be made by pre-defined smart contract rules complemented by AI-based decisions that can quickly analyze data, arrive at the best conclusion, and make the appropriate business decision—a sort of super-CEO that is at the same time predictable but also with tremendous insights! In addition, the benefactors of this super-CEO would be the various stakeholders of the organization. No such organizations currently exist at any meaningful scale; however, if such a business model could be successfully deployed at scale, it would have a transformative impact on the global economy, potentially threatening the primacy of some of the most successful companies to emerge out of the past two decades.

To consider how this might occur, let's examine a hypothetical example of a decentralized competitor to the business model of ridesharing firms like Uber, Lyft, Grab, and Didi. These established ridesharing businesses provide a technology platform that connects a community of drivers with a community of riders. The ridesharing platform sits in the middle, acting as a centralized clearing-house for matching drivers and riders efficiently, facilitating payments between them, and maintaining safety through background checks and reputation management systems. The platform also manages the development and deployment of a range of AI-enabled tools including driver routing and spatiotemporal demand forecasting. For this the platform extracts a fee, in some cases of as much as 25% of the cost of a ride.[3]

A distributed autonomous competitor to a traditional ridesharing app might look a little bit like a traditional cooperative—decentralized and digitized for the modern era—where the ownership rights and the governance of the platform would be managed by a broad group of stakeholders. It could automate a variety of tasks such as the collection of fees and the distribution of payment to drivers. The actual ridesharing operations (the centralized clearing-house for matching drivers and riders) wouldn't necessarily need to happen on the blockchain; however, the ownership and control of that system and its associated intellectual property rights could be tokenized and distributed to its community of users. Some of the decisions that are made by human senior management today could be left to an AI CEO—say to onboard new

---

[3] "Uber Fees: How Much Does Uber Pay, Actually? (With Case Studies)," Ridester, July 9, 2018, https://www.ridester.com/uber-fees/.

drivers or expand into a new city—based on the data and the calculations that it can make.

These ownership rights as well as the governance framework for the organization could be structured in a myriad of ways. One model would be for the tokens of the organization to be held exclusively by the drivers, perhaps with tenure or number of rides driven, conveying greater ownership holdings and decision-making weight. Such a system would allow drivers to directly benefit from the success of the organization, and to have a say in its future direction, unlike today where platform owners can impose unilateral changes on the platform's structure.

Obviously maintaining this platform would still require the work of people, but those individuals would not necessarily need to be employed by the platform in the same way that they are today. For example, AI would continue to play an important role in running the distributed ridesharing service in much the same way it does for centralized platforms today. However, instead of developers and data scientists being directly employed, they could themselves be co-owners of the platform, or receive automated payments from the network via coding bounties. While such an organization would likely still need a core staff, the culture of that organization could be very different than in centralized corporate structures today.

Such a system could create a myriad of problems. Incentives would be challenging to get right and the interactions between stakeholders could easily become fraught. One only needs to look at the message board flame-wars that surround discussions of changes to the governance protocols of today's crypto-assets to wonder if this is really a better way to run an organization than dull quarterly meetings.

Whether or not they succeed, watching future experimentation with these business models will be fascinating. After all, if they can succeed, it won't just be ridesharing incumbents that are at risk. As we discussed in Chap. 16, efforts are underway to shift financial services toward a new digital platform model, with incumbent financial institutions and large technology players likely competitors for the ownership of those platforms. But what if neither one succeeded in owning such a platform because rather than being centralized, it was decentralized and owned by its customers? You might imagine it as a sort of distributed credit union for the twenty-first century. Today it's difficult to imagine such a system, but in a decade, who knows if it will seem quite so far-fetched.

19.3 Blockchain-Based Identity Powered by AI Data Managers

A consistent theme that has run through this text, and that runs through many discussions in both popular media and policymaking circles today, is the need to better manage identity and personal data. As we have seen, the quantity of personal data about our activities, health, and relationships is increasing exponentially through our use of a myriad of devices, sensors, and digital services. At the same time, our economy is increasingly dominated by large AI-enabled platforms all voraciously hungry for that data to enable and refine their business models.

The challenge is figuring out how to manage the trade-off between these two forces. On the one hand, sharing our data with digital platforms allows us to obtain innovative, personalized, and valuable services at no or very low monetary cost. On the other hand, many may not understand the full implications of paying for services with their personal data, while at the same time our data may become more and more difficult to control and subject to breaches or abuse.

Policymakers in many jurisdictions are working to solve components of this problem. For example, in Europe, statutes like the General Data Protection Regulation (GDPR) create strict requirements around the protection of data and the limitations of it use. At the same time, the second payment services direct (PSD2) and other open banking regulations being put in place around the world give customers increased control over the portability of their data (at least in the case of their financial data).

These are important steps, but it may well be that these regulations can only truly empower users if users also have the right tools to manage their data. After all, what is the use of a 'right to be forgotten', as provided under GDPR, if you don't know who has your personal data in the first place? Similarly, just having the right to the portability of data doesn't necessarily mean you have the tools to deploy it effectively, nor does it put you in a strong position to negotiate for its fair monetization.

In this scenario, we can imagine a world where the combination of blockchain and AI allows users to more fully control their data, where a new architecture for identity is established with the help of blockchain technologies and where AI agents help individuals better pick and choose with whom to share their data.

Blockchain advocates have long recognized the need for identity systems, both for the narrow goal of facilitating blockchain-based transactions that require the validation of certain identity data, and for the broader goal of democratizing an individual's control over her identity data. In Chap. 12, we considered the role of non-fungible, non-transferable tokens in the enablement of identity systems such as Sovrin.

Several approaches exist for establishing such a system including 'self-sovereign' identity where an individual directly controls her identity data, and federated models where users entrust their data to a limited number of organizations who make attestations about that data to third parties on the user's behalf. While the detailed workings of these systems are beyond the scope of this book, most solutions seek to shift the architecture of the identity system in favor of users, giving them increased visibility into how their data is being used (and by whom) and offering much higher levels of granularity regarding which aspects of data they wish to share.

But once you have wrested control over your data under this new blockchain-enabled identity architecture, then what? You may still want to use several digital services that plan to monetize your data, but do you really want to have to read the terms and conditions for each one of those services? Moreover, would you really know what they meant if you did? In fact, how would you even know what might be a fair price for your identity data or how you might negotiate with a digital service provider if you thought you deserved a little more in exchange for those pictures from your latest vacation?

The reality is that not everyone's data will be worth the same. For example, the data of someone who has a normal 9-to-5 job in an average suburban city may not be worth as much as the data of a professional triathlete who trains seven days a week or that of a high-stress executive who spends over 150 days a year on airplanes. The unique or rare features of the data may be more interesting to certain organizations (e.g. medical research companies). In certain cases, the data may be worth more simply due to its unique source, say health data from identical twins or from people living at high altitudes.

This is where we can imagine AI capabilities playing a valuable role. In much the same way that a self-driving finance agent as described in Chap. 16 helps you find the right savings instrument or loan to meet your needs, an identity agent could help you to find the right data-sharing arrangements to fit your preferences and avoid those that could put you at risk. Such a system could scan and codify the terms and conditions of digital platforms, incorporating risk analysis and historical news to understand everything from their business practices to the data security of a given digital service provider. At the same time, the agent could analyze your profile and preferences to develop a personalized understanding of the types of data you might be willing to share and the terms under which you might be willing to share it. We could even imagine a world where our agents could come together to collectively negotiate for better terms or monetization arrangements with leading digital services.

Such a system could enfranchise individuals, giving them the transparency to know how their data is being used, the tools to do something about it, and the negotiating power to redefine the terms of the arrangement. The only nagging question left about the world we have imagined pertains to who operates the AI agent?

To be effective, such an entity would need to be subject to close regulatory scrutiny, have a business model not based on data monetization, and be trusted by its customers to act in their interests. It is difficult to imagine what current organization could play this role. Should it be a government agency, a large trusted organization like a Big 4 accounting firm, a law firm, or perhaps a tech company? Or, probably, a type of organization that does not exist yet!

19.4 Data Marketplaces and the Democratization of AI

While the previous example discusses how blockchain allows us to secure our identity and an AI agent allows us to optimize the value of our data, we can also imagine a world where data is more openly shared, data owners automatically compensated, and where AI is accessible and democratized.

As we have seen earlier in this book, while we are generating records amounts of data, one issue we face is that most of this data is owned not by users, but by large technology platforms who have enjoyed unparalleled access to our personal details for years. These large firms are now monetizing user data for their own purposes. For example, Facebook uses profile information to add value to their advertisement packages, leveraging the fact that they can direct the placement of ads to the newsfeeds of those more likely to buy the product. The consumer does not benefit directly apart from having the ability to use that tech platform.

This gives these firms an unfair advantage when it comes to the collection and use of data in the coming years. Big tech currently enjoys a kind of data oligopoly, and it comes with the usual barriers to entry: a new data-driven startup today would have a hard time equaling the data pool that a firm like Tencent or Facebook has, all other resource requirements aside. Bigger firms could suffer as well. Imagine if Google decides in the coming years to become an insurance provider. The dataset it has on the public gives it an unfair advantage when it comes to pricing the actuarial risks.

In addition, these tech firms use data only for limited purposes—say, advertisement or targeted sales. Much more value can be derived from this data, serving wider audiences and solving common problems. For example, what if we could use the data from Facebook for health research or urban planning? Are there patterns of social media usage that could be used for psychological purposes like suicide prevention or mental health research? Can we use localization data from devices like iPhones to optimize urban mass transit or city planning? There are many efficiency gains that are yet to be discovered and can easily be utilized by obtaining access to this data. Just think about the various innovations from which we have benefited as a society when certain datasets and tools have been made publically available. For example, firms like Uber may have not existed if it were not for Google Maps being freely available. While these large tech firms may grant access to part of their data to selected third parties or partners, this does not lead to as efficient an outcome as if the data were publicly available. There are many such arguments in favor of making data available, but few firms are able or willing or give up their data to the public domain for free.

Consider now the concept of a data marketplace, leveraging AI and crypto, where all information could be shared, bought and sold, probably using micro crypto payments and where data providers could be compensated fairly based on pricing determined by AI algorithms. Individuals would be compensated for providing their data to the marketplace and anyone willing to access that anonymized data pool would need to pay for access.

This would level the playing field and allow any individual, startup, government, or corporation to access data and leverage it. The data would not be solely owned by a large tech firm, enabling not only the compensation of data providers, but also productivity and creativity gains, maximizing the value created by the human community. This is particularly true for AI as AI algorithms are derived from large datasets. The availability of data therefore enables the creation of new AI tools.

There are a couple of early stage developments already exploring the combined potential of AI and crypto. For example, the Agorai project is attempting to build this data and AI marketplace on the blockchain, where data is the fuel and AI is the engine. As they put it in their white paper:

> Through Agorai's distributed marketplace, we believe consumers will have access to a broader set of solutions at a lower cost, and producers of AI solutions will have a superior distribution channel and not be required to either sell their solution to a large software firm or spend millions of dollars on an enterprise sales team. We hope that this will allow business of all sizes to operate on a level play-

ing field with access to the benefits that AI can provide. Equally importantly, Agorai plans to create a construct in which individuals and companies can take control of their own data and monetize it in a way that is secure and transparent.[4]

Another example is the SingularityNET project, which is attempting to build an AI marketplace in order to democratize access to AI tools. The project raised US$36 million in less than one minute in an ICO in 2017.[5] Their goal is to "ensure the technology is benevolent according to human standards, and the network is designed to incentivize and reward beneficial players".[6] Imagine if a university researcher in Kenya could access such a platform and use an AI algorithm developed by someone in Canada to further Ebola research in Africa.

While these projects are at the very early stages, they can give an indication of the general direction that we may be heading. However, for this to succeed, finding a way of compensating individuals or organizations for providing their data is key.

Similar to the machine-to-machine economy example that we will discuss later, one efficient way to compensate data owners for sharing this data could be via micro crypto payments. Using the current payment rails may not make sense for transactions that may be worth a fraction of a cent, but they could be worthwhile in a crypto ecosystem, especially when these payments happen automatically.

For example, I may decide to share my health data that is generated by my daily workouts or runs with one of these platforms. I would automatically be compensated for that small piece of data via a micro crypto payment and the value may be determined by an AI algorithm depending not only on my particulars (as we have seen earlier, not everyone's data is worth the same), but also by the simple demand for that type of data. This would happen all seamlessly behind the scenes. In addition, unlike data that is shared with Facebook or Google today, everyone globally could use this data as long as they pay the relevant amount.

There are many issues that need to be tackled before we can even consider such platforms reaching a critical mass, data privacy or data governance being the most obvious. For example, how is the data going to be anonymized? Who will legally own that data? How can the data be revoked and managed? The list goes on. Also, it may be that individuals or corporations are not open

---

[4] https://www.agorai.ai/pdf/Agorai%20White%20Paper%20v8.5.pdf.
[5] https://cointelegraph.com/news/ico-to-build-next-generation-ai-raises-36-million-in-60-seconds.
[6] https://public.singularitynet.io/whitepaper.pdf.

to sharing their data even if they are compensated, as their desire of data protection might be greater than the need for data monetization. The important takeaway is that this is something that is potentially doable and that can be beneficial not only to the owners or providers of the data, but potentially to the broader society and humanity as a whole.

19.5   AI Catalyzing the Adoption of Crypto-assets

As we have seen earlier in this book, there are numerous challenges to the mass adoption of crypto-assets. While some of them are policy driven, say, the lack of regulatory clarity, or technological driven, like some scalability limitations, other challenges can be potentially addressed by AI.

Let's take money laundering for example, which is a risk that is often raised by policymakers globally when talking about the risks involved with crypto-assets. As we have seen earlier in the book, global money laundering transactions are estimated to total US$1–2 trillion a year, with less than 1% seized by authorities.[7] Cryptocurrencies, due to their anonymous nature, could also be used for money laundering. Although when you consider that US$1–2 trillion is multiple times the total market capitalization of all crypto-assets, it is clear that crypto transactions are at worst a drop in the bucket of total global money laundering.

However, as the crypto-asset universe multiplies over the coming years, such assets could be used for money laundering purposes. This is where AI could help. The public nature of crypto transactions, Bitcoin for example, ensures that every single transaction is public and this is where we can use AI-powered solutions to be able to monitor large amounts of transaction data. This allows us not only to identify suspicious patterns of transactions, but also to be able to potentially guess the identity or profile of the end wallet holder. For example, at the time of writing, a number of AI solutions were being developed with a number of basic traceability tools already in use by large crypto players. As these solutions improve in their accuracy and scope in the coming years, we may see regulators and other stakeholders realize the advantages of crypto-assets when we have AI solutions to monitor them.

---

[7] Preeta Bannerjee, "UNODC Estimates That Criminals May Have Laundered US$ 1.6 Trillion in 2009," October 25, 2011, https://www.unodc.org/unodc/en/press/releases/2011/October/unodc-estimates-that-criminals-may-have-laundered-usdollar-1.6-trillion-in-2009.html.

Another example of the combination of crypto-assets and AI is with central bank-backed digital currencies. In such cases, the combination of those crypto-assets and AI can provide policymakers with granular data and market macro and micro visibility that they can only dream of today. For example, a retail central bank-backed digital currency would allow a central bank to have a real-time picture of the economic activity facilitated by this digital currency. Data on the volumes of transactions, sectors of activity, types of transaction, times of transaction, and many other types of input would be available on a real-time basis and, after being analyzed by AI solutions, could provide valuable insights that would help from a policy angle and other perspectives. This would be faster and more accurate than the quarterly and high-level estimates and high-level data that are available today. It could also enable other new capabilities for the central bank, ranging from more effective capital controls to precise quantitative easing that is not possible with today's fiat currencies.

However, at the time of writing and as discussed previously, we are still are far from having central bank–backed digital currencies from major jurisdictions. There are numerous hurdles that we need to jump before this becomes a reality. In addition, many of the AI-powered crypto traceability solutions that are available on the market today are still in the early stages. We need a number of years for these solutions to be more refined and accurate.

19.6   The Machine-to-Machine Payment Economy

For our final scenario, let's consider a financial environment where humans are hardly present, a machine-to-machine world, where AI-enabled devices linked together by networks for the transfer of both data and value engage in complex and dynamic transactions.

On the face of it, such an idea might seem far-fetched, particularly in a world where general AI remains the realm of science fiction. However, as we consider the convergence of some of the trends that we have discussed in previous chapters, the potential for such a transformation begins to come into focus.

First, we know that the ubiquity of computing power and connectivity is facilitating the rapid expansion of the internet of things—a decentralized network of sensors and devices capable of exchanging rich data feeds with one another. Second, we have seen how blockchain creates the potential for the exchange of value across a decentralized network with no need for a centrally trusted party to act as a 'register' of transactions. If we assume a sufficiently scalable blockchain protocol (or another distributed ledger technology model like IOTA or Hashgraph, for example), we can clearly see how the overlay of such a system onto the IoT could allow these devices to exchange streams of value, not just data, with one another. Finally, we have seen that machines are becoming smarter, in the sense that they are able to conduct more and more complex analysis based on rich feeds of unstructured data (such as that originating from the sensors in IoT devices) and to improve their performance of these tasks through a kind a learning.

When we combine these three trends, we can begin to imagine a world where machines conduct transactions with one another to serve the needs of their owners, without any intervention from those owners. For example, let's imagine a smart fridge whose owner has delegated to it the responsibility of always having enough food to feed the household. The fridge could begin to develop a detailed understanding of the household's food preferences, the frequency with which they will be eating at home (perhaps based on an analysis of their calendar), their health goals, and their food budget. At the same time it would need visibility into the pricing of foods from a variety of vendors, the seasonality of those prices, and the quality of various vendors. With all of this data at the fridge's disposal, we can start to imagine how it could be well positioned to make grocery selection decisions on a household's behalf and why a household might choose to delegate control of a share of their food budget to an account or 'wallet' under the fridge's control.

As we zoom out, we can start to imagine a vast network of machines just like this fridge interacting with one another and competing for the best prices through a marketplace of bids and asks. For example, we can imagine a world where our fridge realizes that it needs to restock the household supply of eggs before the weekend, to accommodate for the demands of a planned brunch. As the fridge 'shops' for eggs, it might interact with an entire machine-to-machine supply chain that includes an automated food logistics and delivery service (perhaps powered by drones), an AI-enabled food vendor service connected to those delivery drones, and perhaps even a highly automated egg farm.

In such a system, new factors might start to play an important role in the price you pay. For example, unlike today where the price is the same whether you need the eggs now or in a few days, the urgency of the household's need to restock their eggs might be factored into the propagation of pricing along the supply chain, with a pre-planned brunch able to secure eggs more cheaply than a last-minute one.

As we imagine this world, we can start to draw on other trends that we have explored and consider how they might shape the evolution of a machine-to-machine economy. For example, the self-driving finance agent that we discussed in Chap. 18 could interact with our hypothetical fridge to provide input on the financial goals of the household while health monitoring devices could provide input on an individual's diet and wellness goals.

The use of blockchain as the transactional backbone of this system allows us to consider how capabilities such as tokenization and smart contracts could be incorporated into the machine-to-machine economy. For example, machines could use smart contracts to establish long-term or conditional procurement agreements with one another. New machines might be added to the system in order to act as 'oracles' for such agreements, providing a trusted point of reference for an array of factors, such as weather or traffic, that could be incorporated into the terms of a smart contract. At the same time, while transactions between machines could use payment tokens, such as a stable coin or a retail central bank–backed digital currency, they might just as easily incorporate other forms of crypto-assets, such as investment or utility tokens. We could even imagine a world where a machine pays for an item, or collateralizes a smart contract, with tokens that represent a fractional ownership share in the machine itself.

While we can have little certainty about how this complex network of machine-to-machine interactions might evolve, it is clear that it would have a significant impact on the structure of the financial system. At the core of these changes is a delegation of financial activity to machines as we begin to trust them as our agents, capable of understanding our intent and acting on our behalf. This transfer of responsibility makes machines de facto clients of financial services, and the unique characteristics of machines, in contrast to humans, could create demand for new types of financial products and services.

For example, while an individual might only be able to allocate a few hours a week to the activity of shopping for groceries—or really any item—our hypothetical fridge never needs to stop shopping for groceries. Consequently, unlike human-initiated payments which tend to occur infrequently but with larger ticket sizes, machine-initiated payments might be much smaller but more frequent, requiring a machine-to-machine payment system using crypto-assets to facilitate micro-transactions. For some products and services, it would not be unreasonable for transactions to be usage-based, with a constant stream of low-denomination real-time payments being made by one machine to another so long as a service is being used. Finally, it would be reasonable to expect that this new payment network might seek to enable cross-border payments to a machine halfway around the world with the same ease as those to a machine across the room, particularly when we ponder the ability of an AI-enabled system to consider a much broader array of potential transactional counter-parties than a human.

The advent of machine-to-machine payments enabled by smarter AI and more scalable blockchain technology has the potential provide an array of benefits for consumers, but the concept is not without challenges, and much thought and experimentation would be required to ensure proper governance of such a system. For example, how might the tendency for economies of scale in the development of AI systems distort the highly decentralized model that we have imagined in this scenario? What implications would the optimization of transactions across border have on global capital flows? Who would provide the regulatory control and oversight of transactions within this system, particularly as more and more routine exchanges of data and value might look to occur across borders, particularly for digital goods and services? How could the real-time streams of micro-payments that characterize the system we have described be effectively monitored for emergent price-fixing or cartelization behavior learned by machines as they interact with one another? Perhaps most intriguing of all, what role might the distributed autonomous corporations discussed earlier in this chapter play in a machine-to-machine economy, and would such an organization need human actors to function at all?

A Financial Future Full of Possibilities

Throughout this text, we have explored how new technologies and the business models they enable have transformed the landscape of financial services, as well as the future paths the continued evolution of this process might take. As you have read about these technologies and trends, we hope that new ideas and opportunities have sprung to mind, as you have drawn on your own unique perspective and expertise. Perhaps you have even begun to imagine how you might build a new fintech offering of your own.

The future of financial services is marked by both excitement and uncertainty. Unlocking the full potential of financial innovation will require all stakeholders to work together to ensure that current and future innovations serve the core objectives of the financial system. New innovations should facilitate a more inclusive economy, the effective transfer of risk, the formation of capital for economic growth, the accumulation of saving for retirement and more, all while ensuring that the system for doing so is fair, stable, and secure. Achieving this won't be easy—new innovations can bring just as many risks as they bring opportunities. But if innovators, incumbents, regulators, and consumers all work together, new technologies have the potential to create a transformationally better financial system for all. Welcome to the future of finance!

© The Author(s) 2019
H. Arslanian, F. Fischer, *The Future of Finance*,
https://doi.org/10.1007/978-3-030-14533-0

Bibliography

5 High Profile Cryptocurrency Hacks - (Updated). Accessed January 13, 2019. https://blockgeeks.com/guides/cryptocurrency-hacks/.

6 Charts Breaking Down How Insurers Are Investing in Tech Startups, 2016. https://www.cbinsights.com/research/insurance-corporate-venturing-2016/.

2017 Mobile Payment Usage in China Report, 2017. https://www.ipsos.com/sites/default/files/ct/publication/documents/2017-08/Mobile_payments_in_China-2017.pdf.

2018 Apple Pay Adoption Stats, n.d. https://www.pymnts.com/apple-pay-adoption/.

2018 U.S. Retail Banking Satisfaction Study, 2018. https://www.jdpower.com/business/press-releases/jd-power-2018-us-retail-banking-satisfaction-study.

"A Financial System That Creates Economic Opportunities Nonbank Financials, Fintech, and Innovation." U.S. Department of the Treasury, July 2018. https://home.treasury.gov/sites/default/files/2018-08/A-Financial-System-that-Creates-Economic-Opportunities—Nonbank-Financials-Fintech-and-Innovation.pdf.

"A Guide to Digital Token Offerings." Monetary Authority of Singapore, November 2017. http://www.mas.gov.sg//media/MAS/Regulations%20and%20Financial%20Stability/Regulations%20Guidance%20and%20Licensing/Securities%20Futures%20and%20Fund%20Management/Regulations%20Guidance%20and%20Licensing/Guidelines/A%20Guide%20to%20Digital%20Token%20Offerings%20%2014%20Nov%202017.pdf.

Aadhaar Dashboard. Accessed January 13, 2019. https://uidai.gov.in/aadhaar_dashboard/index.php.

About Revolut, n.d. https://www.revolut.com/it/about.

Abraham, Ronald, Elizabeth S. Bennett, Rajesh Bhusal, Shreya Dubey, Qian (Sindy) Li, Akash Pattanayak, and Neil Buddy Shah. "State of Aadhaar Report 2017-18." ID Insight, May 2018. https://stateofaadhaar.in/wp-content/uploads/State-of-Aadhaar-Report_2017-18.pdf.

© The Author(s) 2019
H. Arslanian, F. Fischer, *The Future of Finance*,
https://doi.org/10.1007/978-3-030-14533-0

Achanta, Ravishankar. "Cross-Border Money Transfer Using Blockchain – Enabled by Big Data." Infosys, 2018.

Acheson, Noelle. "How Blockchain Trade Finance Is Breaking Proof-of-Concept Gridlock." *CoinDesk* (blog), April 30, 2018. https://www.coindesk.com/blockchain-trade-finance-breaking-proof-concept-gridlock.

Acheson, Noelle. *What Is SegWit?* Accessed January 13, 2019. https://www.coindesk.com/information/what-is-segwit.

After Moore's Law | Technology Quarterly, 2016. https://www.economist.com/technology-quarterly/2016-03-12/after-moores-law.

Agarwal, Sulabh. "Will Fintechs Dominate The Cross-Border Payments Market?" Accenture, April 2018.

Aki, Jimmy. "ECash Founder David Chaum Makes Bold Promises with Elixxir Blockchain." Bitcoin Magazine. Accessed January 13, 2019. https://bitcoinmagazine.com/articles/ecash-founder-david-chaum-makes-bold-promises-elixxir-blockchain/.

Alameda, Teresa. *What Is Computer Vision and How Is It Changing the World of Auto Insurance*, 2017. https://www.bbva.com/en/computer-vision-changing-world-auto-insurance/.

Alexander, Doug. "TD Aims for 90% of Transactions to Be Self-Serve in Digital Push." *Bloomberg News*, October 2018. https://www.bloomberg.com/news/articles/2018-10-11/td-aims-for-90-of-transactions-to-be-self-serve-in-digital-push.

Alipay Expands In-Store Mobile Payments to North American Retailers, 2017. https://www.mobilepaymentstoday.com/news/alipay-expands-in-store-mobile-payments-to-north-american-retailers/.

Allison, Ian. *Fidelity Looking to Expand Digital Asset Trading Beyond Bitcoin and Ether*, 2018. https://www.coindesk.com/fidelity-looking-to-expand-digital-asset-trading-beyond-bitcoin-and-ether.

Allstate's Intelligent Agent Reduces Call Center Traffic and Provides Help During Quoting Process, 2015. http://www.kmworld.com/Articles/Editorial/Features/Allstates-Intelligent-Agent-Reduces-Call-Center-Traffic--and-Provides-Help-During-Quoting-Process-108263.aspx.

Amara, Roy. *Roy Amara 1925–2007 American Futurologist*, 2006. http://www.oxfordreference.com/view/10.1093/acref/9780191826719.001.0001/q-oro-ed4-00018679.

Amazon. *All Customer Success Stories*, n.d.-a https://aws.amazon.com/solutions/case-studies/all/.

Amazon. *Public Sector Customer Success Stories*, n.d.-b https://aws.amazon.com/solutions/case-studies/government-education/.

Amazon.com, Inc. *Amazon.Com Announces Third Quarter Sales up 29% to $56.6 Billion*, 2018.

Amy Nordrum, Kristen Clark and IEEE Spectrum Staff. *Everything You Need to Know About 5G*, 2017. https://spectrum.ieee.org/video/telecom/wireless/everything-you-need-to-know-about-5g.

Anand, Shefali. "A Pioneer in Real Estate Blockchain Emerges in Europe." *Wall Street Journal*, March 6, 2018, sec. Markets. https://www.wsj.com/articles/a-pioneer-in-real-estate-blockchain-emerges-in-europe-1520337601.

Anderson, Theo. *How We Shop Differently on Our Phones.* Kellogg School of Management, Northwestern University, n.d. https://insight.kellogg.northwestern.edu/article/how-we-shop-differently-on-our-phones.

Angelica LaVito, Jeff Cox. *Amazon, Berkshire Hathaway, and JPMorgan Chase to Partner on US Employee Health Care.* CNBC, 2018. https://www.cnbc.com/2018/01/30/amazon-berkshire-hathaway-and-jpmorgan-chase-to-partner-on-us-employee-health-care.html.

Ant Financial to Share Full Suite of AI Capabilities with Asset Management Companies, 2018. https://www.businesswire.com/news/home/20180619006514/en/Ant-Financial-Share-Full-Suite-AI-Capabilities.

Anupam, Suprita. *Is Facebook Really Entering The P2P Payments Space In India?*, 2018. https://inc42.com/buzz/messenger-is-facebook-really-entering-the-p2p-payments-space-in-india/.

AP. "Musk Says A.I. Is a 'Fundamental Risk to the Existence of Human Civilization.'" *CNBC*, July 2017. https://www.cnbc.com/2017/07/16/musk-says-a-i-is-a-fundamental-risk-to-the-existence-of-human-civilization.html.

Apple Inc. *Apple Reinvents the Phone with IPhone*, 2007.

Arielle O'shea, Andrea Coombes. *How Much Does a Financial Advisor Cost?*, 2018. https://www.nerdwallet.com/blog/investing/how-much-does-a-financial-advisor-cost/.

Arnold, Martin. *Monzo Poised to Join Ranks of Europe's Fintech 'unicorns'*, 2018. https://www.ft.com/content/ef54082c-a16a-11e8-85da-eeb7a9ce36e4.

Arsenault, Chris. "Property Rights for World's Poor Could Unlock Trillions in 'Dead Capital': Economist." *Reuters*, August 2016.

Arslanian, Henri. *RegTech, LawTech and the Future of Lawyers*, 2017.

"Artificial Intelligence and Machine Learning in Financial Services." Financial Stability Board, November 2017. http://www.fsb.org/2017/11/artificial-intelligence-and-machine-learning-in-financial-service/.

Asia's 1st FinTech MOOC – Introduction to FinTech, n.d. https://www.law.hku.hk/aiifl/asias-first-fintech-online-course-www-hkufintech-com/.

"ASIFMA Best Practices for Digital Asset Exchanges." Asia Securities Industry and Financial Markets Association (ASIFMA), June 2018.

"Asset Management's Fight for 'Alternative Data' Analysts Heats Up." *Financial Times.* Accessed January 17, 2019. https://www.ft.com/content/2f454550-02c8-11e8-9650-9c0ad2d7c5b5.

Austen, Mark, Laurence Van der Loo, Rebecca Carvatt, William Hallatt, Grace Chong, Zennon Kapron, Urszula McCormack, et al. "ASIFMA Best Practices for Digital Asset Exchanges." ASIFMA, June 2018. https://www.lw.com/thoughtLeadership/ASIFMA-best-practices-digital-asset-exchanges.

Author, More by This. *Yearly Mobile Money Deals Close to Half GDP*, n.d. https://www.nation.co.ke/business/Yearly-mobile-money-deals-close-GDP/996-4041666-dtaks6z/index.html.

Average Overdraft Fee. Increase in Average Overdraft Fees, over Time in the United States, 2016. https://media.wiley.com/assets/7349/04/web-Accounts-Average_Overdraft_Fee_US.png.

"AXA Goes Blockchain with Fizzy | AXA." AXA, September 13, 2017. https://www.axa.com/en/newsroom/news/axa-goes-blockchain-with-fizzy%23xtor%3DCS3-9-%5BShared_Article%5D-%5Baxa_goes_blockchain_with_fizzy%5D.

Babu, Pavithra. *What Is IndiaStack and How Is It Set to Change India?* Accessed January 13, 2019. https://razorpay.com/blog/what-is-indiastack-and-how-is-it-set-to-change-india/.

Back, Adam. *[ANNOUNCE] Hash Cash Postage Implementation*, 1997. http://www.hashcash.org/papers/announce.txt.

Bain, Benjamin. "Winklevoss-Backed Bid for Bitcoin-ETF Rejected by Regulators." *Bloomberg News*, July 2018. https://www.bloomberg.com/news/articles/2018-07-26/sec-rejects-winklevoss-twins-request-to-launch-bitcoin-etf.

Baker, Paddy. *Gibraltar Stock Exchange Confirms Move into Security Tokens*, 2018. https://cryptobriefing.com/gibraltar-stock-exchange-security-tokens/.

Bangladesh Population, n.d. https://tradingeconomics.com/bangladesh/population.

Bank of America Revolutionizes Banking Industry from Bank of America, 2014. https://about.bankofamerica.com/en-us/our-story/bank-of-america-revolutionizes-industry.html.

Bank of America Surpasses 1 Million Users on Erica | Bank of America, n.d. https://newsroom.bankofamerica.com/press-releases/consumer-banking/bank-america-surpasses-1-million-users-erica.

Bank, The World. "M-Money Channel Distribution Case - Kenya: Safaricom m-Pesa." The World Bank, January 2017. http://documents.worldbank.org/curated/en/832831500443778267/M-money-channel-distribution-case-Kenya-Safaricom-m-pesa.

Banking Relationship in 2015 (U.S.), 2016. https://media.wiley.com/assets/7350/52/web-Trust-Banking_Relationship_In_2015_US.png.

Bannerjee, Preeta. *UNODC Estimates That Criminals May Have Laundered US\$ 1.6 Trillion in 2009*, 2011.

Baraniuk, Chris. "The Cyborg Chess Players That Can't Be Beaten." *BBC News*, December 2015. http://www.bbc.com/future/story/20151201-the-cyborg-chess-players-that-cant-be-beaten.

Bauguess, Scott W. *The Role of Big Data, Machine Learning, and AI in Assessing Risks: A Regulatory Perspective*, 2017.

Baynes, Chris. *Entire Country Taken Offline for Two Days after Undersea Internet Cable Cut*, 2018. https://www.independent.co.uk/news/world/africa/mauritania-internet-cut-underwater-cable-offline-days-west-africa-a8298551.html.

BBVA Launches First BaaS Platform in the U.S., 2018. https://www.bbva.com/en/bbva-launches-first-baas-platform-in-the-u-s/.

Beattie, Andrew. *The History of Money: From Barter to Banknotes*, 2015. https://www.investopedia.com/articles/07/roots_of_money.asp.

Bech, Morten Linnemann, and Rodney Garratt. "Central Bank Cryptocurrencies." *BIS Quarterly Review*, September 2017. https://www.bis.org/publ/qtrpdf/r_qt1709f.htm.

"Being Open Is the Way" – Ralph Hamers, 2018. https://www.ing.com/Newsroom/All-news/Being-open-is-the-way-Ralph-Hamers.htm.

Berentsen, Aleksander, and Fabian Schar. "The Case for Central Bank Electronic Money and the Non-Case for Central Bank Cryptocurrencies." *Federal Reserve Bank of St. Louis* Second Quarter 2018, Vol. 100, No. 2 (February 2018). https://doi.org/10.20955/r.2018.97-106.

Bergen, Mark, and Jennifer Surane. "Google and Mastercard Cut a Secret Ad Deal to Track Retail Sales." *Bloomberg News*, August 2018. https://www.bloomberg.com/news/articles/2018-08-30/google-and-mastercard-cut-a-secret-ad-deal-to-track-retail-sales.

Bernard, Zoë. "Satoshi Nakamoto Was Weird, Paranoid, and Bossy, Says Early Bitcoin Developer Who Exchanged Hundreds of Emails with the Mysterious Crypto Creator." *Business Insider Malaysia*, May 2018. https://www.businessinsider.my/satoshi-nakamoto-was-weird-and-bossy-says-bitcoin-developer-2018-5/.

Big Decline in Usage of Bank Branches, 2018. http://www.roymorgan.com/findings/7817-big-decline-in-usage-of-bank-branches-201811300632.

Birke, Szifra. *Is Your Financial Advisor Working in Your Best Interest?*, 2017. https://birkeconsulting.com/is-your-financial-advisor-working-in-your-best-interest/.

Bitcoin Block Reward Halving Countdown. Accessed January 13, 2019. https://www.bitcoinblockhalf.com/.

Bitcoin Forum. Accessed January 13, 2019. https://bitcointalk.org/.

Bitcoin History: The Complete History of Bitcoin [Timeline]. Accessed January 13, 2019. http://www.historyofbitcoin.org/.

Bkash in Bangladesh: 24 Million Customers Using Mobile Money, 2018. https://global-paymentsummit.com/bkash-bangladesh-24-million-customers-using-mobile-money/.

"Blockchain Investment Trends in Review." CB Insights Research. Accessed January 13, 2019. https://www.cbinsights.com/research/report/blockchain-trends-opportunities/.

Bohane, Ben. *Yap: Island of Stone Money, Micronesian Song and Just a Trickle of Tourists*, 2016. https://www.abc.net.au/news/2016-03-30/yap-balances-traditional-micronesian-values-with-tourism-push/7285664.

Borghard, Erica. *Protecting Financial Institutions Against Cyber Threats: A National Security Issue*, 2018. https://carnegieendowment.org/2018/09/24/protecting-financial-institutions-against-cyber-threats-national-security-issue-pub-77324.

Brennan, Matthew. *Wechat Red Packets Data Report of 2018 New Year Eve*, 2018. https://chinachannel.co/2018-wechat-red-packets-data-report-new-year-eve/.

Brooks, Rodney. *[FoR&AI] The Seven Deadly Sins of Predicting the Future of AI*, 2017. https://rodneybrooks.com/the-seven-deadly-sins-of-predicting-the-future-of-ai/.

Broughton, Kristin. *Amazon Buying Capital One? Fat Chance, but Fun to Ponder Website*, 2017. https://www.americanbanker.com/news/amazon-buying-capital-one-fat-chance-but-fun-to-ponder.

Browdie, Brian. *Can Alternative Data Determine a Borrower's Ability to Repay?*, 2015. https://www.americanbanker.com/news/can-alternative-data-determine-a-borrowers-ability-to-repay.

Browdie, Brian. *Health Platform Vitality Gets into Banking*, 2019. https://www.dig-in.com/news/the-bank-that-watches-your-every-move-the-rise-of-behavioral-banks.

Brown, Mike. *Best Mobile Payment Apps – Survey & Report*, 2017. https://lendedu.com/blog/best-mobile-payment-app.

Brown, Mike. *Should Amazon Get Into Virtual Currency & Other Products?*, 2018. https://lendedu.com/blog/amazon-virtual-currency-banking-insurance/.

Browne, Ryan. *Fintech Start-up Revolut Grabs 2 Million Users and Plans to Launch Commission-Free Trading Service*. CNBC Europe, 2018. https://www.cnbc.com/2018/06/07/revolut-has-2-million-users-to-launch-commission-free-trading-service.html.

Brynjolfsson, Erik, Yu (Jeffrey) Hu, and Michael D. Smith. "Long Tails vs. Superstars: The Effect of Information Technology on Product Variety and Sales Concentration Patterns." *Information Systems Research* 21, no. 4 (September 2010): 736–747. https://doi.org/10.1287/isre.1100.0325.

Brynjolfsson, Erik, Hu (Jeffrey) Yu, and Michael D. Smith. "Long Tails Versus Superstars: The Effect of IT on Product Variety and Sales Concentration Patterns." MIT Center for Digital Business, September 2010. http://ebusiness.mit.edu/erik/Long%20Tails%20Versus%20Superstars.pdf.

"BTC-USD Historical Prices | Bitcoin USD Stock - Yahoo Finance." Yahoo! Finance. Accessed January 30, 2019. https://finance.yahoo.com/quote/BTC-USD/history/.

Buchko, Steven. *Off to the Races: Crypto's Top 4 Privacy Coins*, 2018a. https://coincentral.com/top-privacy-cryptocurrency-race/.

Buchko, Steven. *Off to the Races: Crypto's Top 4 Privacy Coins*. Coin Central, 2018b. https://coincentral.com/top-privacy-cryptocurrency-race/.

Budworth, David. "Ghosts in the Machine: Revisited." Baker McKenzie, Thought Leadership, 2018. http://www.euromoneythoughtleadership.com/ghosts2.

Bughin, Jacques, Tanguy Catlin, Martin Hirt, and Paul Willmott. *Why Digital Strategies Fail*, 2018. https://www.mckinsey.com/business-functions/digital-mckinsey/our-insights/why-digital-strategies-fail.

Burgess, Rick. *One Minute on the Internet: 640TB Data Transferred, 100k Tweets, 204 Million e-Mails Sent*, 2013. https://www.techspot.com/news/52011-one-minute-on-the-internet-640tb-data-transferred-100k-tweets-204-million-e-mails-sent.html.

Burniske, Chris, and Jack Tatar. *Cryptoassets: The Innovative Investor's Guide to Bitcoin and Beyond*. McGraw Hill Professional, 2017.

"Canada Says No To Blockchain For Now." *PYMNTS.Com* (blog), May 29, 2017. https://www.pymnts.com/news/b2b-payments/2017/bank-canada-interbank-payment-system-blockchain/.

Captain, Sean. *A New Point-and-Click Revolution Brings AI To The Masses*, 2017. https://www.fastcompany.com/3062951/a-new-point-and-click-revolution-brings-ai-to-the-masses.

Caroline Heider, April Connelly. *Why Land Administration Matters for Development*, 2016. http://ieg.worldbankgroup.org/blog/why-land-administration-matters-development.

Casey, Michael J., and Paul Vigna. "In Blockchain We Trust." MIT Technology Review, April 9, 2018. https://www.technologyreview.com/s/610781/in-blockchain-we-trust/.

del Castillo, Michael. *For Blockchain Startups, Switzerland's "Crypto Valley" Is No New York*, 2016. https://www.coindesk.com/blockchain-innovation-switzerland-crypto-valley-new-york.

Chanchani, Madhav. *Alibaba to Hike Stake in Paytm's Marketplace for $177 Million*, 2017. https://economictimes.indiatimes.com/small-biz/money/alibaba-to-hike-stake-in-paytms-marketplace-for-177-million/articleshow/57428717.cms.

Chandler, Clay. *Tencent and Alibaba Are Engaged in a Massive Battle in China Play Video*, 2017. http://fortune.com/2017/05/13/tencent-alibaba-china/.

Chang, Sue. *This Chart Spells out in Black and White Just How Many Jobs Will Be Lost to Robots*, 2017. https://www.marketwatch.com/story/this-chart-spells-out-in-black-and-white-just-how-many-jobs-will-be-lost-to-robots-2017-05-31.

Chaum, David. "Security without Identification: Transaction Systems to Make Big Brother Obsolete." *Communications of the ACM* 28, no. 10 (October 1, 1985): 1030–44. https://doi.org/10.1145/4372.4373.

Chen, Adrian. "We Need to Know Who Satoshi Nakamoto Is," May 2016. https://www.newyorker.com/business/currency/we-need-to-know-who-satoshi-nakamoto-is.

Cheng, Evelyn. "Bitcoin Tops $8,700 to Record High as Coinbase Adds 100,000 Users." *CNBC*, November 2017. https://www.cnbc.com/2017/11/25/bitcoin-tops-8700-to-record-high-as-coinbase-adds-100000-users.html.

"China Bans Initial Coin Offerings." *BBC News*, September 2017. https://www.bbc.com/news/business-41157249.

"China Is Developing Its Own Digital Currency." *Bloomberg News*, February 2017. https://www.bloomberg.com/news/articles/2017-02-23/pboc-is-going-digital-as-mobile-payments-boom-transforms-economy.

"China's Plan to Sideline Bitcoin." *Bloomberg News*, December 13, 2018. https://www.bloomberg.com/news/articles/2018-12-13/china-s-plan-to-sideline-bitcoin.

Citi. "Bank of the Future - The ABCs of Digital Disruption in Finance." Citi Global Perspectives. *Citi Searches for Fraud in Real-Time Transactions with Feedzai Machine*

Learning Tech, 2018. https://www.finextra.com/pressarticle/76809/citi-searches-for-fraud-in-real-time-transactions-with-feedzai-machine-learning-tech.

Citi GPS: Global Perspectives & Solutions. *The Bank of the Future - The ABCs of Digital Disruption in Finance*, 2018. https://www.citibank.com/commercialbank/insights/assets/docs/2018/The-Bank-of-the-Future/124/.

Clarity Money - Champion of Your Money. Accessed January 17, 2019. https://clarity-money.com/.

Clarity. Bringing Societal Impact to Markets. Accessed January 13, 2019. https://clarity.ai/.

Clark, Jack. *5 Numbers That Illustrate the Mind-Bending Size of Amazon's Cloud*, 2014. https://www.bloomberg.com/news/2014-11-14/5-numbers-that-illustrate-the-mind-bending-size-of-amazon-s-cloud.html.

Clifford, Catherine. "Elon Musk at SXSW: A.I. Is More Dangerous than Nuclear Weapons." *CNBC*, March 2018. https://www.cnbc.com/2018/03/13/elon-musk-at-sxsw-a-i-is-more-dangerous-than-nuclear-weapons.html.

Cloud Natural Language. Cloud Natural Language API. Accessed January 16, 2019. https://cloud.google.com/natural-language/.

"CoinDesk ICO Tracker - CoinDesk." Coindesk. Accessed January 31, 2019. https://www.coindesk.com/ico-tracker.

Coldewey, Devin. *Microsoft Hits a Speech Recognition Milestone with a System Just as Good as Human Ears*. TechCrunch, 2016. http://social.techcrunch.com/2016/10/18/microsoft-hits-a-speech-recognition-milestone-with-a-system-just-as-good-as-human-ears/.

Cole, David. "The Chinese Room Argument." In *The Stanford Encyclopedia of Philosophy*, edited by Edward N. Zalta, Spring 2019. Metaphysics Research Lab, Stanford University, 2019a. https://plato.stanford.edu/archives/spr2019/entries/chinese-room/.

Cole, David. "The Chinese Room Argument." In *The Stanford Encyclopedia of Philosophy*, edited by Edward N. Zalta, Spring 2019b. Metaphysics Research Lab, Stanford University, 2019. https://plato.stanford.edu/archives/spr2019/entries/chinese-room/.

Collinson, Patrick. "HSBC Voice Recognition System Breached by Customer's Twin." The Guardian, May 19, 2017. https://www.theguardian.com/business/2017/may/19/hsbc-voice-recognition-system-breached-by-customers-twin.

Collinson, Patrick. "Switching Banks: Why Are We More Loyal to Our Bank than to a Partner?" *The Guardian*, September 2013. https://www.theguardian.com/money/2013/sep/07/switching-banks-seven-day.

Compliance Fines and Penalties, n.d. https://www.gdpreu.org/compliance/fines-and-penalties/.

"Computer History Museum - Zuse Computer Z23." Computerhistory.org. Accessed January 30, 2019. https://www.computerhistory.org/projects/zuse_z23/.

Comtois, James. *BlackRock Puts More of Its Future in Tech*, 2017. https://www.pion-line.com/article/20170403/PRINT/304039990/blackrock-puts-more-of-its-future-in-tech.

Confirmed Transactions Per Day. Accessed January 13, 2019. https://www.blockchain.com/charts/n-transactions.

Cook, James. *UK Fintech Start-up Revolut Reaches 2 Million Users Save*, 2018. https://www.telegraph.co.uk/technology/2018/06/07/uk-fintech-start-up-revolut-reaches-2-million-users/.

"Corda | Training & Certification." Corda. Accessed January 13, 2019. https://www.corda.net/develop/training.html.

Cove, Ricky. "Breaking down Bitcoin and Cryptocurrencies: Key Characteristics." Market Realist, November 21, 2017. https://marketrealist.com/2017/11/breaking-down-bitcoin-and-cryptocurrencies-key-characteristics.

Croft, Jane. "Chatbots Join the Legal Conversation." *The Financial Times*, June 2018.

Crook, Jordan. *Lemonade Wants to Rewrite the Insurance Policy Itself*, 2018. https://techcrunch.com/2018/05/16/lemonade-wants-to-rewrite-the-insurance-policy-itself/.

Crosman, Penny. "How Artificial Intelligence Is Reshaping Jobs in Banking | American Banker." *American Banker*, May 7, 2018. https://www.americanbanker.com/news/how-artificial-intelligence-is-reshaping-jobs-in-banking.

"Cryptography." In *Wikipedia*, January 11, 2019. https://en.wikipedia.org/w/index.php?title=Cryptography&oldid=877811989.

CryptoKitties. "CryptoKitties | Collect and Breed Digital Cats!" CryptoKitties. Accessed January 13, 2019. https://www.cryptokitties.co.

"CryptoKitties: Collectible and Breedable Cats Empowered by Blockchain Technology." White Paper. CryptoKitties, n.d.

"CryptoKitties Cripple Ethereum Blockchain," December 5, 2017, sec. Technology. https://www.bbc.com/news/technology-42237162.

Cuthbertson, Anthony. "Bitcoin Just Got a Boost from the World's Leading Financial Authority." *The Independent*, April 2018. https://www.independent.co.uk/life-style/gadgets-and-tech/news/bitcoin-price-latest-updates-imf-christine-lagarde-blogpost-cryptocurrency-invest-a8308491.html.

Dai, Wei. *BMoney*, 2018a. http://www.weidai.com/.

Dai, Wei. *Wei Dai's Home Page*, 2018b. http://www.weidai.com/.

Dalal, Darshini, Stanley Yong, and Antony Lewis. "Project Ubin: SGD on Distributed Ledger." Deloitte; Monetary Authority of Singapore, 2017.

Dale, Brady. *Even Investors with Access Want ICO Presale Reform*, 2017. https://www.coindesk.com/ico-presales-boost-vc-3iq-multicoin.

Dan Murphy And. "RegTech: Opportunities for More Efficient and Effective Regulatory Supervision and Compliance." Milken Institute, July 2018.

Dan Murphy, Jackson Mueller. "RegTech: Opportunities for More Efficient and Effective Regulatory Supervision and Compliance." Milken Institute, July 2018.

Dastin, Jeffrey. *Amazon Lent $1 Billion to Merchants to Boost Sales on Its Marketplace*, 2017. https://www.reuters.com/article/us-amazon-com-loans-idUSKBN18Z0DY.

"Data Created Worldwide 2005-2025 | Statistic." Statista. Accessed January 30, 2019. https://www.statista.com/statistics/871513/worldwide-data-created/.

Davoodalhosseini, S. Mohammad. "Central Bank Digital Currency and Monetary Policy." Funds Management and Banking Department, Bank of Canada, July 2018. https://www.bankofcanada.ca/wp-content/uploads/2018/07/swp2018-36.pdf.

De, Nikhilesh. *Numbers or Not, Coincheck Isn't Mt. Gox*, 2018. https://www.coindesk.com/numbers-not-coincheck-isnt-another-mt-gox.

"Decentraland." Accessed January 13, 2019. https://decentraland.org/.

"Decentralized Reputation System." White Paper. DREP Foundation, n.d.

Detrixhe, John. *Selling Data to Feed Hedge Fund Computers Is One of the Hottest Areas of Finance Right Now*, 2017. https://qz.com/1082389/quant-hedge-funds-are-gorging-on-alternative-data-in-pursuit-of-an-investing-edge/.

Deutsche Bank Plant Nun Doch Keine Digitalbank, 2018. https://de.reuters.com/article/deutschland-deutsche-bank-idDEKCN1IT1Q8.

Diemers, Daniel, Henri Arslanian, Grainne McNamara, Günther Dobrauz, and Lukas Wohlgemuth. "Initial Coin Offering – A Strategic Perspective." Strategy& PwC, June 2018.

Digital Currencies, 2018. http://www.bankofengland.co.uk/research/digital-currencies.

Dominic J. Moylett, Noah Linden, Ashley Montanaro. "Quantum Speedup of the Traveling-Salesman Problem for Bounded-Degree Graphs." *Physical Review*, 2017.

Dutcher, Jennifer. *Data Size Matters [Infographic]*, 2013. https://datascience.berkeley.edu/big-data-infographic/.

Eckert-Mauchly Computer Corporation. *The UNIVAC System*, 1948.

Editors, History com. *Ford Motor Company Unveils the Model T*, 2009. https://www.history.com/this-day-in-history/ford-motor-company-unveils-the-model-t.

"Encryption." In *Wikipedia*, January 12, 2019. https://en.wikipedia.org/w/index.php?title=Encryption&oldid=878014939.

Ensign, Rachel Louise, Christina Rexrode, and Coulter Jones. "Banks Shutter 1,700 Branches in Fastest Decline on Record." *Wall Street Journal*, February 2018. https://www.wsj.com/articles/banks-double-down-on-branch-cutbacks-1517826601.

ERC-20, 2018. https://en.wikipedia.org/w/index.php?title=ERC-20&oldid=874510987.

"ERC-721." Accessed January 13, 2019. http://erc721.org/.

"Ericsson Mobility Report." Ericsson, June 2018.

"Establishing a Chain of Title - Leveraging Blockchain for the Real Estate Industry." Dentons Rodyk, November 20, 2017. https://dentons.rodyk.com/en/insights/alerts/2017/november/21/establishing-a-chain-of-title-leveraging-blockchain-for-the-real-estate-industry.

European Commission. *Payment Services Directive and Interchange Fees Regulation: Frequently Asked Questions*, 2013.

Everything You Need To Know About What Amazon Is Doing In Financial Services, 2018. https://www.cbinsights.com/research/report/amazon-across-financial-services-fintech/.

FAQ, n.d. https://www.lemonade.com/faq#service.

FAQs, 2018. https://www.marcus.com/us/en/faqs.

"File:Hash Function Long.Svg - Wikimedia Commons." Wikimedia Commons. Accessed January 30, 2019. https://commons.wikimedia.org/wiki/File:Hash_function_long.svg.

Financial, Ant. *Ant Financial Invests in Bangladesh-Based BKash*, 2018. https://www.finextra.com/pressarticle/73644/ant-financial-invests-in-banladesh-based-bkash.

Financial Inclusion Insights Bangladesh 2016 Annual Report (Wave 4 Tracker Survey), 2017. http://finclusion.org/uploads/file/Bangladesh%20Wave%204%20Report_20_Sept%202017.pdf.

Financial Inclusion on the Rise, But Gaps Remain, Global Findex Database Shows, 2018. http://www.worldbank.org/en/news/press-release/2018/04/19/financial-inclusion-on-the-rise-but-gaps-remain-global-findex-database-shows.

FINMA. *FINMA Publishes ICO Guidelines*, 2018. https://www.finma.ch/en/news/2018/02/20180216-mm-ico-wegleitung/.

Fintech and Cross-Border Payments, 2017. https://www.imf.org/en/News/Articles/2017/11/01/sp103017-fintech-and-cross-border-payments.

Fintech Association of Hong Kong. Accessed January 16, 2019. https://ftahk.org/.

"Fintech Experiments and Projects." Bank of Canada. Accessed January 13, 2019. https://www.bankofcanada.ca/research/digital-currencies-and-fintech/fintech-experiments-and-projects/.

Foundation, Thomson Reuters. *IBM Wants to Use AI to Stop Human Trafficking Before It Occurs*, 2018. https://www.globalcitizen.org/en/content/data-human-trafficking/.

Four Billion People Are Excluded from the Rule of Law, 2008. http://www.un.org.za/four-billion-people-are-excluded-from-the-rule-of-law/.

Frankenfield, Jake. *Silk Road*, 2016. https://www.investopedia.com/terms/s/silk-road.asp.

Frankenfield, Jake. *Smart Contracts*, 2017. https://www.investopedia.com/terms/s/smart-contracts.asp.

French, Jordan. "Nasdaq Exec: Exchange Is 'All-In' on Using Blockchain Technology." *TheStreet*, April 23, 2018. https://www.thestreet.com/investing/nasdaq-all-in-on-blockchain-technology-14551134.

Frier, Sarah, and Julie Verhage. "Facebook Is Developing a Cryptocurrency for WhatsApp Transfers, Sources Say." *Bloomberg News*, December 2018. https://www.bloomberg.com/news/articles/2018-12-21/facebook-is-said-to-develop-stablecoin-for-whatsapp-transfers.

"Full-Time MBA | FinTech." NYU Stern. Accessed January 30, 2019. http://www.stern.nyu.edu/programs-admissions/full-time-mba/academics/areas-interest/fintech.

Gara, Antoine. "Wall Street Tech Spree: With Kensho Acquisition S&P Global Makes Largest A.I. Deal In History." *Forbes*, March 2018. https://www.forbes.com/sites/antoinegara/2018/03/06/wall-street-tech-spree-with-kensho-acquisition-sp-global-makes-largest-a-i-deal-in-history/.

Garcia, Adrian D. *Big Banks Spend Billions on Tech But Innovation Lags | Bankrate.* Bankrate.com, 2018. https://www.bankrate.com/banking/jpm-big-banks-spend-billions-on-tech-but-theyre-still-laggards/.

Garside, Juliette. "Is Money-Laundering Scandal at Danske Bank the Largest in History?" *The Guardian*, September 21, 2018, sec. Business. https://www.theguardian.com/business/2018/sep/21/is-money-laundering-scandal-at-danske-bank-the-largest-in-history.

Get Started, 2019. https://www.zellepay.com/get-started.

Gilbert, Mark. "The Hedge Fund King and a Technological Arms Race." *Bloomberg Opinion*, December 2018. https://www.bloomberg.com/opinion/articles/2018-12-27/man-group-ceo-luke-ellis-hedge-fund-king-in-technology-arms-race.

Glaser, April. "Google's Ability to Understand Language Is Nearly Equivalent to Humans." Recode, May 31, 2017. https://www.recode.net/2017/5/31/15720118/google-understand-language-speech-equivalent-humans-code-conference-mary-meeker.

Glazer, Phil. "An Overview of Non-Fungible Tokens." Hacker Noon, April 1, 2018. https://hackernoon.com/an-overview-of-non-fungible-tokens-5f140c32a70a.

Global Asset Management 2018: The Digital Metamorphosis, n.d. https://www.bcg.com/en-ch/publications/2018/global-asset-management-2018-digital-metamorphosis.aspx.

"Global Digital Finance Code of Conduct: Taxonomy for Cryptographic Assets." Global Digital Finance, October 2018. https://www.gdf.io/wp-content/uploads/2018/10/0003_GDF_Taxonomy-for-Cryptographic-Assets_Web-151018.pdf.

Global Fintech Report Q2 2018, 2018. https://www.cbinsights.com/research/report/fintech-trends-q2-2018/.

"Global Hosting and Cloud Computing Market 2010–2020 | Statistic." Statista, 2019. https://www.statista.com/statistics/500541/worldwide-hosting-and-cloud-computing-market/.

Global Payments: Expansive Growth, Targeted Opportunities, n.d. https://www.mckinsey.com/industries/financial-services/our-insights/global-payments-expansive-growth-targeted-opportunities.

Gray, Alex. *Here's the Secret to How WeChat Attracts 1 Billion Monthly Users*, 2018. https://www.weforum.org/agenda/2018/03/wechat-now-has-over-1-billion-monthly-users/.

Great Speculations, Trefis Team. *Five Largest ETF Providers Manage Almost 90% Of The $3 Trillion U.S. ETF Industry*, 2017. https://www.forbes.com/sites/greatspeculations/2017/08/24/five-largest-etf-providers-manage-almost-90-of-the-3-trillion-u-s-etf-industry/#320c41973ead.

Green, Rachel. *Global Merchant Card Acceptance Grew 13% in 2017*, 2018. https://www.businessinsider.com/global-merchant-card-acceptance-growing-2018-12.

Greenberg, Andy. "Your Sloppy Bitcoin Drug Deals Will Haunt You for Years." *Wired*, January 2018. https://www.wired.com/story/bitcoin-drug-deals-silk-road-blockchain/.

Greenemeier, Larry. *How Close Are We–Really–to Building a Quantum Computer?*, 2018. https://www.scientificamerican.com/article/how-close-are-we-really-to-building-a-quantum-computer/.

Grimes, Brittney. "10 Largest Robo-Advisers by AUM." InvestmentNews. Accessed January 30, 2019. https://www.investmentnews.com/gallery/20181107/FREE/110709999/PH/10-largest-robo-advisers-by-aum.

Gwynne, Peter. *Practical Quantum Computers Remain at Least a Decade Away*, 2018. https://physicsworld.com/a/practical-quantum-computers-remain-at-least-a-decade-away/.

Harford, Tim. "Is This the Most Influential Work in the History of Capitalism?" *BBC News*, October 2017a. https://www.bbc.com/news/business-41582244.

Harford, Tim. "What We Get Wrong About Technology." *FT Magazine*, July 2017b. http://timharford.com/2017/08/what-we-get-wrong-about-technology/.

Harper, Colin. *Making Sense of Proof of Work vs. Proof of Stake*, 2018. https://coincentral.com/making-sense-of-proof-of-work-vs-proof-of-stake/.

Healey, Jason, Katheryn Rosen, Patricia Mosser, and Adriana Tache. *The Future of Financial Stability and Cyber Risk*, 2018. https://www.brookings.edu/research/the-future-of-financial-stability-and-cyber-risk/.

Heater, Brian. *Smart Speaker Sales on Pace to Increase 50 Percent by 2019*. TechCrunch, 2018. http://social.techcrunch.com/2018/08/14/smart-speaker-sales-on-pace-to-increase-50-percent-by-2019/.

"Hedge Funds See a Gold Rush in Data Mining." *Financial Times*, August 2017. https://www.ft.com/content/d86ad460-8802-11e7-bf50-e1c239b45787.

Henry, David. *JPMorgan's Dimon Calls Settling Legal Issues "Nerve-Wracking,"* 2014. https://www.reuters.com/article/us-jpmorganchase-dimon-idUSBREA3822W20140409.

Hermann, Jeremy, and Mike Del Balso. *Meet Michelangelo: Uber's Machine Learning Platform*, 2017. https://eng.uber.com/michelangelo/.

Hertig, Alyssa. *Ethereum's Big Switch: The New Roadmap to Proof-of-Stake*, 2017. https://www.coindesk.com/ethereums-big-switch-the-new-roadmap-to-proof-of-stake.

Hertig, Alyssa. *How Do Ethereum Smart Contracts Work?* Accessed January 13, 2019a. https://www.coindesk.com/information/ethereum-smart-contracts-work.

Hertig, Alyssa. *What Is a Decentralized Application?* Accessed January 13, 2019b. https://www.coindesk.com/information/what-is-a-decentralized-application-dapp.

Hertig, Alyssa. *What Is Ethereum? - CoinDesk Guides*. Accessed January 13, 2019c. https://www.coindesk.com/information/what-is-ethereum.

Hileman, Garrick. *State of Bitcoin and Blockchain 2016: Blockchain Hits Critical Mass*, 2016. https://www.coindesk.com/state-of-bitcoin-blockchain-2016.

Hileman, Garrick, and Michel Rauchs. "Global Blockchain Benchmarking Study." University of Cambridge Judge Business School, 2017a. https://www.jbs.cam. ac.uk/fileadmin/user_upload/research/centres/alternative-finance/ downloads/2017-09-27-ccaf-globalbchain.pdf.

Hileman, Garrick, and Michel Rauchs. "Global Cryptocurrency Benchmarking Study." Cambridge Centre for Alternative Finance, 2017b. https://www.jbs.cam. ac.uk/fileadmin/user_upload/research/centres/alternative-finance/ downloads/2017-04-20-global-cryptocurrency-benchmarking-study.pdf.

History of Computing, CSEP 590A. "The History of Artificial Intelligence." University of Washington, December 2006.

Holmes, Frank. *These Are the 5 Costliest Financial Regulations of the Past 20 Years*, 2017. https://www.businessinsider.com/these-are-the-5-costliest-financial-regulations-of-the-past-20-years-2017-5?IR=T#march-2010-foreign-account-tax-compliance-act-fatca-3.

"Home." Sovrin. Accessed January 13, 2019a. https://sovrin.org/.

Home. Accessed January 16, 2019b. https://www.gdf.io/.

Homepage, n.d. https://nest.com/insurance-partners/.

How FinTech Is Shaping the Future of Banking | Henri Arslanian | TEDxWanChai, 2016. https://www.youtube.com/watch?v=pPkNtN8G7q8&t=682s.

How Vitality Works, n.d. https://www.vitalitygroup.com/how-vitality-works/.

HSBC Payment App Users Surpass 1m, 2018. http://www.thestandard.com.hk/breaking-news.php?id=110664&sid=2.

Https://Www.Cbinsights.Com/Research/Europe-Bank-Fintech-Startup-Investments/, 2018. https://www.cbinsights.com/research/europe-bank-fintech-startup-investments/.

Hughes, Eric. "A Cypherpunk's Manifesto." Activism.net, March 1993. https://www. activism.net/cypherpunk/manifesto.html.

Huillet, Marie. *Japan: Nomura Bank Announces Crypto Custody Solution For Institutional Investors*, 2018. https://cointelegraph.com/news/japan-nomura-bank-announces-crypto-custody-solution-for-institutional-investors.

Ian Pollari, Anton Ruddenklau. "The Pulse of Fintech – 2018." KPMG, July 2018.

IANS. "Globally, Just Half of Retail Bank Customers Happy with Services: Report." *Business Standard India*, September 2018. https://www.business-standard.com/ article/finance/globally-just-half-of-retail-bank-customers-happy-with-services-report-118092100610_1.html.

Ingraham, Christopher. "Most People Are Paying off Their Credit Card Debt All Wrong—Are You?" *Washington Post*, January 2018. https://www.washingtonpost. com/news/wonk/wp/2018/01/02/most-people-are-paying-off-their-credit-card-debt-all-wrong-are-you/.

Insights, Bain. *Cutting Through Complexity in Financial Crimes Compliance*. Forbes, 2018. https://www.forbes.com/sites/baininsights/2018/02/14/cutting-through-complexity-in-financial-crimes-compliance/.

International Literacy Day 2017, 2017. http://uis.unesco.org/en/news/ international-literacy-day-2017.

Introduction to FinTech, Provided by University of Hong Kong (HKUx), n.d. https:// www.edx.org/course/introduction-to-fintech.

Irrera, Anna. "Banks Scramble to Fix Old Systems as IT 'cowboys' Ride into Sunset." *Reuters*, April 2017.

Iyengar, Sheena S., Wei Jiang, and Gur Huberman. "How Much Choice Is Too Much?: Contributions to 401(k) Retirement Plans." Pension Research Council, The Wharton School, University of Pennsylvania, 2003. https://pdfs.semantic-scholar.org/04f0/7b37fc9deb167e56c729e1f35e052998ba4a.pdf.

Jayachandran, Praveen. "The Difference between Public and Private Blockchain." Blockchain Pulse: IBM Blockchain Blog, May 31, 2017. https://www.ibm.com/ blogs/blockchain/2017/05/the-difference-between-public-and-private-blockchain/.

Johnson, Khari. *Inscribe Raises $3 Million to Automate Document Fraud Detection*, 2018. https://venturebeat.com/2018/12/12/inscribe-raises-3-million-to-automate-document-fraud-detection/.

Joseph, Michael. *M-Pesa: The Story of How the World's Leading Mobile Money Service Was Created in Kenya*, 2017. https://www.vodafone.com/content/index/what/ technology-blog/m-pesa-created.html#.

Journey of Aadhaar, 2016. https://sflc.in/journey-aadhaar.

JPMorgan Chase Competitive Strategy Teardown: How the Bank Stacks Up on Fintech and Innovation, 2018. https://www.cbinsights.com/research/jpmorgan-chase-c ompetitive-strategy-teardown-expert-intelligence/.

Kabbage and Santander UK Partner to Accelerate SMB Growth, 2016.

Kadlec, Dan. *Why Millennials Resist Any Kind of Insurance*. Time Inc, 2014. http:// time.com/money/3178364/millennials-insurance-why-resist-coverage/.

Kaggle: Your Home for Data Science. Accessed January 16, 2019. https://www. kaggle.com/.

Kahn, Jeremy. "Traders Emulate pro Athletes to Improve Their Game, Hiring Coaches and Metrics Analysts." *The Washington Post*, March 2014. https://www. washingtonpost.com/business/traders-emulate-pro-athletes-to-improve-their-game-hiring-coaches-and-metrics-analysts/2014/03/20/3152baf4-ad3a-11e3-9627-c65021d6d572_story.html.

Kambies, Tracy, Paul Roma, Nitin Mittal, and Sandeep Kumar Sharma. "Analyzing Dark Data for Hidden Opportunities." Deloitte Insights, February 7, 2017. https://www2.deloitte.com/insights/us/en/focus/tech-trends/2017/dark-data-analyzing-unstructured-data.html.

Kharif, Olga. "Bitcoin's Use in Commerce Keeps Falling Even as Volatility Eases." *Bloomberg News*, August 1, 2018, sec. Cryptocurrencies. https://www.bloomberg. com/news/articles/2018-08-01/bitcoin-s-use-in-commerce-keeps-falling-even-as-volatility-eases.

Kharpal, Arjun. *Over 800 Cryptocurrencies Are Now Dead as Bitcoin Feels Pressure*, 2018. https://www.cnbc.com/2018/07/02/over-800-cryptocurrencies-are-now-dead-as-bitcoin-feels-pressure.html.

Kharpal, Arjun. "Stephen Hawking Says AI Could Be 'worst Event' in Civilization." *CNBC*, November 2017. https://www.cnbc.com/2017/11/06/stephen-hawking-ai-could-be-worst-event-in-civilization.html.

Kim, Eugene. *SEC Warns on ICO Scams, "pump and Dump" Schemes*, 2017. https://www.cnbc.com/2017/08/28/sec-warns-on-ico-scams-pump-and-dump-schemes.html.

King, Brett. *Bank 4.0: Banking Everywhere, Never at a Bank.* Marshall Cavendish International Asia Pte Ltd, 2018.

Knight, Will. *A New AI Algorithm Summarizes Text Amazingly Well*, 2017. https://www.technologyreview.com/s/607828/an-algorithm-summarizes-lengthy-text-surprisingly-well/.

Kochansky, Jody. *The Promise of Artificial Intelligence and What It Means to BlackRock*, 2018. https://www.blackrockblog.com/2018/03/08/artificial-intelligence-blackrock/.

Koning, JP. "Fedcoin: A Central Bank-Issued Cryptocurrency." R3, November 2016. https://static1.squarespace.com/static/55f73743e4b051cfcc0b02cf/t/58c7f80c2e69cf24220d335e/1489500174018/R3+Report-+Fedcoin.pdf.

Konish, Lorie. *Fees Could Sink Your Retirement Savings. Here's What to Do about It.* CNBC, 2018. https://www.cnbc.com/2018/02/20/fees-could-sink-your-retire-ment-savings-heres-what-to-do-about-it.html.

Koytcheva, Marina. *Wearables Market to be Worth $25 Billion by 2019*, n.d. https://www.ccsinsight.com/press/company-news/2332-wearables-market-to-be-worth-25-billion-by-2019-reveals-ccs-insight.

Kraft, Owen. *How Natural Language Processing Is Changing Financial Risk and Compliance and Why You Should Care*, 2018. http://www.captechconsulting.com/blogs/how-natural-language-processing-is-changing-financial-risk-and-compliance.

LabCFTC Overview, n.d. https://www.cftc.gov/LabCFTC/Overview/index.htm.

Lagarde, Christine. *Winds of Change: The Case for New Digital Currency*, 2018. https://www.imf.org/en/News/Articles/2018/11/13/sp111418-winds-of-change-the-case-for-new-digital-currency.

Lardinois, Frederic. *Gmail Now Has More Than 1B Monthly Active Users*, 2016. https://techcrunch.com/2016/02/01/gmail-now-has-more-than-1b-monthly-active-users/.

Laszlo Hanyecz. Accessed January 13, 2019. https://en.bitcoin.it/wiki/Laszlo_Hanyecz.

Lee, Emma. *WeChat Pay Tries to Duplicate Domestic Success Overseas with Killer Recipe: Social Networking*, 2018. https://technode.com/2018/03/01/wechat-pay-social-networking/.

Lei Pan, Stefan van Woelderen. *Platforms: Bigger, Faster, Stronger*, 2017. https://www.ingwb.com/insights/research/platforms-bigger,-faster,-stronger.

LendEDU's Venmo Transaction Study: Pizza, Drinks, Fantasy Football ... and Sometimes Strippers, 2016. https://lendedu.com/blog/venmo.

"Leveraging Machine Learning Within Anti-Money Laundering Transaction Monitoring." Accenture, 2017. https://www.accenture.com/_acnmedia/PDF-61/Accenture-Leveraging-Machine-Learning-Anti-Money-Laundering-Transaction-Monitoring.pdf.

Levine, Matt. "SEC Halts a Silly Initial Coin Offering." *Bloomberg Opinion*, December 2017. https://www.bloomberg.com/opinion/articles/2017-12-05/sec-halts-a-silly-initial-coin-offering.

Lewis, Antony. *The Basics of Bitcoins and Blockchains: An Introduction to Cryptocurrencies and the Technology That Powers Them*. Mango Media, 2018.

Libert, Barry, and Megan Beck. *The Machine Learning Race Is Really a Data Race*, 2018. https://sloanreview.mit.edu/article/the-machine-learning-race-is-really-a-data-race/.

Light, John. *The Differences between a Hard Fork, a Soft Fork, and a Chain Split, and What They Mean for The...*, 2017. https://medium.com/@lightcoin/the-differences-between-a-hard-fork-a-soft-fork-and-a-chain-split-and-what-they-mean-for-the-769273f358c9.

Lin, June. "Is a Country Club Membership a Security? | Primerus." Primerus. Accessed January 13, 2019. http://www.primerus.com/business-law-news/is-a-country-club-membership-a-security.htm.

Liu, Jackie. *Blockchain Research: What the Fork? What Happens When the (Block) Chain Splits?*, 2017. https://www.blockchain.tum.de/en/news-single-view/?tx_ttnews%5Btt_news%5D=9&cHash=6d77c31a3e4a8161867eef483b96cdb4.

Liu, Xiao. "Ant Financial to Acquire Stake in Bangladesh's BKash." *Caixin Global*, April 2018. https://www.caixinglobal.com/2018-04-27/ant-financial-to-acquire-stake-in-bangladeshs-bkash-101240395.html.

Lloyd, James. *Regulatory "Sandboxes" Facilitate Optimal Regulation in Asia Pacific*, 2018. https://www.ey.com/gl/en/industries/financial-services/fso-insights-regulatory-sandboxes-facilitate-optimal-regulation-in-asia-pacific.

Lopp, Jameson. "Bitcoin and the Rise of the Cypherpunks." *CoinDesk* (blog), April 9, 2016. https://www.coindesk.com/the-rise-of-the-cypherpunks.

"Love and War - Banking and Fintech." The Economist, December 5, 2015. https://www.economist.com/finance-and-economics/2015/12/05/love-and-war.

Lumens FAQ. Accessed January 13, 2019. https://www.stellar.org/lumens/.

M-Money Channel Distribution Case – Kenya, 2009. http://documents.worldbank.org/curated/en/832831500443778267/pdf/117403-WP-KE-Tool-6-7-Case-Study-M-PESA-Kenya-Series-IFC-mobile-money-toolkit-PUBLIC.pdf.

Magnusson, Niklas, and Amanda Billner. "World Sticks to Cash as Sweden Heads Alone Into Cashless Future." *Bloomberg News*, March 11, 2018. https://www.

bloomberg.com/news/articles/2018-03-11/world-sticks-to-cash-as-sweden-heads-alone-into-cashless-future.

Maguire, Eamonn, David Hicks, Wei Keat Ng, Tek Yew Chia, and Stephen Marshall. "Could Blockchain Be the Foundation of a Viable KYC Utility?" KPMG International, 2018.

Maina, Saruni. *Safaricom FY2017: Data and M-Pesa Were Safaricom's Biggest Earners*, 2017. https://techweez.com/2017/05/10/safaricom-fy-2017-data-m-pesa/.

Manne, Robert. "The Cypherpunk Revolutionary: Julian Assange | The Monthly." The Monthly, March 2011. https://www.themonthly.com.au/issue/2011/february/1324596189/robert-manne/cypherpunk-revolutionary.

Marc Niederkorn, Phil Bruno, Grace Hou, Florent Istace, Sukriti Bansal. "Global Payments 2015: A Healthy Industry Confronts Disruption." McKinsey & Company, October 2015.

Marous, Jim, Co-Publisher of The Financial Br, and Owner/Publisher of the Digital Banking Report. *Banking Needs a Customer Experience Wake-Up Call*, 2017. https://thefinancialbrand.com/63654/banking-customer-experience-research-survey/.

MAS Introduces New FEAT Principles to Promote Responsible Use of AI and Data Analytics, 2018. http://www.mas.gov.sg/News-and-Publications/Media-Releases/2018/MAS-introduces-new-FEAT-Principles-to-promote-responsible-use-of-AI-and-data-analytics.aspx.

Matheson, Rob. *Study: Mobile-Money Services Lift Kenyans out of Poverty*, 2016. http://news.mit.edu/2016/mobile-money-kenyans-out-poverty-1208.

Mathis, Will. *Goldman Sachs Expects Marcus to Get 'Very Big, Very Profitable'*, 2018. https://www.bloomberg.com/news/articles/2018-05-31/goldman-sachs-expects-marcus-to-get-very-big-very-profitable.

McDermott, Darius. "Aberdeen Launches AI Smart Beta Venture." *FTAdvisor - Financial Times*, August 2018. https://www.ftadviser.com/investments/2018/09/05/aberdeen-launches-ai-smart-beta-venture/.

McDowall, Mike. *How a Simple 'hello' Became the First Message Sent via the Internet*, 2015. https://www.pbs.org/newshour/science/internet-got-started-simple-hello.

McWaters, R. Jesse, and Rob Galaski. "The New Physics of Financial Services – How Artificial Intelligence Is Transforming the Financial Ecosystem." World Economic Forum, August 2018. http://www3.weforum.org/docs/WEF_New_Physics_of_Financial_Services.pdf.

Mearian, Lucas. "CW@50: Data Storage Goes from $1M to 2 Cents per Gigabyte (+video)." Computerworld, March 23, 2017. https://www.computerworld.com/article/3182207/data-storage/cw50-data-storage-goes-from-1m-to-2-cents-per-gigabyte.html.

Melendez, Steven. *Insurers Turn to Artificial Intelligence in War on Fraud*, 2018. https://www.fastcompany.com/40585373/to-combat-fraud-insurers-turn-to-artificial-intelligence.

McMillan, Robert, and Cade Metz. "The Rise and Fall of the World's Largest Bitcoin Exchange." *Wired*, November 2013. https://www.wired.com/2013/11/mtgox/.

"Migration and Remittances Factbook 2016 Third Edition." Global Knowledge Partnership on Migration and Development (KNOMAD), World Bank, n.d.

Milano, Annaliese. *E-Commerce Giant Rakuten Is Launching Its Own Crypto*, 2018. https://www.coindesk.com/e-commerce-giant-rakuten-launching-cryptocurrency.

Miller, Ron. *How AWS Came to Be*, 2016. https://techcrunch.com/2016/07/02/andy-jassys-brief-history-of-the-genesis-of-aws/.

Millward, Steven. *Alibaba Launches Online Bank: 'It's for the Little Guys, Not the Rich'*, 2015. https://www.techinasia.com/alibaba-launches-online-bank-mybank.

Mironov, Mikhail, and Steven Campbell. "ICO Market Research Q1 2018." *ICORATING*, 2018, 42.

Mitchell, Robert L. *The Cobol Brain Drain*, 2012. https://www.computerworld.com/article/2504568/data-center/the-cobol-brain-drain.html.

"Mobile Subscriptions Worldwide Q3 2018 – Ericsson Mobility Report November 2018." Ericsson.com, November 20, 2018. https://www.ericsson.com/en/mobility-report/reports/november-2018/mobile-subscriptions-worldwide-q3-2018.

Monero FAQ. Accessed January 13, 2019. https://getmonero.org/get-started/faq/index.html.

MoneroXMR – A Privacy-Focused Code Fork of Bytecoin. Accessed January 13, 2019. https://messari.io/asset/monero.

Mooney, Attracta. "BlackRock Bets on Aladdin as Genie of Growth." *Financial Times*, May 2017. https://www.ft.com/content/eda44658-3592-11e7-99bd-13beb0903fa3.

Moskvitch, Katia. "Inside the Bluster and Lies of Petro, Venezuela's Cryptocurrency Scam." *Wired UK*, August 2018. https://www.wired.co.uk/article/venezuela-petro-cryptocurrency-bolivar-scam.

Motif Thematic Portfolios. Accessed January 13, 2019. https://www.motif.com/products/thematic-portfolios.

Mr Ravi Menon, Managing Director, Monetary Authority of Singapore. *Singapore FinTech Journey 2.0*, 2017.

"Musk Says A.I. Is a 'Fundamental Risk to the Existence of Human Civilization.'" *CNBC*, July 16, 2017. https://www.cnbc.com/2017/07/16/musk-says-a-i-is-a-fundamental-risk-to-the-existence-of-human-civilization.html.

N26 Black, n.d. https://n26.com/en-de/black.

Nakamoto, Satoshi. *Bitcoin: A Peer-to-Peer Electronic Cash System," Http://Bitcoin.Org/Bitcoin.Pdf*, 2009. https://bitcoin.org/bitcoin.pdf.

NEO - An Open Network for Smart Economy. Accessed January 13, 2019. https://neo.org/.

Neogi, Saikat. "Aadhar Verdict: eKYC Curbed; Instant Loan Approvals, MF and Insurance Sales Online Take a Hit." *The Financial Express*, October 2018. https://www.financialexpress.com/money/aadhar-verdict-ekyc-curbed-instant-loan-approvals-mf-and-insurance-sales-online-take-a-hit/1332333/.

News, Kitco. "2013: Year of the Bitcoin." *Forbes*, December 2013. https://www.forbes.com/sites/kitconews/2013/12/10/2013-year-of-the-bitcoin/#2f0b622e303c.

Norry, Andrew. *The History of the Mt Gox Hack: Bitcoin's Biggest Heist*, 2018. https://blockonomi.com/mt-gox-hack/.

"Notice 2014–21. IRS Virtual Currency Guidance." Internal Revenue Service, April 2014. https://www.irs.gov/irb/2014-16_IRB#NOT-2014-21.

One Dollar's Worth of Computer Power, 1980–2010, n.d. http://www.hamiltonproject.org/charts/one_dollars_worth_of_computer_power_1980_2010.

Oprunenco, Alexandru, and Chami Akmeemana. "Using Blockchain to Make Land Registry More Reliable in India." United Nations Development Programme, May 1, 2018. http://www.undp.org/content/undp/en/home/blog/2018/Using-blockchain-to-make-land-registry-more-reliable-in-India.html.

Patel, Sital S. *Citi Will Have Almost 30,000 Employees in Compliance by Year-End*, 2014. http://blogs.marketwatch.com/thetell/2014/07/14/citi-will-have-almost-30000-employees-in-compliance-by-year-end/.

"PayPal Reports Fourth Quarter and Full Year 2017 Results." Press Release. BusinessWire, January 31, 2018. https://www.businesswire.com/news/home/20180131006195/en/PayPal-Reports-Fourth-Quarter-Full-Year-2017.

Peachey, Kevin. "Can a 'bank in a Box' Replace a Branch?" *BBC News*, April 2017. https://www.bbc.com/news/business-39709920.

pengying. *China's Mobile Payment Volume Tops 81 Trln Yuan*, 2018. http://www.xinhuanet.com/english/2018-02/19/c_136985149.htm.

Perez, Sarah. *Zelle Forecast to Overtake Venmo This Year*, 2018. https://techcrunch.com/2018/06/15/zelle-forecast-to-overtake-venmo-this-year/.

Peterson, Paige. *Selective Disclosure & Shielded Viewing Keys*, 2018. https://z.cash/blog/viewing-keys-selective-disclosure/.

Pieniewski, Filip. *The AI Winter Is Well on Its Way*, 2018. https://venturebeat.com/2018/06/04/the-ai-winter-is-well-on-its-way/.

Ping An Insurance (Group) Company of China. *Ping An Financial OneConnect Unveils "Smart Insurance Cloud" To Over 100 Insurance Companies*, 2017. https://www.prnewswire.com/news-releases/ping-an-financial-oneconnect-unveils-smart-insurance-cloud-to-over-100-insurance-companies-300514482.html.

"Ping An Starts Work on Up to $3 Billion OneConnect IPO." *Bloomberg News*, March 2018. https://www.bloomberg.com/news/articles/2018-03-28/ping-an-is-said-to-start-work-on-up-to-3-billion-oneconnect-ipo.

Pinto, Rohan. "The Role of Verified Digital Identities in the Open Banking Ecosystem." *Forbes*, December 2018. https://www.forbes.com/sites/forbestechcouncil/2018/12/11/the-role-of-verified-digital-identities-in-the-open-banking-ecosystem/.

Pollack, Andrew. "Apple's Lisa Makes a Debut." *The New York Times*, January 1983. https://www.nytimes.com/1983/01/19/business/apple-s-lisa-makes-a-debut.html.

Portfolio Companies, n.d. http://santanderinnoventures.com/portfolio-companies/.

Predictive Analytics. Accessed January 13, 2019. https://www.fmglobal.com/products-and-services/services/predictive-analytics.

PricewaterhouseCoopers. "Introduction to Token Sales (ICO) Best Practices." PwC. Accessed January 13, 2019a. https://www.pwchk.com/en/industries/financial-services/publications/introduction-to-token-sales-ico-best-practices.html.

PricewaterhouseCoopers. *PwC Accepts Payment in Bitcoin for Its Advisory Services*, 2017. https://www.pwchk.com/en/press-room/press-releases/pr-301117.html.

PricewaterhouseCoopers. *What Is an Audit?* Accessed January 17, 2019b. https://www.pwc.com/m1/en/services/assurance/what-is-an-audit.html.

"Project Ubin." Singapore Financial Centre | Monetary Authority of Singapore. Accessed January 13, 2019. http://www.mas.gov.sg/singapore-financial-centre/smart-financial-centre/project-ubin.aspx.

Puiu, Tibi. *Your Smartphone Is Millions of Times More Powerful than All of NASA's Combined Computing in 1969*, 2017. https://www.zmescience.com/research/technology/smartphone-power-compared-to-apollo-432/.

Purpose & Strategy, n.d. https://www.ing.com/About-us/Purpose-strategy.htm.

Quantum Computers Will Break the Encryption That Protects the Internet. The Economist, 2018. https://www.economist.com/science-and-technology/2018/10/20/quantum-computers-will-break-the-encryption-that-protects-the-internet.

"Quorum | J.P. Morgan." J.P. Morgan Chase & Co. Accessed January 13, 2019. https://www.jpmorgan.com/global/Quorum#section_1320553510217.

R. Jesse McWaters, Rob Galaski. "Beyond Fintech: A Pragmatic Assessment Of Disruptive Potential In Financial Services." World Economic Forum, August 2017.

Ralph, Oliver, Dan Weinland, and Martin Arnold. "Chinese Banks Start Scanning Borrowers' Facial Movements." *Financial Times*, October 2018. https://www.ft.com/content/4c3ac2d4-d865-11e8-ab8e-6be0dcf18713.

Ray, Shaan. "The Difference Between Traditional and Delegated Proof of Stake." Hacker Noon, April 23, 2018. https://hackernoon.com/the-difference-between-traditional-and-delegated-proof-of-stake-36a3e3f25f7d.

Reback, Gedalyah. *Binance Claims 240,000 New Users in One Hour after Relaunching Service*, 2018. https://www.cointelligence.com/content/binance-claims-240000-new-users-in-one-hour-after-relaunching-service/.

Redrawing the Lines: FinTech's Growing Influence on Financial Services, 2017. https://www.pwc.com/jg/en/publications/pwc-global-fintech-report-17.3.17-final.pdf.

Regtech, n.d. https://www.iif.com/topics/regtech.

Regulation of Virtual Assets, 2018. http://www.fatf-gafi.org/publications/fatfrecommendations/documents/regulation-virtual-assets.html.

Reinventing Insurance for the Digital Generation, 2017. https://www.munichre.com/topics-online/en/digitalisation/reinventing-insurance-digital-generation.html.

Retirement Plans: Last Week Tonight with John Oliver. USA: HBO, 2016.

Reuters. *South Korea Bans All New Cryptocurrency Sales*, 2017. https://www.cnbc.com/2017/09/28/south-korea-bans-all-new-cryptocurrency-sales.html.

Reuters Editorial. *Cash Still King: Swedish Central Bank Urges Lawmakers to Protect Cash Payments,* 2018. https://www.reuters.com/article/sweden-cenbank-cash-idUSL8N1QG79Y.

richbodo. "Usage of the Word 'Blockchain.'" *Richbodo* (blog), September 20, 2017. https://medium.com/@richbodo/common-use-of-the-word-blockchain-5b916cecef29.

Roberts, Jeff John. "Only 802 People Told the IRS About Bitcoin, Coinbase Lawsuit Shows." *Fortune,* March 2017. http://fortune.com/2017/03/19/irs-bitcoin-lawsuit/.

Robinson, Edward, and Matthew Leising. "Blythe Masters Tells Banks the Blockchain Changes Everything - Bloomberg." Bloomberg News. Accessed January 13, 2019. https://www.bloomberg.com/news/features/2015-09-01/blythe-masters-tells-banks-the-blockchain-changes-everything.

Robinson, Matt, and Tom Schoenberg. "Bitcoin-Rigging Criminal Probe Focused on Tie to Tether." *Bloomberg News,* November 20, 2018. https://www.bloomberg.com/news/articles/2018-11-20/bitcoin-rigging-criminal-probe-is-said-to-focus-on-tie-to-tether.

Rooney, Kate. "A Blockchain Start-up Just Raised $4 Billion, without a Live Product." *CNBC,* May 2018a. https://www.cnbc.com/2018/05/31/a-blockchain-start-up-just-raised-4-billion-without-a-live-product.html.

Rooney, Kate. "Fidelity Launches Trade Execution and Custody for Cryptocurrencies." *CNBC,* October 2018b. https://www.cnbc.com/2018/10/15/fidelity-launches-trade-execution-and-custody-for-cryptocurrencies.html.

Rooney, Kate. "Nouriel Roubini: Bitcoin Is 'Mother of All Scams.'" *CNBC,* October 2018c. https://www.cnbc.com/2018/10/11/roubini-bitcoin-is-mother-of-all-scams.html.

Rooney, Kate. "SEC Chairman Clayton Says Agency Won't Change Definition of a Security." *CNBC,* June 6, 2018d. https://www.cnbc.com/2018/06/06/sec-chairman-clayton-says-agency-wont-change-definition-of-a-security.html.

Ross, Joe. "Home." Enterprise Ethereum Alliance. Accessed January 13, 2019. https://entethalliance.org/.

Ross, Sean. *What Major Laws Regulating Financial Institutions Were Created in Response to the 2008 Financial Crisis?,* 2017. https://www.investopedia.com/ask/answers/063015/what-are-major-laws-acts-regulating-financial-institutions-were-created-response-2008-financial.asp.

Routley, Nick. *MAPPED: The World's Network of Undersea Cables,* 2017. https://www.businessinsider.com/map-the-worlds-network-of-undersea-cables-2017-8.

"RSA (Cryptosystem)." In *Wikipedia,* January 6, 2019. https://en.wikipedia.org/w/index.php?title=RSA_(cryptosystem)&oldid=877066365.

Rudin, April J. *The Regtech Revolution: Compliance and Wealth Management in 2017,* 2017. https://blogs.cfainstitute.org/investor/2017/01/12/the-regtech-revolution-compliance-and-wealth-management-in-2017/.

Russell, Jon, and Mike Butcher. "Telegram's Billion-Dollar ICO Has Become a Mess." *TechCrunch*, May 2018. http://social.techcrunch.com/2018/05/03/telegrams-billion-dollar-ico-has-become-a-mess/.

Russell, Jon. *Telegram's Billion-Dollar ICO Has Become a Mess*. Accessed January 16, 2019. http://social.techcrunch.com/2018/05/03/telegrams-billion-dollar-ico-has-become-a-mess/.

S., T. *Why Does Kenya Lead the World in Mobile Money?*, 2015. https://www.economist.com/the-economist-explains/2015/03/02/why-does-kenya-lead-the-world-in-mobile-money.

"SAGE: Semi-Automatic Ground Environment Air Defense System | MIT Lincoln Laboratory." MIT Lincoln Laboratory (Massachusetts Institute of Technology). Accessed January 30, 2019. https://www.ll.mit.edu/about/history/sage-semi-automatic-ground-environment-air-defense-system.

Saïd Business School, University of Oxford. *Oxford Fintech Programme*, n.d. https://www.getsmarter.com/courses/uk/said-business-school-oxford-university-fintech-online-short-course.

Samtani, Manesh. *ASIFMA Publishes Best Practices Guide for Crypto Exchanges*, 2018. https://www.regulationasia.com/asifma-publishes-best-practices-guide-for-crypto-exchanges/.

Satariano, Adam. "Amazon Dominates as a Merchant and Platform. Europe Sees Reason to Worry." *The New York Times*, November 2018. https://www.nytimes.com/2018/09/19/technology/amazon-europe-margrethe-vestager.html.

Satoshi Nakamoto, 2019. https://en.wikipedia.org/w/index.php?title=Satoshi_Nakamoto&oldid=878012844.

Scheck, Justin, and Bradley Hope. "The Man Who Solved Bitcoin's Most Notorious Heist." *Wall Street Journal*, August 2018. https://www.wsj.com/articles/the-man-who-solved-bitcoins-most-notorious-heist-1533917805.

Schreiber, Daniel. *Lemonade Sets a New World Record*, 2017.

Schwab Intelligent Portfolios®, n.d. https://intelligent.schwab.com/.

Schwartzkopff, Frances. "Danske Bank Puts €2.4bn aside for Money-Laundering Case." Independent.ie. Accessed January 24, 2019. https://www.independent.ie/business/world/danske-bank-puts-2-4bn-aside-for-moneylaundering-case-37592181.html.

Schwiegershausen, Erica. *A Brief History of Wearable Tech*, 2015. https://www.thecut.com/2015/04/brief-history-of-wearable-tech.html.

Seamless International Money Transfers with TransferWise, n.d. https://n26.com/en-eu/transferwise.

Securities and Futures Commission Fintech Contact Point, 2017. https://www.sfc.hk/web/EN/sfc-fintech-contact-point/.

Services, Amazon Web. *Deploying Open Banking APIs on AWS*, 2018. https://www.slideshare.net/AmazonWebServices/deploying-open-banking-apis-on-aws?from_action=save.

SFC Sets out New Regulatory Approach for Virtual Assets, 2018. https://www.sfc.hk/edistributionWeb/gateway/EN/news-and-announcements/news/doc?refNo=18PR126.

Shelanski, Howard, Samantha Knox, and Arif Dhilla. "Network Effects and Efficiencies in Multisided Markets." Organisation for Economic Co-operation and Development, June 2017. https://one.oecd.org/document/DAF/COMP/WD(2017)40/FINAL/en/pdf.

Shen, Samuel, and John Ruwitch. "Satellites and Blogs: BlackRock to Raise Game in China Stock Picking." *Reuters*, July 2018. https://www.reuters.com/article/us-china-blackrock-fund-idUSKBN1KE16U.

Shifflett, Shane, and Coulter Jones. "Buyer Beware: Hundreds of Bitcoin Wannabes Show Hallmarks of Fraud." *Wall Street Journal*, May 2018. https://www.wsj.com/articles/buyer-beware-hundreds-of-bitcoin-wannabes-show-hallmarks-of-fraud-1526573115.

Shin, Laura. "Here's The Man Who Created ICOs And This Is The New Token He's Backing." *Forbes*, September 2017. https://www.forbes.com/sites/laurashin/2017/09/21/heres-the-man-who-created-icos-and-this-is-the-new-token-hes-backing/#6b4878d81183.

Shubber, Kadhim. *Peer-to-Peer May Have Changed Banking, but Banking Still Won*, 2016. https://ftalphaville.ft.com/2016/11/16/2179884/peer-to-peer-may-have-changed-banking-but-banking-still-won/.

Siegler, M G. *Eric Schmidt: Every 2 Days We Create As Much Information As We Did Up To 2003*, 2010. https://techcrunch.com/2010/08/04/schmidt-data/.

Simon Jessop, Trevor Hunnicutt. *BlackRock Takes Scalable Capital Stake in Europe "robo-Advisor" Push*, 2017. https://www.reuters.com/article/us-blackrock-scalable-capital/blackrock-takes-scalable-capital-stake-in-europe-robo-advisor-push-idUSKBN19A322.

Simonite, Tom. *What Is Quantum Computing? The Complete WIRED Guide.* WIRED, 2018. https://www.wired.com/story/wired-guide-to-quantum-computing/.

Singleton, Micah. *Nearly a Quarter of US Households Own a Smart Speaker, According to Nielsen.* The Verge, 2018. https://www.theverge.com/circuitbreaker/2018/9/30/17914022/smart-speaker-40-percent-us-households-nielsen-amazon-echo-google-home-apple-homepod.

Skarlatos, Bryan. "Using Bitcoin to Buy a Sandwich Could Trigger a Tax Bill-Commentary," October 2017. https://www.cnbc.com/2017/10/20/using-bitcoin-to-buy-a-sandwich-could-trigger-a-tax-bill-commentary.html.

Skinner, Chris. "Applying Blockchain to Clearing and Settlement - Chris Skinner's Blog," August 2016. https://thefinanser.com/2016/08/applying-blockchain-clearing-settlement.html/.

Skinner, Chris. *Digital Human: The Fourth Revolution of Humanity Includes Everyone.* Marshall Cavendish International (Asia) Private Limited, 2018.

Small Business Loans. Accessed January 13, 2019. https://quickbooks.intuit.com/features/loans/.

Smith, Chris, Brian McGuire, Ting Huang, and Gary Yang. "The History of Artificial Intelligence." *University of Washington*, December 2006, 27.

Son, Hugh. *Consumers Want Tech Firms to Take On the Banks*, 2017. https://www.bloomberg.com/news/articles/2017-11-20/banks-beware-most-customers-suspect-tech-can-do-your-job-better.

"Stablecoin Index." Accessed January 31, 2019. https://stablecoinindex.com/marketcap.

"Standard Chartered Deepens Investments in Digital Solutions." *The Guardian Nigeria Newspaper*, December 2018. https://guardian.ng/business-services/standard-chartered-deepens-investments-in-digital-solutions/.

Stanley, Aaron. *Arizona Becomes First U.S. State To Launch Regulatory Sandbox For Fintech*. Forbes, 2018. https://www.forbes.com/sites/astanley/2018/03/23/arizona-becomes-first-u-s-state-to-launch-regulatory-sandbox-for-fintech/.

State Farm Distracted Driver Detection. Accessed January 13, 2019. https://kaggle.com/c/state-farm-distracted-driver-detection.

"State of the Industry Report on Mobile Money." GSMA, 2017. https://www.gsma.com/mobilefordevelopment/wp-content/uploads/2017/03/GSMA_State-of-the-Industry-Report-on-Mobile-Money_2016.pdf.

Statement on Initial Coin Offerings, 2017. https://www.sfc.hk/web/EN/news-and-announcements/policy-statements-and-announcements/statement-on-initial-coin-offerings.html.

"Statistics." Sveriges Riksbank, January 2, 2018. https://www.riksbank.se/en-gb/notes-and-coins/statistics/.

Stellabelle. *Cold Wallet Vs. Hot Wallet: What's The Difference?*, 2017. https://medium.com/@stellabelle/cold-wallet-vs-hot-wallet-whats-the-difference-a00d872aa6b1.

Stern, Leonard N. *Full-Time MBA | FinTech*, n.d. http://www.stern.nyu.edu/programs-admissions/full-time-mba/academics/specializations/fintech.

Stettner, Barbara. "Cryptocurrency AML Risk Considerations - Allen & Overy." Allen & Overy. Accessed January 13, 2019. http://www.allenovery.com/publications/en-gb/lrrfs/cross-border/Pages/Cryptocurrency-AML-risk-considerations.aspx.

Suberg, William. *John Oliver Compares Bitcoin with Bitconnect, Ridicules Tapscott's 'Dumb' McNugget Metaphor*, 2018. https://cointelegraph.com/news/john-oliver-compares-bitcoin-with-bitconnect-ridicules-tapscotts-dumb-mcnugget-metaphor.

Subscribe to Read. Accessed January 17, 2019. https://www.ft.com/content/4c3ac2d4-d865-11e8-ab8e-6be0dcf18713.

Surane, Jennifer. "Goldman to Add Crypto Contracts Without Trading Bitcoins." *Bloomberg News*, May 2018. https://www.bloomberg.com/news/articles/2018-05-02/goldman-is-said-to-add-crypto-contracts-without-trading-bitcoins.

Swaine, Michael R., and Paul A. Freiberger. "UNIVAC | Computer | Britannica. Com." Britannica, October 7, 2008. https://www.britannica.com/technology/UNIVAC.

Symonds, Jonathan. *Modeling the Future of Regulatory Risk*, 2017. https://www.ayasdi.com/blog/artificial-intelligence/modeling-the-future-of-regulatory-risk/.

Tan, Jessica. *From Ping An to Platform: Technology Innovation for Growth*, 2017. http://www.pingan.com/app_upload/images/info/upload/68a59877-41d3-4fff-a1d3-5f01172bfcdb1.pdf.

Taylor, Adam. *47 Percent of the World's Population Now Use the Internet, Study Says*. The Washington Post, 2016a. https://www.washingtonpost.com/news/worldviews/wp/2016/11/22/47-percent-of-the-worlds-population-now-use-the-internet-users-study-says/.

Taylor, Harriet. *Bank of America Launches AI Chatbot Erica—Here's What It Does*, 2016b. https://www.cnbc.com/2016/10/24/bank-of-america-launches-ai-chatbot-erica–heres-what-it-does.html.

Team / 02.22.18, The Wealthfront. "Investing Just Got Better with Wealthfront." Wealthfront Blog, February 22, 2018. https://blog.wealthfront.com/risk-parity/.

Tepper, Brandon. "Building on the Blockchain: Nasdaq's Vision of Innovation." Nasdaq, March 2016. https://business.nasdaq.com/Docs/Blockchain%20Report%20March%202016_tcm5044-26461.pdf.

"Tether." Accessed January 13, 2019. https://tether.to/.

"Tether – FAQs." Accessed January 13, 2019. https://tether.to/faqs/.

Thake, Max. "What's the Difference between Blockchain and DLT?" *Nakamo.To* (blog), February 8, 2018. https://medium.com/nakamo-to/whats-the-difference-between-blockchain-and-dlt-e4b9312c75dd.

"The Aspen Digital Security Token." Indiegogo Token Sales. Accessed January 13, 2019. https://blockchain.indiegogo.com/projects/aspen/.

The Bank of the Future. Citigroup Inc., 2018. https://www.citibank.com/commercialbank/insights/assets/docs/2018/The-Bank-of-the-Future/60/.

"The Challenger Bank Playbook: How Six Challenger Bank Startups Are Taking On Retail Banking." CB Insights Research, March 8, 2018. https://www.cbinsights.com/research/challenger-bank-strategy/.

The Fed - Report on the Economic Well-Being of U.S. Households in 2017–May 2018, n.d. https://www.federalreserve.gov/publications/2018-economic-well-being-of-us-households-in-2017-preface.htm.

"The Fintech 250: The Top Fintech Startups of 2018." CB Insights Research, October 22, 2018. https://www.cbinsights.com/research/fintech-250-startups-most-promising/.

The Millennial Disruption Index, 2013. https://www.bbva.com/wp-content/uploads/2015/08/millenials.pdf.

The Next Generation of Distributed Ledger Technology. Accessed January 13, 2019. https://www.iota.org/.

"The Pulse of Fintech 2018." KPMG, July 31, 2018. https://assets.kpmg/content/dam/kpmg/xx/pdf/2018/07/h1-2018-pulse-of-fintech.pdf.

"The Race to Build a Quantum Computer | NIST." NIST. Accessed January 30, 2019. https://www.nist.gov/topics/physics/introduction-new-quantum-revolution/race-build-quantum-computer.

"The Shift from Defined Benefit to Defined Contribution Plans." *Greenbush Financial Planning* (blog), July 17, 2015. Accessed January 30, 2019. https://www.greenbushfinancial.com/the-shift-in-retirement-and-importance-of-education/.

The Skeptics: A Tribute to Bold Assertions. Accessed January 13, 2019. https://nakamotoinstitute.org/the-skeptics/.

"The State of Regtech." CB Insights, September 2017.

"The Top 20 Reasons Startups Fail." CB Insights, February 2018.

The trimplement Team. *What Challenges Are Fintech Startups Facing Today*, 2017. https://medium.com/trimplement/what-challenges-are-fintech-startups-facing-today-6e2efef8ecb4.

"The Trust Machine - The Promise of the Blockchain." The Economist. Accessed January 13, 2019. https://www.economist.com/leaders/2015/10/31/the-trust-machine.

The Turk, 2018. https://en.wikipedia.org/w/index.php?title=The_Turk&oldid=867197094.

"The Turk." In *Wikipedia*, January 17, 2019. https://en.wikipedia.org/w/index.php?title=The_Turk&oldid=878918745.

The Unmet Need for Legal Aid, n.d. https://www.lsc.gov/what-legal-aid/unmet-need-legal-aid.

These Figures Show the Incredible Growth of Paytm as Payments Platform, 2018. https://www.businesstoday.in/current/corporate/paytm-transactions-wallet-firm-upi-payments-bank-50-billion/story/280040.html.

Thompson, Patrick. *Bitcoin Mining's Electricity Bill: Is It Worth It?*, 2018. https://cointelegraph.com/news/bitcoin-minings-electricity-bill-is-it-worth-it.

"Top 100 Cryptocurrencies by Market Capitalization." CoinMarketCap. Accessed January 31, 2019. https://coinmarketcap.com/.

TransferWise Content Team. *How TransferWise Works: Your Step-by-Step Guide*, 2018. https://transferwise.com/gb/blog/how-does-transferwise-work.

TransferWise Mission Report Q1 2018, 2018. https://transferwise.com/gb/blog/transferwise-mission-report-q1-2018.

"Transistor Count." In *Wikipedia*, January 26, 2019. https://en.wikipedia.org/w/index.php?title=Transistor_count&oldid=880211715.

Trefis Team. "Five Largest ETF Providers Manage Almost 90% Of The $3 Trillion U.S. ETF Industry." *Forbes*, August 2017. https://www.forbes.com/sites/greatspeculations/2017/08/24/five-largest-etf-providers-manage-almost-90-of-the-3-trillion-u-s-etf-industry/.

Trieu, Huy Nguyen. *Fintech Start-Ups Beware: Customers Are Expensive*, 2016. http://
www.disruptivefinance.co.uk/2016/01/03/fintech-start-ups-beware-
customers-are-expensive/.

Trillo, Manny. *Visa Transactions Hit Peak on Dec. 23*, 2011. https://www.visa.com/
blogarchives/us/2011/01/12/visa-transactions-hit-peak-on-dec-23/index.html.

Trujillo, Jesus Leal, Steve Fromhart, and Val Srinivas. "The Evolution of Blockchain
Technology." Deloitte Insights, November 6, 2017. https://www2.deloitte.com/
insights/us/en/industry/financial-services/evolution-of-blockchain-github-
platform.html.

Two Celebrities Charged With Unlawfully Touting Coin Offerings, 2018. https://www.
sec.gov/news/press-release/2018-268.

Uber Fees: How Much Does Uber Pay, Actually? (With Case Studies), 2018. https://
www.ridester.com/uber-fees/.

"Uncover the True Cost of Anti-Money Laundering & KYC Compliance." LexisNexis
Risk Solutions, June 2016.

Understanding Masternodes. Accessed January 13, 2019. https://docs.dash.org/en/lat-
est/masternodes/understanding.html.

Underwood, Barbara D. "Virtual Markets Integrity Initiative." Office of the New York
State Attorney General, September 2018.

"UNODC Estimates That Criminals May Have Laundered US$ 1.6 Trillion in
2009." UNODC, October 25, 2011. https://www.unodc.org/unodc/en/press/
releases/2011/October/unodc-estimates-that-criminals-may-have-laundered-
usdollar-1.6-trillion-in-2009.html.

UOB Unveils Machine Learning Solution to Combat Financial Crime, 2018. https://
sbr.com.sg/financial-services/news/uob-unveils-machine-learning-solution-
combat-financial-crime.

U.S. Securities and Exchange Commission. *SEC Announces Enforcement Results for
FY 2016*, 2016.

Vagen, Trond. "HSBC Set to Launch Cloud-Based AML System next Year, Says
Senior…" *Reuters*, November 2018. https://www.reuters.com/article/
bc-finreg-hsbc-data-cloud-aml-idUSKCN1NX1KU.

Vaghela, Viren, and Andrea Tan. "How Malta Became a Hub of the Cryptocurrency
World." *Bloomberg News*, April 2018. https://www.bloomberg.com/news/arti-
cles/2018-04-23/how-malta-became-a-hub-of-the-cryptocurrency-
world-quicktake.

Valenta, Martin, and Philipp Sandner. "Comparison of Ethereum, Hyperledger
Fabric and Corda." *Frankfurt School Blockchain Center*, June 2017, 8.

Vallee, Boris, and Yao Zeng. "Marketplace Lending: A New Banking Paradigm?"
Working Paper. Harvard Business School, January 2018. https://www.hbs.edu/
faculty/Publication%20Files/18-067_1d1e7469-3a75-46a0-9520-
bddbfda0b2b9.pdf.

Value Added by Private Industries: Finance, Insurance, Real Estate, Rental, and Leasing: Finance and Insurance as a Percentage of GDP (VAPGDPFI), n.d. https://fred. stlouisfed.org/series/VAPGDPFI.

Vanguard. *Vanguard Introduces Personal Advisor Services, Lowers Minimum to Investors With $50,000*, 2015.

Verhage, Julie. *Wealthfront Valuation Said to Drop About a Third in New Funding*, 2018. https://www.bloomberg.com/news/articles/2018-03-23/wealthfront-valuation-said-to-drop-about-a-third-in-new-funding.

Casey, Michael J. and Paul Vigna. *Mt. Gox, Ripple Founder Unveils Stellar, a New Digital Currency Project*, 2014. https://blogs.wsj.com/moneybeat/2014/07/31/ mt-gox-ripple-founder-unveils-stellar-a-new-digital-currency-project/.

Villanueva, Sandra. *QBE Partners with Cytora to Leverage Artificial Intelligence and Open Source Data*, 2017. https://qbeeurope.com/news-and-events/press-releases/ qbe-partners-with-cytora-to-leverage-artificial-intelligence-and-open-source-data/.

Vision API - Image Content Analysis. Cloud Vision API. Accessed January 16, 2019. https://cloud.google.com/vision/.

Wadhwa, Tina. *One of the Hottest Investment Styles Might Be "Financially Unviable,"* 2016. https://www.businessinsider.com/robo-advisors-may-be-financially-unviable-2016-7?IR=T.

Walden, Stephanie. *Tech Time Machine: Screens and Display*, n.d. https://mashable. com/2015/01/06/screen-display-tech-ces/#e.WJ5m0AguqQ.

Wallace, Benjamin. "The Rise and Fall of Bitcoin." *Wired* 19, no. 12 (November 2011). https://www.wired.com/2011/11/mf-bitcoin/.

Wang, Yue. *Ant Financial Said To Close $150B Funding Round*. Forbes, 2018. https:// www.forbes.com/sites/ywang/2018/05/28/ant-financial-said-to-close-150-b-funding-round/.

Watts, William. *The next Frontier in Investing Is 'Quantamental' Stock Picking*, 2018. https://www.marketwatch.com/story/the-next-frontier-in-investing-is-quantamental-stock-picking-2018-10-03.

Website, n.d.-a https://www.nist.gov/topics/physics/introduction-new-quantum-revolution/race-build-quantum-computer.

Website, n.d.-b https://www.ft.com/content/2d0ba0da-cedf-11e7-9dbb-291a884dd8c6.

Website – Dead Link, n.d.-a https://www.worldpaymentsreport.com/download.

Website – Dead Link, n.d.-b https://historycomputer.com/ModernComputer/ Electronic/SAGE.htm.

Website – Dead Link, n.d.-c https://investor.paypal-corp.com/releasedetail. cfm?releaseid=1055924.

Website – Dead Link, n.d.-d http://www.horst-zuse.homepage.t-online.de/Konrad_ Zuse_index_english_html/rechner_z23.htm.

Website – Dead Link, n.d.-e https://ir.lendingclub.com/Cache/1001230258.PDF?O =PDF&T=&Y=&D=&FID=1001230258&iid=4213397.

Westgard, Kristy. "Two Sigma Hires Google Scientist Mike Schuster for AI Expansion." *Bloomberg News*, April 2018. https://www.bloomberg.com/news/articles/2018-04-16/two-sigma-hires-google-scientist-mike-schuster-for-ai-expansion.

What Are Zk-SNARKs? Accessed January 13, 2019. https://z.cash/technology/zksnarks/.

What Is IndiaStack? Accessed January 13, 2019. http://indiastack.org/about/.

"What Is Natural Language Processing?" SAS. Accessed January 24, 2019a. https://www.sas.com/en_us/insights/analytics/what-is-natural-language-processing-nlp.html.

What Is Natural Language Processing? Accessed January 15, 2019b. https://www.sas.com/en_us/insights/analytics/what-is-natural-language-processing-nlp.html.

"What Is the Difference between DLT and Blockchain? | BBVA." BBVA. Accessed January 13, 2019. https://www.bbva.com/en/difference-dlt-blockchain/.

"What Supreme Court's Aadhaar Verdict Means for You: 10 Points." *Livemint*, September 2018. https://www.livemint.com/Companies/cpSHu1fjQ1WvO-P8vMi27aL/What-Supreme-Courts-Aadhaar-verdict-means-for-you-10-point.html.

"What The Largest Global Fintech Can Teach Us About What's Next In Financial Services." CB Insights Research, October 4, 2018. https://www.cbinsights.com/research/ant-financial-alipay-fintech/.

Where Top US Banks Are Betting On Fintech, 2018. https://www.cbinsights.com/research/fintech-investments-top-us-banks/.

"White Paper: Machine Learning. Modern Payment Fraud Prevention at Big Data Scale." Feedzai, 2013.

Who Are You Calling a 'challenger Bank'?, n.d. https://www.pwc.co.uk/industries/banking-capital-markets/insights/challenger-banks.html.

Wigglesworth, Robin. "The Rise of 'Quantamental' Investing: Where Man and Machine Meet." *Financial Times*, November 2018. https://www.ft.com/content/f1276122-ec19-11e8-8180-9cf212677a57.

Wile, Rob. "Bitcoin's Mysterious Creator Appears to Be Sitting On a $5.8 Billion Fortune." *Time*, October 2017. http://time.com/money/5002378/bitcoin-creator-nakamoto-billionaire/.

Wiley: Bankruption Companion Site Content, 2016. https://www.wiley.com/WileyCDA/Section/id-829480.html.

Will Sweden Become the First Nation to Go Cash-Free?, n.d. https://www.nbcnews.com/mach/science/will-sweden-become-first-country-go-cash-free-ncna809811.

Williams, Sean. *5 Brand-Name Businesses That Currently Accept Bitcoin – The Motley Fool*, 2017. https://www.fool.com/investing/2017/07/06/5-brand-name-businesses-that-currently-accept-bitc.aspx.

Williams-Grut, Oscar. *Hot Foreign Exchange App Revolut Burned through pounds7 Million Fuelling Its Growth Last Year*, 2017a. http://uk.businessinsider.com/fintech-revolut-2016-accounts-loss-revenue-2017-6?IR=T.

Williams-Grut, Oscar. "HSBC Partners with Tradeshift as Banks Increasingly See Fintech as Friends Not Foe." *Business Insider*, March 2017b. https://www.businessinsider.com/hsbc-partners-with-fintech-tradeshift-on-financing-product-2017-3.

Wilmoth, Josiah. *Major Milestone: There Are Now More than 300 Cryptocurrency Funds*, 2018. https://www.ccn.com/major-milestone-there-are-now-more-than-300-cryptocurrency-funds/.

Wilson, H. James, and Paul R. Daugherty. "What Changes When AI Is So Accessible That Everyone Can Use It?" *Harvard Business Review*, January 2018. https://hbr.org/2018/01/what-changes-when-ai-is-so-accessible-that-everyone-can-use-it.

Wininger, Shai. *We Suck, Sometimes*, 2018. https://www.lemonade.com/blog/lemonade-transparency-review/.

Wintermeyer, Lawrence. "The Rise of the Unicorn Challenger Bank You've Never Heard of - OakNorth." *Forbes*, November 2017. https://www.forbes.com/sites/lawrencewintermeyer/2017/11/17/the-rise-of-the-unicorn-challenger-bank-youve-never-heard-of-oaknorth/.

World Bank Group. "Global Findex Report." World Bank, 2017.

"World of Regtech." Raconteur, 2018. https://www.raconteur.net/infographics/world-of-regtech.

"World Payments Report 2018." *World Payments Report* (blog), October 4, 2018. https://worldpaymentsreport.com/resources/world-payments-report-2018/.

Xie, Stella Yifan. "Jack Ma's Giant Financial Startup Is Shaking the Chinese Banking System." *WSJ Online*, July 2018.

Yurcan, Bryan. *The Top Tech Priorities for Banks in 2018*, 2017. https://www.americanbanker.com/news/ai-development-top-of-2018-list-for-many-banks.

Zendrive. Accessed January 13, 2019. http://zendrive.com.

Zhang, Maggie. *Tencent Gets a Licence to Sell Mutual Funds to WeChat's 1 Billion Users in China*, 2018a. https://www.scmp.com/business/companies/article/2126876/tencent-granted-licence-sell-mutual-funds.

Zhang, Shu. *Alibaba-Backed Online Lender MYbank Owes Cost-Savings to Home-Made Tech*, 2018b. https://www.reuters.com/article/us-china-banking-mybank-idUSKBN1FL3S6.

Zhao, Helen. "Own Shares of Brooklyn Building with Tokens Blockchain Real Estate," March 19, 2018a. https://www.cnbc.com/2018/03/19/own-shares-of-brooklyn-building-with-tokens-blockchain-real-estate.html.

Zhao, Wolfie. *Messaging Giant LINE Is Launching Its Own Cryptocurrency*, 2018b. https://www.coindesk.com/messaging-giant-line-is-launching-its-own-cryptocurrency.

Zhao, Wolfie. *PBoC's Yao: Chinese Digital Currency Should Be Crypto-Inspired*, 2018c. https://www.coindesk.com/pbocs-yao-qian-state-digital-currency-can-still-be-cryptocurrency.

Zhao, Wolfie. *Rakuten Is About to Buy a Bitcoin Exchange for $2.4 Million*, 2018d. https://www.coindesk.com/rakuten-seeks-to-acquire-bitcoin-exchange-in-2-4-million-deal.

Zuckerman, Molly Jane. "Andy Warhol Painting to Be Sold via Blockchain in 'World's First' Crypto Art Auction." Cointelegraph, June 7, 2018a. https://cointelegraph.com/news/andy-warhol-painting-to-be-sold-via-blockchain-in-world-s-first-crypto-art-auction.

Zuckerman, Molly Jane. "Swedish Government Land Registry Soon To Conduct First Blockchain Property Transaction." Cointelegraph, March 7, 2018b. https://cointelegraph.com/news/swedish-government-land-registry-soon-to-conduct-first-blockchain-property-transaction.

Index

© The Author(s) 2019
H. Arslanian, F. Fischer, *The Future of Finance*,
https://doi.org/10.1007/978-3-030-14533-0

Printed by Printforce, the Netherlands